1984 3

SOFTWARE
SYSTEM TESTING
AND
QUALITY ASSURANCE

SOFTWARE SYSTEM TESTING AND QUALITY ASSURANCE

Boris Beizer
Data Systems Analysts, Inc.
Pennsauken, New Jersey

Van Nostrand Reinhold Electrical/Computer Science and Engineering Series

VNR VAN NOSTRAND REINHOLD COMPANY
———————— *New York* ————————

Library of Congress Catalog Card Number: 83-10458
ISBN: 0-442-21306-9

Manufactured in the United States of America

Published by Van Nostrand Reinhold Company Inc.
115 Fifth Avenue
New York, New York 10003

Van Nostrand Reinhold Company Limited
Molly Millars Lane
Wokingham, Berkshire RG11 2PY, England

Van Nostrand Reinhold
480 La Trobe Street
Melbourne, Victoria 3000, Australia

Macmillan of Canada
Division of Canada Publishing Corporation
164 Commander Boulevard
Agincourt, Ontario M1S 3C7, Canada

15 14 13 12 11 10 9 8 7 6 5

Library of Congress Cataloging in Publication Data

Beizer, Boris, 1934–
    Software system testing and quality assurance.

    (Van Nostrand Reinhold electrical/computer science
and engineering series)
Includes index.
    1. Computer programs—Testing.   2. Computer programs
—Reliability.   I. Title.   II. Series.
QA76.6.B4328   1984   001.64′25   83-10458
ISBN 0-442-21306-9

To Ruth

Van Nostrand Reinhold
Electrical/Computer Science and Engineering Series
Sanjit Mitra—Series Editor

THE RUNNING OF THREE-OH-THREE

With apologies to Robert W. Service

There are bugs adrift on the midnight shift
That cannot be foretold.
The audit trails have their secret tales
That would make your blood run cold.
Debugging nights have seen queer sights,
But the queerest they ever did see
Was that time on the way to cutover day
I ran test three-oh-three.

Now three-oh-three in its infancy
    Was simple and sublime;
A bit set here or a patch put there;
    All done in record time.
"A trivial test is always best,"
    The experts love to state;
But a test gone sour at the midnight hour,
    Is a test you come to hate.

All through that day we slugged away
    At data errors in store.
Talk about dumps! They lay in lumps
    On every foot of floor.
The printer's stammer beat like a hammer
    In sonic tyranny.
It wasn't much fun and we hadn't yet run
    The infamous three-oh-three.

That very night by the lonely light
    Of the empty Coke machine,
The problems solved, we all resolved
    To embark on the next day clean.
"Just one more test," does the boss suggest,
    "Before we end this session.
You're doing well, I'm proud to tell,
    But humor this last obsession."

We were really beat; we'd been on our feet
    For eighteen hours or more.
Our eyes were glazed and through the haze,

We could not tell "NEITHER" from "NOR."
But he smiled and said, "Before the bed—
    Just one little test to run;
And if you do, and I tell you true,
    Next payday you'll have fun."

Now talk about pay was an eloquent way
    To make our adrenalin rise;
And one little pest of a simple test
    Was trivial enterprise.
We fell for his tact and swore to a pact
    That before the hour would come,
Our victory over three-oh-three
    Would be absolutely won.

We said, "What the heck," and loaded the deck,
    Then toggled the bootstrap switch;
But the ROM was burned and a bit was turned—
    'Twas the ever present hitch.
We keyed-in the code as in days of old,
    With nary an audible murmur;
But beneath our breath, we snarled of death,
    Misery, mayhem, murder.

I loaded the patch; the floppy was scratched,
    Its backup locked in a drawer.
I cursed the slob that did that job,
    A damnable disc destroyer!
We reversed ten yards, picked up the shards
    Of a version he'd discarded.
It rankled like hell—it was sad to tell,
    Each bug was disregarded.

I shouted, "Nix! I refuse to fix
    A bug that's been glossed over!"
I flung my pencil, listing, stencil
    In disgust and went for the door.
But the boss called me back, gave me a pat,
    And said it's a night he'd remember.
He promised booze and great reviews,
    And a bonus in December.

Just one more hour, with tempers sour,
 'Til we could try again.
That code was mangled, tortured, tangled
 Unstructured, dumb, inane.
But after a while we began to smile;
 We'd corrected every blunder.
Just one little test and we could rest
 In sweet repose and slumber.

I hit the key for three-oh-three,
 But the system wouldn't have it.
I tried once more from the monitor,
 On the verge of throwing a fit.
The more I tried, the more I cried
 As the output mocked by silence.
It wasn't fair—I tore my hair;
 The time had come for violence!

I kicked the frame and kicked again;
 The printer burped the beginning.
Ignoring the risk, I stomped the disc,
 Sure now that I was winning.
I relished the hate as I beat the tape,
 Enjoying its rewinding.
That proc knew fear! The fact was clear
 From its internal grinding.

With every hit, I advanced one bit;
 Approaching the conclusion.
My fists were sore, replete with gore,
 Abrasion and contusion.
The tapes were rocking, no more mocking:
 I drove that system, beaming!
And by morning's light, the end in sight;
 I knew I'd soon be dreaming.

But then its bowel began to howl—
 My guts turned into jelly.
The metal shrieked, disk platters streaked
 Across the room pell-melly.
About the hall, from wall to wall,

They dove at us; we cowered,
One did a flip, and in a nip,
　　The boss was disemboweled.

It didn't wait, but threw a tape
　　Which bounded and entangled.
The loops unwound, around and round;
　　My partner died—enstrangled.
The printer dumped, gallumped and thumped,
　　The platen leapt and zoomed.
As in a dream, there was a scream;
　　The analyst was doomed!

There wasn't much fuss for the rest of us—
　　Just fracture and concussion,
An eye gouged out, a busted snout,
　　From which the red was gushin'.
As for the fire, you shouldn't inquire;
　　Nor of the flood that followed.
Those with skin called next of kin:
　　The memory forever hallowed.

There are bugs adrift on the midnight shift
　　That cannot be foretold.
The audit trails have their secret tales
　　That would make your blood run cold.
Debugging nights have seen queer sights,
　　But the queerest they ever did see
Was that time on the way to cutover day
　　I ran test three-oh-three.

PREFACE

This book concerns system software testing and quality assurance methods. The companion volume, *Software Testing Techniques* (BEIZ82), is concerned with structural and functional test techniques that are basic to all testing. The sum is not equal to the whole of its parts: the best designed, implemented, and tested individual units can come together in hopeless chaos in the absence of system-wide test plans, quality assurance, and integration testing. Unit testing, no matter how well done, just isn't enough.

I set out to write a single book that would cover the gamut from testing to quality assurance—from unit to system—and from individual test and quality assurance methods to system testing and quality assurance. It would have been a big, cumbersome book, and holding it to a publishable size would have required unfortunate compromises. The book would have been unsatisfying to me and to most readers. Accordingly, with Van Nostrand Reinhold's concurrence, I declared a book split, which yielded some unexpected dividends. It was no longer necessary to compromise between unit-level and system-level issues or between the programmer's and manager's points of views.

Software Testing Techniques focuses on what the individual programmer can and should do to create reliable software units. It is written for the programmer from a programmer's point of view. I thought at first that *this* book would have a single point of view, but soon found that there were four distinct voices with contradictory demands vying for my attention. The subject of system testing and quality assurance can be seen from the project manager's or the quality assurance manager's point of view and can be addressed to the project manager or to the quality assurance manager—for four voices in all. I quickly put the idea of a four-way split out of my mind—it would have yielded four thin books. I have instead used all four voices in this book. When discussing desk checking, for example, an activity in which I believe quality assurance has no productive role to play, it is as project manager to project manager. The problems of how to select QA personnel and how to shield them from hostility are clearly a conversation between QA managers. The inherent conflicts in system functional testing lead to the crossed conversations. The voice, therefore, changes from section to section, and within sections, without warning. There are so many conflicting goals inherent in system testing and quality assurance that it's essential that all parties in the process understand each other's point of view, and shifting it is one way to help that understanding.

Actually, while there may be beneficial tensions, there are no real conflicts, despite appearances to the contrary, just as there should be no real conflict between the programmer and program manager. In the ideal project, unit testing is well planned, thorough, well documented, and well managed. There is a hierarchy of testing methods from unit to system. The programmer can work in confidence that management and quality assurance methods are in place that relieve much of the uncertainty of interfacing with other programs. Well-wrought pieces of software come together because someone has taken the trouble to emplace the methods that assure that that will be the case. The project manager is not burdened with agonizing over the outcome of thousands of microscopic unit tests, because those tests are developed and executed under a uniform methodology. There is no need to agonize over what might have been forgotten, because quality assurance keeps track of everything. There is no need to worry about what surprises may come from a user's acceptance test, or from the first few months in the field, because quality assurance has savaged the system more than any user ever could, and done it in privacy, where the consequences are merely extra work rather than litigation.

Boris Beizer
Abington, Pennsylvania

Disclaimer and Acknowledgments

The continual references in this book and in *Software Testing Techniques* to "My Favorite Bad Project" should not lead the reader to the false conclusion that it was a Data Systems Analysts project. I am grateful to DSA for the support given to these books and for providing me with the opportunity to experience good programming and testing practices in action. My thanks to A.E. (Ted) Wolf's knowledge of R.W. Service and for helping to make "The Running of Three-Oh-Three" an authentic parody.

CONTENTS

10—ACHIEVING QUALITY SOFTWARE   308

SOFTWARE
SYSTEM TESTING
AND
QUALITY ASSURANCE

1

INTRODUCTION

1. TESTING AND QUALITY ASSURANCE GOALS

1.1. What We Do

The effort to achieve quality is the largest component of software cost. Testing and debugging costs range from 50% to 80% of the cost of producing a first working version of a software package. If the life-cycle cost of the software is considered from inception to retirement, then test and quality assurance related costs are an even larger part of the total cost. A dispassionate observer, a hypothetical person from Mars, might view programming as an activity dominated by testing with occasional lapses into design and documentation. That observer, not knowing what we take for granted, might further ask why the software was retired when it was. The answer would typically be that the program had undergone so many modifications that it was no longer possible to safely adjust it to meet requirements not foreseen by its originators.

"Aha!" says the Martian, "that's a quality assurance failure," and she adds the cost of the replacement program to the original program's cost. This Martian is as compulsive as a human programmer and she proceeds to tote up the cost of the three previous versions, which had also become obsolete, and then projects the cost of the next three versions and adds that in also. The bottom line, as it sees it, is that 99.59% of the cost of this piece of software was incurred as a result of quality assurance failures in the initial design and all through its life. Explaining the mitigating circumstances to these Martian—the difference between short- and long-term goals, the finite schedule and budget, the fact that most managers don't have crystal balls with which to see the future, that superprogrammers are rare, and so on—doesn't change their mind. If you object to Martian accounting, how about this example? A programming group expends ten man-years writing 100,000 instructions, which eventually results in a 20,000 instruction program. Was the group's productivity 10,000 instructions per man-year or 2000?

It's not a question of how hard we work, but of how smart. Smartness in software production is dominated by the ability to avoid past, present, and future bugs.

1.2. Attitudes and Beatitudes

Curse the darkness or light a candle—it's your choice. Blame bugs on the programmer's poor concentration. Insist on greater devotion to the work. Instill guilt and fear over bugs. Create programming standards that only you or a superprogrammer can meet. Listen to the latest snake-oil salesman who promises that if you only use his language (BUGBLAST), design technique (topdown recursive produlation effectors), management controls (cryptographs), and furthermore do them all simultaneously, then there will never again be a bug in your program.

Alternatively, recognize that bugs are rooted in our humanity. Every bug is the result of our human imprecision and our inability to perfectly communicate with one another. That same inability which has led to wars, to the repression of the human spirit, to totalitarian governments, but also to the richness of individual and cultural diversity. The Martians are telepaths and so they don't have wars or bugs; but they are also very dull. But being telepaths and of a single mind and purpose, they don't need computers because they are a computer. In other words, accept the fact that there will be bugs and that the bug's perpetrator is responsible, but not to blame.

But this doesn't mean that you're to accept bugs passively and do nothing about them. Nor should you tolerate sloppy work. The statistics indicate that good programmers will have of the order of one **public bug** per hundred statements (AKIY71, ALBE76, BOEH75B, ENDR75, SHOO75, THAY77).* A **public bug** is one that's discovered after a routine has been declared bug-free. We don't and can't know how many **private bugs** there are—the bugs the programmers keep to themselves. I know how many private bugs I have: approximately 1.5 per statement. What is your ratio of private to public bugs?** Does consideration of that ratio change your attitude towards bugs?

1.3. Productivity and Quality Assurance Goals

Consider the manufacture of a mass-produced gadget. However great the design effort, when it is amortized over a large production run it is a small part

---

*Don't take that 1% bug rate too seriously. Ten bugs in ten lines of complicated control code could be good performance while one bug in 1000 lines of a simple line-by-line report generator could be sloppy work.
**The worst I ever saw was a 500-instruction assembly language routine with an average of 2.2 public bugs per instruction after syntax checking by the assembler. That person, obviously, did not belong in programming.

of the total cost. Once the gadget is in production, every stage of manufacture is subjected to quality control and testing, from the source inspection of components to the final testing prior to shipping. If errors are discovered at any stage, the gadget will be reworked or discarded. The productivity of the assembly line is measured by the sum of costs of the materials, the rework, the discards, and the cost of quality assurance and inspection. There is a trade between quality assurance costs and manufacturing costs. If inadequate effort is devoted to testing, the reject rate will be high and so will the net cost. If, conversely, inspection is so thorough that all faults are discovered, then inspection costs will dominate and again product cost will suffer. The designers of a manufacturing process attempt to set quality assurance costs at a level consistent with the quality assurance objectives for the product and which minimizes the net cost. The cost of quality assurance might be as low as 2% in some consumer products or as high as 80% in products such as spaceships, nuclear reactors, and aircraft, where the cost of failure is measured in human lives.

The relation between productivity and quality in software is distinctly different than in manufactured goods. What does it cost to "manufacture" a copy of a piece of software? The cost of a tape or disc and a few minutes of computer time. Software maintenance is totally unlike hardware maintenance. Software neither fails nor does it wear out. Software "maintenance" consists of two activities: correction of latent defects and installation of enhancements. It is really an extension of the design process executed after the "final" version of the software has been delivered. Software quality assurance, therefore, is aimed completely at the design—either pre- or post-delivery. It is clear that the single largest component of software cost is the cost of bugs: the cost of detecting them, the cost of correcting them, the cost of designing tests that discover them, and the cost of running those tests. Consequently, the aim of software quality assurance should be bug prevention.

Testing is the primary tool of software quality assurance. Not just the act of running a test, but designing tests, establishing standards for tests, corrective procedures for discovered errors, and so on. More than the mere act of testing, the activity required to create a test is itself a powerful bug preventer. The thinking and analysis that must be done to create a useful test can discover and eliminate bugs before they are coded: while they are still private and therefore cheap. The ideal quality assurance activity would be so successful at this that all bugs would be eliminated during test design and there would be no need to run the tests.

Unfortunately, this ideal is unachievable. We are human and there will be bugs. To the extent that quality assurance fails at its primary purpose—bug prevention—it must achieve a secondary goal of bug detection. Bug detection is done by running tests. The test produces an unpredicted result and therefore demonstrates that a bug exists. That leads to the third-level goal of determining the cause of the problem—identifying the actual error, and then invoking the corrective mechanism, followed by **regression testing** to verify that the fix worked.

1.4. Test Design and Design for Test

1.4.1. Test Design

While programmers and programming managers seem to know that code must be designed and tested, many act as if they're unaware that tests themselves must be designed and tested—designed by a process no less rigorous and no less controlled than that used for code. Too often, test cases are attempted without prior analysis or careful consideration of the program's requirements or structure. Such tests (if they deserve the name at all) are no more than a haphazard series of ad-lib cases that are not documented either before or after they are executed. Because they were not formally designed and documented, they cannot be repeated with certainty. After the bug has been ostensibly corrected, no one is sure if the retest was identical to the test that found the flaw. Ad-lib tests are useful during debugging where their purpose is to help locate the bug. However, ad-lib tests, no matter how plentiful or exhausting, are not substitutes for *designed* tests.

The test design phase of programming should be recognized in details proportional to its cost. Why lump half the work under the broad-brush title of "test and debug" but be meticulous with respect to "coding," "design," and "documentation," each of which is only a small part of the whole? The programming process should be described as: design, test design, code, test code, program desk check, test desk check, test debugging, test execution, program debugging, correction coding, regression testing, and documentation. Under this classification scheme, the component parts of programming are of comparable size. Giving test design an explicit place in the scheme of things provides more visibility to that amorphous 50% that now goes under the name "test and debug." It makes it less likely that test design will be given short shrift when the budget's meager and the schedule's tight and there's a vain hope that just this once the system will come together without bugs.

1.4.2. Design for Test

Programming projects are conducted under constraints of time, human resources, and budget. Trades can be made between, and emphases shifted within each of these constraints. If the project's objective is the very short-term goal of producing something that runs without blowing up and that appears to meet the requirements, then emphasis will shift to coding. This seems to be where most programming projects are aimed. A more reasonable objective is to satisfy the requirements of a formal test and show satisfactory performance over a warranty period following the buyer's acceptance of the product. With this goal, the emphasis shifts from merely working code to testable code. A longer-term objective is a product with a long life: then the emphasis shifts to maintainable code. Maintainable code presupposes a base of working, thoroughly tested code and a code structure that can be easily reverified after modification by unknown future programmers. Therefore, maintainable code to a large extent is also testable code. One of the characteristics of all industries as they mature is the shift to longer and longer term goals. Computers and software are not exceptions, and as the goals for software reach further toward a satisfactory lifetime, so too must the emphasis shift from mere workability to testability

2. SOME DICHOTOMIES

2.1. Testing Versus Debugging

Testing and debugging are often lumped under the same heading and it's no wonder that their roles are often confused as a result. The purpose of testing is to show that bugs exist. The purpose of debugging is to find the error or misconception that led to the program's failure and to define the program changes that correct the error. If the program fails a test,* and if the test is correct, then there is at least one bug. There could be several bugs that conspire to cause the program failure, or one bug could cause the program to fail several different tests. While debugging usually follows testing, debugging and testing differ as to goals, methods, and psychology:

1. Testing starts with known conditions, uses predefined procedures, and has predictable outcomes. Only whether or not the program passes the test is unpredictable. Debugging starts from possibly unknown initial conditions, and the end cannot be predicted, except statistically.
2. Testing can and should be designed and scheduled beforehand. The procedures for, and duration of, debugging cannot be so constrained.
3. Testing is a demonstration of error or apparent correctness. Debugging is a deductive process.
4. Testing proves a programmer's failure. Debugging is the programmer's vindication.
5. Testing should strive to be predictable, dull, constrained, rigid, and inhu-

---

*Note that the test didn't fail. The test succeeded because it demonstrated the existence of a flaw. It was the program that failed.

man. Debugging demands intuitive leaps, conjectures, experimentation, intelligence, and freedom.

6. Testing, to a large extent, can be designed and accomplished in ignorance of the design. Debugging is impossible without detailed design knowledge.
7. Testing can be done by an outsider; debugging must be done by an insider.
8. While it is possible to establish theoretical limits to what testing can and cannot do, debugging, so far, has not been amenable to theoretical treatment.

Testing and debugging are not totally separated. Good test design and execution helps debugging because it eliminates fruitless bug hypotheses. Good tests, because they can be repeated and because they start from known initial conditions and follow a predefined sequence of steps, help to reduce the uncertainties of debugging. This book concerns testing and test design and not debugging.

2.2. Units, Subsystems, and Such

The smallest interesting subdivision of a program is a **unit**. The word "unit" as used in this book means:

1. A **unit** is the work of one programmer. Therefore, in addition to technical interfaces such as calling sequences and data-base elements, there is always a human interface.
2. A unit has data inputs. It processes those inputs to produce outcomes.* Inputs and outcomes may be implicit, as when data are in a common data base, or explicit, as when data are passed in a calling or return sequence. If any of these three components (input, process, outcome) is missing, then the unit is incomplete.
3. It is possible, in principle at least, to create a formal specification for every unit, defining input, process, and outcome.

Units are combined to create subprograms and programs. Programs are combined into subsystems, and subsystems are integrated into systems. Once we get into subdivisions larger than units, the definitions get looser. A **subsystem** is a collection of programs that as a collection accomplish some specified processing. Program subsystems are independent of one another. That is, one can draw a boundary around a subsystem such that it can do sensible work in

---

*"**Outcome**" rather than "output" because the execution of some units might result in a state change, interrupt, etc., with no observable output in the usual sense.

the absence of any other subsystem. Except for corrupted data, bugs in one subsystem cannot cause malfunction or error in another subsystem. Each subsystem has independent data validation and formal interfaces with other subsystems. Each subsystem has its own data base, but a data base common to several subsystems is not ruled out. Just as the unit is the work of one programmer, the subsystem is the work of one group of programmers. Therefore, between every pair of subsystems there is, in addition to the technical interface, a managerial interface.

The terms "**program element**" or "**element**" alone when context is clear or "routine" will be applied to all program components (units, programs, subsystems, or systems), when the distinction is not important, or when a concept applies to all levels.

2.3. Testing Versus Integration

Testing is the act of executing tests. Tests are designed and then executed to demonstrate correspondence between an element and its specification. There can be no testing without specifications of intentions. More precisely, since no test or finite sequence of tests can prove correspondence between an element and its specification, testing is an attempt to demonstrate that an element does *not* meet its specification (MYER79).

Integration is a specialized kind of testing applied to interfaces. Integration's purpose is to demonstrate consistency and compatibility between elements. Those elements could be producing garbage, provide no known useful service, or be totally wrong, but could, if they did what they did in a mutually consistent fashion, be successfully integrated. Elements are **unintegrated** prior to the completion of integration tests. Elements that have passed integration testing are **integrated**. Elements that could not be integrated are **disintegrated**. Disintegrated elements may each be correct insofar as their own specifications are concerned, and may even be correct with respect to a higher-level specification that covers them, but as a combination of elements they cannot be correct because there are interface contradictions or ambiguities, or both.

2.4. Structure Versus Function

Tests can be designed from either a functional or a structural point of view. In **functional testing** the element is treated as a black box. It is subjected to inputs and its outcomes are verified for conformance to its specification. The software's ultimate user should be concerned only with function, and the element's implementation details should not matter. Functional testing inherently takes the user's point of view.

Structural testing is intimately tied to the implementation details. Such things as programming style, control methods, source language, data-base design, and coding details dominate structural testing. A test based on following certain paths through an element is structural. A test that exploits peculiarities in hardware, language, or operating system is structural.

There is no controversy between structural and functional testing. Both methods are essential, both are effective, and both have limitations. The two concepts actually represent the extreme points of a spectrum between structure and function. Unit tests tend to be more structural than functional, while the converse is true for system tests. Functional tests can in principle detect all bugs but would take an infinite amount of time to do so. Structural tests are finite, but cannot detect all bugs even if completely executed.

2.5. Designer Versus Tester

Design, coding, and debugging are done by designers. Testing is done by testers. If testing could be completely functional and totally independent of implementation details, then it would be possible to completely separate the designer and tester. Conversely, if testing were totally structural, then the tester would have to know the system as well as the designer, and consequently the tester and designer would have to be one. The less the tester knows about the implemention details (i.e., the more functional the test), the less bias there is in the tests and the more likely that the test will reveal incorrect functions, missing functions, and improper assumptions. Unfortunately, this also means that more tests will be unproductive and inefficient. The problem is that in anything deserving the name "system," there are far more things that could be tested than there is time or money for. All real test plans are incomplete and represent a compromise between thoroughness and budget. The designer's detailed knowledge allows the elimination of countless test cases that would prove nothing. It also brings bias and blindness to strange cases that should be tested but won't be. The independent tester is inherently inefficient because he cannot take advantage of the designer's knowledge. But the independent tester is more likely to find missing functions and incorrect interpretations of the specification.

The extent to which the tester and designer should be separated depends on the level of the test. Independent structural testing of units is wasteful. It can more than double the total labor required to successfully integrate a unit, and can materially *degrade* the unit's quality. Instead of spending half of the time on testing, the programmer must now spend a comparable amount of time with the tester—to explain what the unit should be doing, is doing, and will be doing; to educate the tester and to resolve the tester's many cockpit errors. All that takes as much time as test design and testing; but the tester is spending that time also, and therefore the total labor content is at least doubled. The software is probably worse and the testing not as thorough because the programmer sees the tester as an imposition and may, knowingly or subconsciously, sabotage the tester's effort. And if the tester is any good, she must face the constant frustration of working with a routine that she knows how to design better.

Conversely, to allow system level testing to be done only by the designer is an invitation to self-deception. The designer's motivation guarantees some whitewash. The designer wants to get a program accepted within a specified budget and schedule. Testing interferes with both. Only an angel would not succumb to the more potent pressures of budget and schedule—but angels don't have bugs.

Again, there are no absolutes, but a spectrum. On the unit side of the scale, the need for efficiency and a structural orientation means that there is very little independent testing. At the system level, the need for a functional orientation and verification against specifications dictates the dominance of independent test teams. In between, we hope for cooperation.

2.6. Builder Versus Buyer

Most software is written and used by the same organization. Unfortunately, this situation is inherently dishonest because it clouds accountability. More and more organizations are recognizing the virtue of independent software development because it leads to better software, better security, and better testing. Independent software development does not mean that all software should be bought from software houses or consultants, but that the software development entity and the entity that pays for the software are sufficiently separated as to make accountability clear. I've heard of instances in which the software development group and the operational group within the same company negotiate and sign formal contracts with one another—with lawyers present. If there is no separation between builder and buyer, there can be no accountability. If there is no accountability, the primary motivation for software quality assurance disappears. Just as programmers and testers can merge and become one, so can builder and buyer. There are several other persons in the software development cast of characters who, like the above, can also be separated or merged:

1. The **builder** who designs for and is accountable to
2. The **buyer**—who pays for the system in the hope of making a profit by providing services to
3. The **user**—the ultimate beneficiary or victim of the system. The user's interests are guarded by
4. The **tester**—who is dedicated to the builder's destruction, and
5. The **operator**—who has to live with the builder's mistakes, the buyer's murky specifications, the tester's oversights, and the user's complaints.

3. A MODEL PROJECT

Quality assurance is applied to anything from subroutines to systems that consist of millions of program statements. The archetype system, however, is one that allows the exploration of all aspects of quality assurance without the managerial and organizational complications that have nothing to do with software but that affect any very large project. Testing a stand-alone routine that consists of a few hundred instructions is very different from testing a routine of the same size that must be integrated into a working program of a few hundred thousand instructions. While all the problems of the solitary routine occur for the routine that is embedded in a system, the converse is not true: many kinds of bugs simply cannot exist in solitary routines. The real world of programming is dominated by cooperative efforts and programming staffs of tens to hundreds. There is an implied context for this book—a real-world context, which can be characterized by the following model project:

Application—The specifics of the application are unimportant. It is a real-time system that must provide timely responses to user requests for services. It is an on-line system, which is connected to remote terminals by communication links.

Staff—The programming staff consists of 20 to 30 programmers—large enough to warrant some formality, but not too large to manage effectively—large enough to use specialists for various aspects of the system's design.

Schedule—The project will take 24 months from the start of design to formal acceptance by the buyer. Acceptance will be followed by a six-month cutover period.

Specification—The specification is good. It is functionally detailed without constraining the design. There are, however, undocumented "understandings" concerning the requirements.

Acceptance Test—The system will be accepted only after a formal acceptance test. The application is not new, and therefore part of the formal test already exists. The buyer will initially intend to design the acceptance test, but later it will become the software supplier's responsibility.

Personnel—The staff is professional and experienced in programming and in the application. Half of the staff has programmed for that computer before, and most know the source language. One-third, mostly juniors, have no experience with the application. The typical programmer has been employed by the programming department for two years and knows (likes and dislikes) 25% of the group. The general attitude is open and frank. Management's attitude is positive and knowledgeable about the realities of such projects.

Standards—There are programming standards and they are usually followed. There is an implicit understanding of the role of interfaces and the need for interface standards. Documentation is good. There is an internal, semiformal, quality assurance function. The data base is centrally developed and administered.

Objectives—The system is the first of many similar systems that will be implemented in the future. No two will be identical, but they will have 75% of the code in common. Once installed, the typical system is expected to operate profitably for ten or more years.

History—One programmer will quit before his module is tested. Another programmer will be fired before testing begins. The work will be excellent, but the documentation poor. One module will have to be totally redone after unit testing. It will be a superb piece of work that defies integration. The buyer will insist on five major changes and twenty minor ones. There will be at least one nasty problem that nobody, not buyer, not programmer, not management, nor the hardware vendor suspected. A facility and/or hardware delivery problem will delay testing for several weeks and force second- and third-shift work. Several important milestones will slip, but the delivery date will be met.

In other words, our model is typical of a reasonably well run, successful project with a share of glory and catastrophe. Not a utopian project, but not a slice of hell either.

4. THE SEARCH FOR EL DORADO*

4.1. Do Bugs Exist?

Go back in time to a sixteenth century Spanish or Portuguese port and listen to the debate between the adventurer and his backers. How should the ships be constructed to safely transport such vast hoards of gold? How many barrels will we need to store the precious stones picked off the beaches? The golden armor and plates will have to be melted down, but the curbstones of silver can be used as ballast directly. How many woodcutters will we need, or can the enslaved natives be trusted with axes? All this before it has been ascertained whether or not the fabled El Dorado with its streets of gold exists.

Do bugs exist? I know that atoms exist, as do stars and other things that have physical reality. Bugs do not have that kind of reality. I can argue equally

---

*Being that mythical country in Central or South America whose streets were paved with gold and where precious jewels littered the beaches—searched for in vain by Conquistadores and English pirates. The favorite of the Renaissance con artist, it has yet to be found.

well that all programs have bugs, no matter how simple the program, how good the test, how extensive the quality controls, and that no programs have bugs, no matter how poor the specification, how atrocious the implementation, and how copious the design deficiency reports. All programs have bugs because the specification can be changed to the point where the program no longer matches it. Similarly, no program has bugs because the specification can be revised to accept the most bizarre behavior. You object that I've change the ground rules—I have—and converted the problem to that of a bug-free specification. Are you willing to assert that all specifications are correct and bug-free? You can't prove that a program has or hasn't a bug until you can first prove that the specification is bug-free. Continue in this way and you'll soon ask "What is truth?," leading to fundamental questions in philosophy and theology concerning "good" and "beauty's" definition also. Socrates didn't resolve these questions, nor did Confucius, Kant, Schopenhauer, Lenin, or Mao Tse-tung. Unlike physics and mathematics, where we can strive for absolutes, a physics for bugs is not possible because bugs are a construct of the human mind, and arbitrary as far as the universe is concerned. There can never be an absolute definition for bugs, nor an absolute determination of their existence. The extent to which a program has bugs is measured by the extent to which it fails to be useful. This is a fundamentally human measure and contrary to any notion of absolute certainty.

4.2. Is Complete Testing Possible?

If the objective of testing were to *prove* that a program is free of bugs, then not only would testing be practically impossible, but it would also be theoretically impossible. Three different approaches can be used to attempt to demonstrate that a program is correct: tests based purely on structure, tests based purely on function, and formal proofs of correctness. Each approach leads to the conclusion that complete testing, in the sense of a *proof*, is not theoretically possible, and certainly not practically possible (MANN78).

Functional Testing—Every program operates on a finite number of inputs. Whatever pragmatic meaning those inputs might have, they can always be interpreted as a binary bit stream. A complete functional test would consist of subjecting the program to all possible input streams. For each input, the routine either accepts the stream and produces a correct output, accepts the stream and produces an incorrect output, or rejects the stream and tells us that it did so. Because the rejection message is itself an output, the problem is reduced to verifying that the correct output is produced for every input. However, a ten-character input string has 2^{80} possible input streams and corresponding outputs. So complete functional testing in this sense is clearly impractical.*

Unfortunately, even theoretically we cannot execute a purely functional test this way, because we don't really know the length of the string to which the system is responding. Let's say that the routine should respond to a ten-character string. It should be reset after the tenth character, and the next ten characters should constitute a new test. However, the routine has a huge buffer and is actually responding to a 10,000-character string. The bug is such that the program will appear to provide a proper output for every ten-character sequence the first thousand times and fail on the 1001st attempt. Without a limit to the routine's memory capacity, which is a structural concept, it is impossible even in principle to prove that the routine is correct.

There are two additional problems: the input sequence generator and the output comparator. Is it to be assumed that the hardware and software used to generate the inputs, used to compare the real outcomes to the expected outcomes, and used to document the expected outcomes themselves, are bug-free? Pure functional testing is at best conditional on a nonverifiable assumption that all test tools and test preparation tools are correct and that only the routine being tested is at fault; in the real world of testing, that assumption is silly.

Structural Testing—One should design a sufficient number of tests to assure that every path through the routine is exercised at least once. Right off that's impossible, because some loops might never terminate. Brush that problem aside by observing that the universe and all that's in it is finite. Even so, the number of paths through a small routine can be awesome because each loop multiplies the path count by the number of times through the loop. A small routine can have millions or billions of paths. Total path testing is not generally practical. Total path testing can be done for some routines. Say we do it. This has the virtue of eliminating the problems of unknown size that we ran into for purely functional testing, but it does not eliminate the problem of preparing a bug-free input, a bug-free response list, and a bug-free test observation. We still need those things, because pure structural testing does not assure us that the routine is doing the right thing in the first place.

Correctness Proofs—Formal proofs of correctness rely on a combination of functional and structural concepts. Requirements are stated in a formal language (e.g., mathematics), and each program statement is examined and used in a step of a proof that the routine will produce the correct output for all possible input sequences. The practical issue here is that such proofs are

---

*At one test per microsecond, approximately twice the current estimated age of the universe.

very expensive and have been applied only to numerical routines or to formal proofs for crucial software such as a system's security kernel or portions of compilers. But there are theoretical objections to formal proofs of correctness that go beyond the practical issues. How do we know that the specification is achievable? Its consistency and completeness must be proven, and in general that is a provably unsolvable problem. Assuming that the specification has been proven correct, then the mechanism used to prove the program, the steps in the proof, the logic used, and so on must be proven (GOOD75). Mathematicians and logicians have no more immunity to bugs than programmers or testers have. This also leads to never-ending sequences of unverifiable assumptions.

Manna and Waldinger (MANN78) have clearly summarized the theoretical barriers to complete testing:

"We can never be sure that the specifications are correct."
"No verification system can verify every correct program."
"We can never be certain that a verification system is correct."

4.3. Realistic Goals

Not only are all known approaches to absolute demonstration of program correctness impractical, but they are impossible as well. Therefore, the objective of testing must shift from an absolute proof to a suitably convincing demonstration; from a deduction to a seduction; to the creation of warm feeling in everybody's tummy instead of heartburn. What constitutes a "suitable" demonstration depends on context. What is suitable to a video game is not suitable to a nuclear reactor. What is suitable depends on the buyer's willingness to pay for quality. It also depends on the desired balance between short- and long-term goals. Given all these factors, it should be possible, in principle, to design a quality assurance program that leads to the software quality appropriate to the circumstances. However, the present state of things is not nearly so noble:

1. Much of the software in use and under development has no quality to speak of. Deep philosophical issues aside, they're heaps of garbage crawling with bugs.
2. Testing is often conducted as a meaningless, objectionable ritual that proves nothing, demonstrates less, and is more likely to create dissension than quality.
3. Quality goals are defined after the fact to correspond to the quality observed in the program.

Such a pitiable state of affairs is not realistic either. The prerequisite to quality assurance must be realistic and appropriate quality goals: neither the vain search for absolute perfection as a matter of principle, nor the comatose acceptance of slovenly work; neither the intolerant insistence that all testing and quality assurance effort, at any level, is an automatic part of the job and free of charge, nor shouting "change of scope" whenever an obvious deficiency is pointed out; neither the erection of an obnoxious quality assurance bureaucracy, nor the abrogation of all quality assurance responsibility by delegating it to the individual programmer. Instead, the builder, the buyer, and the tester must strive to establish clear goals, to set firm and realistic prices and schedules for the accomplishment of those goals, and to emplace mechanisms for the discovery, arbitration, and rectification of program flaws.

2

BUGS IN PERSPECTIVE

1. SYNOPSIS

Can bugs be measured? What are the possible consequences of bugs? Bugs are categorized. Statistics on the occurrence of various bugs are given. Some tasks for a quality assurance department.

2. BUG MEASURES

2.1. Can Bugs Be Measured?

Quality assurance for manufactured objects is based on quantitative measurements. The quality assurance department together with the product engineering department establish quantitative objectives for critical aspects of the product: "the shaft must be 0.554 mm plus or minus .0006 mm," "the gain must be 25 db plus/minus one db," "the hardness must be between 7.2 and 7.7," "the pH must be 7.035 plus/minus .03," and so on. Instruments can then be used to determine if an object meets or fails quality objectives. In manufactured physical products, quality can be described quantitatively by a set of measurable parameters. The larger the deviation of those parameters from the standards, the poorer the product. Can such a quantifiable measure be applied to software?

No.

Software products are not physical—they're mental. We don't have mental micrometers for mental constructs. There is no such thing as an "ideal" program or "the" correct program. Ten good programmers working with equal skill to the same specification will produce ten different routines, all of which are acceptable. Therefore, it is impossible to establish a standard against which to measure quality, even if it were measurable in the same way that manufactured products are measurable.

Ignore the problems of a suitable standard for the moment and consider the problem of measurement itself. Let's propose a very simple measure. Count the number of bits by which the "correct" and "incorrect" program differ. It's easy to measure: a simple utility routine can be written for the purpose. But does this measure mean anything? Say that the routine is part of a report generator and that the specification requires every report page to conclude with a line of 100 dashes. The programmer inadvertently uses hyphens. The hyphen and dash characters differ by four bits, therefore the bit difference between the two programs is 400 bits. Right? The programmer should have created the line of dashes in a loop that took six instructions of 32 bits. It took four instructions and a 100-character literal for the "wrong" implementation. The whole thing is wrong, therefore the error is 1120 bits. Right? The next programmer did use a loop, but only had the one character wrong, and therefore the error is only four bits. This measure is beginning to look like a very rubbery micrometer. The same idea can be applied to deviation measures based on instruction differences, data-base differences, structural difference measures of various kinds, or any other quantifiable, measurable, nonsubjective aspect of a program. In all cases you'll find that it is neither possible to establish a suitable standard, nor to do a meaningful measurement of the deviation of the program being examined from that standard. Furthermore, alternative, equally valid implementations will differ from one another by far more than any of them differ from a buggy version of itself. Therefore, perhaps the best we can hope for is a simple count of the number of bugs that are observed without being overly concerned with the structural details of the bits, instructions, and so on that are in error.

2.2. Can Bugs Be Counted?

Surely we can at least count bugs? I'm not so sure. I've spent a lot of time in occasionally acrimonious debates over whether or not a particular test result was indicative of a bug or not. If bug counting was so easy, we wouldn't have so many different interpretations of the same specification. An equation solver provides answers to three significant figures and is also very fast. One user would prefer ten digits of accuracy even if it does slow the solver down, while another will tolerate only two digits if the solver can be made faster. Even in the relatively pure and simple world of mathematics there can be controversy regarding what is or is not a bug. Therefore it shouldn't surprise us that, in the more realistic and humanly oriented world of data processing, bug counting is even more subjective. Ultimately, a bug is a bug only by agreement between builder and buyer (or the quality assurance department). That which is a bug is that which is declared to be a bug after all the arguments are done. Such declarations can and should be recorded and counted.

2.3. Public and Private Bugs

Bugs have scopes that range from private to public, or alternatively from local to global. The scope of a bug is measured by the extent to which it leads to misconceptions that will result in yet more bugs. Programs begin as wholly private thoughts. Setting them down on paper makes them more public. Compiling or assembling them makes them more public yet, because they must interact with the compiler or assembler. As the program progresses from thoughts towards an integrated module it becomes more public. Experience indicates that the cost of correcting a bug is geometrically related to its degree of public exposure. This is independent of the severity of the bug in application terms or the complexity of the fix. Any measure of bugs should be tempered by how public is the routine in which the bug occurs. Any measure of program quality related to bug counting should give higher weight to bugs in proportion to how public they are. The most private bugs, those that the programmer discovers before coding, should be given zero weight because no statistics can be gathered on their incidence. Such private bugs can only be implied from the programmer's productivity. A hundred bugs caught during unit testing are less important than one caught during system integration. If you insist on weighting all bugs equally, whatever their privacy, then you may seriously degrade program quality and circumvent your own efforts. Giving equal weight to bugs of all privacy levels shifts the emphasis in testing, test design, and debugging away from the system level and to the unit level. The result is that the individual programmers become more concerned with covering their asses than with assuring a well integrated system.

I wrote earlier that my private bug rate was approximately 1.5 bugs per statement. I had originally written "one bug per ten statements," thinking that a 10-to-1 ratio between private and public bugs was dramatic enough. However, I decided to check this by an experiment. I kept meticulous track of my private bug rate on several small analytical programs that I was writing in BASIC. I first wrote the programs in ink on paper using pseudo-code and then keyed them into my computer. I kept meticulous track of each syntax error, each erasure, each conceptual error, from the time I started the routine until I believed that it had been thoroughly tested. The routines were small and corresponded to the typical unit-level routine. I did not count honest design changes, revisions made in the interest of improved performance or reduced space, or the like. Just real bugs—in some cases, bugs that failed to materialize because I caught them before I had set them down in pseudo-code. I used the following criterion for such bugs. I asked myself, If the telephone had rung at that moment, might the bug have become imbedded in the code? If yes, it was counted. This is admittedly a highly subjective procedure and prone to self-deception or argument over what did or didn't constitute a bug.* But to paraphrase Louis Armstrong: "If you have to ask what a bug is, you'll never know." I regard myself a good craftsman when it comes to programming, and my public bug rate is less than one per hundred statements. Therefore, counting 1.5 bugs per statement was a shocking but revealing experience.** Although it cannot be verified by sound statistical studies, I am convinced that most humans' private bug rate is comparable—if they were honest about it, to others and to themselves. What matters is not the exact value of the very private bug rate, but the incredible contrast between that rate and the public rate. The impact of this experiment was profound because it more than ever convinced me of the futility of guilt associated with bugs. When the private bug rate is so high, any degree of guilt whatsoever is overwhelming. Therefore, the only rational response to bugs, discovered and otherwise, is to create screens that will sift them out at every stage and prevent them from becoming public. I urge the reader to try this experiment. If honestly conducted, it cannot but help change one's attitude and response to bugs and quality assurance.

2.4. Equal Rights for Bugs?

All bugs are not equal. There is no known relation between the difficulty of fixing a bug and the observed severity of its symptoms. A catastrophic bug may have a trivial fix, and an unimportant functional flaw may have a catastrophic (to budget and schedule) fix. Therefore, bug severity should not be measured in terms of correction cost. A simple count of bugs would be a distortion. A program with ten inconsequential bugs is better than a program with one catastrophic bug. Any method of counting bugs should be tempered by a corresponding, subjective perhaps, measure of the bug's severity. What constitutes severity is highly dependent on context if one insists on technical measures.

---

*I was troubled over what to do with what I thought were bugs but really weren't. Ernie said, "That's two bugs"—and so I counted them.
**The above may seem like a piece of cheap confessional and out of place in a technical book, personal as it is. However, the nature of the experiment is private. I cannot expect any honest corroborative statistics. As the experiment progressed, I found myself not setting things down on paper until I was sure of them—thereby hiding from myself another set of bugs. "Oh, what a tangled web we weave, when first we practice to deceive" (Sir Walter Scott).

However, you can relate severity to human terms and measures, as in the following categories:

1. **Mild**—The symptoms of the bug offend us aesthetically: a misspelled output or a badly aligned printout.
2. **Moderate**—Outputs are misleading or redundant. The bug has a small but measurable impact on the system's performance.
3. **Annoying**—The system's behavior, because of the bug, is dehumanizing. Names are truncated or arbitrarily modified. Bills for $0.00 are sent. Operators must use unnatural command sequences and must trick the system into a proper response for unusual, bug-related cases.
4. **Disturbing**—It refuses to handle legitimate transactions. The money machine refuses to cash your paycheck. My credit card is not accepted at the bookstore.
5. **Serious**—It loses track of transactions: not just the transaction itself (your paycheck), but the fact that the transaction occurred. Accountability is lost.
6. **Very Serious**—Instead of losing your paycheck, the system credits it to another account, or converts a deposit into a withdrawal. The bug causes the system to do the wrong transaction.
7. **Extreme**—The above problems are not limited to a few users or to a few transaction types. They occur frequently and arbitrarily, instead of sporadically for strange cases.
8. **Intolerable**—Long-term, irrecoverable corruption of the data base occurs. Furthermore, this corruption is not easily discovered. Serious consideration is given to shutting the system down.
9. **Catastrophic**—The decision to shut down is taken out of our hands. The system fails.
10. **Infectious**—What can be worse than a failed system? One that corrupts other systems even though it does not fail itself; one that erodes the social or physical environment; one that melts nuclear reactors or starts wars; one whose influence, because of malfunction, is far greater than expected, or wanted; a system that kills.

These philosophical consequences must be interpreted in terms peculiar to the application. They will be modified by the program's audience—the human population with which the program directly and indirectly interacts. They must be modified to conform to legal definitions of severity regarding consequences, as in banking, credit management, air traffic control, and so on. They must be modified by management's mind-set regarding severity—does management's attitude reflect "to hell with the customer" or "the customer is always right"? Clearly, the "human terms" of programming as conducted in the Soviet Union are not to be compared to the human terms of a public information system in a free society.

3. A TAXONOMY FOR BUGS

3.1. General

This section establishes technical categories for bugs. A more detailed version of the same can be found in BEIZ82. It's important to establish categories for bugs if you take the goal of bug prevention seriously. If a particular kind of bug (in technical terms) recurs or seems to dominate the kinds of bugs you have, then it's possible through education, training, new controls, revised controls, documentation, inspection, and a variety of other methods to reduce the incidence of that kind of bug. If you have no statistics on the frequency of bugs in your organization, you cannot have a rational perspective on where and how to allocate your limited bug-prevention resources. Using statistics gathered from another shop, or published statistics, is a valid starting point when you have nothing better to go on, but ineffectual in the long run. As corrective measures are applied to reduce the incidence of one kind of bug, the statistics perforce change. The change in bug statistics is the only way you can determine if a quality assurance method is effective—the incidence of the kind of bug the measure is intended to prevent is reduced.

The taxonomy presented here is only a starting point. There is no universally correct way to categorize bugs. This taxonomy is not rigid. Bugs are difficult to categorize because they usually have several symptoms. A given bug can be put into one or another category depending on the history of the bug and the programmer's state of mind. For example, a one-character error in a source statement changes the statement, but, unfortunately, it passes syntax checking. As a result, data are corrupted in an area far removed from the actual bug. That in turn leads to an improperly executed function. Is this a keypunch error, a coding error, a data error, or a functional error? The broad categories are: function bugs, system bugs, data bugs, and code errors. The function bugs can be subdivided into specification errors, incorrect functions, testing errors, and validation-criteria errors. System bugs include external interfaces, internal interfaces, hardware-architecture problems, operating system problems, software architecture problems, control and sequence bugs, and resource-management bugs. Process errors can involve basic manipulations, initialization, control and sequence, and static logic.

3.2. Function-Related Bugs

3.2.1. Specification Problems

Specifications can be incomplete, ambiguous, or self-contradictory. They can be misunderstood or incapable of being understood. The specification may assume, but not mention, additional specifications and prerequisites which are known to the specifier but not the designer. And specifications that do not have these flaws may change while the design is in progress. The designer has to hit a moving target and occasionally misses.

3.2.2. Function Errors

Specification problems usually create corresponding functional problems. A function can be wrong, missing, or superfluous. A missing function is the easiest to detect and correct. A wrong function could have deep design implications. Extra functions were at one time considered desirable. It is now recognized that "free" functions are rarely free. Any increase in generality that does not contribute to software reliability, modularity, maintainability, and system robustness should be suspected. Gratuitous enhancements can, if they increase the system's complexity, accumulate into a fertile compost heap that breeds future bugs, and they can burrow holes that can be converted into system security breaches. Conversely, one cannot rigidly forbid additional features that might be a consequence of good design. Removing the features might complicate the software, require additional resources, and foster additional bugs. For example, if the present system is built on a base of a well-tested previous system, taking the unwanted functions out of that base might incur more bugs than leaving them in.

3.2.3. Testing

Testers have no immunity to bugs; neither do specification writers. Tests, particularly system-level functional tests, require complicated scenarios and data bases. They require code or the equivalent to execute, and consequently they can have bugs. The virtue of independent functional testing is that it provides an unbiased point of view. But that lack of bias creates an opportunity for different, and possibly incorrect, interpretations of the specification. While test bugs are not system bugs, it's hard to tell them apart, and considerable labor can be expended in making the distinction.

3.2.4. Test Criteria

The specification is correct, it is correctly interpreted and implemented, and in principle a proper test has been designed. However, the criterion by which the system's behavior is judged is incorrect or impossible. How would you, for example, "prove that the entire system is free of bugs"? The more complicated the criteria, the more likely they are to have bugs.

3.2.5. Remedies

Most function-related bugs are rooted in human-to-human communication problems. One of the proposed solutions being researched is the use of high-level, formal specification languages (BOEH79, FISC79, YEHR80). Such languages may or may not help. If the specification language were really good, and it were possible, even theoretically, to create an unambiguous, complete specification with an unambiguous, complete test, and completely consistent test criteria, then a specification written in that language would be theoretically capable of automatic conversion into code (ignoring efficiency and practicality issues). But this is just programming in HOL squared. The specification problem has been shifted to a higher level but not eliminated. The real impact of formal specification languages will probably be that they will influence the design of ordinary programming languages so that more of the specification can be formalized. This will reduce, but not eliminate, specification-related errors.

Assurance of functional correctness is provided by an independent interpretation of the specification and independent, system-level, functional testing. The remedy for test bugs is testing and debugging the tests. The differences between test debugging and program debugging are not fundamental. Generally, test debugging is easier, because tests, when properly designed, are simpler than programs and do not have to make concessions to efficiency. Programmers have the right to ask how quality in independent testing and test design is monitored. Should we implement test-testers and test-tester tests? This sequence does not converge. Methods for test quality assurance are discussed in Chapter 10.

3.3. System Bugs

3.3.1. External Interfaces

The external interfaces are the means the system uses to communicate with the world. These include devices, actuators, sensors, input consoles, printers, and communication lines. Often there is a person on the other side of the interface. That person may be ingenious or ingenuous, but often malevolent. The principal design criterion for an interface with the outside world is robustness. External interface errors include: invalid timing or sequence assumptions related to external signals; misunderstanding external input and output formats; insufficient tolerance to bad input data.

3.3.2. Internal Interfaces

Internal interfaces are in principle not different from external interfaces, but there are differences in practice because the internal environment is more controlled. While the external environment is fixed, and the system must adapt to it, the internal environment, which consists of interfaces with other programs, can be negotiated. Internal interfaces have the same problems that external interfaces have and a few more that are more closely related to implementation details: protocol-design errors, input- and output-format errors, inadequate protection against corrupted data, wrong subroutine call sequence, call-parameter errors, misunderstood entry or exit parameter values.

Internal interfaces should be standardized and not just allowed to grow. They should be formal, and there should be as few as possible. There is an inherent trade between the number of different internal interfaces and the complexity of the interfaces. One universal interface would have so many parameters that it would be inefficient and subject to abuse, misuse, and misunderstanding. Unique interfaces for every pair of communicating routines would be efficient, but N programmers could lead to N^2 interfaces, most of which wouldn't be documented and all of which would have to be tested (but wouldn't be). The primary objective of integration testing is to test all internal interfaces.

3.3.3. Hardware Architecture

It is neither practical nor economical for every programmer in a large project to be knowledgeable in all aspects of the hardware architecture. Software bugs related to hardware architecture arise mainly from misunderstanding how the hardware works. Here are examples: paging mechanism ignored or misunderstood, address-generation error, I/O-device operation or instruction error, I/O-device address error, misunderstood device-status code, improper hardware simultaneity assumption, hardware race condition ignored, data format wrong for device, wrong format expected, device protocol error, device instruction-sequence limitation ignored, expecting the device to respond too quickly, waiting too long for a response, ignoring channel throughput limits, assuming that the device is initialized, assuming that the device is not initialized, incorrect interrupt handling, ignoring hardware fault or error conditions, ignoring operator malice.

The remedy for hardware architecture and interface problems is twofold: 1) good programming and testing, and 2) centralization of hardware interface software in programs that are written by hardware interface specialists.

3.3.4. Operating System

Program bugs related to the operating system are a combination of hardware architecture and interface bugs, mostly due to misunderstanding what it is the operating system does. And of course, the operating system could have bugs of its own. The remedy for operating system interface bugs is the same as for hardware bugs: use operating system interface specialists, and use explicit interface modules or macros for all operating system calls. This may not eliminate the bugs, but at least it will localize them and make testing easier.

3.3.5. Software Architecture

Routines can pass unit and integration testing without revealing software architecture bugs. Many of these bugs are load dependent and occur only when the system is stressed. They tend to be the most difficult kind of bug to find and exhume. Here is a sample of the causes of such bugs: assumption that there will be no interrupts, failure to block or unblock interrupts, assumption that code is reentrant or not reentrant, bypassing data interlocks, failure to close or open an interlock, assumption that a called routine is resident or not resident, assumption that a calling program is resident or not resident, assumption that registers or memory were initialized or not initialized, assumption that register or memory location content did not change, local setting of global parameters, and global setting of local parameters.

The first line of defense against these bugs is the design. The first bastion of that defense is that there *be* a design for the overall software architecture. Failure to create an explicit software architecture is an unfortunate but common disease. The most elegant test techniques will be helpless in a complicated system whose architecture "just growed" without plan or structure. All test techniques are applicable to the discovery of software architecture bugs, but experience has shown that careful integration of modules and subjecting the system to a brutal stress test are particularly effective.

3.3.6. Resource Management Problems

Memory is subdivided into dynamically allocated resources such as buffer blocks, queue blocks, task-control blocks, and overlay buffers. Similarly, external mass storage units such as discs are subdivided into memory-resource pools. Here are some resource usage and management bugs: required resource not obtained (rare), wrong resource used (common, if there are several resources with the same structure or different kinds of resources in the same pool), resource already in use, race condition in getting a resource, resource not returned to the right pool, fractionated resources not properly recombined (some resource managers take big resources and subdivide them into smaller resources, and Humpty Dumpty isn't always put together again), failure to return a resource (common), resource deadlock (a type A resource is needed to get a type B, a type B is needed to get a type C, and a type C is needed to get a type A), resource use forbidden to the caller, resource linked to the wrong kind of queue.

A design remedy that prevents bugs is always preferable to a test method that discovers them. The design remedy in resource management is to keep the resource structure simple: the fewest different kinds of resources, the fewest pools, and no private resource management. The second design remedy is to centralize the management of all pools, either through centralized common resource-management subroutines or subprograms, resource-management macros, or a combination of these.

3.4. Process Errors

3.4.1. Arithmetic and Manipulative Bugs

These bugs include arithmetic errors and their extension into algebra, function evaluation, and general processing. Many problems in this area are related to incorrect conversion from one data representation to another. This is particularly true in assembly language programming. Other problems include: ignoring overflow; ignoring the difference between positive and negative zero; improper use of greater, greater-than-or-equal, less-than, less-than-or-equal; assumption of equality to zero in floating point; and improper comparison between different formats, as in ASCII to binary or integer to floating point.

The best design remedy is in the source language. A **strongly typed language**, that is, language that does not permit the inadvertent combination of different data types or that warns the programmer when such operations are attempted, can minimize this kind of error. If such language facilities are not available, the use of macros and arithmetic subroutines, particularly in assembly language programming, are effective.

3.4.2. Initialization Bugs

Initialization-related bugs are among the most common. Both the failure to initialize properly and superfluous initialization occur. The latter tends to be less harmful but can affect performance. Typical errors are: forgetting to initialize working space, registers, or data areas before first use or assuming that they are initialized elsewhere; error in the first value of a loop-control parameter; accepting an initial value without a validation check; and initializing to the wrong format, data representation, or type.

The remedies here are in the kinds of tools the programmer has. The source language is also helpful. Forcing explicit declaration of all variables, as in Pascal, helps to reduce initialization problems.

3.4.3. Control and Sequence Bugs

These are similar to control and sequence errors at the system level, but they are usually easier to test and debug, because they tend to have more localized effects: paths left out, unreachable code, improper nesting of loops, loop-back or loop-termination criteria incorrect, missing process steps, error in process step, duplicated processing, unnecessary processing, improper assumption about processing byproducts, and unwanted byproducts.

Control and sequence errors at all levels are caught by testing, particularly structural testing, combined with a bottom-line functional test based on a specification. The problem at the unit level is that there often is no formal specification of what is wanted. While informal or absent design specifications are appropriate for throwaway code, even small routines in a large system must have formal design specifications.

3.4.4. Static Logic

Static-logic errors are errors in logic, particularly those related to misunderstanding how case statements and elementary logic operators behave singly and in combinations: nonexistent cases, improper layout of cases, "impossible" case is not impossible, a "don't-care" case matters, improper negation of boolean expression (for example, using "greater than" as the negation of "less than"), improper simplification and combination of cases, overlap of exclusive cases, confusing "exclusive-or" with "inclusive-or."

These errors are not really different in kind from arithmetic errors. They are more likely to occur than arithmetic errors because programmers, like most people, have less formal training in logic at an early age than they do in arithmetic. The best defense against this kind of bug is a systematic analysis of cases.

3.5. Data Errors

3.5.1. General

Data errors include all errors that arise from the specification of data objects, their formats, the number of such objects, and their initial values. Data errors are as common as code errors, but they are often treated as if they did not exist at all. The underestimation of the frequency of data-related bugs is due to bad bug accounting. In some projects, bugs in data declaration statements are simply not counted, and for that matter, data declaration statements are not counted as part of the code.

Software is evolving toward programs in which more and more of the control and processing functions is stored in tables. Because of this, there is an increasing awareness that coding errors are only half the battle and that data-base problems should be given equal attention. Examine a piece of contemporary source code—you may find that half of the statements are data declarations. Although these statements do not result in executable code, because they are specified by humans they are as subject to error as operative statements. If a program is designed under the assumption that a certain data item will be set to zero and it isn't, while the operative statements of the program are not at fault, there is still an initialization error, which, because it is in a data declaration, could be much harder to find than if it had been an error in executable code.

The first step in the avoidance of data-related errors, whether that data is used as pure data, as parameters, or as pseudo-code, is the realization that *all* source statements, particularly data declarations, must be counted, and that all source statements, whether or not they result in object code, are bug prone.

The categories used for data bugs are different from those used for code bugs. Each way of looking at data provides a different perspective on the possible bugs. These categories for data bugs overlap and are no stricter than the categories used for code bugs.

3.5.2. Dynamic Versus Static

Dynamic data is transitory. Whatever its purpose, it has a relatively short lifetime, typically the processing time of a single transaction. A storage element may be used to hold dynamic data of different types, with different formats, attributes, and residues. Failure to properly initialize a shared structure will lead to data-dependent bugs because of possible residues from a previous use of that object by another transaction. Note that the culprit transaction is long gone when the bug's symptoms are discovered. Because the effect of corruption of dynamic data can be arbitrarily far removed from the cause, such bugs are among the most difficult to catch. The design remedy is complete documentation of all shared data structures, defensive code that does thorough data-validation checks, and centralized resource managers.

Static data is fixed in form and content. Whatever its purpose, it appears in the source code or data base, directly or indirectly, as, for example, a number, a string of characters, or a bit pattern. Static data need not appear explicitly in the source code. Some languages allow **compile-time processing**. This is particularly useful in general-purpose routines that are particularized by inter-related parameters. Compile-time processing is an effective measure against parameter-value conflicts. Instead of relying on the programmer to calculate the correct values of interrelated parameters, a program which is executed at compile time (or assembly time) calculates the parameter's values. Alternatively, if compile-time processing is not a language feature, then a specialized preprocessor can be built which checks the parameter values and calculates those values that are derived from others.

All new software must be subjected to rigorous testing, even if it is not part of the application's mainstream. Static data can be just as wrong as any other kind and can have just as many bugs. Do not treat a routine that creates static data as "simple" because it "just stuffs a bunch of numbers into a table." Subject such code to the same degree of rigorous testing that you use for running code.

3.5.3. Information, Parameter, and Control

Static or dynamic data can serve in one of three roles, or in a combination of roles: as a parameter, for control, or for information. What constitutes control or information is a matter of perspective and can shift from one processing level to another.

Information is usually dynamic and tends to be local to a single transaction or task. As such, errors in information (when data are treated as information, that is) do not constitute bugs. The bug, if any, is in the lack of protective data-validation code. The only way we can be sure that there is data-validation code in a routine is to put it there. Assuming that the other routine will validate data invites latent bugs and maintenance problems. If a routine is vulnerable to bad data, the only sane thing to do is to block such data within the routine or to redesign it so that it is no longer vulnerable.

Lack of data validation often leads to finger pointing. The calling routine's author is blamed, the called routine's author blames back, they both blame the system's operators. This leads to a lot of ego confrontation and guilt. It's neither effective nor necessary to blame programmers or to inculcate guilt. Nature has conspired against us, but also given us a convenient scapegoat. One of the unfortunate side effects of large-scale integrated circuitry stems from the use of microscopic logic elements that work at very low energy levels. Modern circuitry is vulnerable to electronic noise, electromagnetic radiation, cosmic rays, neutron hits, stray alpha particles, and other noxious disturbances. No kidding—alpha particle hits that can change the value of a bit are a serious problem, and the semiconductor manufacturers are spending a lot of money and effort to reduce the random modification of data by alpha particles. Therefore, even if programmers do thorough, correct data validation, dynamic data, static data, parameters, and code can be corrupted. Put in the data-validation checks and blame the need on sunspots and alpha particles!

3.5.4. Contents, Structure, and Attributes

Data specifications consist of three components:

Contents—The actual bit pattern, character string, or number put into a memory location or data structure. Content is a pure bit pattern and has no meaning unless it is interpreted by a hardware or software processor. All data bugs result in the corruption or misinterpretation of content.

Structure—The size and shape and numbers that describe the data element, i.e., the memory locations used to store the content: 16 characters aligned on a word boundary, 122 blocks of 83 characters each, bits 4 through 14 of word 17, and so on. Structures can have substructures and can be arranged into superstructures. A given hunk of memory may have several different structures defined over it—e.g., a two-dimensional array treated elsewhere as N one-dimensional arrays.

Attributes—The specification of meaning, i.e., the semantics associated with the contents of a data element. For example: an integer, an alphanumeric string, a subroutine.

The severity and subtlety of bugs increases as we go from content to attributes, because things get less formal in that direction. Content has been dealt with adequately earlier in this section. Structural errors can take the form of declaration errors, but these are not the worst kind of structural bugs. A particularly serious potential for bugs occurs when data are used with different structures. Here is a piece of clever design. The programmer has subdivided the problem into eight cases and uses a three-bit field to designate the case. Another programmer has four different cases to consider and uses a two-bit field for the purpose. A third programmer is interested in the combination of the other two sets of cases and treats the whole as a five-bit field that leads to 32 combined cases. We cannot judge, out of context, if this is a good design or an abomination. However, we can note that there is a different structure in the minds of the three programmers and therefore a potential for bugs. The practice of interpreting a given memory location under several different structures is not inherently bad. Often, the only alternative would be a large increase in the amount of memory needed and many additional explicit data transfers.

Attributes of data are the meanings we associate with data. While some bugs are related to misinterpretation of integers for floating point and other basic representation problems, the more subtle attribute-related bugs are embedded in the application. Consider a 16-bit field. It could represent, among other things, a number, a loop-iteration count, a control code, a pointer, or a link field. Each interpretation is a different attribute. There is no way for the computer to know that it is proper or improper to add a control code to a link field to yield a loop count. We have used the same data with different meanings. In modern parlance, we have changed the **data type**. It is generally incorrect to logically or arithmetically combine objects whose types are different. Conversely, it is almost impossible to create an efficient system without doing so. Shifts in interpretation usually occur at interfaces, particularly the human interface that is behind every software interface. See GANN76 for a survey of **type errors**.

The preventive measures for data-type errors are in the source language, documentation, and coding style. Explicit documentation of the contents, structure, and attributes of all data is essential. The data-base documentation should be centralized. All alternate interpretations of a data object should be listed along with the identity of all routines that access that object. A proper **data dictionary** (which is what the data-base documentation is called) can be as large as the narrative description of the code. The data dictionary and the data base it represents must also be designed. This design is done by a high-level design process which is as important as the design of the system software hierarchy. It is an integral part of the system's architecture. My point of view here is admittedly dogmatic. Individual routines should not have their own data declarations.* All data structures should be globally defined and centrally administered. Exceptions, such as a private work area, should be ruled on and justified individually. Under no circumstances should such private data structures ever be used by any other routine. If there is more than one user, then the structure should be documented in the data dictionary.

It's impossible to properly test a system of any size (say more than 10,000 instructions) without central data-base management and a controlled data dictionary. I was once faced with such a Herculean challenge, and my first step was to try to create the missing data dictionary preparatory to any attempt to define tests. The act of dragging the murky bottoms of a hundred minds for hidden data declarations and semiprivate space in an attempt to create a data dictionary revealed so many data-type and structure bugs that it was evident that the system would defy integration. I never did get to design tests for that project—it collapsed, and a new design was started surreptitiously from scratch.

The second remedy is in the source language. **Strongly typed languages** pro-

---

*Except as required by the language—e.g., COMMON in BASIC or FORTRAN. However, in such cases the declarations should be maintained separately and inserted by a text editor.

hibit the mixed manipulation of data that are declared as different types. A conversion in usage from pointer type to counter type, say, requires an explicit statement that will do the conversion. Such statements may or may not result in object code. Conversion from floating point to integer would, of course, require object code, but conversion from pointer to counter might not. Strong typing in a language forces the explicit declaration of attributes and provides compiler facilities to check for mixed-type operations. The ability of the programmer to specify types, as in Pascal, is mandatory. These data-typing facilities force the specification of data attributes into the source code, which makes them more amenable to automatic verification by the compiler and to test design than when the attributes are described in a separate data dictionary. In assembly language programming, or in source languages that do not have programmer-defined types, the remedy is the use of **field-access macros**. No programmer is allowed to directly access a field in the data base. Access can only be obtained through the use of a field-access macro. The macro code does all the extraction, stripping, justification, and type conversion necessary. If the data-base structure has to be changed for any reason, the affected field-access macros are changed, but the source code that uses the macros does not (usually) have to be changed. The attributes of the data are documented with the field-access macro documentation. In one system, the data dictionary is automatically produced from the specifications of the field-access macro library.

3.6. Code Errors

Code errors of all kinds can create any of the above bugs. Syntax errors are generally not important in the scheme of things, if the source language translator has adequate syntax checking. Failure to catch a syntax error is a bug in the translator. A good translator will also catch undeclared data, undeclared routines, dangling code, and many initialization problems. Errors that are normally caught by the translator (assembler, compiler, or interpreter) do not materially affect the design and execution of tests, because testing cannot start until such errors are corrected. Whether it takes a programmer one, ten, or a hundred passes before a syntactically valid, testable routine is achieved should concern software management but not test design. However, if a program has many source-syntax errors, we should expect many logic and coding errors as well—after all, a slob is a slob is a slob.

Given good source-syntax checking, the most common pure coding errors are typographical, followed by errors due to misunderstanding the operation of an instruction or statement or the by-products of an instruction or statement. Coding errors are the wild cards of programming. Unlike logic or process errors, which have their own perverse rationality, wild cards are arbitrary.

3.7. Testing and Style

This is a book on testing and quality assurance, yet this chapter has dealt heavily with programming style and design. You might wonder why the productivity of one programming group is as much as ten times higher than that of another group working on the same application, the same computer, in the same language, and under similar constraints. It should be obvious. Bad designs lead to bugs, and bad designs are difficult to test; therefore, the bugs remain. Good designs inhibit bugs before they occur and are easy to test thoroughly. These two factors are multiplicative, which explains the large productivity differences. The best test techniques are useless when applied to abominable code and systems that were not designed. It is sometimes easier to totally redesign a bad routine than to attempt to create tests for it. The labor required to produce new code plus the test design and execution labor for the new code can be significantly less than the labor required for the design of thorough tests for an undisciplined, unstructured monstrosity. Good testing works best on good code and good design. And no test technique can ever change garbage into gold.

4. SOME BUG STATISTICS

The frequency of bugs taken from several different sources (DNIE78, ENDR75, RUBE75, SCHN79A) shows approximately 1.6 public bugs per hundred statements. However, because most of the sample did not include nonexecutable statements, the real value is probably lower. The norm appears to be one per hundred statements. A further breakdown into categories, especially the categories discussed in this chapter, is difficult to achieve, because different schemes were used to categorize the bugs. The breakdown shown in Table 2-1 is rough and is based on interpreting the reported results according to my categories. The biggest swing could occur between process-level errors and system-level errors. Most of the data did not distinguish between them. I suspect that many of the control/sequence errors, which I ascribed to individual processes, were actually system-level errors. The low value for data errors is also likely to be apocryphal, because part of the source data (ENDR75) was based on a combination of new code and modified code, in which the impact of data errors would be somewhat less than for new code. You should examine the sources for these statistics yourself so that you can rearrange the categories to better match your own situation. Other references with useful statistics are: AKIY71, BELF79, BOEH75A, BOIE72, ELSH76B, GANN76, GILB77, GOEL78B, HAUG64, HOFF77, ITOH73, LITE76, REIF79, SCHI78, SCHN75, SCHW71, SHOO75, THAY77 (especially), and WAGO73.

Table 2-1.   Sample Bug Statistics.

SIZE OF SAMPLE—126,000 STATEMENTS (MOSTLY EXECUTABLE)
TOTAL REPORTED BUGS—2070
BUGS PER STATEMENT—1.63%

FUNCTIONAL		
Specification	404	
Function	147	
Test	7	
Total	558	27%
SYSTEM		
Internal Interface	29	
Hardware (I/O devices)	63	
Operating System	2	
Software Architecture	193	
Control or Sequence	43	
Resources	8	
Total	338	16%
PROCESS		
Arithmetic	141	
Initialization	15	
Control or Sequence	271	
Static Logic	13	
Other	12	
Total	560	27%
DATA		
Type	36	
Structure	34	
Initial Value	51	
Other	120	
Total	201	10%
CODE	78	4%
DOCUMENTATION	103	5%
STANDARDS	166	8%
OTHER	62	3%

5. TASKS FOR A QUALITY ASSURANCE DEPARTMENT

1. Define a measure of bug publicness on a scale of 1 to 5 based on the publicness of the program element(s) in which or between which the bug is found. Base the measure on objective criteria such as testing level completed, degree of integration testing completed, appearance in documentation, and the scope of such documentation. A publicness index of 1 is a bug caught at the unit level, in unit-level tests designed and conducted by the programmer. A level of 5 is a bug caught in the field after the program has been accepted by the buyer. Establish a follow-on program that allows you to relate repair cost to publicness. Travel costs, long-distance telephone, down-time, and so forth should be included in the cost. Expect the costs to range from 1 to 125 for publicness of 1 to 5.

2. Propose a measure of bug severity on a scale of 1 to 10 based on the application, the environment, business concerns, management goals, applicable legal concerns, and moral issues. Explore these measures with upper management and obtain concurrence on their applicability. Explore them with software development management and senior staff and get concurrence on their applicability and practicability. Resolve the inevitable differences by arbitration until you get a mutually agreeable set of bug-severity measures. Publish the measure and educate the programming staff regarding its interpretation and application.

3. Design a set of technical bug categories that programmers can live with. Make it as easy as possible for them to report the bug type. Don't get trapped into ten-page bug-reporting forms. If you can't list the categories on one page, they're too detailed. Use a few senior programmers to generate the first set and then subject it to criticism by a broader group. Iterate until mutual dissatisfaction is achieved.

4. Establish a reporting mechanism to gather statistics on the technical bug categories defined in 3 above. Analyze the statistics to discover what kinds of bugs occur with what frequency. Temper that analysis by weighting the type by publicness and severity to obtain a perspective on the effort worth spending in preventing such bugs. Define **importance** as proportional to the product of **severity, frequency,** and **publicness**. Design education plans, test methods, documentation, and reporting structures in keeping with the importance of each kind of bug.

5. Recognize that everything you do, from gathering raw data to implementing QA measures, impacts the publicness, frequency, severity, and type of bug that will occur, and therefore invalidates the data you've already gathered. If the data remains stable over a period of years and through several projects, you have failed, because you are not influencing the software's quality. The number of bugs should decrease, their publicness should

decrease, their severity should decrease, and their categories should change. If not, you are being ignored and there are severe quality assurance bugs.

6. Count your private bug rate as honestly as you can. It helps to make a game of it. Do it for a small program or subroutine, because you'll find that your productivity will drop dramatically during this experiment. Study the results and then burn them. Assume that you're not much better or not much worse than all other humans. Reflect on the difference between humans and machines.

3

OVERVIEW OF TEST TECHNIQUES

1. SYNOPSIS

Being an overview of test techniques that can be used to catch various kinds of bugs at different levels ranging from unit to system.

2. IS THERE A BEST METHOD?

This chapter is a summary of the test techniques detailed in *Software Testing Techniques* (BEIZ82). That book, while almost three hundred pages long, is not definitive because it only covers techniques that have gained general acceptance and that are likely to apply to most programming projects. Test techniques are as varied as programmers and applications, and it's natural to ask if there is a "best method" or a small set of "best methods." The answer is a clear NO!

A program can be looked at from different points of view: you can focus on processing or control, or you can emphasize data structures or data validation. Each way of looking at the program leads to different test techniques that can reveal different kinds of bugs. No one method, no one set of methods, can guarantee finding all bugs. The issue in test techniques is not that there be a single best method, but that there be a varied enough set of techniques available to the programming staff to assure catching as many bugs as necessary to meet quality objectives.

While no one testing method is sufficient, one method is a minimum, mandatory base for all other testing: structure-based path testing, as discussed in the next section.

3. PATH TESTING

3.1. General

Path testing is the cornerstone of all testing. It is the minimum, mandatory foundation of any effective test plan. A **path** through a routine is any executable sequence of instructions through that routine. The word "path," however, is usually used in the more restrictive sense of an executable instruction sequence that starts at the routine's entrance and ends at its exit. The objective of path testing is to exercise enough different paths to demonstrate that the routine's actual structure matches its intended structure. In theory, this could require an infinite number of tests. Every decision can double the number of paths. Every case statement multiplies that number by the number of cases, and every loop is potentially infinite. Given any routine and any proposed finite set of test paths, it is possible to create a bug that cannot be caught by that set of tests. Consequently, absolute assurance can only be obtained through an unachievable and unrealistic set of path tests. Path testing, therefore, is conducted over a much smaller set of paths so chosen that they serve to demonstrate the correspondence between intention and reality, and, failing that, to catch most of the bugs that can be caught by unit-level tests. The issue in path testing is to select and exercise that small but sufficient set of test paths.

Path testing is a structural test technique that focuses on control structures rather than processing. The control structure of a program is conveniently represented by a flowchart, whose elements are shown in Figure 3-1.

A **process** has one entry and one exit. It performs one or more operations on data. It can consist of one instruction or a long sequence of instructions unbroken by program branches or junctions. From the point of view of path testing, a one-instruction process and a 1000-instruction process are equivalent—they are both processes.

A **decision** is a point in the program at which the flow diverges. Conditional branch instructions, case statements, IF-THEN-ELSE constructs, and UNTIL components of a loop statement are examples of decisions.

A **junction** is a point in the program where the control flow merges. The target of a GOTO, or a jump or skip target in assembly language, are examples of junctions.

It is convenient to abstract the notion of path further and to deal with a **graph** representation of a program. Junctions and decisions are replaced with the more abstract and simpler notion of **node**. A **node** is any point in the program where the control flow either merges or diverges or both. Nodes are joined by **links**. Processes, as defined above, are examples of links. However, a link may do no actual processing. For example, a conditional branch instruction consists of a node (the decision instruction) and two links (the flowchart lines that depict the branch alternatives.) The graph representation is more convenient because it depicts only labels or addresses and the path segments that join them. The graph of a program can be automatically generated from its source code (assuming that the program does no address calculations that affect the control flow) for most higher-order languages and for most parts of assembly language code. The resulting graph is a simpler depiction of the program control flow than the typical flowchart or code because most processing

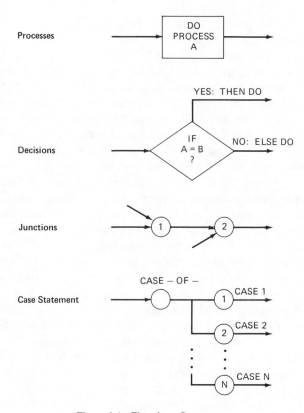

Figure 3-1. Flowchart Components.

components are ignored. It is not unusual to compress a 30- or 40-page flow-chart to a single page when represented by a graph. This alone is beneficial because it removes the clutter and can make an obscure control structure clear.

3.2. Fundamental Path Selection Criteria

Path testing as a minimum requires enough paths to assure that:

1. Every instruction in the routine has been exercised at least once.
2. Every decision (branch or case statement) has been taken in each possible direction at least once.

These are not redundant specifications. It can be shown that satisfying the one does not guarantee the other (BEIZ82). A set of paths that meets these criteria is said to provide **cover** or **complete cover**. Do not confuse complete cover with testing all paths. A routine could have millions of possible paths but still be covered by only a handful. Complete cover does not imply complete testing, because complete cover is itself insufficient. Complete cover assures that every instruction in the program has been exercised at least once and that every alternative has been attempted at least once. This is equivalent to having tested the components out of which all paths must be created, but not all paths.

I have on occasion been told that to insist on complete cover as a minimum mandatory starting point for all other testing is unrealistic; that it is not always possible to assure that all instructions in a program have been exercised. And they point to this or that guru who still writes in terms of "percentage of code covered" as if anything less than 100% had any meaning at all. One-hundred-percent coverage is not assurance of 100% testing by a long shot. It is at best, assuming that it's properly done, an assurance that half of the latent bugs in that code have probably been discovered. The incidence of bugs in code which is not to be tested is not less than the incidence of bugs in code which is to be tested. Actually it's probably far higher, because the code not scheduled for testing is deemed relatively unimportant and will receive relatively less care in design, desk check, and all the rest. Consequently its initial bug rate will be higher than for code scheduled for testing.

It's true that there are a lot of systems with untested code, and it's also true that there are a lot of system failures and a lot of bad systems. Untested code is perforce bad code and perforce has an uncomfortably high probability of not working as intended. Therefore, what use is it? What is worse is that untested code corrupts good code which would otherwise work. This can happen directly in assembly language programs, or indirectly, typically through data-base problems and data corruption, in higher-level language programs. Further-more, untested code, because its bugs *do* show all through system test and integration, erodes confidence and increases integration labor; time will be wasted to confirm that a particular unit-level routine or path that had not been 100% covered was not a source of problems discovered at the higher level. The bottom line is that effort appears to have been saved at the unit level but emerges later in extra expense at higher testing levels or in field changes after delivery. It is better to leave untested code out altogether than to falsely claim program completion through the insertion of untested garbage: because untested code is garbage and remains so until tested. If you still believe that it's possible to test and integrate a system without meeting the minimum standard of 100% coverage, then there's no point in continuing with this book. There is a philosophical chasm between this writer and the reader that only the reader's future bitter and expensive experience will bridge.

Any rational unit-level test plan must therefore include an uncompromising requirement that complete coverage be assured. This can be demonstrated by a table such as 3-1 whose graph is shown in Figure 3-2. The program or its

Table 3-1.   Node and Link Coverage for Figure 3-2.

PATHS	DECISIONS				PROCESS–LINK												
	4	6	7	9	a	b	c	d	e	f	g	h	i	j	k	l	m
abcde	YES	YES			✓	✓	✓	✓	✓								
abhkgde	NO	YES		NO	✓	✓		✓	✓		✓	✓			✓		
abhlibcde	NO, YES	YES		YES	✓	✓	✓	✓	✓			✓	✓			✓	
abcdfjgde	YES	NO, YES	YES		✓	✓	✓	✓	✓	✓	✓			✓			
abcdfmibcde	YES	NO, YES	NO		✓	✓	✓	✓		✓			✓				✓

flowchart has been reduced to a graph that consists of nodes and links. Each link is named by a lower-case letter and each node by a number. A path is then a succession of link names or, equivalently, a succession of node numbers. The table lists every decision and every link (process) and the paths that the programmer has selected. If a link is exercised on some path, put in a check mark. Similarly, mark every decision with a "YES" or "NO" as appropriate to the path. Case statements and multi-direction GOTO statements must be marked with all possible alternatives. The test plan achieves coverage if every decision has been marked with all possible alternatives and if every link has been checked at least once.

Associated with each path must be a specification of the inputs that will force that path (more on that later) and a specification of all outputs and database changes for that path. Detailed tactics on path selection to satisfy the fundamental criteria are given in Chapter 3 of BEIZ82. The gist of those tactics are:

1. A sufficient number of paths to achieve coverage.
2. Selection of short, functionally sensible paths.
3. Minimizing the number of changes from path to path—preferably only one decision changing at a time.
4. Favor more but simpler paths over fewer, complicated paths.

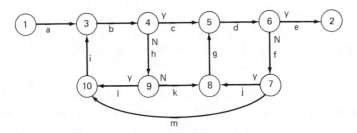

Figure 3-2. A Graph Example for Path Testing.

3.3. Loop Testing

3.3.1. General

Loop testing is an aspect of path testing aimed at exposing bugs that typically occur in loops. In theory, path testing should make specialized loop testing unnecessary. In practice, it pays to augment minimal cover paths with a more extensive loop covering. Furthermore, loop testing must be expanded to consider the possible interaction between multiple loops, especially when such loops are nested. Loop bugs can be divided into two major categories:

1. End point bugs.
2. Initialization bugs.

Every loop, directly or indirectly, has a loop control variable. At the simplest, it is the variable that controls the FOR in a FOR $I = 1$ TO N statement, as an example. Indirectly, that variable may be the result of a process executed within the loop. It may be a more complicated result and may not necessarily be numerical. The variations are endless. To simplify loop testing, it is convenient to treat each loop as if there were a single variable or process that controlled the number of times that the routine traversed that loop. That number can range from zero to infinity.

3.3.2. Fundamental Loop Test Criteria

Unless covered by other forms of path testing, testing for a single loop should as a minimum contain the following cases:

1. Bypassing the loop altogether—that is, a set of input values that will cause an immediate exit or that attempts to cause an immediate exit if the immediate exit case is supposedly impossible.
2. One pass through the loop—many initialization problems are caught by this test.
3. Two passes through the loop before exiting. Some initialization problems will surface only with two or more passes through the loop (HUAN79).
4. A typical number of passes through the loop, unless covered by some other test.

The next tests are based on the assumption that there is a maximum number of possible passes through the loop. If there isn't a maximum number, then what prevents a set of input values that will cause the program to loop forever? Every realistic program must directly or indirectly impose a limit on the time spent in loops.

5. One less than the maximum number of passes.
6. The maximum allowable number of passes.
7. Attempt one more or two more than the maximum number.

Whether or not these cases are possible is not the issue. They should be set up and attempted even if they could not come about in normal operation. They can occur because the program has bugs, because other programs have bugs, because equipment can malfunction, or because of alpha particles. If any of the cases between the minimum and maximum number of loopings are forbidden or impossible, then the test plan should be augmented by end-point checks in the neighborhood of such excluded values (i.e., one less than the forbidden value, the forbidden value, and one more).

3.3.3. Nested Loops

The most obvious example of nested loops occurs when one loop is inside another. However, this is not the only possibility. In complicated loop structures (which are better avoided) it may not be possible to distinguish between an "inner" and "outer" loop. Nested loops or coupled loops are treated as combinations of single loops. In principle, the cases are designed as if the loops were independent, and then every combination of the cases for the one loop with every case of the other loop forms a new test case. While practical for a pair of nested loops, for three nested loops and more this becomes an impossible prescription. The number of cases can be cut down by the following stratagem without significant sacrifice in test thoroughness:

1. Set all but one loop to a typical value and run through the single-loop cases for that loop. Repeat for all loops.
2. Do minimum values for all loops simultaneously.
3. Set all loops but one to the minimum value and repeat the test cases for that loop. Repeat for all loops.
4. Do maximum looping values for all loops simultaneously.

This last prescription could lead to running times measured in centuries. If the running time for maximum simultaneous values is excessive, then further investigation and testing are warranted. See Section 3.4 below.

3.3.4. Unstructured Loops

Complicated loops can be created by the onerous practice of jumping into or out of the middle of routines or loops. There are no simple rules for testing such loops. Structured programs lead to relatively simple, at worst nested, loop structures that can be tested with easily specified tests. Unstructured code leads to complicated test specifications that seem to defy generalization. Because unstructured code is more bug prone than structured code, and because it is harder to design proper tests for such code, the more frequent bugs are more likely to remain. This is a multiplicative effect.

3.4. Test Execution Time

Computers execute hundreds of thousands to millions of instructions per second. The typical routine tested at the unit level is a few hundred instructions long. The execution time for such routines is of the order of milliseconds or seconds—not hours and days. Path selection, particularly for routines with multiple and nested loops, could lead to projected execution times measured in centuries (for methods to predict the execution time, see BEIZ78). For example, say that a routine has four nested loops, and each has a maximum value of 1000. At one pass through the loop per millisecond, the execution time for testing all four loops achieving the maximum value simultaneously is over thirty years. The programmer should always make a quick mental check (or detailed analysis, if necessary) of the expected test execution time. If it's more than a few seconds, then run parameters must be changed to bring the test execution time down to reasonable values. This can usually be done without sacrificing test integrity. For instance, in the nested loop example, the test issue is the logic of all four loops achieving their maximum loop values simultaneously and not that they all hit the specific number 1000 simultaneously. If that maximum value is changed to 10, say, by program patches, code modification, data-base changes, declaration changes, and so on, the test will take a few seconds and should still prove the same point—that the routine behaved correctly when all four loops reached the maximum value simultaneously. Excessive test execution times can occur for file copying and initialization, file restructuring, sorting, queue scanning, file searching, and so on. Usually there's not one test, but many tests that result in excessive execution times. Therefore, create a special test data base or do a special assembly or compilation with program parameters that lead to reasonable test durations. This works most of the time, but has the following dangers.

1. More than one test data base, test program version, and such must be created. There is no assurance, without testing, that the versions are identical except for the modified parameters.
2. Location-dependent bugs may be hidden.
3. Timing-dependent bugs may be obscured.
4. Certain program paths or operating system functions may not be invoked with the smaller parameter values.
5. Overlay relations are changed.

It's a trade. If only a few routines or paths have the excessive execution time, then it's probably more effective to allow the long runs than to spend the time debugging variant data bases and program versions. If all such tests can be lumped into one small test data base and program version, then the extra test setup debugging is worthwhile.

3.5. The Rest of Path Test Design

3.5.1. Path Sensitizing

Selecting a path through a routine does not guarantee that the path is achievable. Furthermore, of itself, selecting a path does not specify the input values that must be supplied to cause the program to follow that path. The act of deriving the path-forcing input values is called **sensitizing** the path. That act is as important as selecting the path. If all decisions were independent of one another and if the outcome of all decisions depended only on the input values and not on any processing done within the routine, then all paths would be achievable. However, the presence of loops, program switches, and the fact that the same decision may recur several times in a routine, can materially reduce the number of paths through the routine, to the point where seemingly sensible paths are not achievable. In simple programs the act of sensitizing is so trivial that it can be unrecognized as an explicit activity. The path is traced and the values that force that path are obvious. However, in complicated routines considerable effort may be needed to find values that force the specified path. It can be done either in forward or backward direction. The forward method starts at the routine's entrance. As each decision along the specified path is reached, the broadest set of values that will force the decision in the desired direction, and that does not contradict the values previously chosen, is taken. With each decision, the choices are narrowed. Occasionally the choices may be narrowed to the point that there are no choices, which means that the particular path attempted is not achievable. The backward method is essentially the same, but it starts at the exit and traces the path in reverse. As each decision is reached, the broadest set of values that could have led to that path is determined, thereby imposing conditions on subsequent values in the reverse traversal of the path. Again, some paths may prove unachievable.

If the paths are selected in accordance with the path selection criteria given earlier, then all selected paths should be achievable, and the fact that a path is not achievable could be indicative of a bug, but at least a misconception of what it is the routine should be doing. If short, functionally sensible paths are chosen to achieve cover, then sensitizing those paths should be trivial. If not, then either there is a bug or the chosen paths are not functionally sensible. Therefore there is either a bug or a misconception. Misconceptions invariably lead to bugs, particularly at interfaces and in data bases. Therefore, an unachievable, supposedly functionally sensible path is almost always indicative of a bug.

Inputs to a routine should not be restricted to the explicit inputs that are passed to the routine in a calling sequence. Inputs, in the context of testing, include any data objects on which the routine's decisions can be based. Typically that includes all the data base objects that the routine accesses.

3.5.2. Outcome Prediction

Testing is like playing pool. There's real pool and kiddie pool. In kiddie pool, you hit the balls and whatever pocket they happen to fall into, you claim as the intended pocket. It's not much of a game and although suitable to ten-year-olds it's hardly a challenge. The object of real pool is to specify the pocket in advance. Similarly for testing. There's real testing and kiddie testing. In kiddie testing, the tester says, after the fact, that the observed outcome was the intended outcome. In real testing *the outcome is predicted and documented before the test is run*. If the programmer cannot reliably predict the outcome for a specified path, then that programmer has misconceptions as to what it is the routine should be doing and is doing. Such misconceptions perforce lead to bugs.

Any sensible unit test plan must include, in addition to path selection and path sensitizing, outcome prediction. The outcome of a routine, like the inputs, may be direct as in a calculated value; or indirect as in modification of database objects; or it may pass control to other routines, calling certain subroutines; or it may be a combination of all of these. A routine's outcome is rarely just a simple calculated value.

3.5.3. Instrumentation

Selecting a set of paths, deriving sensitizing input values for those paths, and predicting the outcome for all selected paths does not guarantee that the routine will be covered. That is, even with all of the above work it's possible that some code may be unexercised and some branches not taken. This seems like a contradiction on the surface, but it isn't. All the work done in designing path tests is done on what we think the routine is, rather than what it really is. That work is based on the fallacious assumption that the routine is bug-free—in which case, what's the point of testing? This bug-free assumption is the only rational basis for selecting paths. Consider the alternative. If we were to select paths on the basis of some hypothetical bugs, we would have to postulate the bug. The very fact that you can postulate a bug guarantees that the bug will not occur. If the thought occurs to the programmer, then it's a trivial enterprise to check the routine to see if that specific bug does or does not exist. One can postulate an infinite number of bugs, and no one postulated bug is likelier than any other. Therefore, the supposedly bug-free structure is used as a basis for path testing, recognizing that the presence of bugs changes that structure. The actual outcome of the routine can be usually corroborated with the predicted outcome without difficulty. But the *path* by which that outcome was produced cannot be determined solely on the basis of comparing predicted outcome to actual outcome. "What's the point of bothering with the path by which an outcome is produced if the outcome is correct?" you ask. Here's the reason: whatever paths you select represent only a small sample of the possible paths and outcomes. The idea behind path testing is that if the covering paths prove correct, then untested combinations of those paths will probably be correct. If you don't know that the covering paths were actually traversed as predicted to produce the outcome, then there can be no confidence that the combinations of the covering paths, combinations that correspond to cases too difficult or numerous to test directly, will be correct. There is also the possibility that the same outcome could be produced by several different paths.

Path confidence is obtained by **instrumenting** the paths to assure that they were followed. The simplest way to instrument the paths is to run the routine under a trace. There are several problems with traces, however, as instrumentation tools:

1. The output of a typical trace is too voluminous. It gives us much more data than we want, and the sheer mass thereof can make it difficult to verify that the path was actually followed.
2. Traces destroy timing relations through the imposition of an extremely high overhead. Some routines, such as interrupt handlers, device handlers, and communications interfaces, may not work in trace mode.
3. Traces may change location dependencies. A bug may exist without the trace and disappear when the trace is invoked (a **peek-a-boo bug**).

Some higher-order languages and assemblers provide an elegant instrumentation tool: **assertion statements**. These statements are used to check properties of specified variables, states, registers, flags, and so on, but do not otherwise modify the control flow. For example, an assertion statement might state that a given variable was a positive integer within a specified range at a specified program point. If the assertion is active, then the property will be checked and the routine will go to an error location or halt if the assertion proves false. **Conditional assembly** and **compilation** can also be used to provide similar facilities. The instrumentation code is activated only when assertion statements are activated, or when specially marked (for conditional processing) classes of statements are activated by run-time control parameters. The point of such facilities is not that they do things which cannot be done by inserting ordinary code, but that they make the instrumentation process less bug prone. Alternatively, particularly in higher-order languages, a preprocessor program can be used to insert and remove instrumentation statements.

Two different things must be determined by instrumentation: the path and variable values along the path. The full interpretive trace dumps all values and explicitly identifies all link traversals. Path information can be gathered by a variety of methods, with increased effectiveness and complexity. Here are some suggestions:

1. A master counter that is incremented at the start of every link. One of the outcomes must be the proper count of link traversals. If not as predicted, then the routine achieved the correct outcome by the wrong path.
2. Two master counters, one incremented at the start and another at the end of every link. Now both counts must be correct at the end of the path, and furthermore, equal. If not equal, then there are unsuspected or missing links.
3. Link flags and markers—a bit flag or equivalent for each link. The correct number of bits must be set, and the right bits must be set. A little better is two flags per link, one for the beginning and one for the end, to catch broken paths and unsuspected paths.
4. Traversal markers—a marker, say a character in an array or an integer in an array, to mark the name or number of each link as passed. The correct number of markers, the correct markers, and in the correct order, must be verified. Again, doubling this with beginning and end markers helps catch path problems.

Continuing in this way, it is clear that with ever more elaborate instrumentation you approach the full interpretive trace. You cannot be dogmatic about the extent of instrumentation to use because:

1. It is additional labor and can be easily carried to excess.
2. Each piece of code inserted in the interest of instrumenting paths changes the routine being instrumented. The more instrumentation, the less the correspondence between the instrumented version and the real program.
3. Instrumentation can have bugs of its own.
4. Instrumentation can hide bugs.

When planning instrumentation, it's important to keep its purpose in sight— to demonstrate that the actual outcomes were achieved by the specified paths; any more than that is superfluous. More important than actual instrumentation is the principle of instrumentation. If all test paths are not instrumented, for practical reasons, then the programmer should be aware of the possibility of selective instrumentation and/or other means of proving that the desired paths were achieved.* The most important thing about instrumentation is that effective tools and options be available and that the programming staff is knowledgeable regarding their use and limitations.

3.5.4. Automatic Path Generation and Random Paths

There are programs available that purport to automatically produce a set of covering paths—obviating much of the labor required to create valid unit tests. Such programs are to be distinguished from very useful test drivers that organize the inputs, the outputs, instrumentation, data storage, and the like, but which are based on the programmer-supplied paths, inputs, and results. Automated path selection misses the point entirely. The automated path generator perforce works on the real routine—the one with bugs—and therefore, achieving coverage over a buggy routine proves nothing except possibly that the routine did not loop indefinitely or did not cause the system to crash by some other means. No automated test tool can ever read the programmer's mind, and therefore no automated test data generator can ever distinguish between the intended program and the actual program. The point of path testing is to demonstrate that actuality matches intentions—not just that the routine can be covered, or that it does not crash.

Another form of automated path testing is the use of a random data generator that will force arbitrary but achievable paths through a routine. Is this a substitute for designed paths? It is not.

1. Random paths do nót correlate with coverage. It is possible to run random data through a routine for years and not cover the code (MORA78).
2. Random paths again only prove that the routine is not likely to loop indefinitely or to cause crashes. It proves nothing about whether or not what the

---

*The need for instrumentation, or at least the threat thereof, was demonstrated to me by the following unfortunate experience. One programmer's work proved very difficult to integrate. Time and again during system integration, the problem would turn out to be in one of his routines. In addition to being expensive, this was demoralizing to the other programmers in the group, and more and more of my time was spent in fielding their justifiable complaints. That programmer had devised and executed seemingly correct unit test plans, complete with path selection, sensitizing values, and documented outcomes. And yet time and again the problem was in his routines. The predicted outcomes had been achieved by a path that I had never considered. It had all been faked! He had never been logged into the system. The results had been laboriously typed in by hand with the terminal in local mode—inputs, responses, and all the rest were meticulously simulated, while the actual routine had not been tested at all. Had I required instrumentation, that would have been a simulation too laborious and too difficult for any person. It would have been much easier to test the program and correct its manifold errors.

routine does is correct, because there is no prediction of outcome for specified inputs (i.e., it's a form of kiddie testing). If there were a prediction of outcome, it could only be provided by an outcome predictor program—which, if you think about it, is no better, or worse, or simpler, than the program being tested.

3. Many random paths are not achievable because the combination of data produced by the random data generator is not sensible. If the data generator can be guaranteed to produce only sensible data, then there is the additional burden of providing it with bug-free specifications for that data. A random data generator that produces only the path-forcing values that are legitimate for the unit under test can be shown to be *exactly* equivalent to the routine it purports to test. Similarly, a specification that produces only valid strings is also exactly equivalent to the routine that recognizes those strings.

Quasi-random data is useful when done as part of load and stress testing, as discussed in Chapter 8. It is not, however, a substitute for properly designed path tests.

3.5.5. Effectiveness and Limitations of Path Testing

Approximately 65% of all bugs can be caught in unit testing, which is dominated by path testing. Precise statistics based on controlled experiments on the effectiveness of path testing are not available. What statistics there are show that path testing catches approximately half of all bugs caught during unit testing or approximately 35% of all bugs (BOEH75B, ENDR75, GANN79, HOWD76, HOWD78D, KERN76, MILL77C, THAY77). When path testing is combined with other methods, such as limit checks on loops, the percentage of bugs caught rises to 50% to 60% in unit testing. But the statistics also indicate that path testing as a sole technique is limited. Here are some of the reasons:

1. Planning to cover does not mean you will cover. Path testing may not cover if you have bugs.
2. Path testing may not reveal totally wrong or missing functions.
3. Interface errors, particularly at the interface with other routines, may not be caught by unit-level path testing.
4. Data-base errors may not be caught.
5. The routine can pass all of its tests at the unit level, but the possibility that it interferes with or perturbs other routines cannot be determined by unit-level path tests.
6. Not all initialization errors are caught by path testing.

3.6. Tasks for a Quality Assurance Department

1. Convince project management, programmers, upper management, the buyer, and yourself that 100% coverage in path testing is the starting point of testing and not the unachievable end.
2. Design unit test plan standards that include (but are not limited to):
   a. Specification of the paths that are intended to provide cover.
   b. Specification of path sensitizing input values.
   c. Specification of the outcomes for each path included in the test.
   d. Specification of instrumentation code, source language facilities, test tools, or a combination of these to supply the range of instrumentation necessary to verify paths and intermediate outcomes.
   e. Specification of test drivers and other tools or procedures to organize and automate all aspects of path testing that do not rely on telepathic programs.
3. Augment unit test plan standards with loop testing standards that include:
   a. Identification of the loops and the inputs that determine the number of times the routine will loop.
   b. Identification of the minimum and maximum number of times the routine is allowed to loop, as well as any intermediate forbidden values.
   c. Explicit listing or table of input values for all zero, one, two, and near-end point passes. Specification of outcomes for all cases.
   d. Identification of preventive or defensive measures in the code that prevent infinite looping or exclude "impossible" cases and combinations.
   e. Specification of procedures and tools used to drive the tests, to count the number of times looped, and to validate the predicted outcomes.
   f. Identification of intertwined and nested loops and tabulated values for combined cases.
   g. Justification for not using combinations of looping values for structurally nested loops—for example, if the loops, though nested, have little or no interaction and the combination will not prove much, if anything.

4. TRANSACTION FLOW TESTING

4.1. General

A flowchart is usually used as a representation of a program's logical structure and is therefore usually a structural description of the program. The same elements (process, decision, junction) can also be used as a functional description of a program's behavior. When what the system does is described this way, we are using a **transaction flow** representation of the behavior, which leads to **transaction flow testing**. Path testing is structural and is more effective the closer we get to the unit level. Transaction flow testing is functional and gets better as we approach the user's point of view. Yet the techniques and methods used in both are almost identical. Coverage must be provided, special attention should be paid to loops, extreme cases must be considered, paths must be sensitized and instrumented, and so on.

4.2. Transaction Flows

4.2.1. Definitions

A **transaction** is a unit of work seen from a system user's point of view. A transaction consists of a set of operations, some of which are performed by a system, persons, or devices that are outside of the system. A transaction typically consists of a set of operations that begins with an input and ends with one or more outputs. At the conclusion of the transaction's processing, the transaction is no longer in the system, except perhaps in the form of historical records. A transaction for an on-line information retrieval system might consist of the following steps or **tasks**:

1. Accept input.
2. Validate input.
3. Transmit acknowledgment to requester.
4. Do input processing.
5. Search file.
6. Request additional directions from user.
7. Accept input.
8. Validate input.
9. Process request.
10. Update file.
11. Transmit output.
12. Record transaction in log.

   The user sees this scenario as a single transaction. From the system's point of view, the transaction consists of twelve steps and ten different kinds of subsidiary tasks.

   Tasks in a transaction flow correspond to processing steps in a control flowchart. As with control flows, there can be conditional branches, unconditional branches, and junctions.

4.2.2. Example

Figure 3-3 shows part of a transaction flow. A microcomputer is used as a terminal controller for several VDU terminals. The terminals are used to process orders for parts, say. The order forms are complicated. The user specifies the wanted action, and the terminal controller requests the proper form from a remotely located central computer. The forms may be several pages long and may have many fields on each page. The form is transmitted by the central computer in a code designed to minimize communication-line usage. The form is then translated by the terminal controller for the user's benefit. The terminal controller only transmits the answers (i.e., the contents of the blanks) back to the central computer. As each page of the form is completed, the terminal controller transmits the answers to the central computer, which either accepts or rejects them. If the answers are not valid, a diagnostic code is transmitted by the central computer to the terminal controller which, in turn, translates the code and informs the user at the terminal. Finally, the terminal allows the user to review the filled-out form.

Decision D1 in Figure 3-3 is not part of the process as such—it is really a characteristic of the kinds of transactions that the terminal controller handles. However, there is a decision like this somewhere in the program. Process P1 probably consists of several subsidiary processes that are completed by the transmission of the request for an order form from the central computer. The next step is "Process P2," which involves no real processing. What the terminal controller will do here depends on the software's structure. Typically, transactions for some other terminal will be processed. Process P3 is a real processing step, as is P4, which does the translation. Process P6 is another wait for input. This has no direct correspondence to a program step. Decisions D2 and D4 depend on the structure of the form. Which branch is taken at decision D3 is determined by the user's behavior. The system does not necessarily have actual decisions corresponding to D1, D2, D3, D4, or D5. D1 and D5 could be implemented by interrupts caused by special keys on the terminal.

The most general case of a transaction flow, then, represents by a flowchart or a graph a scenario between people and computers.

4.2.3. Usage

Transaction flows are indispensable for specifying the functional requirements of complicated systems, particularly on-line systems. Very big systems, such as an air traffic control system, have not hundreds but thousands of different transaction flows. The flows are represented by relatively simple flowcharts, many of which have a single straight-through path. Loops are relatively infre-

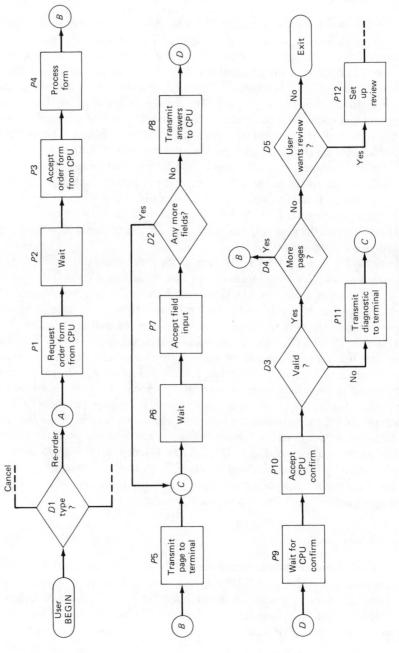

Figure 3-3. A Transaction Flow Example.

quent compared to ordinary flowcharts. The most common loop is used to request retries after user-input errors.

4.2.4. Complications

While in simple cases transactions have a unique identity from the time they are created to the time they are completed, in many systems one transaction can create several others, and transactions can also merge. The simple graph elements are inadequate to represent transaction flows that split and merge: a Petri-net model (PETE76) can be used. However, the available methodology for test case design based on Petri nets is not as well developed as that based on graphs. Most such problems can be reduced to a set of flows that can be represented by graphs. If a transaction splits at some point, say into two parts that then go on independently, treat it as three different transactions—one transaction type that starts at the beginning and ends at the split and two more that start at the split and end at their ends. Treat merging transactions the same way: from the point where they were created to the merger, and from the merger to the end. Document the split or merger to keep track of the test cases and to assure that the correlation of the merged and split components is kept correct.

4.3. Transaction-Flow Testing

4.3.1. Get the Transaction Flows

Complicated systems that process a lot of different, complicated transactions should have explicit representations of the transaction flows, or the equivalent, documented. If transaction flows are part of the system's functional specification, half the battle is won. Don't expect to get pure transaction flows, and don't insist on only that form of representing the system's processing requirements. There are other, equivalent representations, such as HIPO charts and Petri nets, that can serve the same purpose (PETE76). If these representations are available and if they are done correctly, it will be easy to create the transaction flows from them. The objective is to have a very high-level trace of what happens to transactions—a trace of the progression of actions.

Designers ought to understand what they're doing. And it's obvious that if they don't, they're not likely to do it right. I've made it a practice to ask for transaction flows for the, say, ten most important transactions that a system is to process, preparatory to designing the system's functional test. I hope that that information is in the specification. If it isn't, it's likely that there will be some disagreement as to what the system is supposed to be doing. More important, the system's design documentation should contain an overview section that details the transaction flows (all of them, it is hoped). If I can't find that or the equivalent, then I don't need a lot of complicated tests to know that the system will have a lot of complicated bugs. Detailed transaction flows are a mandatory prerequisite to the rational design of a system's functional test.

Like so much in testing, the act of getting the information on which to base tests can be more effective at catching and exterminating bugs than the tests that result from that information. Insisting on getting transaction flows or the equivalent is sometimes a gentle way of convincing an inept design group that they don't know what they're doing. These are harsh words, but let's face it: superb code and unit testing are useless if the overall design is poor. And how can there be a rational, effective design if no one on the high-level design team can walk you through the more important transactions, step by step, alternative by alternative? I'm sure that mine is a biased sample, but every system I've seen that was in serious trouble had no transaction flows documented, nor had the designers anything that approximated that kind of functional representation.

4.3.2. Test Design

Once you have a complete set of transaction flows, test design proceeds exactly as it does for path testing. You must test every link, every decision's outcome, every process. Links now encompass actual processes and the queues on which transactions wait for processing. Decisions and case statements are actions taken by the scheduler, dispatcher, or operating system, and do not necessarily correspond directly to instructions. In some systems, all queue entries may not go via a central dispatcher but may be linked directly from one process to the next. This is not necessarily bad, but it should be reckoned with. Coverage is essential and usually easy to achieve with functionally sensible paths. Loops are relatively rare, and when they do occur, there is usually some mechanism that limits the maximum number of iterations.

4.3.3. Path Selection

Path selection for system-level functional testing based on transaction flows should have a distinctly different flavor than path selection done for unit-level tests based on flowgraphs. Forbidden paths were a bother at the unit level and made path sensitizing difficult. Each forbidden path was suspected because a more structured design might have eliminated the duplication of decisions that caused the path to be unachievable. In transaction flow testing, in addition to coverage, you must look for achievable paths that should be forbidden. I've written harsh words about unit-level programmers who jumped into the middle of code to save a few instructions. At the system level, however, we expect to merge transaction flows, use common parts, and do various things that we would condemn at the unit level. It is more justified at the system level because the alternatives could mean large increases in program and data space, increased control complexity, a badly tuned system, and a host of other things. Consequently, it is not unusual to have paths deliberately blocked in order to use a common part for several different kinds of transactions. Furthermore, because the operation of the transaction flow is not localized to a single program but is distributed over several programs and results from their interaction, and because many more person-to-person interfaces are involved, it's more likely that essential interlocks that prevent various paths will be missing, abused, or misunderstood. Finally, because some of the conditional branches in the transaction flows may be executed by humans whose actions are unpredictable, even though they are represented in the transaction flows, it may be impossible to guarantee decent structure for those flows.

Select a covering set of paths based on functionally sensible transactions as you would for program path testing. Confirm these with the designers. Now do exactly the opposite of what you would have done for unit-level tests. Try to find the most tortuous, longest, strangest path from the entry to the exit of the transaction flow. Create a catalog of these weird paths. Go over them not just with the high-level designer who laid out the transaction flows, but also with the next-level designers who are implementing the modules that will process the transaction. It can be a gratifying experience, even in a well-designed and well-managed system. The act of discussing the weird paths will expose missing interlocks, duplicated interlocks, interface problems, programs working at cross purposes, duplicated processing—a whole lot of stuff that would otherwise show up only during the final acceptance tests, or worse, after the system was operating. The entire cost of independent testing can be paid for by a few such paths for a few well-chosen transactions. This is best done early in the game, while the system design is still in progress, before processing modules have been coded. I try to do it just after the internal design specifications for the processing modules are done and just before those modules are coded. Any earlier than that, you'll get a lot of "I don't know yet" answers to your questions, which is a waste of both yours and the designer's time. Any later, it's already cast into code and correction has become expensive.

This process has diminishing returns. Most competent designers won't be caught twice. You have only to show them one nasty case and they'll review all their interfaces and interlocks and you're not likely to find any new bugs from that module—but you can catch most modules and their designers once. Eventually the blatant bugs have been removed, and those that remain are due to implementation errors and wild cards.

The covering set of paths belong in the system functional tests. I still try to cover with weird paths in preference to normal paths, if I possibly can. It gives everybody more confidence in the system and its test. I also keep weird paths in proportion to what I perceive to be the designer's lack of confidence. I suppose it's sadistic hitting a person who's down, but it's effective. Conversely, you do get fooled by supremely confident idiots and insecure geniuses.

4.3.4. Hidden Languages

At the system level, you can't expect to find neat decision boxes and junctions as in a low-level flowchart. The actual decision may be made (usually is) in a process module, and the central dispatcher is usually indifferent to the transaction flows. Alternatively, the dispatcher may direct the flows based on control codes contained in the transaction's control block or stored elsewhere in the data base. Such codes actually constitute an internal language. If an explicit mechanism of this kind does exist, the transaction flows are indeed implemented as "programs" in this internal language. A commercial operating system's job-control language or the set of task-control codes combined with execution files are examples of such "languages."

The trouble is that these languages are often undeclared, undefined, undocumented, and unrecognized. Furthermore, unlike formal higher-order languages and their associated compilers or interpreters, neither the language's syntax, semantics, nor processor has been debugged. The flow-control language evolves as a series of ad hoc agreements between module designers. Here are some of the things that can go wrong:

1. The language is rarely checked for self-consistency (assuming that its existence has been recognized).
2. The language must be processed, usually one step at a time, by an interpreter that may be centralized in a single routine but is more often distributed in bits and pieces among all the processing modules. That interpreter, centralized or distributed, may have bugs.
3. The "program," i.e., the steps stored in a transaction-control table, may have bugs or may become corrupted by bugs far removed from the transaction under consideration. This is a nasty kind of bug to find. Just as a routine may pass its tests but foul the data base for another routine, a transaction may pass all of its tests but, in so doing, foul the transaction-control tables for other transactions. This can be insidious, because the program will work the first time but not the second.
4. Finally, any module that processes the transaction can have bugs.

If transaction-control tables are used to direct the flow, it is effective to treat that mechanism as if an actual language had been implemented. Look for the basic components of any language—processing steps, conditional-branch instructions, unconditional branches, program labels, possibly subroutines (i.e., the tables can direct processing to subtables which can be used in common for several different flows), loop control, and so on. Assuming you can identify all of these elements, document a "syntax" for this primitive, undeclared language and discuss this syntax with whoever is responsible for implementing the trans-action-control structure and software. The pseudo-language approach was used to provide flexibility in implementing many different, complicated, transaction flows. Therefore, it is reasonable to expect that any syntactically valid "state-ment" in this language should make processing sense. A syntactically valid, arbitary statement might not provide a useful transaction, but at the very least, the system should not blow up if such a transaction has been defined.

4.3.5. Instrumentation

Instrumentation plays a larger role in transaction flow testing than in unit-level path testing. Counters are not useful, because the same module could appear in many different flows and the system could be simultaneously processing dif-ferent transactions. The information of the path taken by a transaction must be kept with that transaction. This can be recorded either by the dispatcher or by the individual processing modules. What is needed is a trace of all the pro-cessing steps for the transaction, the queues on which it resided, and the entries and exits to and from the dispatcher. In some systems, such traces are provided by the operating system. In other systems, a running log that contains exactly this information is maintained as part of normal processing. You can afford heavy instrumentation compared to unit-level testing instrumentation, because the overhead of such instrumentation is typically small compared to the processing.

4.4. Tasks for a Quality Assurance Department

1. Make a transaction flow walk-through a mandatory part of the preliminary design review. The walk-through should include:
   a. Discussion of a sufficient number of different transaction types (i.e., paths) to account for 98% of all transactions with which the system is expected to contend. The designers should name the transaction, provide a transaction flow for it, identify all processes, branches, loops, and so on.
   b. Discussion of each flow or path through the various flows in functional, rather than technical, terms. If a nontechnical buyer's representative who understands the application but not necessarily the implementation is present, so much the better. The discussion should be understandable, relatively nontechnical, and to a great extent, design independent.

   c. Have the designers relate the selected transaction flows to the specification and show how that transaction, directly or indirectly, follows from specified requirements. However, don't insist on a slavish one-to-one correspondence, because that could result in a poor system or implementation.

2. Make transaction flow testing the cornerstone of system-level functional testing just as path testing is the cornerstone of unit-level structural testing. For this you need a sufficient number of transaction flowcharts to cover *all* possible transactions. Select a sufficient number of paths through those transaction flows to assure complete coverage in the sense of every link and every decision being exercised at least once.

3. Select additional paths beyond coverage to take care of loops, extreme values, and boundaries.

4. Select additional paths to correspond to weird cases and very long, potentially troublesome transactions.

5. Publish and distribute the selected paths as early as possible so that they will have the maximal beneficial effect on the project.

6. Get concurrence from the buyer that the execution of these paths will constitute an adequate system-level functional test. Augment the test paths as necessary to achieve buyer concurrence, or alternatively, demonstrate how specific paths of interest to the buyer are more effectively covered by the selected set of paths.

7. Be sure that the designers know in general which paths will be selected, but not the details of those paths. You can, for example, start with an unrealistically large set of loosely specified paths with the understanding that the number of paths will be decreased as they are developed in further detail. The designers should have enough information to investigate and test the general situation, but not so much information that they can develop an explicit "Mickey Mouse" fix that covers a specific test case but which is otherwise useless.

5. INPUT VALIDATION AND SYNTAX TESTING

5.1. The Hostile World

5.1.1. A Protest

I think one of the worst cop-outs ever invented by the computer industry is "garbage-in equals garbage-out." We know when to use that one! When our system screws up in a nasty way. People are inconvenienced by the host of subsidiary problems that result. A big investigation is launched and it's discovered that an operator made a mistake, an improper tape was mounted, the source data was inconsistent, or something like that. That's the time to put on the guru's mantle, shake your head from side to side, disclaim all guilt, and mutter, "What do you expect? Garbage-in equals garbage-out."

Do we have the right to say that to the families of the passengers on an airliner that crashes? Will you offer that explanation for the failure of the intensive care unit's monitor system? How about a nuclear reactor meltdown, a supertanker run aground, or a war? GIGO is no explanation for anything except our failure to install good data validation checks, or worse, our failure to test the system's tolerance for bad data. The point is that garbage shouldn't get in at all—not in the first place or in the last place. Every system must contend with a bewildering array of internal and external garbage, and if you don't think the world is hostile, how do you plan to cope with alpha particles?

5.1.2. Casual and Malicious Users

Systems that interface with casual, nontechnical users must be especially robust and consequently must have prolific data validation checks. It's not that the users of cash machines, say, are willfully hostile but that there are so many of them; so many of them and so few of us. The more users, the less knowledgeable they are, the more likely that eventually, on pure chance, they'll hit every spot at which the system is vulnerable to bad inputs.

There are a few malicious users in every population—nasty people who delight in doing strange things to the systems they use. They're out to get *you.* Some of them are even programmers. They are persistent and systematic. A few hours of attack by one of *them* is worse than years of ordinary use and bugs found by chance. And there are so many of them; so many of them and so few of us.

Then there is crime. It's estimated that computer criminals (using mostly hokey inputs) are raking in hundreds of millions of dollars annually. Some criminals could be doing it from a telephone booth in Arkansas with an acoustic coupled portable computer. Every piece of bad data unknowingly accepted by a system, every crash-causing input sequence, is a chink in the system's armor that knowledgeable criminals can use to penetrate, corrupt, and eventually suborn the system to their own purposes (LEIB74). There aren't many of them, but they are smart, highly motivated, and possibly organized.

5.1.3. What to Do

Data validation is the first line of defense against a hostile world. Good designers will design their system so that it just doesn't accept garbage—good testers will subject their systems to the most creative garbage possible. Input-tolerance testing is usually done at the system level, such as in a formal functional test or in a final acceptance test, and consequently, the tester is usually distinct from the designer.

5.2. Principles

5.2.1. Objectives, Methods, and Principles

Input data validation and syntax testing is primarily a functional test technique and consequently usually appears as part of a formal system functional test or acceptance test. However, just as path testing was useful as a structural test technique for units and also as a functional test technique on transaction flows at the system level, syntax testing may also be useful at the unit level, in system integration, or as part of structural testing.

In **syntax testing**, the object under test, the program or system, say, is treated as a black box that can accept certain kinds of inputs, reject others, and process some. The emphasis is not on what the program or system does with the inputs, or even that it processes them correctly. Rather, the emphasis is on the system's vulnerability to bad inputs. Unlike most other testing, in which most of the inputs are "good," in syntax testing, the inputs are mostly creative junk. The object of syntax testing is to demonstrate the following, in order of decreasing importance:

1. The element does not fail (e.g., crash or loop indefinitely) when subjected to bad inputs.
2. The element does not cause another element to fail, even though it does not fail itself when subjected to bad inputs.
3. The element does not corrupt the data base when subjected to bad inputs, even though it does not fail itself.
4. The element rejects all bad inputs and accepts all good inputs.
5. It performs the correct processing on good inputs.

Correct processing has been put last, and you might object that it should have been put first. However, syntax testing tests only one aspect of the system's behavior. It is not a method to the exclusion of other methods. Proper functioning should be demonstrated in the context of other kinds of tests.

5.2.2. Formal Description of Syntax

The set of inputs to which an element responds, those data input strings it must accept, and those it must reject, can always be formally defined and must be formally defined in order to generate good syntax-directed tests. One popular and effective method of describing the syntax is to use a metalanguage such as **Backus-Naur form**. This is described in detail in BEIZ82. While it may seem imposing at first, it is nothing more than a systematic way of defining the input strings which a routine is to accept and reject. BNF defines higher-level syntactic elements in terms of simpler or more primitive elements as in the following example:

$$line ::= (alpha{:}character)_7^{80} \ end{:}line$$
$$alpha{:}character ::= A/B/C/D/E/F/G/H/....W/X/Y/Z$$
$$end{:}line ::= cr \ cr \ lf \ / \ cr \ lf \ lf$$

An input string called "*line*" is defined as ("::=" means "is defined as") 7 to 80 repetitions of an object called "*alpha:character*" followed by a field called "*end:line.*" The "*alpha:character*(s)" are defined as the letters "A," "B," "C," and so on; "*end:line*" is defined as two carriage returns followed by a line feed or a carriage return followed by two line feeds. Additional notation is provided to specify alternatives, options, conditional options, zero or more repetitions, a potentially infinite number of repetitions, and the like. In its most developed form, BNF is used to define the entire syntax of a higher-order language, such as COBOL, FORTRAN, BASIC, and so on. While BNF is the most prevalent, and probably the easiest such notation to use, its use is not essential to the development of formal syntax tests. What is needed is any reasonably complete method of specifying the input syntax. Any such method must describe the following:

1. Identify all the input strings to which the element under test is to respond.
2. For each string, identify the fields and combinations of fields which can occur, and the format or syntax of each field, e.g., number of characters, what kind, optional characters, variations, and so on.
3. Identify all correlated fields—fields that must appear together and dependent fields—e.g., if field A appears, then so must B, C, and D.
4. For each field, identify the permissible numerical or alphanumerical values. If these are interrelated, specify the relation in detail.

The emphasis is on specifying all formats by a relatively few simple, but rigid, rules. Verbiage here gets in the way, and the closer you can approach a completely formal specification, such as BNF, the better.

5.3. Test Case Generation

5.3.1. Generators, Recognizers, and Approach

A data validation routine is designed to recognize strings that have been explicitly or implicitly defined in accordance with a formally specified input format. It either accepts the string, because it has recognized it as a valid string, or rejects it and takes appropriate corrective action. The routine is said to be a **string recognizer**. Conversely, the test designer attempts to generate strings and is said to be a **string generator**. There are three possible kinds of incorrect actions:

1. The recognizer does not recognize a good string.
2. It accepts a bad string.
3. It may accept or reject a good string or a bad string, but in so doing, it fails.

Even small specifications lead to many good strings and far more bad strings. There is neither time nor need to test them all. Strings' errors can be categorized as follows:

1. *High-level syntax errors.* The strings have violations of the topmost level in a syntax specification, typically through inappropriate combinations of fields.
2. *Field-syntax errors.* Syntax errors associated with an individual field, where a **field** is defined as a string of characters that has no subsidiary syntax specification other than the identification of characters that compose it. A field is the lowest level at which it is productive to think in terms of syntax testing.
3. *Delimiter errors.* Violation of the rules governing the placement and the type of characters that must appear as separators between fields.
4. *Field-value errors.* Not syntax errors, but errors associated with the contents of a field.
5. *Syntax-context errors.* When the syntax of one field depends on values of other fields, there is a possibility of an interaction between a field-value error and a syntax error. For example, when the contents of a control field dictate the syntax of subsequent fields.
6. *Field-value correlation errors.* The contents of two or more fields are correlated by a functional relation between them. There is not full freedom in picking their values. The value of one field is restricted by another field's value.
7. *State-dependency errors.* The permissible syntax and/or field value is con-

ditional on the state of the system or the routine. A command used for start-up, say, may not be allowed when the system is running.

5.3.2. Syntax Errors

Say that the topmost syntax level is defined as:

$$item ::= atype \mid btype \mid ctype \mid dtype\ etype$$

Here are some obvious test cases:

1. *Do it wrong.* Use an element which is correct at some other, lower syntax level, but not at this level.
2. *Wrong combination.* The last element is a combination of two other elements in a specified order. Mess up the order and combine the wrong things:
   dtype atype / btype etype / etype dtype / etype etype / dtype dtype
3. *Don't do enough*:
   dtype / etype
4. *Don't do nothing.* No input, just the end-of-command signal or carriage return. Amazing how many bugs you catch this way.
5. *Do too much*:
   atype btype ctype dtype etype / atype atype atype / dtype etype atype / dtype etype etype / dtype etype[128]

5.3.3. Delimiter Errors

Delimiters are characters or strings of characters placed between two fields to denote where one ends and the other begins. Delimiter problems are an excellent source of test cases. Therefore, it pays to identify the delimiters and the rules governing their syntax.

1. *Missing delimiter.* This kind of error causes adjacent fields to merge. This may result in a different, but valid, field or may be covered by another kind of syntax error.
2. *Wrong delimiter.* It's nice when several different delimiters are used and there are rules that specify which can be used where. Mix them up and use them in the wrong places.
3. *Not a delimiter.* Includes any character or string that is not a delimiter but which could be put into that position. For example: cr X lf. Note the possibility of changing adjacent field types as a result.
4. *Too many delimiters.* The number of delimiters appearing at a field bound-

ary may be variable. This is typical for spaces, which can serve as delimiters. If the number of delimiters is specified as 1 to N, it pays to try 0, 1, 2, N–1, N, N+1, and also an absurd number of delimiters, such as 127, 128, 255, 256, 1024, and so on.

5. *Paired Delimiters.* Another juicy source of test cases. Parentheses are the archetypal **paired delimiters**. There could be several kinds of paired delimiters appearing within a format. If paired delimiters can nest, as in "(()( )," there is a set of new evils to perpetrate. For example: "BEGIN, BEGIN, END," "BEGIN, END, END." Nested, paired delimiters provide opportunities for **matching ambiguities**. For example, "(( )(( )))" has a parenthesis-matching ambiguity and it's not clear where the missing parenthesis belongs.

5.3.4. Field-Value Errors

We've been able to keep away from any notion of meaning up to this point. None of the test cases described above took into account what the fields meant. Fields do have meaning, and that meaning is not normally part of the field-syntax specification. Fields are treated like loops. Every field should have a specification for the range of permissible values. We can consider the field as if its contents are numbers. Nothing is lost by this assumption, because we can convert everything to equivalent numerical values if we choose to.

1. *Boundary values.* Bugs congregate at the edges of fields just as they do at the ends of loops. The obvious cases to try are: minimum –1, minimum, minimum +1, typical good value, maximum –1, maximum, maximum + 1, a whole lot more than the maximum.
2. *Excluded values.* Test excluded field values like excluded values for loops. Divide the range into allowed and excluded subranges and do boundary checks on each subrange.
3. *Troublesome values.* Dig into the implementation and particularly into the data base and see how the field is stored. The boundary values for the storage element are excellent choices for tests. For example: 0, 15, 16, 31, 32, 63, 64, 127, 128.

5.3.5. Where Did the Good Guys Go?

Syntax-directed test design is like a lot of other things that are hard to stop once you've started. A little practice with this kind of test design and you find that the most innocuous format leads to hundreds of tests. I use format validation test design as basic training for persons new to a test group. With little information and training they can churn out hundreds of good tests. It's a great confidence builder for people who have never done formal test design before and who may be intimidated by the prospect of subjecting a senior designer's masterpiece to a barrage of calculated heartburn. There are, however, several dangers to this kind of test design.

1. *It's easy to forget the normal cases.* I've done it often. You get so entangled in creative garbage that you forget that the system must also be subjected to good inputs. I've made it a practice to explicitly check every test area for the normal cases.
2. *Don't go overboard with the combinations.* It takes iron nerves to do this. You have done all the single-error cases, and in your mind you know exactly how to go about creating the double- and triple-error cases. And there are so many of them that you can create an impressive mound of test cases in short order. "How can the test miss anything if I've tried 1000 input-format errors?" you think. Keep reminding yourself that any one test approach is inherently limited to discovering certain types of bugs. Keep reminding yourself that all those N^2 double-error cases and N^3 triple-error cases may be no more effective than trying every value from 1 to 1023 in testing a loop. Don't let the entire test become top-heavy with syntax errors at the expense of everything else just because syntax tests are so easy to design.
3. *Don't ignore structure.* Just because it's possible to design thousands of test cases without looking at the software that's going to handle those cases doesn't mean you should do it that way. Knowing the program's design may help you eliminate error combinations wholesale without sacrificing the integrity and thoroughness of the test. As an example, say that operator-command mnemonics are validated by a general-purpose preprocessor routine. The rest of the input-character string is passed to the appropriate handler for that operator command only after the mnemonic has been validated. There would be no point to designing test cases that deal with the interaction of command mnemonic errors, the delimiter between the mnemonic and the first field, and format errors in the first field. You don't have to know a whole lot about the implementation. Often, just knowing what parts of the format are handled by which routines is enough to avoid designing a lot of impressive but useless error combinations that won't prove a thing. The bug that could creep across that kind of interface would be so exotic that you would have to design it. If it takes several hours of work to postulate and "design" a bug that a test case is supposed to catch, you can safely consider that test case as too improbable to worry about—certainly in the context of syntax testing.
4. *There's more than one kind of test.* Each model of the system's behavior leads to tests designed from a different point of view, but many of these overlap. Although redundant tests are harmless, they cost money and little is learned from them.

5.4. Running, Validation, and Ad-lib Tests

5.4.1. Running Syntax Tests

Syntax tests are easy to design but hard to run. Every character is important. Every character must be documented, as must each step in the test scenario. Manual inputs are almost hopeless. It's just not possible to type thousands of character sequences, many of which contain subtle errors, some of which use nonprinting characters, with any acceptable degree of reliability and consistency. All inputs must be prepared in advance and be meticulously desk checked and confirmed. Often, the easiest way to confirm the input's validity (actually, design invalidity) is to dry run the test. Fan-fold mylar paper tape is an excellent test tool for this kind of test. Each test sequence is punched on tape and checked. If test errors are found (and this kind of test has more errors than any other kind of test I know of), the tape can be corrected by patching and splicing. Each test has its own tape. The high-quality tape will take abuse. This is such an excellent medium for inputting syntax test data that it's worth buying a paper-tape-equipped terminal for just this purpose, even if it has no other use later in the system's life. Card inputs, where applicable, are almost as good as paper tape. Less convenient, but still acceptable, is to record all the test cases on a magnetic cassette or a floppy disc, used in conjunction with a smart terminal or a microcomputer dedicated to the purpose. Note that there is more hardware and software between the tester and object under test, and consequently, more opportunities for testing bugs. Least acceptable, but unfortunately common, is the use of manual input. If you are forced into this, three persons should be used to do the job—one who calls out the test sequence, one character at a time; the second who actually inputs it; and the third who sees to it that the input is correct. Do not underestimate the practical difficulties of manual inputs for syntax testing. It is possible to extend a formal validation test by weeks or months because the many input errors (such as an inadvertently correct input) may mean that much time is spent chasing ghosts, i.e., why didn't the system reject that input?

5.4.2. Validation

Three of the five test objectives of syntax testing are easy to validate. The others are not.

1. *Show that the element does not fail when subjected to bad inputs.* This should be easy to confirm.
2. *Show that the element does not corrupt another element even though it does not fail itself.* This is inherently difficult to show and can take a lot of instru-

mentation. A way out of this difficulty is to use background and stress testing, as discussed in Chapter 8. If the system is kept busy enough handling correct transactions at the same time that it's handling bad transactions, then corruption of other elements may result in system crashes and restarts. Another approach is to enter several bad transactions simultaneously from different terminals. Statistically, if another program element is corrupted, it will show up. It is not practical to do a detailed audit of all other elements to prove that they did not fail or were not corrupted.

3. *Show that the data base was not corrupted by inputs.* Structure part of the test data base so that it contains simple, completely repetitive data. That part of the data base should not be used in other test transactions. You want a lot of identical or simple data-base entries which can be easily confirmed by a program written for the purpose. Fill all of memory with this data. After you do several hours of syntax testing (or any other kind of testing), run the validation routine. Inadvertent data-base modifications then become obvious.

4. *Show that the element rejects all bad inputs and accepts all good inputs.* There should be no difficulty with this aspect of validation. You may have to put in some instrumentation code or log the results if the fact is not obvious from the terminal's behavior.

5. *Correct processing.* This is best shown under tests designed for that purpose. If correct processing can be demonstrated in the context of syntax testing, without undue difficulty, then by all means do so. Typically, though, demonstration of correct processing is best shown in the context of testing designed for that purpose (e.g., path testing).

5.4.3. Ad-Lib Tests

Whenever you run a formal system test there's always someone in the crowd who wants to try ad-lib tests. And almost always, the kind of test they want to ad-lib is an input-syntax error test. I used to object to ad-libbing because it didn't prove anything—I thought. It doesn't prove anything substantive about the system, assuming you've done a good job of testing—which is why I used to object to it. It may save time to object to ad-lib tests, but it's not politic. Ad-libbing does prove you have confidence in the system and the test. Because a system-wide functional demonstration should have been through a dry run in advance, the actual test execution is largely ceremonial (or should be) and the ad-libbers are part of the ceremony, just as hecklers are part of the ball game—it adds color to the scene.

You should never object if the buyer has designed his own set of tests. If they're carefully constructed, and well-documented, and all the rest, you should welcome yet another independent assault on the system's integrity. Ad-lib tests aren't like that. The buyer has a hotshot operator who's earned a reputation for crashing any system in under two minutes, and she's itching to get her mitts on yours. There's no prepared set of tests, so you know it's going to be ad-libbed. Agree to the ad-libbing, but only after all other tests have been done. Here's what happens:

1. 90% to 95% of the ad-lib tests will be input strings with format violations, and the system will reject them, as it should.
2. Most of the rest are good strings that look bad. The system will accept the strings and do as it was told to do, but the ad-lib tester won't recognize it. It will take a lot of explanation to satisfy the buyer that it was a bona fide cockpit error.
3. A few seemingly good strings will be correctly rejected because of a correlation problem between two field values or a state dependency. These will also take a lot of explanation.
4. At least once, the ad-lib tester will shout "Aha!" and claim that the system was wrong. It will take days to dig out the documentation that shows that the way the system behaves for that case is precisely the way the buyer insisted it behave—over the designer's objections.
5. Another time the ad-lib tester will shout "Aha!" but, because the inputs weren't documented and because nonprinting characters were used, it won't be possible to reproduce the effect. The ad-lib tester will be forever convinced that the system has a flaw.
6. There may be one problem, typically related to the interpretation of a specification ambiguity, whose resolution will probably be trivial.

This may be a bit harsh to the ad-lib testers of the world, but such testing proves little or nothing if the system is good, if it's been properly tested from unit level on up, and if there's been good in-house quality control. If ad-lib tests do prove something, then the system's so shaky and buggy that it deserves the worst that can be thrown at it.

5.5. Application

Although syntax testing is most obviously applicable to input routines and explicit data validation routines, opportunities for effective use of syntax testing techniques abound at all system levels. Here are some examples:

1. All user interfaces, particularly terminals and input devices—the more naive the user, the more extensive should the tests be.
2. Operator command processing.
3. All communications interfaces and protocols.

4. Internal interfaces and protocols such as formal calling sequences to an application executive.
5. Internal job control and transaction control languages, even when not formally specified.
6. Higher-order user languages, specialized operator languages, application specific languages and command sets.
7. Dedicated data validation routines and programs.
8. All interfaces with new devices or with equipment not part of the mainframe supplier's product line.

5.6. Tasks for a Quality Assurance Department

1. Define guidelines for the use of syntax-directed testing at the unit level, for integration testing, and at the functional level. Educate the staff regarding syntax testing's applicability and methodology.
2. Obtain management's and/or the buyer's guidance regarding the degree of garbage tolerance appropriate to each product. Measure that tolerance in terms of consequences, damages, and the severity thereof. Make sure that there is unanimity regarding objectives.
3. Adopt a standard for the specification of all syntax in the system. Don't invent new notations or make a research project out of it. It doesn't really matter what you use as long as you use something and use it consistently.
4. Identify all system elements for which syntax-directed testing might prove beneficial.
5. Obtain or create a formal specification of the appropriate syntax for each such element. Evaluate the specification for consistency and thoroughness. Obtain buyer concurrence. (This entire step is where most of the action is.)
6. Design appropriate single-error test cases, and far fewer double- and higher-order error combinations. Obtain approval regarding the cutoff level. It can go either way—the powers that be (those who foot the bill) may not want to go far enough, but if they've been burned, they may want to go much too far. Projected testing costs and duration are useful to set a perspective.
7. Establish reliable methods for conducting this kind of test and for validating the results.

6. LOGIC-BASED TESTING

6.1. Definitions and Notation

Table 3-2 is an example of a **limited-entry decision table**. It consists of four areas called the **condition stub**, the **condition entry**, the **action stub**, and the **action entry**. Each column of a decision table is a **rule** that specifies the con-

Table 3-2. An Example of a Decision Table.

CONDITION ENTRY

		RULE 1	RULE 2	RULE 3	RULE 4
CONDITION STUB	DECISION 1	YES	YES	NO	NO
	DECISION 2	YES	I	NO	I
	DECISION 3	NO	YES	NO	I
	DECISION 4	NO	YES	NO	YES
ACTION STUB	ACTION 1	YES	YES	NO	NO
	ACTION 2	NO	NO	YES	NO
	ACTION 3	NO	NO	NO	YES

ACTION ENTRY

ditions under which the actions named in the action stub will take place. The condition stub is a list of names of program decisions or tests. These could be direct decisions or the result of a more complicated process executed by a subroutine. Decisions are usually **binary**—that is, they can be reworded into questions that can be answered with a "YES" or "NO." Binary decisions are not a strict requirement, but things are generally simpler with binary decisions. A rule specifies the answer required of a decision for the rule to be satisfied. The required answer can be specified as "YES," "NO," or "I," which means that the result of the decision is **immaterial** to the satisfaction of the rule.

The **action stub** is a list of names of the actions the routine will take or initiate if the corresponding rule is satisfied. If the action entry is "YES," the action will take place; if "NO," the action will not take place. An immaterial entry (I) in the action stub is meaningless. Table 3-2 can be translated as follows:

   a. Action 1 will take place if Decisions 1 and 2 are satisfied and if Decisions 3 and 4 are not satisfied (Rule 1), or if Decisions 1, 3, and 4 are satisfied (Rule 2).
   b. Action 2 will take place only if none of the decisions are satisfied (Rule 3).
   c. Action 3 will take place if Decision 1 is not satisfied and Decision 4 is satisfied (Rule 4).

It is not obvious from looking at this specification whether or not all 16 possible combinations of the four decisions have been covered. In fact, they have not; a combination of YES, NO, NO, NO, for decisions 1 through 4 respectively, is not covered by these rules. In addition to the stated rules, therefore, an ELSE condition must be provided. The ELSE condition is a set of entries that specifies the **default** action when all other rules fail. The default case for Table 3-2 is shown in Table 3-3. Decision tables can be specified in specialized languages that will automatically create the default rules. Consequently, when programming in such languages, it is not necessary to make an explicit default specification. However, when decision tables are used as a tool for test case design and specification analysis, the default conditions must be explicitly specified or determined even if the decision language processor creates the default cases. If the set of rules covers all the combinations of YES/NO for the decisions, a default specification is not needed.

6.2. Decision Tables as a Basis for Test Case Design

Decision tables can be automatically translated into code and, as such, constitute a higher-order language. The decision table's translator examines the specifications (given as a decision table) for consistency and completeness and fills in any default rules that may be required.

If a specification is given directly as a decision table, it follows that decision tables should be used for test case design. Similarly, if a program's logic is to be implemented as decision tables, decision tables should also be used as a basis for test case design. But if that's the case, the consistency and completeness of the decision table can and should be checked by the decision-table translation processor; therefore, there would be no need to design those test cases.

The use of a decision-table *model* to design test cases is warranted when:

1. The specification is given as a decision table or is easily converted to one.
2. The order in which the decisions are evaluated does not affect the interpretation of the rules or the resulting action; that is, any arbitrary permutation of the decision order will not, or should not, affect which action takes place.

Table 3-3. Default Cases for Table 3-2.

	RULE 5	RULE 6	RULE 7	RULE 8
DECISION 1	I	NO	YES	YES
DECISION 2	I	YES	I	NO
DECISION 3	YES	I	NO	NO
DECISION 4	NO	NO	YES	I
DEFAULT ACTION	YES	YES	YES	YES

3. The order in which the rules are evaluated does not affect the resulting action; that is, any arbitrary permutation of rules will not, or should not, affect which action takes place.
4. Once a rule has been satisfied and an action selected, no other rule need be examined.
5. If multiple actions can result from the satisfaction of a rule, the order in which the actions take place is immaterial.

What these seemingly restrictive conditions mean is that the action is selected strictly on the basis of the combination of decision values and nothing else. It might seem at first that these restrictions would eliminate many potential applications and many potential usages for test case design. However, the order in which rules are evaluated is often immaterial. For example, if I use a cash machine, the card must be valid, I have to enter the right password, and there must be a sufficient balance in my account. It really doesn't matter in which order these things are checked. The specific order chosen may be sensible in that it can reduce processing or increase efficiency, but the order is not an inherent part of the program's logic.

The above conditions have further implications: 1) the rules are complete in the sense that every combination of decision values, including the default combinations, are inherent in the decision table, and 2) the rules are consistent if and only if every combination of decision values results in only one action or set of actions. If the rules were inconsistent, that is, if at least one combination of decision values was implicit in two or more rules, then the action that would take place could depend on the order in which the rules were examined, in contradiction to Requirement 3 above. If the set of rules were incomplete, there could be a combination of input values for which no action, normal or default, was specified and the routine's action would be unpredictable.

6.3. Expansion of Immaterial Cases

Immaterial entries (I) are the source of most contradictions in decision tables. If a decision's value (YES/NO) is immaterial in a rule, the satisfaction of the rule does not depend on the answer. It does not mean that the case is impossible. For example, say the rules are:

R1—"If the persons are male and over 30, then they shall receive a 15% raise."

R2—"But if the persons are female, then they shall receive a 10% raise."

It's clear that age is material for determining a male's raise, but immaterial for determining a female's raise. No one would seriously suggest that females either under or over 30 are impossible. If there are n decisions there must be 2^n cases to consider. You find the cases by expanding the immaterial cases.

Table 3-4. Expansion of Immaterial Cases.

	RULE 2.1	RULE 2.2	RULE 4.1	RULE 4.2	RULE 4.3	RULE 4.4
	RULE 2		RULE 4			
DECISION 1	YES	YES	NO	NO	NO	NO
DECISION 2	YES	NO	YES	YES	NO	NO
DECISION 3	YES	YES	YES	NO	NO	YES
DECISION 4	YES	YES	YES	YES	YES	YES

This is done by converting each I entry into a pair of entries, one with a YES and the other with a NO. Each I entry in a rule doubles the number of cases in the expansion of that rule. Rule 2 in Table 3-2 contains one I entry and will therefore expand into two equivalent subrules. Rule 4 contains two I entries and will therefore expand into four subrules. The expansion of Rules 2 and 4 are shown in Table 3-4.

Rule 2 has been expanded by converting Decision 2's I entry into a separate Rule 2.1 for YES and 2.2 for NO. Similarly, Decision 2 was expanded in Rule 4 to yield intermediate Rules 4.1/4.2 and 4.3/4.4, which were then expanded via Decision 3 to yield the four subrules shown.

The key to test case design based on decision tables is to remove all immaterial entries by expansion and to generate tests that correspond to all the subrules. If some decisions are three-way decisions, an immaterial entry expands into three subrules. Similarly, an n-way, immaterial case statement expands into n subrules.

If no default rules are given, then all cases not covered by explicit rules are perforce default rules (or are intended to be). If default rules are given, then you must test the specification for consistency. The specification is complete if and only if n (binary) decisions expand into exactly 2^n unique subrules. It is consistent if and only if all rules expand into subrules whose decision combinations do not match those of any other subrule.

6.4. Test Case Design

The design of test cases by decision tables begins with examining the specification's consistency and completeness. This is done by expanding all immaterial cases and checking the expanded tables. Efficient methods for doing this are given in Chapter 10 of BEIZ82. Once the specifications have been proven correct, the objective of the test cases is to show that the implementation provides the correct action for all combinations of decision values.

1. If there are n binary decisions, there are 2^n cases to consider—no more and no less. Each case is a test case. Find input values that will force each case and confirm the action. Expand the decision table as required for the default cases, which should be treated as just other actions.
2. It is not usually possible to change the order in which the *decisions* are evaluated because that order is built into the program. If, however, the implementation does allow that order to be modified by input values, augment the test cases by using different decision-evaluation orders. Try all pairs of interchanges for a representative set of values. For example, if the normal order is decision A followed by B, then try a test in which B is followed by A. For N decisions, there will be $N(N-1)/2$ interchanges for each combination of values of the decisions.
3. It is not usually possible to change the order in which the *rules* are evaluated because that order is built into the program. If, however, the implementation does allow the rule-evaluation order to be modified, test different orders for the rules by pairwise interchanges. One set of decision values per rule should be sufficient.
4. Identify the place or places in the routine where rules are invoked or where the processors that evaluate the rules are called. Similarly, identify the places where the actions are initiated. Instrument those paths so that you can show that the correct action was invoked for each rule.

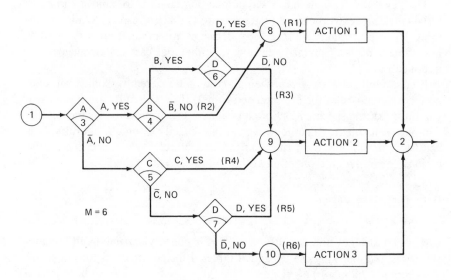

Figure 3-4. Example for Decision Table Analysis.

Table 3-5. Decision Table for Figure 3-4.

	RULE 1	RULE 2	RULE 3	RULE 4	RULE 5	RULE 6
DECISION A	YES	YES	YES	NO	NO	NO
DECISION B	YES	NO	YES	I	I	I
DECISION C	I	I	I	YES	NO	NO
DECISION D	YES	I	NO	I	YES	NO
ACTION 1	YES	YES	NO	NO	NO	NO
ACTION 2	NO	NO	YES	YES	YES	NO
ACTION 3	NO	NO	NO	NO	NO	YES

6.5. Decision Tables and Structure

Decision tables can also be used to examine a program's structure (GOOD75). Figure 3-4 shows a program segment that consists of a tree of decisions. These decisions, in various combinations, can lead to actions 1, 2, or 3. Does this flowchart correspond to a complete and consistent set of conditions?

The corresponding decision table is shown in Table 3-5. You can almost read it from the flowchart. If the decision appears on a path, put a YES or NO as appropriate. If the decision does not appear on the path, put in an I. Rule 1 does not contain Decision C, therefore its entries are: YES, YES, I, YES. Expanding the immaterial cases for Table 3-5 leads to Table 3-6.

Sixteen cases are represented in Table 3-6 and no case appears twice. Consequently, the flowchart appears to be complete and consistent. As a first check, before you look for all sixteen combinations, count the number of Y's and N's in each row. They should be equal.

Table 3-6. Expansion of Table 3-5.

	R1	RULE 2	R3	RULE 4	R5	R6
DECISION A	Y Y	Y Y Y Y	Y Y	N N N N	N N	N N
DECISION B	Y Y	N N N N	Y Y	Y Y N N	N Y	Y N
DECISION C	Y N	N N Y Y	Y N	Y Y Y Y	N N	N N
DECISION D	Y Y	Y N N Y	N N	N Y Y N	Y Y	N N

6.6. Logic and Boolean Algebra in Test Design

The tabular procedures used to manipulate and analyze decision tables can be better done by converting the decision table to equivalent boolean algebra expressions. Notations, rules, and methodology are detailed in BEIZ82. The methods described show how to develop one or more boolean algebra expressions that correspond to the logical behavior of the routine as viewed from every entry to every exit. As a desk-checking technique, it leads to the following determinations for most programs:

1. Is the logic complete and consistent or are there ambiguities and contradictions?
2. More effective and efficient ways of organizing path sensitization.
3. Discovery of harmless but unnecessary complications and redundancies in logic and decision code.
4. Discovery of input values that could cause indefinite looping.

The use of boolean algebra leads to the notion of **logical coverage**. If a routine is based on n different binary factors, some of which may be examined at more than one program decision point, then there are at least 2^n different combinations to consider. However, this does not necessarily lead to 2^n paths, because combinations of factors could result in immaterial cases. A routine is **logically covered** if the test cases used directly or indirectly explore all 2^n combinations of decision factors. Logical coverage may or may not correspond to path coverage. Path sensitization should be based on logical coverage when the routine appears to be dominated by TRUE-FALSE alternatives and combinations thereof, such as when a decision table is a natural way of expressing the routine's behavior. Logical coverage is not *instead* of path coverage, but *in addition* to it.

Logical coverage is a good bottom-line (functional) test method. A program whose outcome depends on, say, 8 factors is not usually written as a full dissection of the 256 cases, followed by jumps to the program segments that provide the correct processing. That would be a clear but needlessly complicated way of implementing. Furthermore, that extra code would be burdened with typographical errors, so that the benefits gained from the simpler structure would be destroyed by the sheer mass of additional code. Programmers are much cleverer and organize the program's logic so that it's done in a tight and efficient manner. If a program is based on n factors, there are 2^n cases to consider and of the order of 2^{2^n} different, correct, ways of implementing that logic. Programmers can expend a lot of effort and much ingenuity to find efficient ways of implementing complicated logic. Logic-based testing, with the idea of using logical coverage (either based on decision tables or boolean algebra) cuts through all those implementation alternatives and tests the logic functionally, case by case, without regard to implementation. It is, therefore, a predominantly functional test technique.

6.7. Tasks for a Quality Assurance Department

1. Define guidelines for the use of logic-based testing at each testing level.
2. Translate specifications that are dominated by logic and combinations of cases into either decision tables or boolean algebra and develop functional test cases from those representations.
3. Examine specifications with respect to logical consistency and ambiguity. Obtain explicit concurrence on all seemingly impossible cases and immaterial cases.
4. Identify logic- or combination-dominated routines and functions. Insist on test plans that provide logical coverage for such routines.

7. STATE TRANSITION TESTING

7.1. General

7.1.1. States

The word "**state**" is used in much the same way it's used in ordinary English, as in "state of the Union" or "state of health." The Oxford English Dictionary defines "state" as "A combination of circumstances or attributes belonging for the time being to a person or thing."

A program that detects the character sequence "ZCZC" can be in the following states:

1. Neither ZCZC nor any part of it has been detected
2. Z has been detected
3. ZC has been detected
4. ZCZ has been detected
5. ZCZC has been detected

States are represented by circles, or nodes. The states are numbered or may be identified by words or whatever else is convenient. Figure 3-5 shows a typical state graph. A state usually depicts a combination of attributes or conditions of interest. Each additional factor that has alternatives multiplies the number of states by the number of alternatives. Because most interesting factors are

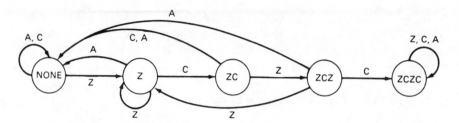

Figure 3-5. ZCZC Sequence Detection State Graph.

binary, and because each new factor doubles the number of states, state graphs are most useful for relatively simple functional models involving at most a few dozen states and only a few factors.

7.1.2. Inputs and Transitions

That which is being modeled is subjected to inputs, and as a result of those inputs, the state changes, or is said to have made a **transition**. The transitions are denoted by links that join the states. The input or inputs that caused the transition are marked on the link. The ZCZC detection example can have the following kinds of inputs:

1. Z
2. C
3. Any character other than Z or C, which we'll denote by A.

The state graph of Figure 3-5 is interpreted as follows:

1. If the system is in the "NONE" state, any input other than a Z will keep it in that state.
2. If a Z is received, the system transitions to the "Z" state.
3. If the system is in the "Z" state, and a Z is received, it will remain in the "Z" state. If a C is received it will go to the "ZC" state, and if any other character is received, it will go back to the "NONE" state because the sequence has been broken.
4. A Z received in the "ZC" state progresses to the "ZCZ" state, but any other character breaks the sequence and causes a return to the "NONE" state.
5. A C received in the "ZCZ" state completes the sequence and the system enters the "ZCZC" state. A Z breaks the sequence and causes a transition

back to the "Z" state; any other character causes a return to the "NONE" state.

6. No matter what is received in the "ZCZC" state, the system stays there.

As you can see, the state graph is a compact representation of all this verbiage.

7.1.3. Outputs

An output, action, or outcome can be associated with every combination of input and transition. An output is denoted by a letter or label and is separated from the input by a slash as follows: "input/output." If every input associated with a transition causes the same output, then denote it as: "input 1, input 2, input 3/output." If there are many different combinations of inputs and outputs, it's best to draw a separate parallel link for each output.

7.2. Good State Graphs and Bad

7.2.1. General

We must deal not with good state graphs, but with bad ones. What constitutes a good and a bad state graph is to some extent biased by the kinds of state graphs that are likely to be used in a software test design context. Here are some principles for judging:

1. The total number of states is equal to the product of the possibilities of factors that make up the states.
2. For every state and input there is exactly one transition specified to exactly one, possibly the same, state.
3. For every transition there is one outcome specified. That outcome could be trivial, but at least one outcome does something sensible.
4. For every state there is a sequence of inputs that will drive the system back to the same state.

Figure 3-6 shows examples of improper state graphs.

None of the examples showed output codes. There are two aspects to state graphs: 1) the states with their transitions and the inputs that cause them, and 2) the outputs or outcomes associated with specific transitions. Just as in the flowchart model we concentrated on the control structure and tended to ignore the processing that did not directly affect the control flow, in state testing we may ignore outcomes, because it is the states and transitions that are of pri-

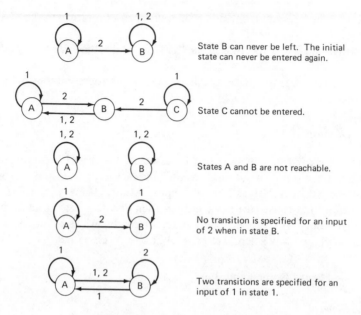

Figure 3-6. Improper State Graphs.

mary interest. Two state graphs with identical states, inputs, and transitions could have vastly different outputs, yet from a control point of view and from a state testing point of view, they would be almost identical. Consequently, we reduce the clutter caused by explicit output specifications if outputs are not interesting at the moment.

7.2.2. State Bugs

Number of States

The number of states in a state graph is the number of states we choose to recognize or model. However, in practice, the state is directly or indirectly recorded as a combination of values of variables that appear in the data base. As an example, the state could be composed of the value of a counter whose possible values ranged from 0 to 9, combined with the setting of two bit flags, leading to a total of $2 \times 2 \times 10 = 40$ states. When the state graph represents an explicit state-table implementation, this value is encoded, and consequently, bugs in the number of states are less likely. However, the encoding can be wrong. Failing to account for all the states is one of the more common bugs related to software that can be modeled by state graphs. Because an explicit state-table mechanization is not typical, the opportunities for missing states abound. Find the number of states as follows:

1. Identify all the component factors of the state.
2. Identify all the allowable values for each component.
3. The number of states is the product of the number of allowable values of all the components: Period—Exactly—Precisely.

Before you do anything else, before you consider a single test case, go over the number of states you think there are with the number of states the programmer thinks there are. Differences of opinion are common. There's no point in designing tests that are intended to check the system's behavior in various states if there's no agreement on how many states there are. And if there's no agreement on how many states there are, there must be disagreement on what the system does in which states and on the transitions and the outputs. If it seems that I'm giving undue emphasis to the seemingly trivial act of counting states, it's because that act often exhumes fundamental design deficiencies. You don't need to wait until the design is finished. A functional specification is usually sufficient—as state testing is primarily a functional test tool. Read the functional specification and identify the factors and then the number of possible values for each factor. Make up a table, with a column for every factor, such that all combinations of factors are represented. Before you get concurrence on outputs or transitions or the inputs that cause the transitions, get concurrence from the designer that every combination listed makes sense.

Impossible States

Some combinations of values may appear to be impossible. Say that the factors are:

GEAR	R, N, 1,2,3,4	= 6 values
DIRECTION	Forward, reverse, stopped	= 3 values
ENGINE	Running, stopped	= 2 values
TRANSMISSION	Okay, broken	= 2 values
ENGINE	Okay, broken	= 2 values
TOTAL		= 144 states

However, a broken engine cannot run, and consequently, the combination of values for engine condition and engine operation yields only 3 rather than 4 states, so the total number of states is at most 108. A car with a broken transmission won't move for long, thereby further decreasing the number of feasible states. The discrepancy between the programmer's state count and the tester's state count is often due to a difference of opinion concerning "impossible states."

We should say "supposedly impossible" rather than "impossible." There are always alpha particles to contend with, as well as bugs in other routines. The implicit or explicit record of the values of the factors in the computer is not always the same as the values of those factors in the world—as was learned at Three Mile Island. One of the contributing factors to that fiasco was a discrepancy between the actual position of an actuator and the reported position of that actuator. The designers had falsely assumed that it was "impossible" for the actuator's actual position to be at variance with its reported position. Two states, "Actuator-UP/Actuator-Indicates-DOWN" and "Actuator-DOWN/Actuator-Indicates-UP," were incorrectly assumed to be impossible.

Equivalent States

Two states are **equivalent** if every sequence of inputs starting from one state produces exactly the same sequence of outputs when started from the other state. This notion can also be extended to sets of states. Figure 3-7 shows the situation:

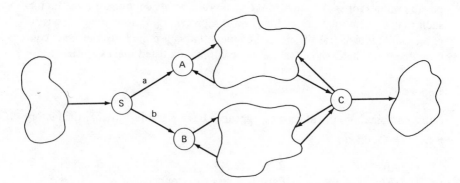

Figure 3-7. Equivalent States.

Say that the system is in state S and that an input of **a** causes a transition to state A while an input of **b** causes a transition to state B. The blobs indicate portions of the state graph whose details are unimportant. If, starting from state A, *every* possible sequence of inputs produces *exactly* the same sequence of outputs that would occur when starting from state B, then there is no way that an outside observer can determine which of the two sets of states the system is in without looking at the record of the state. The state graph can be reduced to that of Figure 3-8 without harm:

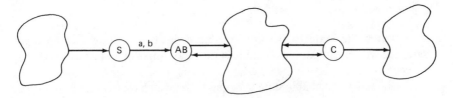

Figure 3-8. Equivalent States Combined.

The fact that there is a notion of state equivalency means that there is an opportunity for bugs to arise from a difference of opinion concerning which states are equivalent. If you insist that there exists another factor, not recognized by the programmer, such that the resulting output sequence for a given input sequence is different depending on the value of that factor, then you are asserting that two nonequivalent sets of states have been inadvertently merged. Conversely, if you cannot find a sequence of inputs which results in at least one different outcome when starting from either of two supposedly inequivalent states, then the states *are* equivalent and should be merged if only to simplify the software and thereby reduce the probability of bugs. Be careful, though, because equivalent states could come about as a result of good planning for future enhancements. The two states are presently indistinguishable but could in the future become distinguished as a result of an enhancement that brings with it the distinguishing factor.

Unspecified and Contradictory Transitions

Every input/state combination must have a specified transition. If the transition is impossible, then there must be a mechanism that prevents that input from occurring in that state—look for it. If there is no such mechanism, what will the program do if, through a malfunction or an alpha particle, the impossible input occurs in that state? The transition for a given state/input combination may not be specified because of an oversight. *Exactly one transition must be specified for every combination of input and state.* However you model it or test it, the system will do *something* for every combination of input and state.

A program (as distinguished from a program's model or specification) cannot have contradictions or ambiguities. Ambiguities are impossible because the program will do *something* (right or wrong) for every input. Even if the state does not change, by definition this is a transition to the same state. Similarly, real software cannot have contradictory transitions because computers can only do one thing at a time.

Unreachable States

An **unreachable state** is like unreachable code. It is a state that no input sequence will reach. An unreachable state is not impossible, just as unreachable code is not impossible.

An isolated, unreachable state here and there, which clearly relates to impossible combinations of real-world state-determining conditions, is acceptable. However, if you find groups of connected states that are isolated from others, there is reason for concern. There are two possibilities: 1) there is a bug; some transitions are missing, 2) the transitions are there, but you don't know about it; there are other inputs and associated transitions to reckon with. Typically, such hidden transitions are caused by software operating at a higher priority level or by interrupt processing.

Dead States

A **dead state**, or set of dead states, is a state which once entered cannot be left. This is not necessarily a bug, but it is suspicious. If the software was designed to be the fuse for a bomb, we would expect at least one such state. A set of states may appear to be dead because the program has two modes of operation. In the first mode it goes through an initialization process that consists of several states. Once initialized, it goes to a working set of states, which, within the context of the routine, cannot be exited. The initialization states are unreachable to the working states, and the working states are dead to the initialization states. The only way to get back might be after a system crash and restart. Legitimate dead states are rare. They occur mainly with system-level issues and device handlers. In normal software, if it's not possible to get from any state to any other, there's reason for concern.

7.2.3. Outcome Errors

The set of states, the transitions, and the inputs that cause those transitions could be correct, there could be no dead or unreachable states, but the outcome for the transition could be incorrect. Outcome must be verified independently of states and transitions. That is, you should distinguish between a program whose state graph is correct but has the wrong outcome for a transition and one whose state graph is incorrect. The most likely reason for an incorrect outcome is an incorrect call to the routine that executes the outcome. This is usually a localized and minor error. Errors in the state graph are more serious because they tend to be related to fundamental control-structure problems. If the routine is implemented as a state table, both types of errors are of comparable severity.

7.2.4. *Impact of Bugs*

Let's say that a routine is specified by a state graph and that the state graph has been verified as correct in all details. Code or tables or a combination of both must still be implemented. A bug can manifest itself as one or more of the following symptoms:

1. Wrong number of states.
2. Wrong transition for a given state-input combination.
3. Wrong outcome for a given transition.
4. Pairs of states or sets of states are inadvertently made equivalent (factor lost).
5. States or sets of states are split to create nonequivalent duplicates.
6. States or sets of states become dead.
7. States or sets of states become unreachable.

7.3. State Testing

7.3.1. *General Principles*

The approach for state testing is analogous to that used for path testing. Just as it's impractical to go through every possible path in a flowchart, it's impractical to go through every path in a state graph. A **path** in a state graph, of course, is a succession of state-to-state transitions caused by a sequence of inputs. The notion of coverage is identical to that used for flowcharts—pass through each link (i.e., each transition must be exercised). Assume that some state is particularly interesting—call it the **initial state.** Most realistic state graphs are **strongly connected**; that is, it should be possible to go through all states and back to the initial state, when starting from there. The starting point of state testing is:

1. Define a set of covering input sequences that get back to the initial state when starting from the initial state.
2. For each step in each input sequence, define the expected next state, the expected transition, and the expected outcome.

A set of tests, then, consists of three sets of sequences:

1. Input sequences
2. Corresponding transitions or next-state names
3. Outcome sequences

7.3.2. Limitations

Just as node-link coverage in a flowchart model of program behavior did not guarantee complete testing, **state-transition coverage** in a state-graph model does not guarantee complete testing. However, things are slightly better because it's not necessary to consider any sequence longer than the total number of states. In general, one must use longer and longer covering sequences to catch transition errors, missing states, extra states, et cetera. The theory of what constitutes a sufficient number of tests (i.e., input sequences) to catch specified kinds of state-graph errors is still in its infancy and is beyond the scope of this book. Meanwhile, we have the following experience:

1. Simply identifying the factors that contribute to the state, calculating the total number of states, and comparing this number to the designer's notion catches some bugs.
2. Insisting on a justification for all supposedly dead, unreachable, and impossible states and transitions catches a few more bugs.
3. Insisting on an explicit specification of the transition and output for every combination of input and state catches many more bugs.
4. A set of input sequences that provide coverage of all state graph nodes and links is a mandatory minimum requirement.
5. In executing state tests, it is essential that means be provided (e.g., instrumentation software) to record the sequence of states (e.g., transitions) resulting from the input sequence and not just the outputs that result from the input sequence.

7.3.3. What to Model

Because every combination of hardware and software can in principle be modeled by a sufficiently complicated state graph, this representation of software behavior is applicable to every program; the utility of such tests, however, is more limited. The state graph is a behavioral model—it is functional rather than structural and is therefore far removed from the code. As a method of testing, it is a bottom-line method that ignores structural detail to focus on behavior. However, it is advantageous to look into the data base to see how the factors that create the states are represented in order to get a state count. More than most test methods, state-graph tests yield their biggest payoffs during the design of the tests rather than during the running thereof. Because they can be constructed from a design specification long before design and coding, they help catch deep bugs early in the game when correction is inexpensive. Here are some generic situations in which it may prove useful to design state-graph tests:

1. Any processing where the output is based on the occurrence of one or more sequences of events, such as detection of specified input sequences, sequential format validation, and other situations in which the order of inputs is important.
2. Most protocols between systems, between humans and machines, between modules within a system.
3. Device handlers such as tape handlers, disc handlers, and the like, that involve complicated retry and recovery procedures if the action depends on the state.
4. Transaction flows where the transactions are such that they can stay in the system indefinitely. For example, online users, tasks in a multi-programming system.
5. High-level control functions within an operating system. Transitions between user states, supervisor's states, and so on. Security handling of records, permission for read/write/modify privileges, priority interrupts and transitions between interrupt states and levels, recovery issues and the safety state of records and/or processes with respect to recording recovery data.
6. The behavior of the system with respect to resource management and what it will do when various levels of resource utilization are reached. Any control function that involves responses to thresholds where the system's action depends not just on the threshold value, but also on the direction in which the threshold is crossed. This is a normal approach to control functions. A threshold passage in one direction stimulates a recovery function, but that recovery function is not suspended until a second, lower threshold is passed going the other way.
7. Whenever a function is directly and explicitly implemented as one or more state-transition tables.

8. TASKS FOR A QUALITY ASSURANCE DEPARTMENT

1. Explore and then select a limited number of effective test techniques (not more than 10) that:
   a. Have been proven in practice.
   b. Appear to apply to your context.
   c. Can be easily understood by programmers, designers, and testers.
2. Establish a training program to instruct programmers and quality assurance personnel in the use, limitations, objectives, and most likely areas of application of the various test techniques.

3. Establish nonbinding guidelines for the use of different test techniques in the circumstances to which they best apply—e.g., functional/structural, unit/system level, etc.

4. Review test plans for correspondence to test method guidelines and investigate seeming deviations. Don't be dogmatic about using the "right" test design method. The programmer could be very astute or very stupid, or your guidelines could be wrong.

5. Monitor the effectiveness of the methods you use with respect to:
   a. The number of bugs caught.
   b. The severity and publicness of those bugs.
   c. The level (unit to system) at which the bug was caught.
   d. The application context.

   Tune your methods in accordance to the data gathered and emphasize the methods that have the best payoff. Remember, though, every method, if it works, is self-defeating and will change the bug statistics. Therefore be resigned to continually retuning your methods as the application, staff, and bug mix changes. I call this the **quality assurance uncertainty principle**.

6. Listen to the programmers and designers for test method suggestions and keep on top of the test literature—you need all the help you can get, so be ready, willing, and able to adopt and implement any method that works.

7. Denounce any single, monolithic, ostensibly universal test technique for the nonsense it is. Prove it by creating a bug it can't catch.

4

UNIT TESTING, ELEMENT TESTING, AND QUALITY ASSURANCE

1. SYNOPSIS

Unit testing is put into perspective with respect to goals, methods, and conduct. It is seen as a microcosm that reflects the overall system testing and quality assurance problem.

2. SOFTWARE SOCIOLOGY

2.1. Unit Testing

2.1.1. Unit Definition

A **unit** is a system software component that has the following attributes:

1. It is, or is intended to be, the work of one programmer.
2. It has a documented specification that includes as a minimum:
   a. Input definition
   b. Processing definition
   c. Outcome definition
   d. Data base definition
   e. Interface specification
3. It is a visible, identifiable product that will be explicitly integrated into the program of which it is a part.
4. It can be compiled or assembled and tested separately from other units, except such subunits as it might call.
5. It is necessary.

2.1.2. Unit and Subunit Prevention

If the highest goal of software quality assurance is bug prevention, then its most effective method should be code prevention. Deciding whether or not a unit is necessary is primarily a design responsibility and not a quality assurance concern. However, while a unit itself may be essential, it may call subunits such as common subroutines, or use common macros, or contain within itself subroutines or macros. Every private subroutine or macro is a candidate for elimination, and, in this sense, the justification of such subunits is a quality assurance concern.

Software design as practiced (as distinct from preached) proceeds simultaneously from the top down and from the bottom up. The top-down component divides the unmanageable whole into manageable parts. In so doing, the designer sees opportunities for units—e.g., for common subroutines and macros—that can serve as building blocks. The fact that there are such blocks influences the partition of the system to take advantage of them. A typical approach might have one senior designer sketching the system while another defines the common subroutines and a third does the data base. A pure top-down approach denies the possibility of common subroutines and would result in a proliferation of almost identical subunits which in turn would result in high integration and system testing cost. A pure bottom-up approach denies that there are global concerns to which the units must be subservient. It also falsely assumes that if the units are good then so must be the system. A good building cannot be built from bad bricks, but good bricks do not obviate the need for architecture.

As the project continues, implementation details are passed down further and further and close communication between the unit implementers is more difficult and less likely. While new common subunits may be added, there is usually no mechanism in place that will search for these if the opportunity for them is not recognized. The quality assurance department is usually the only entity that is required to look at all units in detail, cutting across project boundaries and program subdivisions. It is, therefore, uniquely placed to recognize the potential for new common subunits and, in so doing, to reduce design cost and testing cost, and to improve quality. It should act in an advisory capacity and bring such opportunities to the designer's attention. Assuming a cooperative design staff, that's all that's necessary to give the proposed common subunit a fair examination.

2.1.3. Unit Puberty Rites

Unit testing is a rite of passage in which the unit is transformed from the private to the public domain. Judging from the difficulty some programmers have with this rite and the agony for them that attends it, it is not all that unlike walking across a bed of hot coals or facing the discomfort and privation that are part of the puberty rites of many aboriginal cultures. Like puberty and adolescence, unit testing is not a singular event that takes place on a certain day (e.g., "Today I am a man"), but it is, rather, the progression of a complex of interrelated events and rituals that begins with a private thought and ends only when the routine is no longer in use.

The following words show what happens to a unit and its programmer as they, together, go from the private to the public domain:

PRIVATE	PUBLIC
informal	formal
variable	fixed
ambiguous	concrete
incomplete	finished
disorder	order
isolated	integrated
discordant	concordant
not accountable	responsible
weak	robust

All of these changes and more occur in that passage. Furthermore, as the unit progresses towards a public life, the costs of correction, anxiety, and stress increase geometrically. This pattern, and its associated factors, does not stop with unit testing. It is repeated for each unit, each assembly of units, program, subsystem, and the entire system as each goes from private to public. Unit testing is not only the starting point of testing but it is also a microcosm of the testing process as a whole. Everything that's to be said about unit testing applies to the higher levels of testing in one form or another. Just as the individual passes from childhood through adolescence to maturity and then senescence, so does the family, the band, the clan, the tribe, and the culture. Unit-level quality assurance should be dedicated to the achievement of the transition from private to public by the least costly and, hopefully, least traumatic path.

2.2. Subjective Goals

Underlying the concrete and objective goals of unit testing, such as a working routine that meets requirements, are subjective goals that must simultaneously be achieved if a routine is to be admitted to the society of public routines.

Certainly a feeling of satisfaction by the programmer over a job well done is an important subjective goal of unit testing. However, in the context of quality assurance, the reduction of uncertainty, or equivalently, achievement of trust and confidence in the unit, is the most important subjective goal. It is not enough that the unit works—it must also be *trusted*. Once a unit is public, it will interact with other units. That interaction is stressed in integration testing. The integrator perceives a bug. It could be in any one of several units, or result from their interaction. The debugger must determine which. Debugging is a cyclic process consisting of the following steps:

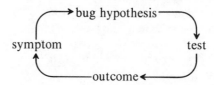

The debugger designs an ad hoc test intended to confirm or falsify the hypothesized bug. The results of that test lead to new symptoms, new hypotheses, new experiments, and so on. Unfortunately, there are an infinite number of possible bugs for any given set of symptoms. The debugger starts (or should) with what is perceived to be the simplest explanation of the symptoms. If these fail to explain the bug, more complicated hypotheses are posited and checked. Bugs contained within a unit are usually simpler than bugs that arise from the interaction of units. There is, therefore, a rational tendency to look to the unit first for the error, before examining the interactions. If unit testing has been correctly and thoroughly done, and done and made public in such a way as to instill a deserved trust in that unit, then the integrator can dismiss the simpler hypothesis of bugs within the unit and hypothesize the more complicated and more likely inter-unit bug. Conversely, if there is no trust in the unit, even if it has no bugs the debugger will waste valuable time redoing unproductive unit tests. The debugger's reworking of unit testing is neither formal nor complete, and is typically less efficient than predesigned unit tests. If trust is really poor, then not only may the debugger do a slew of ad hoc unit tests, but he may go back through the entire unit test procedure to confirm that the unit deserves trust or to prove that trust is undeserved.

Trust is subjective. We trust ourselves and our own units best. We trust those units more after unit testing. A may distrust B as a person, and consequently, A may distrust B's routine no matter how well B has tested it. If they distrust each other, they may express that distrust by engaging in exhaustive fratricidal testing at every opportunity. The result is not necessarily better software—it may be just more inefficient integration testing. This is where quality assurance comes in. It has no ax to grind—rather, it grinds all programmers equally roughly on the same stone. There is no love or hate between programmers to get in the way of trust—quality assurance is universally despised and feared. If formal unit testing is conducted under recognized quality assurance standards (but not necessarily by quality assurance personnel), then the unit has officially earned trust. Unit testing establishes a mark, a ritual totem that states that the unit is fixed, finished, robust, and correct. It has been through the ceremony with honor and is believed to be a mature and responsible component of the system. And this is attested to by the quality assurance witch doctor who directed the ceremony.

The perception of trust must be true and not merely an appearance. It doesn't pay for the programmer to create false confidence by trickery, white-wash, and superficial testing. That kind of lie is soon discovered, and such units will be forever mistrusted: time and again in higher levels of testing, needless labor will be expended to yet again demonstrate that the unit was not at fault. Similarly, if the mark of acceptance conferred on the unit by quality assurance is not true because quality assurance is superficial, a rubber stamp, then there is no trust in quality assurance's marks and no trust in the units. Witch doctors have no power over disbelievers.

2.3. Objective Goals

2.3.1. Proving There Are Bugs

If there is one theme in the recent literature of testing, it's that the objective of testing is to prove that there are bugs and not to prove that the unit is bug-free (MYER 79). This is inherently a difficult point of view for programmers to take. It asks them to participate in self-immolation. It doesn't take years of experience to convince programmers that they can't write bug-free code. Programmers have nagging doubts about their routines forever, no matter how vigorously they protest when their unit is accused of having a bug. They know that it's an impossible task to prove a unit bug-free, but that doesn't make them any more comfortable with the idea of proving that their unit *does* have bugs. There's an inherent conflict of interest here which, depending on the programmer's mind-set, can lead either to ludicrous overtesting, or superficial testing and cover-ups. Both of these extremes destroy quality and/or productivity. One of the virtues of independent testing is that it alleviates this psychologically untenable position. However, independent unit-level testing is not practical as a rule. The programmer is forced to face the conflict. What can the programmer, quality assurance, and management do to make the job of proving that there are bugs more palatable?

The programmer can:

1. Make a game out of it.
2. Consciously switch roles between tester and programmer—it pays to be schizoid.
3. Keep the embarrassment private by more thorough private testing.

4. Work in closely coupled teams of two or three and do mutual testing—not truly independent testing, but semi-independent testing.

Quality assurance and management can:

1. Establish clear guidelines for unit testing, defining not only minimum standards, but maximum standards too.
2. Reward the programmer's discovery of bugs—say "Great!" when a bug is discovered and brought to your attention. Cheer when a bug is found instead of scowling.
3. Artificially formalize the conclusion of unit testing so that the mark thereof is tangible—make a ceremony out of it, pass out certificates of merit or gold stars.
4. Avoid guilt induction. Don't be judgmental.

2.3.2. Further Objective Goals

The following should also be achieved as a result of the unit testing process. These objective attributes of a complete unit can be verified by quality assurance and are signs by which the unit can be admitted to public life.

1. Does the program's intention match the requirements?
2. Does the execution match the intentions?
3. Does the unit conform to published interface conventions and calling sequences?
4. Is the unit consistent to the data base?
5. Are all private data items (e.g., data objects not in the data dictionary) justified?
6. Are all absolute addresses, relative addresses, address modifications, and other potentially dangerous constructs justified?
7. Does the unit meet performance and size objectives (if specified)?
8. Is the documentation complete and meaningful (rather than verbose but inadequate)?
9. Was the test plan published in advance?
10. Was the test plan followed?
11. Are all identified bugs corrected?
12. Was the test plan revised to reflect the correction?
13. Was regression testing done to verify the corrections?

2.3.3. Subsidiary Goals

The following can be verified as part of the unit testing process and/or as part of unit testing review. A unit may work well even though it does not conform to a project's stylistic conventions and standards. However, such units are harder to integrate and maintain. Adherence to conventions is in the interest of long-term viability and maintainability. Verifying such conventions is a subsidiary goal and is subservient to the goals described in 2.3.2 above. Unfortunately, sometimes quality assurance loses sight of this and adherence to conventions is treated as if it's more important than proper function.

1. Does the coding conform to published project style standards?
2. Are mnemonic and label conventions followed?
3. In assembly language programs, are registers and absolute data object restrictions and usage specifications followed, and justified if not?
4. In higher-order language source code programs, are all assembly language inclusions justified?

2.3.4. Auxiliary Goals

The following should also result from the unit testing process. These are auxiliary goals because they do not in themselves affect the quality of the unit. However, quality assurance and management need information to tell them how the project is going. Part of that information can be produced as a byproduct of unit testing.

1. Start the bug counter. Unit testing, because it is formal, is the first place where reliable bug data can be gathered. QA needs bug counts to predict system quality (see Chapter 9). Management needs bug counts to predict testing costs and duration, and programmer quality.
2. Gather data on: bug types by established categories, bug severity, and bug correction costs.
3. Obtain feedback on the effectiveness of test techniques used, bug prevention methods employed, and quality assurance efforts.
4. Revise estimates of labor, elapsed time, project completion costs, testing resource requirements, and testing schedules.

2.3.5. Keeping Things in Perspective

As we progress from the primary goal of proving that the unit has bugs and correcting those bugs to the further objective goals, the subsidiary goals, and then the auxiliary goals, we move further and further away from the central issue of producing a working unit—which is the paramount goal. The programmer is inherently concerned with the paramount goal. However, management and quality assurance tend to be concerned with visibility and therefore lean to the satisfaction of subsidiary and auxiliary goals, sometimes to the detriment of working routines produced on time and within cost. There's a delicate balance. If the programmer just produces a working routine without proof and documentation and all but the primary goals are ignored, quality cannot be measured and management is impossible. Conversely, if the subsidiary and auxiliary goals dominate, management and quality assurance seems satisfied, but there's little or no working code to evaluate and manage. You can't burden programmers with filling out thousands of forms—you can try, but it won't work. Here are some suggestions of how to have your cake and eat it also.

1. Let the initiative for documentation and reporting come from the programmers—at least let them think that it does. Let them participate at all levels—in the definition of forms, reports, and the rest. It's harder to bitch about self-imposed discipline than externally imposed discipline.
2. Automate as much of data gathering and reporting as possible. The use of test driver tools, for example, can automate data collection on bug incidence and test failure.
3. Use nontechnical clerical help to gather data, organize it, produce reports and summaries, wherever possible.
4. Be willing to sacrifice some detailed information in the interest of making data gathering more palatable.
5. Give the programmers feedback based on the gathered data. Publish bug summaries by types (never by individuals). Publish data on the relative effectiveness of test techniques used. Let the programmers know where they, as a group, stand with respect to percentage of testing completed. In other words, use the data they've gathered to give them information that concerns them.

3. SOFTWARE ANTHROPOLOGY

3.1. Prerequisites

3.1.1. Specifications

Every unit that is to go through formal unit testing must have a formal specification. It is only by comparing the unit's behavior with its specified behavior that we can tell if the unit is acceptable. A rough draft of the specification should have been produced before work on the unit started. However, you can't blindly insist on total adherence to that initial specification. Some change in requirements is inevitable and must be accepted. You can't expect the designer who first specified the unit to foresee all problems and contingencies. Effective design and implementation depends on the fact that, at each level of implementation, the programmers will contribute to the further refinement of the requirements. There is a point, however, early in the unit's life it is hoped, that the requirements are frozen (at least jelled). That may not occur until after some private unit testing. How loose and how tight the initial specification might be is a programming management and design concern. It is with the supposedly complete specification that quality assurance should be concerned. That final specification is the one that other programmers will work with. It is the unit's public specification. It should be tied down, documented, and available for distribution prior to formal unit testing.

3.1.2. Testable Code

Testable code does not necessarily mean complete code. While it's desirable that the unit be completely tested in unit testing, prior to integration, it's not always possible. This is especially true for I/O device handlers. The physical device which the unit controls may not be available. In interrupt processing, for example, some paths can't be tested out of the context of an almost complete system. Testable code means enough code and enough functions implemented to produce a workable unit with respect to those components that have been formally tested. A unit may have to go through several stages of unit testing as devices and other software become available, and it's not always effective from the point of view of project schedule to hold the project up by insisting that all unit testing for every unit be complete prior to integration.

3.1.3. Private Testing and Independent Unit Testing

It should be assumed that programmers will have conducted some private, informal testing prior to formal unit testing. You can't impose documentation and standards on what a programmer does in private. It's counterproductive. You can only suggest techniques that have proved effective in the past. If you encroach too heavily on the private domain, breathing down the programmers' necks as they code, that's counterproductive. If you believe in private errors, then let them stay private. There's nothing wrong with a programmer going through the entire formal unit test plan in private, correcting all discovered bugs and revising the unit specification and/or the test plan as a result. And there's much to be said for it. If the programmer does all that, then running the unit tests should be nothing more than a formal and seemingly pointless ritual. It is perhaps a ritual, but it's not pointless. It shows that the programmer is willing to go public with the unit. It establishes a recognizable basis for trust. We can only take a programmer's word when he says he's done thorough private testing. We can only assume that that's his sincere belief. Sincerity, however, doesn't substitute for facts, and only a formal test can provide facts.

I encourage complete private testing prior to formal unit testing, and I also expect to find *no* unit-level bugs during formal unit testing. This has several benefits and demerits:

1. The unit appears to take longer to finish. Actually it doesn't, because private debugging and testing eliminates a lot of paperwork and overhead. However, if progress is judged superficially, then the untested routine appears to have been finished earlier; it will also be buggy longer.
2. Visibility is lost and protracted. That's good for the programmer's ego but makes prediction and planning more uncertain.
3. It takes longer to discover incompetence and to effect corrections; but productivity and quality are better. Good programmers get better; bad programmers get worse.

If you use private testing prior to formal unit testing, then it must be done uniformly. If you have reason to distrust a programmer, or have no prior experience with that programmer on which to judge how well she will do in private testing, then start her on a relatively short, simple routine before committing her and yourself to several months of work. Private testing is based on the supposition that programmers are competent and conscientious. Reduce the risk with unknown programmers by calibrating them on an unimportant piece of work. You'll root the bad apples out in short order.

If you use private testing, you must also compensate for the relative freedom given the programmers by a more uncompromising attitude towards any bugs caught during formal unit-level testing. There shouldn't be any. That doesn't mean the unit is bug-free—only that its bugs were not capable of exposure by the unit tests that were run. One has to be relatively serious about bugs caught during formal testing if prior private testing was used, because it could mean that:

1. The private tests weren't really run.
2. Test plans were not revised to reflect changes that came about as a result of discovered bugs.
3. Proper verification testing on the corrections was not done.
4. Documentation is faulty.

Private testing means that the formal unit test is a ritual which, if sufficient test plan documentation is provided, could be run by any qualified individual. That's true, but it's not the same as independent unit testing. When we talk about independent unit testing, we are really talking about independent unit test *design* and not the relatively trivial act of running the unit test. While the actual running of a formal unit test can be done by another person, the proper design of unit tests requires a lot of knowledge about that unit. Furthermore, testing, debugging, and correction is an interactive and interrelated job best done by the unit's designer.

3.1.4. Unit Test Plans

Unit-level test plans should be designed and documented sufficiently well to allow another programmer to run them if necessary. It will happen to some extent during integration and as part of installing enhancements in the future. Finally, if the unit's designer has to redo the tests after a hiatus of several months, then the test is effectively being rerun by a new person.

A unit is not ready for formal unit testing until there is a formal unit test plan document. That document should contain:

1. Identification of the unit, its programmer, the module of which it is a part, the date submitted for formal unit testing, version number, and any other information required to properly track it.
2. A *brief* statement of its purpose and function and references to the unit's formal requirements specification.
3. A *brief* description of how it works and references to the detailed documentation.
4. Assumptions and prerequisites for testing. For example, program version, data base, hardware configuration, special test gear, and so on.
5. The total number of unit tests to be run. Identification of the unit tests required to provide coverage. Number of tests attempted, percentage passed, list of bugs or deficiences found, percentage of coverage achieved thus far.

The test plan consist of many tests—from a few to hundreds, depending on the complexity of the unit, the number of paths, and the kind of unit it is. I prefer a separate test sheet for each test, with the following information:

1. Test number and type (path test, syntax test, state test, functional test, and so on).
2. Date attempted, outcome (pass/fail), rework or corrective action with dates, reschedule date.
3. Data-base prerequisites.
4. Initialization method or initial conditions assumed.
5. Inputs.
6. Outcomes.
7. Method of verifying outcomes.

8. Instrumentation plan.
9. Context of runs.

This last point requires explanation. A unit can be tested in a simulated environment or in the context of a working system. The latter is more stringent, but rarely possible in the initial phases of unit testing. For example, it may be necessary that a unit be reentrant. In the context of unit testing done in a simulated environment, it may not be possible to really test reentrancy. When integration problems show up, the context of the initial unit test is important for clues to possible bugs—the integrator will correctly look to the differences between the initial test environment and the integration environment.

The test plan should be reviewed prior to execution. That implies three different reviews, with three different objectives:

1. By the programmer.
2. By the programmer's supervisor or peers.
3. By quality assurance.

Of these, the second is the most important. I advocate doing it at that point at which the programmer is ready to start private testing. An informal and casual review of the planned test can reveal many bugs and many holes in the test. Alternatively, a peer review system can be used (see Section 4.4.6 below), which is as effective and less threatening. If the second review has been competently done (and redone as necessary), then the final review by quality assurance should be nothing more than another formality.

3.1.5. Acceptance and Conditional Acceptance

Acceptance of a unit cannot always be based on the sole criteria of having passed all unit-level tests. You have to make allowances for **conditional acceptance** or **acceptance with reservations**. This may be necessitated by a schedule problem. The unit has not passed all the unit-level tests but it is on the critical paths for other units that depend on it. The project can't be held up. It's my observation that in this tug of war between project progress and quality assurance, quality assurance usually loses. If there's blind insistence on passing all aspects of unit testing in meticulous detail before going on, the project will grind to a halt. If the project management exercises muscle to get the unit into use despite known deficiencies, then there's a fair chance that those deficiencies will be glossed over in the future and never corrected. The remedy is to formalize acceptance with reservations. The unit is marked as acceptable with respect to those functions that have been thoroughly tested, but documentation is also marked to indicate that the unit's test status is incomplete. It's a way of saying that you can trust the unit with respect to A, B, and C, but not with respect to D, E, and F. It is then up to quality assurance to:

1. Require a schedule for the completion of D, E, and F.
2. Reach agreement on how much of the original unit test plan will have to be rerun.
3. Identify all units whose acceptance may be conditional on this unit's acceptance and the retesting that will have to be done.

The completion schedule is the most important item. Conditional acceptance should only be granted with the understanding that work on that unit will continue uninterrupted until done. The programmer should not be allowed to drop the unit with the intention of picking it up again at some future unspecified time. The schedule should be in terms of days or weeks, not months. The longer you allow an untested routine to wander about in the system, the more likely it is that the warnings issued, the fact that acceptance was conditional, and all the rest will be forgotten—until system testing—or until the user screams. One of quality assurance's jobs, then, is to keep track of incomplete units and units incompletely tested, and to nag project management until such units are complete and completely tested or unit requirements have been redefined. You can be diplomatic about the nagging, though. Let's say that you issue a weekly report for each subsystem, and for the system as a whole, that shows the percentage of unit testing complete (see Chapter 9). How should a unit which is 50% complete or 50% tested be rated? Multiply the completion percentage by the testing percentage and square the result. Thus, a unit which has been accepted for 50% of unit testing is rated as 25% complete, as is a half-finished unit completely tested. A unit which is 50% complete, of which half is tested, is granted a measly 6% completion $(.5 \times .5)^2$ rather than an unrealistic 50%. It's a fair measure because the remaining bugs will provide at least the square of the trouble. Nagging can consist of showing two curves—the first with full credit for testing and completion and the other using the square rule for partially tested and incomplete units.

3.2. Mores and Taboos

3.2.1. Standards, Style, and Rigidity

Standards and style are the civilizing factors in that society which we call a system. They are the taboos and mores of that society. Following them makes the routine acceptable and capable of function in the system. It can be understood by other components of the system and by other programmers. Like all such rules of behavior, programming style and standards are to a great extent arbitrary. They can come in a bewildering variety of different, but workable forms. Often what is good style to one is junk to another; just as when two alien cultures meet, they each profess the other to be barbaric. They are both right, because that which is barbaric is that which doesn't fit and that which doesn't fit won't work in a system. Therefore, not only must the unit satisfy the subjective goals of unit testing, pass through the formalities of the puberty rites, and satisfy the objective goals, but it must also be civilized.

Styles and standards are imposed rules for the construction of code. Style differs from standards. The implication of "standards" is that of relative rigidity. "Style" implies choice and the ability to violate stylistic rules if necessary. Standards are usually concerned with the tactics of coding, while style is usually concerned with strategy. The fact that there is a rational, system-wide plan for mnemonics and labels is style; the specific conventions used are governed by a standard. Standards, then, are rules created to nudge the system to a particular style.

The question for quality assurance should be how rigidly should style and standards be enforced. To what extent should a unit's acceptance be conditional upon following style and standards? It's not a simple question. Stylistic rules and standards are incomplete. They are established to make most programming easier for most programmers most of the time. They cannot, not even theoretically, encompass all situations. Some violations are inevitably justifiable. Cultural mores and taboos are also like that. They are rules agreed upon by society, which, on the whole, make society workable. If the environment changes, if the society must be rearranged to meet new goals, then so must the society's mores. Every advance involves a challenge to the established rules. A society changes through the action of its radicals, but is kept from the destructive potential of ill-conceived experiments through the reluctance of its conservatives. Both are essential. Blind adherence to style and standards and the blind enforcement thereof will lead to poor code and stultify advances. A lackadaisical attitude, conversely, leads to chaos as programmers wander off and do their own things. Violations of style and standards should be permitted, but it shouldn't be an easy thing to do. Style should be enforced by persuasion—by demonstrating that the style is workable and that the programmer can get more good code working in less time by following stylistic conventions instead of flouting them. If that can't be demonstrated, then either the conventions are wrong or the pedagogy is wrong.

3.2.2. Standards

Standards are rules that govern the details of coding. Relatively inflexible standards must be adopted for interfaces, access to data base objects, and any other system component that must be used by many different programmers. There's no time to waste in fruitless discussions of how two programs should interface. It usually doesn't matter which field comes first, which comes second, and so on. Left to their own devices, N programmers who must interface will propose N^2 different interfaces, and those that are adopted will be based more on who has the louder voice than who has justice on their side. It's better to short circuit the arguments and impose inter-unit standards from above.

More interesting are internal coding standards. Can we allow programmers to "do their own thing" within the context of their own unit? Not really. It's their unit only as long as it's private. Once public, it must be familiar and understandable to all other programmers who may have to interface with it, test with it, or modify it.

Programming standards should govern the following aspects of coding:

1. Mnemonics. Detailed standards should be established for mnemonics used for program labels and data objects. Every character should have a conventional meaning so that you can pick up a piece of source code at random and know that it belongs to a particular subsystem, program within that subsystem, and specific unit. In any system worthy of the name, wordlike mnemonics usually fall apart. Every programmer will use "BEGIN," "ERROR," "TEST," "LOOP," and so on. It's better to say such things in comments than to try to cram them into labels and variable names. Typically, mnemonic conventions are hierarchical. A pair of characters identify the subsystem, another character identifies the program, two more the unit, and perhaps two or three characters are left for the programmer's use. Stylistic conventions can govern these also, such as using I, J, K, L, M, N for integers, T for test, and so on.
2. Use of macros and common subroutines should be enforced wherever possible. While a programmer might be able to squeeze space by private code, or save processing time by avoiding a common subroutine, these tactics are rarely necessary and rarely pay.
3. Methods of handling error conditions should be governed by standards. Errors should be categorized as correctible within the unit's scope, correctible within the subsystem, fatal, and so on. There should be standard handlers for each error type.
4. Parameters should be identified as to function and value. Wherever possible, parameters should be system-wide and global. Programmers should not be allowed to use an immediate operand for the parameter value (unless generated by reference to a global declaration).
5. Hooks for future enhancements should be identified and treated in a standard way. For example, say a feature has two alternatives and a binary decision could be used to distinguish between them. However, it's known that the number of alternatives will increase in the future and the same

decision will be handled by a case statement. Then either all instances of that decision should be implemented as binary decisions, or all as case statements with error returns for the unimplemented cases. Allowing each programmer freedom in this respect is an invitation to future chaos.

6. Coding restrictions such as forbidding absolute and relative addressing (except where unavoidable), use of privileged or executive mode instructions, and so on. Each programmer works not with the entire source language but with a defined subset of the source language. Every coding restriction is a reduction of that language and should be carefully considered and explained. The bulk of the standards will be in this area.

7. Memory access restrictions. This is extended in the general sense to include registers, cache memory, main memory, files, and the like. Whether a programmer can have actual access or access only through a memory management function and so on.

8. Declarations. Where declarations are required by the source language to be part of the unit definition (as in FORTRAN and BASIC), there should be detailed rules governing what is to be declared, how, and where. Common declarations should be supplied as predefined source code segments and inserted by text editing.

9. Patching conventions—specification and use of patch areas and method used to get to, and return from, the patch area.

10. Test code. Code to be inserted only for test purposes should be guided by standards as to labels, placement, and method of activating and deactivating. For example, using conditional compilation or assembly, or converting running code to comments in FORTRAN and BASIC.

11. Comments—the placement and contents of comments. Too often, a subroutine call instruction such as:

JSB *label*

is commented as:

JSB *label*; Jump to subroutine *label*

Comments like that don't deserve the name. Every statement is worthy of comment, and it's easy to specify such a rule but difficult to assure that useful comments will result.

Checking and enforcing standards is a difficult and thankless task with relatively little payoff. One of the features of some newer higher-order languages and their associated processors is the ability to define coding standards and to automatically check conformance to such standards. It's essential that any standards or style checker allows translation to proceed even if there are violations. Violations should be marked but allowed. Then if the violation is legitimate, it can remain.

3.2.3. Style

Stylistic rules are statements of preferred programming constructs. For example:

1. Jumping into the middle of loops and decision segments is not allowed.
2. Multi-entry and/or multi-exit routines are forbidden.
3. No routine shall have more than 50 object-level instructions.
4. No routine shall have a complexity metric exceeding N (see Chapter 9).
5. GOTO's are forbidden.
6. All programmers shall use a string of IF-THEN-ELSE constructs to implement logical cases.
7. Recursive calls are forbidden.
8. Every case statement shall have an associated explicit boundary range check on the case variable and an explicit common point for forbidden and impossible cases.
9. All case statements of more than four cases shall use a jump table implementation.
10. Each level of a nested IF-THEN-ELSE construct and each nested loop shall be indented five spaces.

While I agree with the intent of each of the above rules, I hate them all, because I've seen each of them backfire in one context or another, leading to bad code, impossible testing, or poor performance. Rigid stylistic rules do not guarantee good code. You can, with some work, take the best-intentioned set of stylistic rules and create a patently abominable piece of code that adheres to them strictly, and is abominable because it does adhere to the rules; alternatively, you can create a clear, concise, testable, efficient piece of code that violates every rule. As in writing, style is a guide that works most of the time and usually produces workable, clear code. The most important thing about style in a project, though, is that there be a written manual of style so that one programmer can readily understand another's work. All stylistic rules are limited and simplistic and attempt to convert the programming art into a few simple rules that can be followed mechanistically. Programming admits of no such simple codification. Yet we can't do without style guides—how else is a novice programmer to learn what usually works and what usually doesn't? Writing style usually results in clearer prose, and coding style usually results in better programs. However, just as the sensitive editor can recognize when a violation of style rules works, the sensitive project leader or quality assurance personnel should recognize when style rules are violated with good results.

We're in a transitional period now. Having come out of a dark age in which style was unknown and unrecognized, we find that the pendulum has swung the other way and style is offered as a panacea that will cure all bugs. One good-sounding rule after another is proposed and sometimes enforced with disastrous results. Perhaps, in a decade or two or three, the programming community will have learned which stylistic rules are really beneficial and which are harmful. Codifying grammar has taken centuries for each language for which it was done (Latin, Greek, Hebrew, Arabic, English, French, Spanish, and so on), but the codification of writing style provides ample opportunities for continued debate between critics in all languages: it just hasn't been done yet. Why are we programmers so arrogant and so impatient to think we can do it for programming languages in a few years?

Don't be misled into thinking that programming style is more important than well-wrought, well-tested code. Don't let stylistic standards get in the way of quality. Don't let style become the end-all and do-all of a programming project.* It's at best worth a few percent of the total. As General Patton said upon reviewing the glamorous parade of the Algerian Camel Cavalry, "They sure are pretty, but can they fight?"

3.3. Environment

3.3.1. Real Versus Simulated Environment

Unit testing isn't done in a vacuum. It's done in an environment that encompasses tools and other units. The most important test tool is the system itself. It's an uncompromisingly real environment. However, unit testing must begin before enough of the real system is available for testing. Any unit testing done outside of the real system is done in a simulated environment. The simulated environment has some advantages and disadvantages:

1. It's available early in the project. This is its greatest benefit.
2. Test aids and debugging aids are usually part of the simulated environ-

---

*My favorite bad project had standards and style—and not much else. They believed the rain-maker and his wagonload of tricks. That code was structured up to yin-yang, and so modular it took your breath away. But it didn't work. The pieces didn't fit. What did fit was slow and what wasn't slow took an obscene amount of space. As an example, we traced a do-nothing call to a data-base item—fetch it, change a bit, restore it. It took more than 2500 subroutine calls, with the depth exceeding 200 levels. It's hardly conceivable that things could have been worse had there been no stylistic rules and standards—but considering the project, it's entirely possible.

ment—e.g., unit testing under a debug package. Tools and facilities are more convenient.
3. Timing relations are incorrect. Interrupt and race conditions are incorrect. Reentrancy is typically not the same (e.g., stack management) as in the real system. Inadvertent location dependencies may not be discovered.
4. Resource management is often done by a utility subsystem rather than by the real resource management program. Other executive functions are handled by a simulated executive rather than by the real.

The simulated environment gains convenience but loses reality. Therefore, all units whose unit testing was done under a simulated environment are suspect. If the unit is one of the central units, such as a resource management function, a scheduler, I/O driver, and so on, then there will be no need to do regression testing because the act of integrating the system's backbone and subsequent system-level testing should root out most of the problems that were not caught at the unit level. However, application routines should be scheduled for some retest in the real environment if at all possible. This does not necessarily mean explicit new tests. For example, a unit is thoroughly tested in a simulated environment. It is further exercised as part of the system test, this time in the real environment. Even though the system tests are primarily functional, they will cover part or most of the unit's code. If unit-level instrumentation is available for that unit during system or integration testing, you can record the coverage that has been achieved during the higher-level tests. Therefore, only a few more paths or repetitions of unit-level tests may be needed to re-achieve coverage in the real environment.

While there can be profound differences between a real and simulated environment, the kinds of bugs that show up in the real but not the simulated environment are the same bugs that tend to be discovered during integrations and system testing. Therefore, good records that track how various units were, in effect, retested by higher-level tests may be all that's needed, rather than explicit scheduling of redundant unit tests.

3.3.2. Prerequisite and Corequisite Units

Only the lowest-level subroutines call no other subroutines and have no prerequisite or corequisite routines. While unit testing is intended to be a test of the unit without regard to other units, it is not always practical to do unit testing that way. Rational scheduling may force testing before all prerequisites are met. If prerequisites are not available at unit-test time, then their action must be simulated. A dummy routine, or **stub**, is used to replace the missing prerequisite unit. The simulated prerequisite, the stub, provides prestored responses for the calling unit. There are several severe limitations to this approach, as necessary as it may be at times:

1. A whole new host of bugs can result from the incorrect simulation or construction of the stub.
2. The stub is itself a unit and, although intended to be simpler than the real unit, it must nevertheless be unit tested and validated. Sometimes it's easier to test and debug the real prerequisite unit.
3. The stub is a simulation, and any simulation can have simulation bugs in addition to real bugs.

The way to avoid the redundant work of creating prerequisite simulators is to properly schedule the unit testing process. Figure 4-1 shows an aid to the scheduling (the similarity to a PERT chart is obvious). The routines are represented by nodes. The arrows show which unit depends on which. Scheduling can be suggested by starting with the deepest (longest branch) on the tree and working upwards until a fork, which indicates the latest point in time at which the next set of prerequisites must be completed. There are many feasible schedules for Figure 4-1a and much freedom. For example, a scheduled order of

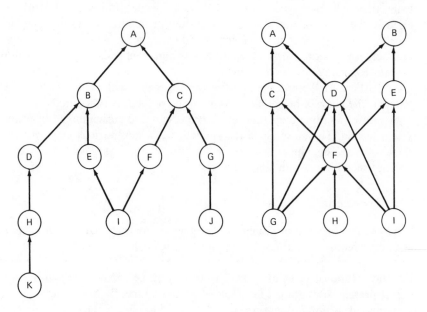

(a.) Partly Ordered.   (b.) Non–Partly Ordered.

Figure 4-1. Partly Ordered and Non–Partly Ordered Prerequisites.

KHIJDEFGBCA is reasonable, as is JGIFCEKHDBA. Figure 4-1b, however shows a more complicated and realistic set of dependencies. While G, H, and I can be tested in any order, F must come next. This kind of dependency constrains the schedule, or alternatively, forces the use of stubs or prerequisite simulation to achieve a reasonable schedule.

Two units that require each other's presence, either directly or indirectly, are **corequisite units**. For example, B provides the data A needs but B need not be in A's call tree or vice-versa. Corequisite units can occur in a loop that forces an entire set of units to be tested simultaneously. Any direct or indirect recursive call creates this type of prerequisite structure. While such loops are not desirable, that kind of construction can be effective, even if not theoretically required. For example, most compilers and parsers would be more complicated if recursive calls were not permitted.

It's possible that a unit may be ready for testing long before any of its prerequisites are started. A typical large system has preceding systems, or may be a variation of an already existing system. The designers will try to retain as much of the existing code as they can. It's not unusual to have a large system started with 40% to 50% of the code, typically common subroutines, available after minor modifications. This completely rearranges the schedule, so that units are ready for testing at all levels in the tree. Use the tree as a basis for scheduling the tests nevertheless, but mark those units that are done or available when working the schedule out. The scheduling criteria, then, are:

1. Start with the bottom of the tree first, if at all possible.
2. Try to build up uniformly from the bottom, layer by layer—except as this may conflict with integration strategies (see Chapter 5).
3. Recognize corequisite routines or sets of corequisite routines. Try to find a single routine that breaks the loop and do initial testing with only that routine simulated.
4. All other factors being the same, favor paths that do not require simulated prerequisites over paths that do.
5. Give preference to routines that require fewer prerequisites over routines that require many; test the simpler prerequisite structures first.
6. Identify those units that are prerequisite to many, such as F, and give those preference in the schedule over those that are prerequisite to few (note: this is not a contradiction to 5 above).

While unit test scheduling is not a direct quality assurance concern, and is properly a design and project management responsibility, the question of whether a unit was tested with real or simulated prerequisites *is* a quality assurance concern. This fact should be recorded. Acceptance should be conditional until the unit has been tested with real prerequisites. Often this will occur only during integration testing. It's important that such facts be documented as part of the unit's test status.

3.3.3. Resources and Facilities

Resources such as terminals, computer time, test facilities, and the like present a recurrent problem during testing. They are usually inadequate and often force "round-the-clock" testing. Such resources must be centrally managed by the project management and allocated in an equitable manner. This is nevertheless a quality assurance concern because:

1. Testing controlled and devised by quality assurance is often given a low priority or forced into the undesirable shifts (e.g., 2 AM Saturday to 8 PM Sunday).
2. No time is allowed in the schedule for retesting.
3. No time is allowed for independent confirmation of unit tests, if, unfortunately, that proves necessary.
4. No time is allowed for test-testing and debugging.

Assuming that quality assurance is independent of design—as it should be—then there are two groups with conflicting demands for the same facilities. In the beginning, the facilities are dominated by the designers doing unit testing and integration. As the project progresses, testing responsibility shifts further and further in favor of quality assurance and independent testing. It's important that this be known and understood. If resources are not available for quality assurance, then the entire thing becomes an academic exercise in futility. I know of no better and easier way to completely short-circuit a quality assurance department than by denying it adequate test resources. Get the following agreed to early in the game, and in writing:

1. Create a test schedule and resource requirement projection for testing just as you would for code development. Have it ready for discussion at the same time that program development has their schedule ready.
2. Allow blocks of time for contingencies and retesting.
3. Be sure that facility control and schedule is a mutual affair. Arrange to have voice in proportion to the time required at each phase in the project. For example, initially design has 80% of the say, but later the schedule is taken over by quality assurance with 80% of the clout.
4. Allocate good time and bad time equitably in proportion to the time used.
5. Be reasonable in test scheduling in order to avoid needlessly complicated setups and data-base shifts from project usage to quality assurance usage.

Cooperate to create mutually satisfactory setups and data bases. Design the test data base jointly.

6. A retest initiated and witnessed by QA is a QA test even if run by project personnel.
7. Be firm, but not obnoxious.

4. UNIT TESTING PROCEDURES AND EXECUTION

4.1. General

Unit testing is a model for testing at all levels. Every procedure, tool, and technique used in unit testing has its counterpart, albeit in a more complicated form, at the higher levels of testing. Things are simpler at the unit level because units are simpler than systems—interactions and interfaces are more limited, as are objectives. System quality assurance must be based on a solid foundation of unit quality assurance methods. Unit testing is not just the execution of unit tests, but a complex of activities that have four main components, executed in roughly the following order:

1. Mechanical analysis (e.g., syntax checking).
2. Manual analysis (e.g., desk checking).
3. Audits and reviews.
4. Execution, correction, and refinement.

These components do not occur as singular events or necessarily as distinguishable activities. They are also repeated several times as the unit progresses from private to public.

4.2. Mechanical Analysis

4.2.1. Static Versus Dynamic Analysis

The term "**static analysis**" encompasses all processing done on source code which results in useful test and debugging information, short of executing that code, as distinguished from a **dynamic analysis**, which is processing done under execution. A cross-reference list is the result of a static analysis, while a trace is the archetype dynamic analysis.

4.2.2. Source Language Processor

The source language processor and translator, such as a compiler, assembler, or interpreter, is the single most important static analysis tool, although its role in this respect is often overlooked. Source language processing and the translation to object code consists of the following steps, each of which can yield useful test and debugging information, and each of which can catch the majority of typographical and wild-card errors.

1. Statement identification—identifying the statements of which the code is composed.
2. Lexical scan and conversion to tokens—examination of each statement and the keywords and symbols within that statement, followed by the conversion of recognized keywords and symbols to simpler, typically single-character tokens.
3. Parsing—confirming that the arrangement of keywords and symbols follows the specified syntax of the source language.
4. Construction of symbol tables and label tables.
5. Conversion from infix form to prefix or suffix form.
6. Replacement of tokens by macros, calls, or code segments.
7. Address calculations and assignment, typically to relative address form.

Each step (they do not necessarily occur in the above order) yields different kinds of source code bug detection. Examples include:

1. *Statement identification*: missing BEGIN-ENDs, missing right quotes on string literals, missing statement numbers, end of statement delimiters, improper or incomplete block structures, improper loops.
2. *Lexical scan*: keyword typographical errors, invalid symbols (e.g., "#" instead of "+"), label formation error, variable name structure error.
3. *Parsing*: missing operators or operands, extra operators or operands, missing or wrong delimiters, parenthesis mismatch.
4. *Symbol table and label tables*: undeclared variable, variable type errors, unreferenced labels, reference to nonexisting labels, dangling code.

Testing cannot begin until the source code has been successfully translated. Successful translation, however, does not guarantee syntactic correctness. For example, FORTRAN and BASIC I/O statements are partially interpreted at run time. The source code may be syntactically correct insofar as those checks that can be done at compile time, but the error is discovered by the run-time resident portion of the compiler only under execution.

The compiler and assembler are powerful bug detectors, yet their role in this respect is often overlooked and programmers are not given adequate access to them. Immediate, hands-on access to the translator is essential and is a fundamental test tool. The programmer should be able to get immediate turnarounds on syntax checking by using an on-line terminal. Much time is lost when programmers are forced to use batch mode compilation or assembly of units. Often the detection of a single syntax error may make the programmer realize that there are several related errors not caught by syntax checking, which should be immediately corrected. If there is a two- or three-day turn-around, rather than a few minutes or seconds, the idea may be lost and the correction not made.

The most efficient method I know of is to have the programmer code directly into the terminal, with instant syntax checking done on each statement as it's typed in; for example, as in many BASIC interpreters. Barring that, almost instant compilation of short routines should be accessible. It is not unreasonable to use twenty to thirty turnarounds to get a 250-statement routine syntactically correct. There's no point in doing manual syntax checking, because the compiler is much better at it. In constructing a FORTRAN system, I kept track of the number of turnarounds per line of code used by the programmers. I found that 0.1 turnarounds per statement was efficient. If the turnaround rate was of the order of 0.25 or higher, then the programmer was not being careful enough and desk checking was insufficient—not just with respect to syntax checking but with respect to all desk checking. If the turnaround rate fell below 0.05, then the programmer was spending too much time in the wrong kind of preliminary desk checking. As an experiment, checking the number of turnarounds used to complete syntax checking was a reasonable thing to do, but I do not advise it as a practice because it is a clear intrusion on the programmer's privacy. It's embarrassing and makes what should be private bugs public.

Some operating systems provide two or more versions of the compiler. One version, used for syntax checking, is optimized to provide very good diagnostics, references, and checking. This is done at the expense of relatively loose and inefficient object code. The other version provides only rudimentary diagnostics but produces highly optimized object code. It's difficult to design a compiler that does both jobs well, still runs in a reasonable amount of time, and takes a reasonable amount of space: the two compiler approach is a fair compromise.

As important as the source language translator is as a principal test tool, it is the tool with which the programmer is most often shortchanged. Programmers are asked to work in batch mode with assemblers and compilers that have virtually remained unimproved since Grace Hopper and the days of UNIVAC I. There are still compilers out there that refuse to continue syntax checking after the first error is discovered, forcing a turnaround for each syntax error. Compilers that produce no cross references. Translators whose only diagnostic message is "SYNTAX ERROR" and which don't even identify the character in the statement at which the error was discovered. Compilers that refuse to do syntax checks on program segments or incomplete programs. Sophisticated microcomputers can be purchased for a few hundred dollars, but we waste a hundred times that in lost programmer productivity and high bug rates by forcing programmers to work with a primitive tool and to use batch methods that were obsolete two decades ago. Don't expect good programmers to do good work if they have to punch the bits out by hand using stone axes. If you want quality software, you had better look to quality tools and start with the source language translator and its access method as the first step.

4.2.3. Cross Reference Generators

Good assemblers and compilers produce extensive cross-reference lists. Two main lists are produced: **label cross-references** and **variable cross-references**. But several other useful lists can also be produced as a by-product of the translation process.

1. *Label Cross-Reference.* This is a listing of all program labels, declared and otherwise. Items should be listed either in order of appearance or in lexicographic (e.g., alphabetical) order. All undefined label references should be marked. All unreferenced labels should be marked. All label relative references (as in assembly language) should be marked. If a label reference is outside the unit's scope (e.g., global label), it should also be marked. Computed label references such as COMPUTED and ASSIGNED GOTO's in FORTRAN and ON statements in BASIC should be marked.
2. *Variable Cross-Reference.* One beneficial stylistic measure is to insist on an explicit declaration of all variables, even if not required by the source language syntax. Furthermore, all such declarations should be grouped by type (integer, array, floating point, etc.). This measure makes the resulting variable cross-reference a more useful diagnostic tool. The cross-reference should provide listings in any of the following orders: 1) appearance, 2) lexicographic, or 3) type. If all variables are declared and grouped, then typographical errors in names are obvious when checked against the appearance order listing. The listings should include markings for all undeclared or implicitly declared variables, the variable type, and unused variables. A further breakdown that distinguishes the appearance of the variable on the right-hand side of an assignment statement is also useful. Explicit identification of COMMON, global, or privileged variable references should be provided.
3. *Subroutine, Macro, and Function List.* A listing by subroutine, macro, or function of the statement in which they are called or referenced. Identification and listing of call parameters in a list following each subroutine.
4. *Equate Lists.* Explicit listing of all labels and variables that have been equated by equate statements or the equivalent.
5. *Constants.* Listing of all numerical or alphanumerical constants and the statement in which they are first defined by virtue of appearing on the left side of an assignment statement or in a data statement.

4.2.4. Flowcharters and Graph Generators

Most flowcharting programs are only of moderate help in test design. Flowcharts were intended to aid the visualization of control structures and not as an alternate form of code. The problem with most automatically produced flowcharts is that they are one-to-one with the source statements. Typically the flowcharter will create decision points and process boxes and fill them with the comment associated with that line of source code. The result is the replacement of a one- or two-page listing with several dozen pages of flowcharts and a tangle of off-page connectors. If anything, the control structure that the flowchart was intended to clarify has been made even more obscure. Most programmers do not use flowcharts. They prefer to look at code. Most flowcharts, to the programmers, serve the sole purpose of satisfying a contractual documentation specification.* Are programmers wrong or is it flowcharts?

Some flowchart programs are more elaborate and allow production of flowcharts to varying degrees of detail, based on commands or controls inserted with the source code. These can be more useful. The happy extreme of this kind of flowcharter is a control graph generator that shows the pure control structure and only the labels which are decision targets and the decisions that lead to those labels. The rest of the program is represented by simple links. A control flow graph generator such as this is very useful because it produces the abstraction of the program on which path testing must be based. Furthermore, because all unnecessary details have been left out, unwanted code, unreachable code, superfluous code, extra links, and such can be easily seen. Of course, flowcharters are perforce limited to static analysis. Therefore, their utility in assembly language programming, much of which cannot be evaluated by static analysis (especially if it has bugs), is similarly limited. For similar reasons, when the control flow can be interrupted by higher-priority processing which does not necessarily return to the interrupted point, flowcharter and graph-generated outputs may hide much of what is important. While it's not desirable to jump out of code via interrupts and not return to the same point, if the reason for jumping is related to an error condition, for example, where further processing on that path would be harmful, then again, control structures which spanned more than one priority level would not be represented. Unfortunately, it's in things like interrupt processing where many bugs tend to congregate.

4.2.5. Style and Standards Checker

Stylistic rules and standards can be looked upon as an informal extension of the source language syntax—an extension which limits the definition of good

---

*Talk about hard-dying fads!

statements. If the source language processor supports the formal specification of stylistic rules and standards, then the parser will typically be augmented to check style and standards as well. Alternatively, a special preprocessor program can be used to do a second pass over the source code and, much in the way that a compiler operates, check the source code for possible style and standards violations. Such violations will typically constitute bugs. A programmer is more likely to violate a label- or variable-naming convention as a result of a simple typographical error than because of willful intent. Jumping into the middle of loops is more likely to be a bug than a misguided attempt to save code. There are some things a style and standards checker should not do:

1. Stop processing after the first violation.
2. Prevent translation on a violation.

There are several reasons for this:

1. The program may be in part constructed out of previous code that preceded the adoption of the standards or that was written to different standards. Rigid enforcement of rules may prevent the incorporation of well-tested, reliable, previous code.
2. The set of stylistic rules and standards are rarely as well thought out as the syntax of a source language.* The rules will be incomplete and possibly inconsistent. Unless you know that the rules have been thoroughly tested and debugged, prudence mitigates against rigid enforcement.
3. Junk code or test code, inserted in the interest of test and debugging, may not follow the rules, nor need they. Similarly for throwaway code used to simulate a part that's to be detailed later. In fact, temporary code should be written to different standards so that it can be easily identified.
4. Patching under standards may be difficult. And don't think you can enforce a ban on patches.
5. Some seemingly good standards and stylistic guidelines may prove in retrospect to be more trouble than they're worth, or just plain wrong. A flexible approach to enforcement will allow you to recover from such errors.

There's no real data yet on what percentage of bugs are caught by style/standard checkers or style/standard check portions of source language processors. My guess is that 95% of standards violations (assuming rational stan-

---

*There isn't room to tell the horror stories or to describe the abominable code that can result from the rigid adoption of ill-conceived and inconsistent stylistic rules.

dards) are bona fide bugs, as are 75% of style violations. Consequently, style and standards checkers are probably less trouble than they're worth.

4.3. Desk Checking

4.3.1. General

Desk checking is probably the least understood, most poorly executed, and most troublesome phase of programming, and yet it is probably, when properly done, the single best catcher of private bugs. Desk checking is often an indeterminate and interminable process. Too often the programmer thinks (and is encouraged to think) that desk checking is to be a manual simulation of the computer's behavior. People are people and computers are computers and it's unfair and ineffectual to ask the one to try to do the other's job. Desk checking should consist only of operations that cannot be done by computer. Consequently, *anything* that can be automated should not be a part of desk checking.

4.3.2. What Desk Checking Shouldn't Do

1. *Syntax Checking.* Humans are terrible syntax checkers. If they were any good at it, they wouldn't have so many syntax errors. Testing can't begin until all the source syntax errors have been corrected. Such bugs are clearly private. Manual syntax checking is a waste of human resources and bespeaks either inadequate tools or a concept of computer time costs that's several decades out of date.
2. *Style and Standards Checking.* This is just an extension of the syntax checking issue. If stylistic rules and programming standards are to be specified and enforced, then it pays to have an automatic checker. In most projects that warrant the name "system" the purchase or construction of such a tool is far cheaper than attempting to find stylistic and standards errors manually.
3. *Play Computer.* An inherently futile game. It's much easier to let the computer play at computer and to take dumps of intermediate and interesting values. Playing computer may be effective as an adjunct to debugging, but it has no place in desk checking.
4. *Produce the Flowchart or Graph from the Code.* An abstracted version of the control structure, such as an abbreviated flowchart or control graph, is useful in desk checking (see below). The actual control flow should be compared to the intended flow, but the actual flow should be produced automatically by a flowcharter or graph generator and not by hand. If done by hand, it's more likely that the programmer will merely reproduce the intended flow (that which he thinks he has) rather than the actual flow.

4.3.3. An Agenda for Desk Checking

Desk checking should be a finite activity, predictable, human, and humane. Here is an agenda for desk checking in accordance with these principles:

1. *Variable Cross-Reference List Examination.* Examine the variable cross-reference list paying particular attention to undeclared variables and variables whose mnemonics violate standards. If the standards included declaring variables in alphabetical order, then undeclared and incorrect variables can be easily spotted. Check the lengths of all mnemonics to see if they make sense. Check the references to the variables, one at a time, against the code to see if every reference makes sense. Check the sequence of usages to assure that temporary variables are not inadvertently overwritten on some path. Confirm local, global, and privileged variables.
2. *Label Cross-Reference List Examination.* Justify all absolute labels. Justify all relative labels. Justify every point in the program that jumps to the specified label. Justify and examine all label-naming violations.
3. *Subroutines, Macros, Function Cross-References.* Justify every call and the point called from. Confirm that a subroutine, macro, or function exists for each call. Confirm that subroutines are called by subroutine calls, macros invoked by macro calls, and functions by function calls. Check the calling sequence for every call to insure that the parameters are in the right order, the right number, and of the right type.
4. *Equates.* Check all equated variables for type consistency and explain any that involve a type difference. Confirm conflicting equates and multiple equates. Explain all equates that are local to the routine, rather than a local item equated to a global label or variable (the typical case).
5. *Constants.* Confirm the value, type (e.g., integer, alpha), and format (e.g., hex, decimal, octal, octal by character) of every constant. Examine all constants that have the same value. Examine all absolute and immediate operands implicitly declared as constants. Confirm every call to every constant as correct with respect to value, type, and format. Explain why each constant is a constant rather than equated to a global parameter.

All of the above presuppose decent tools, extensive cross-referencing facilities, and plentiful computer access. The above checks are essential components of desk checking and worth doing even without automatically generated cross-reference lists of the kind recommended. I assume that as a minimum there is a basic variable and label cross-reference list (hopefully separate). With that as a base, the programmer can manually mark each entry in the list as to type (variable, subroutine, macro, and so on) and do the rest of the checks by hand.

6. *Standards Violations.* Justify each standards violation flagged by the standards checker. If there's no standards checker or standard checking by the source language processor, then this job should be done manually by the programmer's supervisor or peer as part of a review.

7. *Stylistic Violations.* Justify every stylistic violation. The comments of the standards checker apply here.

8. *Control Flow Comparison.* Compare the source flowchart (or PDL) control structure or graph with that produced by the flowcharter or control graph generator. Every difference must be explained, documentation changed, or bug corrected.

9. *Path Sensitizing.* Select the paths based on the source control flow but sensitize the paths from the code or from a code-based control graph or flowchart. If the selected paths cannot be sensitized based on the actual flows (rather than the intended flow), there's probably a bug. Path sensitizing in this way assures that every line of code and every instruction will be examined. That is, it assures that desk checking will have achieved coverage.

10. *Detailed Comparison.* The ugliest part of desk checking and still essential. **READ THE CODE!** Don't just scan it, but *read* it—a character at a time, a statement at a time. Savor each instruction or statement and ask if it makes sense. It doesn't always. The comparison is between the source code as seen by the computer and the source code in the programmer's mind. If the code was entered by the programmer directly at a terminal (which is best), then the comparison is really between intentions and actuality. If there was an intermediary keypunch operator and the original code was written on a coding sheet,* then the comparison is a true, character-by-character comparison. Ugly but essential. *READ THE CODE.* **READ THE CODE.**

READ THE CODE

4.3.4. Documentation

Documentation is not usually considered part of desk checking, but it should be. The act of documenting forces the programmer to be explicit about what the routine does and how it does it. This act can reveal many bugs. Documentation, aside from the first, superficial program design documentation, is usu-

---

*An altogether too frequent practice of benefit only to the coding sheet printing cartel and the international keypunch operator's conspiracy.

ally done after the routine has been completely tested. It is argued that this is the most efficient time to do documentation, because at that time that which is documented is correct. If you document any earlier, it's argued, you'll have to completely revise the documentation because of the bugs discovered. That argument was valid when documentation was handled by secretaries and had to be typed, revised, and so on by hand. But in the world of sophisticated text editors, word processors, and an available on-line terminal for every programmer (is there any other way?) most of those inefficiency arguments go out the door. We have come to insist on some level of documentation before the fact (of programming), at the system level, in the form of design documents, data dictionaries, and the like. Why not insist on the same kind of thing at the unit level? Early, although admittedly incomplete, documentation, if done in the context of desk checking, can be a beneficial catcher of bugs, and furthermore, those bugs are caught in the private domain. Here are some suggestions of what "desk-check" documentation can consist of:

1. A miniature data dictionary that explains every data structure, variable, register usage, and so on that are peculiar to that program. At the least, those data assumptions, structures, and variables that will not become part of the global data dictionary. Create the list and check the cross-reference listing against the list. Expect to find duplicated usages, duplicated elements, contradictory uses of elements, and missing elements.
2. Discussion of the principal paths and the more important exception paths. This is an aid to providing coverage and sensitizing values, and can give insight into instrumentation.
3. Discussion of logical cases where the routine is logic driven—similarly for other test techniques. Let the appropriate test technique dictate the approach to the documentation, e.g., state driven, syntax driven, etc.
4. Discussion of the routine in purely functional terms—input/outcome. This provides a clearer relation of the routine to its specification.
5. Discussion of all known restrictions and assumptions.
6. Discussion of all interfaces and interface assumptions.

The method has benefits in several directions:

1. The act of setting things down on paper provides a commitment which spurs the programmer to be "right"—in other words, it enhances self–quality control.
2. When things are hard to write, it's because the concept is unclear in the writer's mind. Things get simpler and easier with greater understanding. If I can't explain how a routine works (at least to myself), it's usually because

it's a lousy piece of code and not because it's a complicated task. The act of writing makes it clearer and helps discover private bugs.

3. Each area written about (data, paths, logic, function, and so on) is a subconscious test and exercise of the routine. Writing about the different areas is like subconsciously exposing and testing from that point of view—more private bugs caught.

4. Test design is too much like programming and consequently may retain the same misconceptions and self-delusions that lead to the bugs. Writing is so different (for most programmers) from programming that the same self-deception that led to the bug's not being caught in the test design context will not work in the writing context—ergo, more private bugs caught.

5. This initial documentation is an early-warning indicator of quality, completeness, test approach, and a strong indication of how aware that programmer is of the issues surrounding that routine.

HOWEVER:Don't muck things up by insisting on proper grammar, spelling, arbitrary forms, rules of usage, complete sentences, and all the other accouterments of good writing. That just gets in the way at this point and will inhibit many programmers. Also don't confuse verbosity with quality, nor terseness with cleanliness. There's probably no correlation.

Some people are just naturally wordy and can tear off a fifty-page description in a few days. That description could be superb or just fifty pages of meandering, repetitive junk that's full of holes (just like the code). Conversely, a short, terse description consisting only of nouns and verbs could be excellent or incoherent. There's no automated tool that will tell you if the documentation is good or bad. You can't apply arbitrary rules such as the ratio of syllables to instructions, or the average number of syllables per word, or similar garbage. Documentation has to be read and understood (if possible) to be evaluated. Keep in mind, though, that the purpose of *this* documentation is to force the programmer to explain the routine to herself—the more formal public documentation should come later, but can be based on this initial, private documentation.

4.3.5. How Good and How To

Meticulous desk checking appears to be capable of catching 30% of all bugs and is particularly effective against wild cards and typographical bugs. Most programmers receive no formal training in desk checking, just as they receive no formal training in testing. The prevailing attitudes to desk checking appear to be a holdover from the early days of programming when manual syntax checking was not only more efficient, but in some cases essential. From the era when two or three weeks might elapse from the completion of the code to the first assembly—what else was there to do in the meanwhile? Desk checking should be done systematically and under an explicitly defined procedure, such as that detailed above. It should be started after the element passes all syntax checks and prior to unit test design. When properly done, it will take longer than coding—perhaps twice as long for experienced programmers. In fact, it's one of the marks of the more experienced programmer. They have the instruction repertoire at their fingertips and don't have to look up formats, options, and syntax rules. They code at a dead run, at one or two hundred instructions per hour—but then take days to desk check. Ask the programmers to create a desk-checking standard. Split the group into senior and junior, and examine the recommendations. Collate them, augment the result. Get a consensus, and publish them in a practices and procedures handbook.

4.4. Reviews and Audits

4.4.1. Objectives and Differences

A **review** is a public, verbal, interpersonal examination of a program element. An **audit** is an impersonal verification of tangible evidence such as documentation. The review presumes that the programmer is honest but possibly misguided. The audit presumes that the programmer is possibly dishonest or sloppy. The review is an aid to quality, and the audit is a confirmation that quality objectives have been achieved. Both reviews and audits are essential parts of software quality assurance, but the intentions and methods for each are distinctly different.

The primary beneficiary of the review is the reviewee. Properly conducted reviews help the programmer catch his own errors by helping him to verbalize his intentions. It is essentially an interpersonal affair, and its success depends on the personal dynamics between reviewee and reviewers. Once intentions have been clarified, it is possible to compare intentions with execution, with requirements, and to spot contradictions and ambiguities, or clumsy and inefficient implementations. In properly conducted reviews it is the programmer who most often detects the problems, and not the reviewers. An ideal reviewer is not judgmental and recognizes that the primary benefit of a review is the act of "talking out" the program or unit. It may not matter whether or not the reviewer actually understands the program.

The primary benefit of an audit is that the audit is to take place. An audit should be totally impersonal and should be based only on tangible evidence such as code listings, cross-reference listings, documentation, data dictionary, test plans, test execution logs, and so on. There should be *no* input from the programmer lest such inputs cloud the auditor's objectivity with good intentions, persuasive chatter, or wishful thinking. In a well-run project with good cooperation between programming and quality assurance staffs, the only thing an audit should show up are oversights and honest mistakes. It should, by and large, be a mechanical procedure done in accordance with a predefined check list. The mere fact that there is to be an audit should prompt programmers to go over that check list themselves, thereby obviating the audit's purpose.

Audits tell us the state of things, and reviews tell us what that state is likely to become. Actual progress in testing should be based on audited results, but projections and planning can be based on a combination of audits and reviews. Potential or actual bugs caught in a review are still private relative to the element (e.g., unit, program, subsystem) and can therefore be handled privately. Deficiencies exposed by an audit are perforce public and must be corrected through formal change procedures, notification, and reverification testing as appropriate to the element level. Reviews focus on prevention and audits focus on correction.

4.4.2. Contents

The subject matter of reviews and audits are the same, the difference is that the audit concentrates on documentation and the review on explanations. The reviews should cover all that material that cannot be put into documentation. The content should include:

1. Review of specifications and requirements documents—do they exist, are they understandable, what is the element supposed to be doing?
2. Major problems and risk areas—identification of the components of the element that are tricky, complicated, or risk prone. For example, programming that was forced to start before a crucial interface was properly defined.
3. Principal design assumptions. Review of all assumptions made by the programmer, to the extent that these can be verbalized (for a review) or documented (for an audit).
4. The design and the code.
5. Data-base structures and items peculiar to the element, or put into the global data base for this element.
6. Interfaces with other elements, especially if the interfaces are nonstandard.
7. Prerequisite subelements, corequisite elements, elements which depend on this element—e.g., this subroutine is used by . . .
8. Test plans—type of tests (syntax, path, state, and so on), test objectives, test environment (real or simulated), test data base.

9. Previous history, if appropriate—e.g., this unit is a rework of a previous routine.
10. Performance and resources. Expected execution time per item processed if part of the specification, expected space consumed, I/O operations, and so on, as appropriate.
11. Operating assumptions and environment—reentrant, recursive, absolute, relocatable, operating system version or imbedding program version, hardware prerequisites, computer model number, and so on.
12. Optimization goals. The element was optimized for maximum speed, for minimum space, for minimum programming time, for flexibility, for maintainability, and so on. Relative weight of each goal.

4.4.3. Element Level, Hostility, and Privacy

Reviews range in a spectrum from very private to public. The most private is the programmer's desk check. The most public is a formal review conducted before the buyer on which the system's acceptance may be based. The higher the element level (e.g., unit, program, subsystem), the more public the review. Several other factors shift along a continuum as we go from unit to system:

1. *Number of reviewers.* Because the element is more public, there are more interested parties, and therefore the number of reviewers increases relative to the number of reviewees. Large groups tend to operate at knowledge's least common denominator (i.e., large groups are collectively stupid). Therefore, large public reviews can't be effective at spotting detailed technical problems. If a large public review focuses on the operation of a few lines of code, it will merely be a waste of time. Big reviews should be reserved for big issues and small reviews for details. Any big review should be conducted under the guidance of a chairman who assures that the review will not get bogged down in microscopic details at the wrong level.
2. *Formality.* The larger the reviews, the more formal they must be.* Small, private reviews need no agenda, no formal preparation, no rehearsals, or expensive graphics. Conversely, system-level reviews are a shambles without adequate preparation.
3. *Anxiety.* Because the issues are bigger as we go from unit to system, anxiety also increases. The most private review should engender no anxiety. Its pur-

---

*MFBP (my favorite bad project) had copious reviews—at the unit level, for unit integration, programs, subsystems, and the like. These were held weekly. Wednesday was spent discussing the coming review. Thursday preparing the graphics. Friday was the review itself. And on Monday they rehashed Friday's outcome. They programmed on Tuesday, I think.

pose is to help the programmer. The programmer is not helped if the environment and ground rules of the review promote anxiety. The more detailed the material to be reviewed, the more its purpose is to aid the programmer. Therefore, the detailed review is not to be judgmental or critical, but supportive. One reason for reviews not working is that objectives are misunderstood, useless anxiety promoted, and the programmer clams up instead of finding the problems.

4. *Hostility.* Hostility can be beneficial, particularly at the higher system levels. In a sense, then, as the review type shifts from private to public, there is an increase in the level of criticism. It shifts from the objective of support to the programmer to criticism, and therefore a degree of warranted hostility. The degree of criticism must be kept appropriate to the element level. There's no point in attacking a programmer's unit from the point of view of global system issues. The programmer may not be competent to discuss such issues, or if competent, may have implemented the program as directed.

It's important, therefore, to be clear about the objectives of a review. What level is being reviewed? Is it to be supportive or critical? Is the criticism appropriate to the unit's level and the programmer's scope? Is the level of detail appropriate to the competence of the participants? Is the degree of formality and preparation appropriate? Is the level of stress conducive to the objectives, or counterproductive? The bottom line, however, must be: will this review improve quality and productivity, or hinder it?

4.4.4. Review Design and Documentation

No one review technique can be universal. Every organization must establish the levels, formality, and type of reviews conducted for itself because too much depends on staff, training, personalities, management style, history, application, and so on. The reviews discussed below are intended to provide signposts along the spectrum from private to public, which should be modified as necessary to achieve a policy with regard to reviews. Whatever is decided should be formalized to the extent that all programmers are aware of what kinds of review are to be conducted at what point in the program's progress. Who is to participate, what the ground rules are, and so on. These review specifications should be published in a practices handbook. Most important of all, however, is that a review policy be consistently administered. Too often a policy is officially adopted but ignored. The reviews are conducted haphazardly until it is perceived that the system has serious quality problems. Then panic ensues and tiger teams are called in to grill the programming staff with long, hostile reviews. It's too late then. The damage's been done. All that the review will do is show how bad things are.

4.4.5. Colleague Reviews

The least threatening review is one conducted by a programmer's colleagues. The programmer seeks a person with whom to discuss the program. The simple act of verbalizing the program's intentions and operations exposes many bugs.* The colleague asks questions, seeks clarification, and points out possible problem areas. The programmer should look at the colleague's face. If there's a blank look, the colleague doesn't understand—such blank stares can be clues to possible bugs. You probably don't have to implement a colleague review system because it's probably happening right now. Programmers discuss their problems with one another and informally seek each other's approval. However, it's not being done uniformly nor is it an approved practice. Therefore, some programmers may forgo this process because there's guilt associated with it. Remove the guilt. Make a practice of it. Encourage it; but control it. It must not be allowed to become an excuse for continuous coffee klatches. The manager should control who reviews whom, under what circumstances, and how often—not a formal control, mind you, but informal control through suggestions and direction, rather than through rules and directives.

The reviewers and reviewees should be of comparable competance and rank. They should not be working on the same program lest they wander down the primrose paths of misconceptions together. They should be compatible individuals who have nothing to lose by exposing themselves to one another.

The way in which the review is initiated is important. If A is the reviewee and B the reviewer, you can't say to B, "I want you to review A's work." This sets up a conflict which will destroy the review's objectives. Instead, say to A, "Why don't you talk the program over with B?" or "Have you discussed the program with B?" The first move must appear to come from the reviewee and not the reviewer. That move must come only when the programmer feels comfortable with the idea. Be flexible with who reviews whom and let the compatible pairs seek each other out. You may have one or more individuals on the

---

*I've conducted hundreds of interviews in support of system performance modeling. In such reviews, we are interested only in the high probability paths; most complicated logic associated with errors and exception conditions (which is where the bugs tend to be) are deliberately ignored. Because the objective of the interview is to obtain detailed timing data and is not at all related to quality assurance objectives, we strive to make the interview as nonjudgmental and benign as possible. The interviews are usually conducted around the time of unit testing and the beginning of integration. I've yet to go through a few hundred lines of code with a programmer without his discovering a bug or problem. In this context, the ratio of bugs the programmer discovers to those I discover is at least 100 to 1. It's clear to me that it's nothing I'm doing that's of benefit. It's just the fact that I'm another human being, without an ax to grind, with whom the program can be discussed that's important.

staff who seem particularly effective in the reviewer role—a confessor type; use them to advantage, but make it clear that time spent in such reviews is a legitimate part of their job and adjust their productivity expectations and schedules accordingly. You must encourage those who are secretive or inhibited and discourage those who'd rather talk than program. Finally, don't ever call them "reviews." Call them "program discussions" or anything else that's nonthreatening and that implies mutual participation between reviewer and reviewee.

4.4.6. Peer Review

A **peer review** is a more public and formal review of a program conducted by the programmer's peers. Peers, like colleagues, are of comparable competence and rank to the reviewee. The purpose of a peer review is to get a more public exposure of the element and to obtain the benefits of divergent points of view. A peer review is not, however, a critique. Like the colleague review, its primary purpose is to help the reviewee spot the problems. Peer reviews must not include management or project leader participation. The peer review should be a nonthreatening kind of review, even though it is conducted with some formality. Some suggestions for peer reviews are:

Peer Review Group. Programmers from different sections should be formed into peer review groups. All members of the group review each other's programs. Each member has equal say and weight.

Chairmanship. A chairman is essential to keep the group on track, to prevent personal squabbles, to avoid getting bogged down in unnecessary details, to adjudicate honest differences of opinion and stylistic differences, and to maintain the review's objectivity. In keeping with the idea of peer groups, rotate the chairmanship.

Agenda and Report. The group works to a formal agenda that includes: items left over from previous meetings, the program to be discussed or reviewed that session, schedule for the next session, agenda for the next session, chairman selection, follow-up of previous problems. Minutes are kept for each meeting, and results are published in an informal report. The report is for the peer group's benefit and should not be integrated into the project's formal documentation.

When. These reviews should be applied mostly at the unit level, after private unit testing but before formal testing.

Follow-up. The group confirms, by a private check list, that all problems brought up at previous meetings have been corrected or otherwise properly disposed of. The follow-up is mutually supportive and provides self-regulation, which is always cheaper and more beneficial than external regulation.

Regularity and Duration. Most programs can be adequately reviewed in one or two hours. Review only one program or several small related routines by one programmer at each session. Because the review is tied to the stage in which the program is, it is the program's progress that dictates the review's schedule; regular formal meetings are neither necessary nor effective. There is more activity during unit testing and less as the project progresses. Higher-level elements can also benefit from peer reviews; these occur later, and the peer group might have to be drawn from outside the project.

4.4.7. More Public Reviews

Leader Review. Like the colleague review, this is a one-on-one review. The main difference is that it's conducted by the programmer's direct supervisor. The content and agenda are the same as the colleague review. The principal difference is that any fault discovered cannot help but influence the leader's evaluation of the programmer's competence. While the leader should strive to alleviate anxiety, some stress is inevitable, just by the facts of the situation. The leader review should be conducted after private testing, after any corrections discovered by the peer review, and after the leader's preliminary audit. At this point, the programmer should have full confidence in the results of the forthcoming formal test. The success and effectiveness of this kind of review depends significantly on the leader's management style. An autocratic put-down artist will accomplish little, as will an overly permissive leader.

QA Review. This is like a cross between the peer review and the leader review. The differences are in who the reviewers are, when it's done, and what the reactions are. QA reviews are typically used at higher system levels and are most effective at system-level testing and in preliminary acceptance testing. QA staffs the review team using individuals from QA, a QA chairman, and possibly technical experts from other projects or external consultants. The entire programming staff that produced the element is on the line. The only caution is that it is the review of a group's effort, and QA should avoid putting the person who happens to present that effort personally on the spot.

Adversary Team. The adversary team is a team of experts who are directed to be hostile. It is the reviewee's job to convince this hostile group and to leave them smiling. This kind of review sould be reserved for the highest level of system testing and conducted only prior to a formal customer acceptance test. The adversary team should be external to QA, because its activity is also a test of how well QA has been conducted. An adversary team puts everybody's ass on the line.

4.4.8. Audits

Every formal passage of a program element from one level to the next more public level should be accompanied by a formal audit of the documentation and accomplishments appropriate to that passage. Each audit should be conducted in accordance to a prepared check list of items. The audit, like the system, is hierarchical. Successful audit at a level includes checking lower-level audits. The contents of the audits, at various levels include:

Unit Level: Unit requirements specification, a coded and tested unit, unit test plans, unit testing logs, data-base dictionary components, successful correction of all bugs discovered, unit description and documentation, completion of specified reviews (peer review, project leader review, and so on), style and standards, performance objectives (size, speed).

Program Level: Requirements, documentation, and data base as for units; unit integration test plans, test logs, bug correction, completion of reviews, completion of all unit-level audits, performance objectives.

Subsystem Level: All program audits completed, all pertinent reviews, subsystem test plans, subsystem integration, subsystem data base, interface test plans, test logs, completion of problem reports, performance objectives, detailed verification of functional requirements against a requirements check list for that subsystem.

Almost every audit will reveal holes and oversights. The completion of an audit is therefore marked by an auditor's report that lists all problems by categories such as: function, testing, documentation, interface testing, test logs, actual bugs, and so on. Audit reports should be clearly marked as to whether or not they are complete and what is missing. For example, incomplete or inadequate documentation should not be reason for rejecting the unit and certainly should not be given the same weight as incomplete testing or test plans. A follow-up procedure for deficiencies discovered by audits should be implemented.

4.5. Execution, Correction, and Refinement

Unit testing is not a single event. It is a process. It employs both formal and informal methods and private and public activities. It progresses at varying rates and may appear to retrogress at times. The element moves towards perfection by a sequence of step-wise refinements, starting with a minimum functioning backbone to which features are added or confirmed. Each step in the element's integration requires new tests and reveals new bugs. Each bug requires correction and retest. It is not the superficial and arbitrary signposts in that process which we create as tags for our convenience that are important (e.g., desk check, unit test design, unit test, and so on) but the entire process.

4.6. Implementation

Both private and public, formal and informal methods for unit-level testing and quality assurance are required. Informal methods do not mean haphazard or ad hoc methods. The methods used must be planned, carefully considered, and regulated, whether formal or informal, public or private. This is not a contradiction, although it might seem so at first. Desk checking, as I advocate it, is a private affair, but that doesn't mean that every programmer should learn through trial and error what works and what doesn't. One of the serious limitations to quality assurance as practiced is an excessive concern for formal and public methods to the detriment of more effective private and informal methods which catch most of the bugs. No wonder quality assurance is so often despised or ignored—they're beating the wrong drum. Private and informal methods are private and informal only as conducted, and not as planned. They must be implemented by indirect methods:

1. Planning and careful consideration of each method's objectives and structure so that you know what it is you want to implement. If it isn't clear in your mind, it won't work. Develop written guides for all informal and private methods and publish them in a programming practices handbook.
2. Education—don't leave it to the programmers to learn how to design tests—teach them. Don't assume they'll do it right—show them.*
3. Exploit leadership—get the natural leaders to adopt the practice by having them participate in the design. QA didn't create the standards, the programmers themselves did it. Leadership in this context has to do with respect and not hierarchy.
4. Peer pressure—works wonders if peers agree with objectives, wreaks havoc otherwise.
5. Strategic seeding—create disciples and distribute them. Start with the most receptive groups, not with the most hostile. Start with the least problematic project, not with the toughest.
6. Patience—don't expect to implement everything at once or on one project.

---

*Rose-Ann instructed her programmers in great detail, including exactly how to tear out and replace an update page in the system design documentation and handbooks. It seemed like an overly autocratic and insulting thing to do at first, but her group's bug rate was noticeably lower than the average. All of her programmers worked to exactly the same documentation. The little things do count.

Be sensitive to what works and what is rejected, even if it does work. Expect results to be measured across years, not weeks. Push to get more and more of your methods accepted and implemented, an increment at a time so that each project is better than the previous. Plan and direct evolution, don't expect revolutions.

5. HIGHER LEVEL ELEMENT TESTING

5.1. General

All that's been said about unit testing, as to scope, techniques, and objectives, applies after integration (see Chapter 5), with little modification, to testing higher-level elements.

5.2. Decision Nodes and Path Testing

Decision nodes at the higher levels of flow can arise by one of several mechanisms:

1. Actual decisions at the instruction or statement level, in the higher-level flowgraph or transaction flows.
2. The choice of multiple exits from a multi-exit routine.
3. A direction-forcing exit parameter or data-base object value interpreted by the executive which then directs the flow to the appropriate routine.
4. An implicit or explicit exit parameter which is interpreted by the called routine to select paths within that routine.

Coverage is required at the higher element levels just as it is at the lower. Every exit from a multi-exit routine must be covered in the higher-level flows. Every indirect decision, as interpreted by the executive, must be covered. In this context, ignore the details of the executive's operation and just how the decision in the higher-level flow is implemented, and concentrate only on the fact that different alternatives are possible. Direct code or instructions are treated exactly as they are at the unit level. However, subroutine or subelement calls are handled differently. It is not possible to exercise every path through the subelement in the higher-level test. Say that two routines A and B are called in sequence. If A and B each require 30 paths for coverage, then the combination of covering paths is of the order of 1000. Actually, the combination can probably be covered by 30 paths, but even that's too many. The higher-level element paths are defined by an appropriate higher-level flowgraph or transaction flow. These are the paths to be covered at the higher level. These paths must be sensitized and instrumented just as they are at the lower levels. Choose entry parameter values to the subelement that are as broad as possible and consistent with the requirements of the higher-level paths. Within the called subelement, choose the simplest and most direct path consistent with the higher-level flow. If adequate instrumentation is available so that lower-level element path coverage executed in higher-level tests can be recorded, as the element progresses to higher and higher levels of testing, there will be a measure of just how much coverage was accomplished at the higher levels. Ideally, not only should coverage have been achieved at the unit level, but it should have also been reaccomplished when system testing is completed. Everything that's done at the unit level is done for a higher-level purpose. Consequently, the unit-level paths should also all be ultimately exercised at higher levels of testing.

5.3. Syntax Directed Testing

Syntax-directed testing has a relatively small role to play at the higher levels of element testing. It should be restricted to those aspects of syntax that result from the interaction of elements. For example, an input command sequence process starts with a parse routine that identifies the command. Once the command is isolated, the rest of the input string is passed to individual analyzers in accordance with the command type. The command parser has been tested at the unit level with appropriate syntax-directed testing, as have the individual analyzers. What remains to be tested in the higher-level test is the logic by which the input string passes from the parser to the individual analyzers. Although it's a syntax-directed test and in principle purely functional, the syntax errors which it pays to test at this level cannot be determined without examining the program structure.

5.4. Logic-Based Testing

The use of decision tables and boolean algebra to determine logical coverage at the higher levels of element testing proceeds as it does for unit-level testing. However, the logic may be more indirect, particularly due to the interposition of executive or operating system functions. As with path testing, you should attempt to ignore the details of the interposed executive and concentrate only on the resulting truth values produced. If the program is reasonably modular and well designed, then the higher-level decisions will tend to occur at higher levels. A combination of lower-level truth values will resolve, at the higher levels, to a simple TRUE/FALSE. This provides a clear separation of lower-level logic from higher-level logic and makes testing and confirmation of higher-level consistency and completeness relatively easy. If, conversely, a decision variable occurs at many levels, then complexity increases as we progress from low-level elements to higher-level elements, and with it, test and verification complexity increase also.

5.5. State Testing

State testing becomes more difficult as one progresses from lower-level to higher-level elements because the state-controlling variables become increasingly more implicit and diffuse. As with unit-level state testing, the most important part of the job is to identify the factors that go into the state and to count the states. Given that, it then remains to design and execute tests that provide state-transition coverage.

The biggest problem in identifying state factors is getting trapped into including lower-level components in the higher levels. For example, at a higher level the state factor for a transaction might be GOOD/BAD/ILLOGICAL. Each GOOD state has many substates because there are many ways in which a transaction can be GOOD or BAD or ILLOGICAL. What constitutes a higher-level state factor is that all substates share one or more characteristics in common (e.g., GOOD, BAD), without regard to the details of what makes the state GOOD or BAD. State test design then consists of identifying groups of states and groups of transitions between these groups of states, all of which are controlled by the same higher-level control variable. If a set of states are to be merged into a single higher-level state, then that set cannot have any states in common with another set of states similarly grouped. If a set of transitions are to go from superstate A, say, to superstate B, then every state in A must go to some state in B (not necessarily the same state), for the same value of the higher-level control variable.

5.6. The Question of Stratification

Higher-level element test design is plagued by the problem of nonstratification. It would be nice if a set of logical parameters, say, could be grouped so that a higher-level one could examine the truth or falsity of the set rather than its individual components. Similarly, a path-forcing variable ideally should be applicable at one level, and when we get to the next level up it should be possible to ignore that variable because it cannot affect a higher-level flow. An assembly of elements that exhibit this behavior is said to be **strictly stratified**. For example, consider a common subroutine that has two exits (or equivalently, a binary-valued exit parameter), say NORMAL and ERROR. Trace the level of the call to that routine from the highest system level down. Say that it's called at level N (see Figure 4-2). The level N routine uses the common subroutine as a decision node (directly or indirectly). It then appears in the level N test, and presumably disappears in the next-higher-level test, N-1. Unfor-

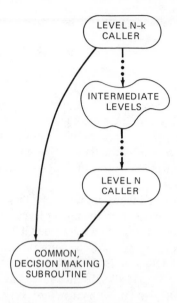

Figure 4-2. Unstratified Calls.

tunately, strict stratification rarely exists because the same common subroutine is also called at some higher call level, say N-k. Therefore, having tested the controlling factor at level N does not mean that it can be ignored at level N-k. That would be possible only if every call to the subroutine occurred at exactly the same level in the call tree; only if the entire system were strictly stratified. It is theoretically possible to achieve strict stratification by the artifice of introducing artificial subroutines whose only function is to pass the call down to the next level, so that every call to subroutine A, say, appears at level N. This would certainly be slow, and the introduction of all those extra calls and dummy subroutines would add so much additional code and interfaces that the net result would be a serious degradation rather than an enhancement of software quality.

The problem of nonstratification occurs for every aspect of higher-level element testing, be it path testing, syntax testing, logic-based testing, state testing, or any other form of testing applied at the unit level. Without stratification of some sort, the tester is forced to carry more and more details to higher and higher levels. This is impractical. Therefore, what is done is to partition the higher-level element testing into sets that can be stratified. For example, say that a level N element cannot be stratified because a subroutine is called at two different levels. Testing of the element, however, can be divided into two sets of tests, each of which can be stratified. Say test set A in which the routine is called at level N and test set B in which the routine is called at level M (see

Figure 4-3). A set of tests is designed and executed for the A set and a separate set is done for the B set. There may be some overlap. However, because both test sets can now be stratified, in neither the A set nor the B set is it necessary to consider the details of the subroutine's operation. Therefore, the number of combinations is reduced (truth values, paths, state transitions, states, data input errors, or what have you) and the testing effort is reduced without sacrificing effectiveness.

Stratification usually follows element boundaries. To a great extent, stratification is achieved by the very fact that functions are subdivided into subprograms, programs, and the like. Occasionally, artificial partition of an element will be needed to achieve stratification and a workable test set. The principle here is that there is no need to force testing of an element to be conducted at a single level or from only one point of view. Partition of the set of tests in the interest of making it possible to ignore lower-level interactions with higher-level issues can considerably reduce test labor. Although such partitions will usually follow functional lines, there is no need that they do so. For example, say that in a higher-level path test, stratification can be achieved by dividing the set of covering paths into three subsets, each of which allows ignoring some lower-level details. While the three sets of paths will probably reflect functional differences and it is preferable if they do, there is no need to reject a partition of

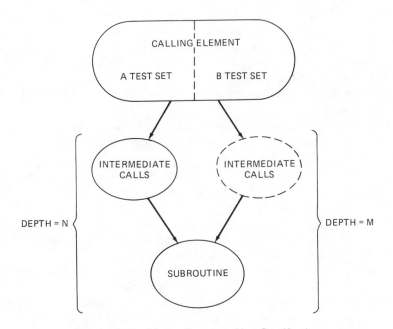

Figure 4-3. Partitioning Tests to Achieve Stratification.

the paths that seems to have no clear functional significance. Nor need the set of paths be divided according to the values of a control variable. The sole significance of the partition could be that it permitted stratification and therefore the avoidance of low-level detail at the higher levels of testing.

5.7. Stratified Designs

Because stratification permits simplification of testing by allowing the tester to ignore low-level issues in higher levels of testing, designs biased to stratification, where it can be done without sacrificing simplicity or function, or without increasing interfaces, should be encouraged. A stratified design is achieved by top-down thinking (although not by strict top-down design). Step-wise refinement of specifications, where each level is defined in increasing detail to the level below, abet stratified designs, as does the use of clearly defined, independent elements (i.e., modular programming). The following also contribute to stratification:

1. An explicit data-base design with a controlled data dictionary, rather than allowing the data base to come into being as programming progresses.
2. A top-down subdivision of functions into subfunctions and the avoidance of functions that cross boundaries.
3. Explicit consideration of transaction and system states and explicit subdivision of such states into mutually exclusive subsets.
4. Clear-cut separation of input validation into different syntactic and semantic elements. That is, emulation of the design principles used in all well-designed contemporary compilers.
5. Early identification of logical variables and a top-down subdivision into subsidiary variables.
6. Explicit design of a common subroutine library. Similarly for macros and functions. Grouping of subroutines into common subfunctions of a higher order where possible.
7. Monitoring the design to avoid unnecessary nonstratification, level skipping, and the like. For example, a decision can be based on either a single character, or on individual bits within that character. If at all possible, and sensible, the whole character should be used for the decision at the higher level, even if a lower-level examination can provide the same information. As another example, a number can be tested for positive or negative, or alternatively the sign bit can be examined. The higher-level test should be based on the word, and only lower-level tests on the sign bit.
8. Examining the partitions created in the interest of artificial stratification and making them explicit if they can be explained in functional terms.

While stratification and modularity are beneficial because they simplify element testing, they should not be allowed to become the do-all and end-all of design and testing. Artificially imposed stratification that increases the total amount of code, the number of interfaces, and call depths will, by the sheer addition of complexity, reduce reliability and make testing more difficult. As with anything else, it's possible to go over the hill and be on the wrong side of a trade-off.

6. TASKS FOR A QUALITY ASSURANCE DEPARTMENT

1. Establish methods for finding potential common code and the avoidance of redundant program elements.
2. Define the ritual and the steps therein by which a unit is admitted as a trustworthy public element. Create the ceremony and the signs by which such units can be recognized.
3. Educate the programming staff, group leaders, section heads, and management as to the objective, subjective, subsidiary, and auxiliary goals of unit testing.
4. Define in detail the minimum unit-testing procedures and associated forms and documents.
5. Establish a reward system for discovered bugs.
6. Define the objective goals to be verified by programmers, group leaders, and QA.
7. Define QA data-gathering forms and procedures that are effective but not obnoxious. Distribute collective results periodically in a QA bulletin.
8. Define standards and procedures for testing partially complete code and for follow-up of incomplete units and incompletely tested units.
9. Define standards and procedures for conditional unit acceptance.
10. Define unit test plan standards, associated documents, and forms.
11. Define unit test plan review procedures—what, with what, how, and by whom.
12. Define style guides.
13. Define coding standards.
14. Work with programming management to:
    a. Get adequate test tools, resources, facilities, and schedules.
    b. Get a fair share of those tools and resources for QA's use.
15. Define the test environment (e.g., real versus simulated) for unit testing. Create methods to track the environment in which tests were run.
16. Agitate for good automated analyzers. Agitate for enough on-line computer time so that the analyzers and test tools can be used effectively.
17. Stop keypunching source code. Let the programmers code at a terminal.

18. Define desk-checking objectives, procedures, and methods. Educate programming staff, group leaders, and managers regarding desk checking.
19. Define initial documentation objectives.
20. Create standard agendas for reviews at every level, defining who, what, and when.
21. Define and publish what is to be covered by each type of audit and the procedures for deficiencies found by audits.
22. Plan a grand strategy of implementation in which QA appears to have the least contribution—wherever possible, let the programmers believe that they are initiating QA measures. Accept and incorporate any sensible suggestion you get from programming staff and be sure they get the credit for it.
23. Don't ignore the importance of informal and private practices—that's where most of the unit-level bugs are caught. It works. Don't fight it. Just try to make it better.

and

READ THE CODE

5

INTEGRATION

1. SYNOPSIS

Integration testing is aimed at showing inter-element consistency under the assumption that the elements themselves satisfy element requirements and have passed element level testing. Tactics and strategy for integration testing are discussed.

2. OBJECTIVES

Integration is the act of taking a set of subelements and combining them into larger, self-consistent elements. **Integration testing** is the testing done to show the existence of integration bugs, which is to say, the existence of inconsistencies between the subelements.*

Whatever testing is done at the unit level applies, with suitable modification, to higher-level elements, as discussed in Section 5 of Chapter 4. If integration testing is just testing the integrated unit, structurally and functionally, then there is little to be said which I have not already said. A higher-level element test, either structural or functional, makes no sense until there is reasonable confidence concerning the compatibility and consistency of its subelements. Why even attempt a path test, say, that traverses several units until you believe the call sequences to be correct? Why attempt end-to-end functional verification until you know that the subelements of the element under test all use the same data-base object in a consistent way? How can you propose a state-transition test until you know that the state is based on a consistently used set of

---

*This definition is not in keeping with the usual but vague definition of integration which includes element-level testing as well as the question of subelement consistency. Sometimes the term "integration" is used to include all system-level testing. The problem with such broad and vague definitions is that they obscure the very important problem of subelement consistency and do not address the possibility that all subelements are correct but the assemblage is not.

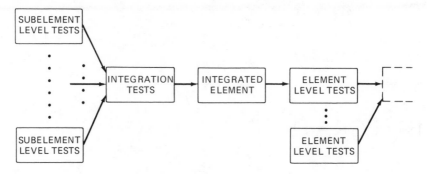

Figure 5-1. Integration Procedure.

state controlling variables? The procedure in our definition of integration test-ing is shown in Figure 5-1.

Integration testing assumes:

1. All subelements to be integrated have successfully completed element-level tests—or risk is accepted in proportion to those that have not completed element-level testing. The subelements are assumed to be self-consistent and correct.
2. Integration tests are designed to explore the direct and indirect interfaces and the consistency of the subelements to one another.
3. Integration testing and debugging continue interactively until a mutually consistent set of subelements is achieved. This may involve one level or sev-eral levels. The integrated set of subelements may or may not work in a functional sense.
4. The integrated element is tested as an element from the point of view of structure and function, with tests appropriate to that level.
5. The process is iterated until the entire system has been tested and integrated.

This prescription is ideal and not real. If carried out exactly as defined, each addition of an element would require complete retesting of that which had already been integrated. It would effectively prevent any form of parallel test-ing. Integration testing is a chicken-and-egg situation. Most of what is to be integrated must be successfully integrated before integration testing can take place. It is often necessary to assume that A and B are integrated in order to test C's integration, to assume that A and C are integrated in order to test B's integration, and to assume that B and C are integrated in order to test A's integration. We make an inherently nonverifiable assumption in integration testing:

If A is consistent with B and B is consistent with C, then A is consistent with C.

If in addition to this act of faith we assert that every element is self-consistent, then we can be assured that every assemblage of elements is consistent.*

3. INTEGRATION TACTICS

3.1. Graphs and Standards

3.1.1. Who Calls Whom?

Despite the designer's intentions, it is not generally completely known at integration time which elements call which. Common subroutines are defined with strict usage rules (it is to be hoped), and programmers are encouraged to use these routines wherever possible. Similarly, at higher levels, common subfunctions are implemented—that is, specific paths through various elements that accomplish some common stated purpose. Again programmers are encouraged to use these common paths. The result is that there is incomplete knowledge concerning the actual way in which routines call each other. With few exceptions, this information is not difficult to get, and the getting can be automated. The result is a **subroutine call graph** or **call tree** which is the starting point of integration. It displays, either as a list or as a graph, every call made by every routine, every call made by every lower-level routine, and so on until routines are reached that call no other routines. Similarly and of equal importance are function call graphs and macro call graphs. Note that macros can call subroutines and vice-versa, so that it's not always possible to disentangle the two graphs—similarly for function calls.

An automated tool that produces the entire call graph down from a specified

---

*For the mathematically minded, we've asked for reflexivity and transitivity for element consistency, which is sufficient to assert that the consistency of which we speak (assuming it can be defined as a recursive predicate) applies on every path, and therefore for the graph as a whole. In general, consistency cannot be so defined, things aren't always transitive (because of bugs), and we can't be sure that every subelement is self-consistent. That is why higher levels of testing are required. Note that we haven't asked for symmetric relation because, in general, symmetric calls (e.g., co-routines) are rare and A's compatibility to B does not imply B's compatibility to A. If we had symmetry, the consistency relation would define an equivalence relation and provide a sensible guide to the way elements could be integrated into higher-order elements—helas, that's not the way it is. See HECH77B.

point (i.e., the element to be integrated) is a useful adjunct to the design of integration tests. Barring that, the call graph can and should be developed manually. In most higher-level language programs the entire call graph can be developed automatically based on static analysis. In assembly language programs, where the identity of the called routine can be the result of a calculation, only dynamic analysis can determine the call tree with certainty.* The presence of bugs, however, can also throw a static analysis off in a higher-order language. For example, the way in which the interpreter handles an out-of-bounds value in a BASIC ON...GOSUB statement can result in strange paths and calls. If the out-of-bounds condition is not checked, control can revert to the next executable statement number following the correct range, inadvertently creating a new subroutine. You could argue that that's a bug in the interpreter, and so it is, but analogous problems are found in FORTRAN, COBOL, and other higher-order languages. In other words, the call tree we get is not necessarily the real call tree, but the call tree we think we have in the absence of bugs or the call tree that can be developed by a static analysis. Still, it's better than no call tree at all.

Given the call tree from the element to be integrated down, it is a simple matter to strike out all parts of the tree below elements that have been already integrated at that level. The remaining pruned tree is the tree of routines that are to be subjected to integration testing. Note that the act of getting the call tree implied a considerable amount of integration. The agglomeration of units was deemed acceptable to the compiler and/or assembler, the linkage editor, and the loader—no small accomplishment. Just as real testing can't begin until the unit has passed the compiler's syntax testing, integration testing can't begin until the elements to be integrated have been successfully loaded and are ready for integration testing.

3.1.2. Data Dependency Graph

Data that's local to a given element should have been tested in an element-level test. What remains is data that's global to several subelements. What we want for any given element is the identity of all data-base items that affect it and which it affects. Just like subroutine calls, no one really knows this structure until integration time, because programmers are urged to define and use global data wherever possible. A data dictionary is an indispensable aid to determin-

---

*Higher-order languages can, of course, have calls in which the called routine's identity is the result of a calculation. However, the user is not likely to input that identity. The called routine must be identified and declared someplace in the program. In assembly language, an indirect subroutine call instruction can go almost anyplace in memory with any value. Strictly speaking, it's a matter of degree as to whether static or dynamic analysis will suffice to analyze a program.

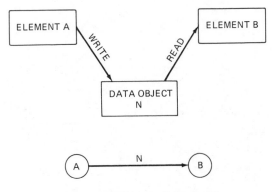

Figure 5-2. Data Dependency Graph.

ing the data dependencies, because it at least lists the intended properties and usage of every data object in the system. Integration is a nightmare without a data dictionary.

The first step in obtaining a data dependency graph is to find out what data objects an element calls and whether that call is a read or a write. A read call can only affect paths within the calling element, but the object itself is not changed.* A write call must be assumed to have modified the object, and can therefore cause interactions with other elements—with any element that makes a read access. The ideal tool for this purpose starts with the element identity and establishes all the direct read and write accesses made by that element. It then augments this by all the accesses made by subelements and so on until the lowest-level element is reached.

A different data dependency graph is needed, in principle, for every object referenced. If subelement A writes to an object and subelement B reads that object, then the data dependency graph shows an arrow from A to B (Figure 5-2). Alternatively, a combined graph that annotates the link between A and B by all the object names that cause a data dependency can be used. Note that the data dependency path between elements A and B can be indirect, as when a subelement of A writes to an object, which is then read by a subelement of B.

The ideal tool for this purpose does not exist, and in any case would be limited to static analysis. However you obtain it, a necessary preparation to integration testing is to have a complete listing of how the elements affect one another (static analysis) through the data base.

---

*Not strictly true. Some systems may modify an object as a result of a read operation. For example, a floating point process (hardware or software) that renormalizes the number on every read.

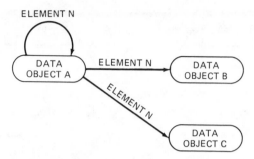

Figure 5-3. Process Dependency of Data Objects.

3.1.3. Process Dependency Graph

We can turn the whole thing inside out and consider how objects in the data base are transformed by processes (Figure 5-3). Object A is read by element N and transformed by it. It also, by processing, causes potential modification to objects B and C. Determining such relations, while possible, tends to be severely incomplete when restricted to static analysis. Furthermore, the resulting graph tends to show that all objects are dependent on one another via the action of all elements. It can be useful in limited cases, when the object in question is transformed in a relatively simple way by the action of several elements that operate on it in sequence. For example, the history of an entire data block, a transaction control block, or a queue block.

3.1.4. Interface Standards and Interfaces

Every interface between elements should be controlled by, and documented in, an interface control document. This can be part of a data dictionary or part of the system documentation for that element. Furthermore, every interface must follow relatively inflexible interface standards. The interface standards cover:

1. What kinds of items are to be passed implicitly in the data base and which are to be passed in a calling sequence.
2. Ordering of object by type within a call—for example, all inputs before all outputs, control before data, local data before global data, and so on. The rules themselves aren't as important as the fact that rules exist.
3. Format of the calling element—hex for control, decimal for numerical values, octal for bits—again the convention doesn't matter as long as some convention is followed.
4. Who validates the inputs—the caller, the called, both, neither, and under what circumstances?

5. What kind of resources are to be used for parts of the call when parameters are passed indirectly by reference? Is this based on the number of parameters to be passed, or the type of parameter passed?
6. Rules governing the use of call by value and call by name. That is, is the parameter's value to be passed, in which case the parameter itself is not changed, or is its name to be passed, in which case the called routine could modify it.
7. Call syntax rules—some languages allow a call to be made in several different ways—with a fixed or variable number of parameters; a subelement can be simultaneously a subprogram or a subroutine, with different call methods; different call types can occur in assembly language, and so on.

The interface to an element should be detailed in that element's documentation. It is assumed that any caller of that element will follow the interface rules for that element and that any violation thereof constitutes a bug. It's not possible to design and test a system in which subelement interface conventions are left to the individual programmers: it leads to a proliferation of ad hoc interfaces. Higher levels of integration are usually done by integration test teams that may not include any of the subelements' programmers. Ad hoc interfaces make it impossible to tell at a glance if the interface code is correct or not. The integrators must go back to the documentation of both elements each time, assuming that such documentation exists. Undisciplined interface design also further broadens the scope for bugs. The result is that the debugger has too many feasible hypotheses to deal with, and consequently the search for a bug's cause is prolonged. Rigid interface standards limit the type of bugs that can occur at interfaces and thereby increase the probability that a hypothesized cause will be correct.

3.2. What to Test

3.2.1. Object Compatibility

Object Range. Every object in the data base can be considered as if it were a binary number. The source element can produce objects that fall within defined numerical limits. The destination element expects to receive numbers that fall within other limits. The range of the source must be included in the range of the destination—see Figure 5-4. Tests consist of finding values that set the source output to the extremes of the source range, and to any excluded values within that range.
Type Compatibility. Every object has a type such as binary, BCD, alphanumerical, floating point, and so on. In addition to the built-in types provided by the hardware or the language, there are user-defined types. For example,

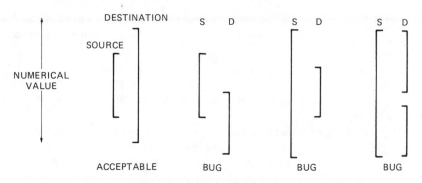

Figure 5-4. Source/Destination Range Compatibility Bugs.

a given number might represent a priority, a security, or another kind of category. Every type difference between source and destination is a potential bug. Strongly typed languages provide automatic facilities for user definition and explicit declarations of object types. Furthermore, type conversions, which may or may not require run-time code, must also be explicitly specified in such languages. These facilities reduce type errors, particularly at interfaces. If such facilities don't exist, then type compatibility between objects must be confirmed and checked manually. The source and destination element's documentation is examined to determine the type. If the types of every object used by both are compatible, then range checks will suffice. If the types are incompatible, then additional tests of the interface should be run, in which the source provides call values which are excluded or meaningless for the real destination.

Representation. The source element assumes a number to be represented in octal, while the destination element assumes it to be in decimal, say. Such representation difference may be converted into an equivalent range check. If the ranges are compatible, then additional checks, such as the source providing a decimal 89 to a destination that expects octal, can be used to test representation compatibility.

Number of Parameters. This applies to calls in which some of the source parameters are in an explicit calling sequence. The number of parameters must match. If the destination element can accept a variable number of parameters in the call, then the range of the number of parameters provided by the source must be compared to the range of the number of parameters expected by the destination. If the ranges are incompatible (e.g., source can deliver 7 to 12 parameters and destination can accept 5 to 9 parameters), then tests must be used that force the number of source parameters outside of the range of the number of parameters acceptable by the destination.

Input/Output Parameters. In calls by reference, the address of the object is passed to the called element. Consequently, the value of that object may be changed as a result of the call. The fact that the intention is to read the object rather than to modify it is, in the presence of bugs, no assurance that it has not been inadvertently modified. Similarly, the same parameter could be used for input and output, as in FORTRAN. If the called element (and the element it in turn calls) is not supposed to modify a parameter, and if input and output are shared, then explicit tests are required to confirm the fact that no modification took place.

Object Order. The source may provide the objects in variable order, and the destination may be able to accept the objects in variable orders. This can be done through the action of one or more control parameters in the call that dictate the format used. Each alternate format must be tested to assure that the order of the parameters in the call is correct.

Method of Transfer. Parameters can be transferred in different direct and indirect ways. Values can be transferred by reference or as actual values. The transfer can be via memory, via resources, registers, cache memory, the data base, accumulators, and so on. Compatibility of the way in which the parameter is transferred must be confirmed for every call. In many languages (higher order or assembly) the different methods of transfer may be a matter of only one or two characters in the source statement. Multiple levels of indirection can be used so that it is possible to confuse the address of the address of an object with, say, the object's address.

Variable Element Name in a Call. A call can either directly or indirectly include an element name. For example, a control parameter directs the called element to execute one of several different subroutines based on the transferred value. As another example, the symbolic element name (e.g., a subroutine) is transferred directly as part of the call. Because the called routine can be called from several different places, one call may not allow all possibilities. The set of subroutines that can occur in the call must be a subset of the subroutine names that can be accepted by the called routine. This fact must be confirmed by tests.

3.2.2. Call Graph Cover

The call graph of an element is generated based on static analysis and consequently does not neccessarily represent the entire call graph as actually programmed, even if there are no bugs. An element cannot be considered integrated until every path in its real, dynamic, call graph has been explored under test. As with path testing, this consists of two parts:

1. Every element in the tree has been called on some path in the call graph.
2. Every called element has been called by all possible callers.

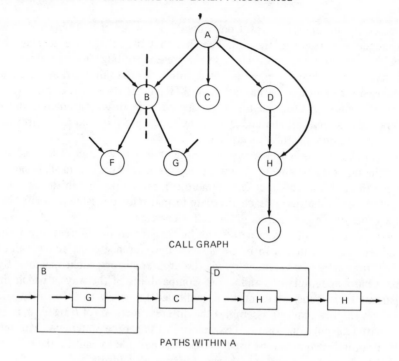

CALL GRAPH

PATHS WITHIN A

Figure 5-5. Call Graph Testing and Cover.

Figure 5-5 shows a segment of a call graph for element A which is being integrated with B, C, D, F, G, H, and I. Element A calls G indirectly via B. Elements B, F, G, and H are also called by other elements, not shown in this portion of the call graph. A test based on the integration of A exercises a B call, but not all the B calls. Similarly, calling B in a test does not test the F call because in the context of A, F is not called at all. In testing the H calls, not only must the direct call of H by A be exercised, but values that force the indirect call of H via D must also be used. Elements such as B, F, and H cannot be considered successfully integrated until *all* links in all the call graphs that lead to them have been tested. If proper path testing is done for all elements at all levels, and path coverage is provided, then when all calling elements have been tested, all calls to a routine such as B will have also been tested and **call graph cover** will have been achieved. However, it is not possible to assert on the basis of one element's test, or a few elements' tests, that B's call graph has been covered. This should be more a matter of record keeping than anything else. If cross-reference lists can be provided that show each call to the element (static calls, that is) then there is a basis to monitor call graph coverage as integration proceeds.

3.2.3. Multi-Entry and Multi-Exit Routines

Multi-entry and multi-exit routines complicate integration testing, and that's sufficient reason to avoid them. It's better to implement multi-entry routines as single-entry routines with a control parameter in the call that internally directs the routine to the proper point. Similarly, multi-exit routines are better implemented as single-exit routines with an exit parameter.

Each entry point of a multi-entry routine should be treated as if it were a totally separate element. This is the safe, worst-case approach. Produce a separate call graph for each entry and provide call graph coverage for each entry, or do separate record keeping for each entry. Multi-entry subroutines fool us into thinking that because code is shared, the same routine is being tested. Element-level testing for the multi-entry and/or the multi-exit routine should have provided complete path cover for every path from every entry to every exit (i.e., testing a routine with three entries and four exits is equivalent to testing twelve routines). If these have been confirmed under test, then integration testing is still needed to show that the right entry has been selected in each call. This is often a source of bugs.

Multi-exit routines are more troublesome than multi-entry routines. Typically, only one or two of the possible exits in a multi-exit routine are valid for any given call. Each exit, then, operationally makes the routine behave as if it is a different routine in which only a subset of the possible paths are correct. Figure 5-6 shows the general situation. Element A has a single entrance and can be called either by element X or Y. It has three exits, labeled 1, 2, and 3. Exits 1 and 2 are valid for the X call and 2 and 3 are valid for the Y call. We really have two different routines, A and A'. Element-level testing of A should have also confirmed that only exits 1 and 2 were taken for the input values corresponding to an X call and that only exits 2 and 3 could be taken for the input values corresponding to a Y call. Unfortunately, when A was unit tested, say, it was not known which calls would be made, by which element, and with which range of values. Consequently, if such tests have not been made at the element level, they must be done during integration testing.

Multi-exit routines have their place, particularly for handling illogical con-

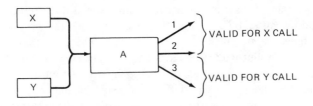

Figure 5-6. Invalid Paths in a Multi-Exit Routine.

ditions or other catastrophic situations. The routine has the normal exit and the exception or illogical exit. Several different error exits might be provided depending on the severity of the illogical condition detected. These exits may totally bypass the normal return paths either by direct jumps to the exception condition handler, or more drastically, by changes in priority level or partition—e.g., a jump that involves a level change from user mode to executive mode. Such paths must also be exercised as part of integration testing.

3.3. Data Corruption and Residues

3.3.1. Residues

An element operates on data which resides in a global data base, in registers, in locations specified by the call, or in main and mass memory resources. The element must also use storage areas for itself. Let's use the word "memory" in this context to mean any kind of memory, from cache to disc—this will avoid a lot of extra words in the following discussion. The element may be free to corrupt the contents of some locations and has no burden to restore what had been in there at the beginning of the call. Other locations must have the same content at the return that they had at the entry. It is incumbent on the element to safely store such locations and to restore their content prior to exit. This is a common source of errors. The element does not properly restore disturbed locations. Often this happens because the restoration is done on what is assumed to be a common exit path, but in reality there are sneak paths which can bypass the restoration process. A clear specification of what locations are apt to be destroyed should be part of the element's specification, and this should be confirmed by element-level tests—that is, not only are correct outputs produced, but no data are inadvertently destroyed that must not be destroyed. It's relatively easy to check this in element-level testing for things such as registers or unique data areas in memory. However, if the object is a dynamically allocated resource, the fact that it was corrupted may not be determinable except in higher-level testing.

If you know that memory is being modified and should be restored, then it's relatively easy to confirm this fact. Instrumentation and halts can be installed and the locations of interest confirmed as unchanged upon return. Data corruption can be caused by bugs, and there's no hint that this occurs. For example, eight flags are stored in a single character. The programmer intends to clear the one flag, but inadvertently does so by clearing the entire character. Similarly, there is a multiple location clear instruction and the programmer clears more than should be cleared. Element-level tests may not show this problem. Theoretically, we could freeze the system after the return and examine every memory location and confirm their contents. This is not practical. A more reasonable alternative is to create dummy entries in the data base with known contents and to examine their contents after a batch of integration tests have been run. If the contents are modified, then the routines or paths in the routines that may have caused the problem have been localized.

3.3.2. Data Base Integration

There's a tendency to focus on processing element integration, and it's somehow hoped that data structure integration will take care of itself. Just as the integration of elements must proceed in an organized manner, so must the integration of the data-base objects used by those elements. Explicitly passed parameters have been adequately covered in the preceding. Whenever a parameter is indirectly passed via the data base, there is an opportunity for data-base corruption, destroyed values, and unwanted residues.

Data structures can be integrated using the same principles used to integrate program elements: one object at a time. Initially, wherever possible, the unintegrated units communicate with one another by means of explicit statements. For example, A and B are communicating elements that pass a parameter "X" as a value in the data base. Integration of data-base item X proceeds in four steps:

1. A passes the value of X directly to B in the call. B reads the value by an explicit statement inserted for that purpose.
2. A passes the value of X to location Y which is read by B. Location Y is not in the data base. The instructions used to write and read are as close as possible to the eventual instructions.
3. A passes the value of X to B via the data-base structure, but by a controlled and specific object, rather than a general object that might be dynamically allocated.
4. The actual communication process is used.

In FORTRAN or BASIC, for example, this transformation is achieved by delaying the creation of COMMON. Initial testing is done with all data transfers explicit. Only after the elements are successfully integrated from a processing point of view is COMMON created and the transfers made implicit. This should be done a few objects at a time rather than the entire data base at once. Implicit transfers are more bug prone than explicit transfers. Furthermore, explicit transfers are easier to debug, because there's code rather than operations and paths to look at. By making as many transfers explicit as possible in the initial stages of integration, the possibility of data corruption is reduced, but more important, problems that occur after the explicit transfer testing is done and transfers are converted to implicit, can be reasonably ascribed to the method in which the transfer was made implicit.

The penalty for a piecemeal data-base integration is either a proliferation of test data bases or control over the order in which the test data bases will be created and used. The latter is preferred. Different versions of the test data base are produced, starting from a data base with nothing in COMMON and concluding with a fully integrated data base. The entire process is considerably simplified if data access macros are defined and their use enforced. Every data access is done through a defined access macro. In the earlier data-base versions, where everything is not integrated, the macro is modified (for test purposes) to transfer the data directly between the two elements. Later the macro is replaced with a transfer to the parameter passing area that simulates the data base (Step 2), then to a controlled common area (Step 3), and finally the access macros are replaced by the real access macros. Each data-base version, then, has its own corresponding set of macros, and the source code need not be changed as data-base integration proceeds.

3.4. Special Problems

3.4.1. Reentrance

Fully reentrant routines can be interrupted at any point or quit at specified points and the same code be executed again as if the first call had not occurred. The key point of reentrance is that reentrant routines must not have any private data areas. That includes registers, cache areas, or any other locations where data can be stored. Typically, data are stored in a stack (or pointers to data are stored in a stack) so that a unique stack position corresponds to the inter- rupted call. Reentrant elements should be explicitly tested for satisfactory reentrance by use of a driver that will invoke the routine, allow it to proceed to a point, say by means of a timer, and then interrupt it. If this is done in a loop, it can provide satisfactory element-level testing of reentrance. Violations of reentrance rarely occur at the level of the reentrant routine itself. The prob- lem occurs in the subelements called by the reentrant routine. In an assembly language program, for example, written for a machine that has no floating point hardware, there could be two different multiply subroutines—one that guarantees reentrance and one that does not. If at some point, several levels down the call tree, the wrong routine is called, then reentrance may be violated and the higher-level calling routine may work normally, but not when it's reen- tered. The countermeasure to this kind of bug is to create usage conventions that identify what memory locations and/or registers must be presumed destroyed as a result of each subroutine's operation. Furthermore, every routine must be labeled as reentrant or non-reentrant. A reentrant routine that has non-reentrant subroutines in its call tree must be treated with suspicion. Reen- trant subroutines can be counted upon to destroy that which they claim to destroy and to protect that which they claim not to be destroyed. If this has been verified at every level of the integration process, then higher level reentrancy can be assumed with confidence.

3.4.2. Interrupts

Most complicated systems have interrupts. The programmer cannot assume that a program will be uniquely and continuously executed. This can be assumed only if interrupts are blocked and unblocked for those parts of the processing that require unique access. For example, a reentrant routine must block interrupts while it is saving the values required to guarantee reentrance. Most systems employ at least two distinct priority levels, and many have 7, 8 or more priority levels. Say that the hardware provides 8 levels, with level 1 the highest and level 8 the lowest priority. The element in question operates at level 5. At critical points in its operation it may block interrupts from level 3 down, say. At other times, any level higher than 5 is allowed to interrupt the routine. A routine then can be classified as to whether or not it's interruptable and from what level. An interruptable routine can be resumed at the interrupted point, but a non-interruptable routine must be restarted if interrupted. Reentrant routines are typically interruptable.

The integration problem caused by interrupts is an almost infinite increase in the number of possible paths. *Every instruction in every routine can be considered as if it is followed by a jump to every possible routine that can interrupt it.* The return is not necessarily to the next instruction in the interrupted routine, nor can the interrupting routine be counted on (because of bugs) to leave the interrupted routine's data and registers unharmed. Furthermore, the interrupting routine may itself be interrupted, compounding the problem. Usually, protecting the interrupted routine's registers is a task accomplished by the interrupting routine—but it can have bugs.

3.4.3. Background Testing

There is no practical way to consider the vast proliferation of additional paths that can be created through the action of interrupts. There is no practical way to test all the conditions in which reentrance could be violated or compromised. But the difficulty must be recognized, as is the fact that an element successfully integrated in the absence of interrupts may or may not work when interrupts are allowed. Similarly, a routine tested for reentrance in a quasi-static, uniprocessing environment may or may not prove reentrant in the more realistic and more dynamic real environment. Initial integration testing should be conducted without allowing interrupts and without raising issues of reentrancy. Once satisfactory operation has been demonstrated in this context, retesting can be done—in fact, the element level tests should be repeated under a background load that simulates the system's actual operation.

The action of interrupts makes element integration at best conditional, and therefore element acceptance is also conditional. In principle, it would be necessary to redo all element level testing with background transactions running to be sure that the element works correctly. In practice, this is impractical: typically, only elements such as executive routines, resource allocation routines, and other global routines, will be reconfirmed in the more complicated, realistic environment.*

4. INTEGRATION STRATEGY

4.1 Objectives

Integration starts when there are two or more units to integrate and ends only when the system is ready for system level testing. There's really no sharp dividing line between integration and system testing. You're integrating when you're trying to put elements together and show that they're compatible. You're system or element testing when you take a set of integrated elements and show that they do what they're supposed to do and don't do anything that they shouldn't do. The ultimate objective of integration is a working system. However, there is an important intermediate objective which should dictate integration strategy. *The best possible test tool is a working system.* It's easier to test a modification to a working system than to test that modification in a simulated environment. The working system provides the means of creating and/or accepting inputs, recording results, and producing outputs. When augmented with instrumentation for data logging, halts, and manual interventions not built in to the system, a truly flexible test tool results. Therefore, the intermediate objective of integration should be to achieve enough of a working system to facilitate subsequent integration and testing. This partial system, the **backbone**, has the following facilities:

1. Method for entering test data, manually or automatically—terminal interfaces.
2. Output terminals and devices for observing and recording outcomes.
3. Allocation and de-allocation of memory resources.

---

*Real-time multiprocessing systems pass through three distinct points during testing. You hold the first, small party when a transaction finally makes its way through from input to output. The big bash that marks the *beginning* of system testing is held only after the system simultaneously processes two or more transactions. I've been to more first parties than second parties. Some systems never make it there. The last party comes after acceptance, but that's usually a letdown. It's the second party that counts.

4. Read/write access to files, file creation.
5. Event recording or logging.
6. Operator or run controls.

4.2. Top-Down Integration and Testing

4.2.1. The Pure Method

Each of the integration strategies presented are to some extent based on myths regarding what bugs dominate the system. In pure **top-down testing** and integration, there is no unit testing as such. Integration starts with the topmost element, which is tested as would be a unit. All called subelements are simulated by **stubs**, which are simplified programs designed to provide the response (or a response) that would be provided by the real subelement. When the equivalent of unit testing has been done for that top-level element, the stubs of the next level are replaced with the real element, and retesting is done to confirm that the new element is working correctly. This continues one element at a time until the entire system has been integrated and tested.

4.2.2. The Myths

1. *Most bugs are related to control problems. Top-down design limits the complexity at any one level, and therefore top-down integration and testing limits testing complexity.*
   At best 15% of the bugs are related to control problems (see Table 2-1). Many of these would be eliminated by suitable element-level tests at the lower levels. The control problems eliminated and tested by a pure top-down integration strategy are only a few percent of the whole.
2. *Complexity decreases uniformly from top-down. The most complex level is at the top, the least complex is at the bottom.*
   Just plain untrue. A well-designed, modular, table-driven executive is very simple. Complexity typically rises to a peak at about three or four levels down the calling tree and then decreases from there on.
3. *There is a single executive or calling program—the system as a whole is treelike.*
   Not true. Real systems have no single "top," may have multiple executive structures, alternate control programs, and may use elements in a complex way. There may be no single top-down path for testing.
4. *Testing with stubs is easier than with real routines.*
   Only if the stubs are much simpler than the real routines. Then there's the cost of debugging the stubs. Most real programs have data dependencies

which make a correct stub no less complicated than the real routine. Stubs are useful only if trivial or if the schedule forces testing without the real elements.

5. *The system is the best test driver. Top-down testing provides this in short order.*

Partially true. However, how much of the system will have to be tested before it can be used as a test driver? Also, why not use good test driver tools if the real system's not available?

6. *Top-down testing is a natural adjunct to top-down design. If top-down design is used, it follows that testing should be top-down also.*

The only thing they have in common is the word "top-down."* How do we accommodate a pre-existing library of fully tested subroutines? How do we accommodate high-level functional subprograms that only need minor modification? How do we schedule and implement parallel testing? How do we take advantage of unit-level programmers that are soon to be reassigned to another project?

4.2.3. Where to Use It

Does the above diatribe against top-down testing mean that there's no place for it? Decidedly not! Top-down testing can help debug control structures. As a preliminary step to integrating an element, it may pay to use stubs (or better yet, to use the real subelements with paths jumped out) and do initial testing for that element top-down. This will help confirm that there is a control structure (the element being integrated) and that the basic facilities needed to do the rest of that element's integration testing are working correctly. The integration procedure now looks like this:

1. Mechanical integration—compilation, linkage editing, loading.
2. Paths in subelements jumped out or replaced with stubs to reduce testing complexity.
3. Top-down testing of the control structure to the point where the element seems to support integration testing.
4. Subelement interface testing, interface of element to called subelements—replace subelement stubs or modified subelements with real or unmodified subelements one at a time, until all interfaces are verified.
5. Element-level structural and functional testing as appropriate.

---

*The **principle of similarity** is the most important principle in magic, witchcraft, and voodoo. Objects and persons are manipulated through the principle of similarity by performing operations on a facsimile of the object—e.g., by sticking pins in a likeness of the hated person. To say that top-down testing follows from top-down design is to invoke the thaumaturgic principle of similarity to programming.

4.3. Bottom-Up Testing and Integration

4.3.1. The Method

Pure bottom-up testing and integration starts at the bottommost part of the call tree and integrates those elements. The integrated elements are then integrated with new elements, and so on until the topmost level has been successfully integrated and tested. The pure method assumes thorough unit tests and element tests at each integration level.

4.3.2. The Myths

1. *If the pieces are thoroughly tested and carefully integrated, then so must the whole. The whole is equal to the sum of its parts.*
   That's wishful thinking. Bridges don't fall down because of bad steel, but because of bad architecture. Level A may be consistent with B, and B consistent with C; but only in an ideal bug-free world does that imply that level A is consistent with C.*
2. *Complexity increases from bottom to top. Get the simple stuff taken care of and the complicated problems become simple.*
   Bugs don't know if things are simple or complicated.
3. *Once a bug is corrected at the lower level, it remains corrected throughout and up to the topmost level.*
   Would that it were so. The bug may first show at level 17 (the bottom) and be corrected. The correction may be proven wrong at level 8, and be recorrected. Proven wrong again at level 2, showing that the original version was correct *in the first place*, and that it was levels 16, and 9 that were wrong.
4. *Test drivers are easy to build.*
   Not really easier than stubs. It's all a matter of point of view.

4.3.3. When to Use It

Bottom-up testing has several distinct advantages. It allows a maximum amount of flexibility in scheduling and parallel testing. It's a good way to get elements integrated, particularly if the subelements have been subjected to rig-

---

*MFBP chose a strict bottom-up approach to integration. All units were modular and coded in accordance with rigid rules of structured style and were subjected to what they believed was adequate unit testing (path cover wasn't deemed practical or essential). There was no data dictionary. All interfaces were the results of ad hoc agreements between programmers, documented on brown paper bags, if at all. They had modularity, structured code, and bottom-up integration. How could anything go wrong? Testing and integration was assumed to be such a trivial task that an idiot could do it—so they gave the job to QA.

orous element-level tests. It makes incorporating preexisting or modified preexisting code relatively easy. The principal deficiencies are that testing is done in a simulated environment, and control problems or fundamental architectural problems may not surface until late in the game.

4.4. Big-Bang Testing

4.4.1. The Method

In its purest (and vilest) form, **big-bang testing** is no method at all—"Let's fire it up and see if it works!" It doesn't, of course.

4.4.2. The Myths

1. *It's no method at all and never works.*
   If it's no method at all, why does everybody do it? I want all the closet big-bangers of the world to come out and confess. Here's my confession: I *always* big-bang, usually earlier than later, as soon as I've got enough with which to make a bang. This is followed by a lot of little big-bangs (mini-bangs? big-plinks?) as each new element is added. Does everybody do it because they're ignorant and undisciplined or because there's something to it?
2. *Bugs are random, so no integration strategy biased to one class of bugs will help—you might as well start integrating at random, using big-bang.*
   Testing is confusing and bugs are unpredictable—but holding on to that confusion and uncertainty by refusing a disciplined approach in favor of unrestrained big-bang can't reduce the confusion. An optimum test and integration strategy should be bias-free and work well against all bugs.

4.4.3. Where and How to Use It

Unrestrained big-bang at its most ludicrous would avoid all unit testing until all code had been written. Then the whole thing would be compiled and tested in one dramatic pass.*

---

*A programmer and her minions worked for a year and produced four large trays (20,000 FORTRAN source statements) of code. There was no unit testing, no integration, no data dictionary, no documentation, not a hint of how it was supposed to work—just the original specification to which the so-called program had been written. She zapped it through the compiler, got rid of the compile-time syntax errors, announced that the program was done except for routine testing, and quit, taking her dwarfs with her. I was honored with the task of verification testing and getting rid of a "few minor" bugs. What else to do except big-bang? I tried for a week and couldn't even get it to fizzle or pop. So I threw the cards into the wastebasket, in front of the boss, and was immediately fired. He relented. A year later, with the help of ten others, we had a working system.

The act of attempting to compile, link-edit, load, and execute a program is a big-bang act that usually reveals some bugs. These must be fixed before any organized testing begins. The systematic integration tests are based on the assumption that the program works, or at least that it provides some rudimentary test support facilities. You really can't start organized tests until the simple paths run to output—that attempt is also a big-bang act that reveals bugs. In other words, the act of attempting to get the element to the point where it can accept some input, do output, record the results, allow control over the test case and paths, is at the boundary between testing and debugging, and is a form of big-bang testing.

The principal advantage of **restricted big-bang integration** is that an element and most of its subelements are brought to an integrated form very quickly. Much more quickly, say, than if each subelement was integrated one step at a time, one subelement at a time. Big-bang integration, if limited to the objective of bringing the element up to the point where predefined, formal testing can be used, is an efficient and effective use of time.* Note, however, that if a test case has been attempted, successfully, in the context of big-bang, it should nevertheless be repeated under more formal integration and element-level tests.

4.5. An Integration Strategy

Integration proceeds not a single level at a time, but in blocks that encompass several levels, usually identifiable with a system administrative partition such as a subprogram, program subsystem, or system. As usual, the word "element" is to be taken to mean any and all of these. The following strategy applies at all levels and is to some extent repeated as we continue. The overall pattern is bottom-up, but big-bang and top-down are also important components. The strategy is:

**BOTTOM-UP THE SMALL; TOP-DOWN THE CONTROLS;
BIG-BANG THE BACKBONE; AND REFINE.**

1. *Bottom-Up the Small.* Thorough unit testing is essential, if only to reduce the scope of possible bugs and eliminate fruitless bug hypotheses. Unit testing is an archetypal bottom-up technique. Small assemblies of units can be integrated by bottom-up techniques, when the driving control structure is not too complicated.

---

*I don't think I've suggested anything new by advocating restricted big-bang integration. I've merely suggested that programmers continue doing what they've been doing and will be doing, but not to feel guilty about it.

2. *Top-Down the Controls.* Where control structures are complicated (at whatever level, not necessarily the executive), where the element seems to lend itself to state testing, and where stubs are indeed little more than canned responses in predefined locations, use top-down with stubs and then integrate the real elements. Top-down should only extend one or two levels down.

3. *Big-Bang the Backbone.* Define the backbone—that which you need for further testing (input, output, memory management, recording, and control)—and big-bang it after good element-level testing on the backbone's subelements. Trying to compile, link-edit, and load the backbone will reveal many bugs. Fix them.

4. *Test the Backbone.* Do enough structural and functional testing on the backbone to confirm its suitability as a primary test tool. Avoid all paths that could be troublesome if they are not backbone paths.

5. *Integration Testing of the Backbone Elements.* Confirm the backbone elements by integration and interface testing.

6. *Refine the Backbone.* Complete the structural and functional testing of all functions and structures in the backbone. Many paths will not be possible because of missing or unintegrated elements.

7. *Continue Integration/Testing.* Add one or a few related additional elements to the backbone to expand its functionality beyond the raw backbone—put flesh on the backbone. Each new set of functions will require several additional elements, each of which should have gone through prior element-level testing. Add related elements as a group, in a mini-big-bang, debug, do integration testing, then structural and functional testing. Continue refining until the entire element that can be constructed on that backbone is complete. That element is now ready for the next level of integration testing.

5. WHO INTEGRATES?

Integration is the point at which the work of several programmers, programming sections, or programming groups come together. Once successfully integrated and element-level functional and structural testing begins, the element is again under the purview of one programmer or group—the one that wrote the calling program. Integration testing, because it focuses on compatibility issues between elements, is largely structure-independent, and therefore does not require deep and detailed knowledge of how the elements to be integrated work. Integration, because it focuses on compatibility issues between elements, is inherently conflict-ridden. Each party to the incompatibility will righteously and properly assert that theirs was not the misconception that led to the incompatibility that integration testing revealed. The incompatibility exists because human languages are imperfect. The incompatibility exists because we want programmers to use their brains in order to avoid having to spell everything out in detail.

The conflict inherent in integration leads to the need for arbitration, or more efficiently, a third party to act as a mediator. Here, then, is an effective place to employ independent testing and independent test design. This does not mean, however, that the integration is done by QA and structural and functional testing by programming staffs. However, just as the individual programmer has a personal, built-in QA function, each programming section and group should have designated individuals concerned with QA roles, even if not part of a QA department. That QA role can be fixed or variable, and it can change or rotate among all programmers (it's good experience). Staffing and procedures then look like this:

1. Individual programmers (group, section, as appropriate to the element level) do individual element-level tests.
2. A set of elements to be integrated are big-banged to get a working backbone—this job should be done by a good debugger, who may or may not be the calling program's designer.
3. Formal integration test design and integration testing that validates subelement consistency is conducted by the QA entity at that level—it is a form of independent testing.
4. The integrated element is turned over to the element's designer for element-level functional and structural testing.

A variation on a theme of this procedure keeps the element under independent testing longer. We can take advantage of the fact that functional testing does not require deep knowledge of the program's structure.

4a. The integrated element goes through detailed functional testing by the QA entity which also designs the functional tests for that level.
4b. The integrated and functionally tested element is then turned over to the element designer for detailed structural testing.

6. TASKS FOR A QUALITY ASSURANCE DEPARTMENT

1. Define integration testing at each level, stating objectives, what is to be tested and verified, and by whom.
2. Identify the element level at which independent integration and/or functional testing is to be used. For each level, specify the entity that is to design and/or execute the independent tests (e.g., another programmer, section QA, group QA, project QA, independent QA department).

3. Define in detail all aspects of all formal interfaces that must undergo formal integration testing (e.g., range compatibility, type compatibility, and so on).
4. Review project interface standards for completeness, consistency, and effectiveness. Monitor conformance. If there are no interface standards, define them, and create and implement enforcement methods.
5. Create call graphs for all elements. Record call graph cover progress as elements are integrated.
6. Define integration guidelines that specify the extent to which top-down, bottom-up, and big-bang methods are to be used, in what combinations and under what circumstances.
7. Define ground rules for the use of stubs, versus modified real subelements, versus unmodified real subelements, for that part of integration that is to be dominated by top-down methods.
8. Assure the existence of adequate test tools and test drivers for conducting that part of integration that is to be dominated by bottom-up methods.
9. Make the written definition of the backbone part of the specification of element-level integration and testing.

6
SYSTEM TESTING

1. SYNOPSIS

A fully integrated system that has been thoroughly tested at every level is not enough. It represents the halfway mark.

2. WHAT'S LEFT TO TEST?

I defined unit testing in Chapter 4 and stated that the same procedures, the same kind of functional and structural tests, must be done at every level from the lowest-level unit to the entire system. Integration testing was defined as a preparatory step to higher-level element testing aimed at exploring the incompatibilities between the subelements of an element. If all elements from unit to system have been thoroughly tested, functionally and structurally, and no known incompatibilities between elements remain, what then is there left to test at the system level that has not already been tested? Approximately half of the testing and QA effort remains to be expended in the following tests:

1. System-level functional verification by the programming staff and/or QA.
2. Formal acceptance test plan design and execution thereof by the buyer or a designated surrogate.
3. Stress testing—attempting to "break" the system by stressing all of its resources.
4. Load and performance testing—testing to confirm that performance objectives are satisfied.
5. Background testing—retesting under a real load instead of no load—a test of proper multi-programming, multi-tasking systems.
6. Configuration testing—testing to assure that all functions work under all logical/physical device assignment combinations.

7. Recovery testing—testing that the system can recover from hardware and/or software malfunctions without losing data or control.
8. Security testing—testing to confirm that the system's security mechanism is not likely to be breached by illicit users.

System-level functional testing, formal acceptance testing, and stress testing are required for every system. Background testing is required for all systems but the simplest uniprocessing batch systems. Background testing is usually not required (but is desirable) for application programs run under an operating system. Load and performance testing is required for all on-line systems. Configuration testing is required for all systems in which the program can modify the relation between physical and logical devices and all systems in which backup devices and computers are used in the interest of system reliability. Recovery testing is required for all systems in which data integrity despite hardware and/or software failures must be maintained, and for all systems that use backup hardware with automatic switchover to the backup devices. Security testing is required of all systems with external access.

Configuration, recovery, and security testing are discussed in Chapter 7. Stress testing, background testing, and performance testing have many techniques and problems in common and are treated in Chapter 8. The rest of system testing is treated in this chapter.

3. CROSS-REFERENCE CONSTRUCTION

3.1. Objectives

Prior testing at all levels has probably tested every system function not only once but several times. However, all through element-level test and integration, retesting after bug correction is limited to what are perceived to be potential problem areas. It is not practical to go back through all levels of testing in all detail for every change. For this reason alone, a complete system run-through is essential. There's another equally important reason. The system's specification has been changing all through the project's life. The changes are mostly detailed and should not be profound. However, the accumulation of such changes in the functional requirements means that some functions that were tested early are not completely correct at the end of integration. A third reason for doing a system-wide functional test (actually retest) is that the process of designing that test can itself be a major contributor to system quality. Finally, even if the design team has done a thorough and conscientious job of system-level functional testing, every system benefits from an independent verification of functionality. The objectives of system-level functional testing are therefore:

1. Independent verification of the system's functions.
2. Retesting.
3. The test design process as a quality assurance method.

3.2. Specification Cross Reference

3.2.1. What Is It?

The specification cross-reference is an index file that cross-references the entire specification under as many technically meaningful terms as possible. It is a large file, say on a rotary card index that details every aspect of the system's required functions. Specifications are imperfect. They are necessarily linear documents that purport to specify functions that are interconnected in a complicated way. Thus, operator commands, as an example, can legitimately appear under operator commands, interfaces, input error tolerance, the specific operator command (e.g., open file), the command options (e.g., open history file), operator training, and who knows what else. A specification writer takes a point of view with respect to each subject. The subject heading is picked from the point of view of what that writer believes is most important, but many other factors creep in, or may be left unstated. Therefore, any one paragraph such as "operator commands" may also impact other subjects (e.g., file structure). Conversely and coincidentally, any one subject may appear in parts of many specification paragraphs. You could postulate a specification language that would not have these limitations—a language that had built-in cross-reference features that would have each subject appear in only one place. Such a specification would probably be as complicated as the program that would have to be written from it, and even then perfection could not be guaranteed.

A further problem is that the specification is never really frozen. It is actually a statement of intent. If there is cooperation between the builder and the buyer, then they will accommodate each other as the project progresses, to get better functions, remove poorly conceived functions, and eliminate contradictory and unimplementable requirements. It's no good to rail against shifting specifications or to wish for an ideal world with perfect specs. If the buyer could write a perfect spec, then the buyer would probably not need the implementers. The buyer relies on the implementer's expertise and experience to correct the minor contradictions and to produce a system that meets the buyer's intentions rather than the buyer's statement of requirements—"Build what I need, not what I said."

3.2.2. How to Produce It

I can't speak for the rest of the world and can only give my own experience in producing a useful specification cross-reference. I use a personal computer (Hewlett Packard 85) that has a pin-feed printer that can print in a small font. A cross-reference program is used to produce various index cards. The program has the following controls:

1. Increment page number.
2. Increment paragraph number (allowing for multi-point paragraphs such as "3.4.5.6.17a").
3. Change page number.
4. Change paragraph number.
5. Enter subject keys.
6. Enter note.
7. Control to assign the card to a test area or group.

A sample card is shown in Figure 6-1.

The key to the cross-reference is the keys. I allow many keys. They are entered as a sequence of phrases or words separated by slash marks (/). Other controls in the key field create duplicate cards and special cards as discussed in the sequel.

You produce the cross-reference index by reading the specification a line at a time and creating a new entry for each line or paragraph as appropriate. Enter the keys that make sense, and as many keys as make sense, so that all the possible subject headings under which this paragraph might appear are covered. This is a tedious operation. A complete specification cross-reference for a large-scale communication system with a 200-page, single-spaced specification took ten weeks to produce. The result was a 5000-card rotary file.

The program creates, on command, one card for each cyclic permutation of the keys. If there are ten keys, then ten cards will be produced. These are filed alphabetically by subject according to the lead key for that card. This may seem a primitive method to use, when an on-line information storage and retrieval system might be more effective. It is admittedly primitive, but has a high payoff. It proved effective to do completely manually, before a personal computer was available. The rotary card file provides great flexibility and access to any subject area in under two seconds—it takes a powerful computer to provide such rapid access. A more sophisticated on-line information storage and retrieval system that permitted more elegant key structures would be welcome, and would result in even further improvements, but is not necessary.

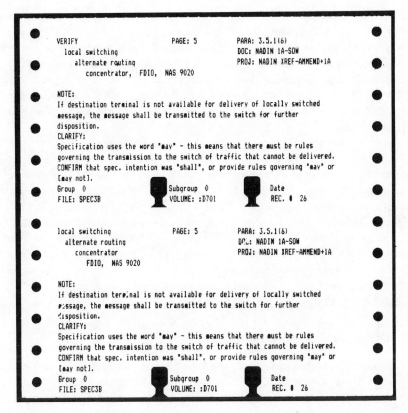

Figure 6-1. Sample Cross-Reference Index Card.

3.2.3. When, by Whom, and for Whom

The specification cross-reference should ideally be started when the project is started—say when the system is proposed to the buyer—and refined as the specification is refined. If that's not possible, then it should be started as early as possible so that maximum benefit will be obtained from it.

The cross-reference should probably not be done by project personnel, but by knowledgeable quality assurance personnel. Doing it this way provides an early, independent, unbiased evaluation of requirements. It can be done by one person if the system is small enough, or by several persons with expertise in different areas for a large system. The advantage of using a computer is that the card formats and structure will be consistent. If several different persons do this job, then it's necessary to create a glossary of keywords. Alternatively, if the entire specification is available in processable form (e.g., on word processor discs) then a keyword extract program can be used to generate the glossary. I don't think it's effective to turn the whole job over to a machine because a machine misses too much. I've found that half the keys are prompted by the meaning of the paragraph, or its intent, but the keys do not even appear in the paragraph. For example, you may realize that a paragraph has implications in operator training, but there may be no appearance of "operator training" in that paragraph.

The cross-reference is a living document and must be updated as the specification changes. In fact, once you have the cross-reference, it can be used to determine the impact of every proposed specification change. At least two copies should be maintained: one for project personnel reference and the other for quality assurance. A third copy, for the buyer, is a politic investment. A cross-reference index of the specification is an essential document that will be referred to again and again through the project's lifetime. It eliminates many arguments over what the spec said where. As a project resource it helps prevent missing functions and features, it helps assure that the functions programmed match the specification, it's an aid to documentation, and it's a great help in acceptance test design.

3.3. Design Documentation Cross-Reference

The same method used to produce the specification cross-reference is used to produce a design documentation cross-reference. This starts with the first preliminary release of the system design overview and continues in ever greater detail as the design progresses. It's done the same way—by reading the design documentation and creating appropriate index entries, with the appropriate keys, as you read. There are some differences though. Whereas the entire specification should be cross-referenced in detail, the same should not be done for the design. Much of the design documentation deals with issues that have no direct functional significance—that is, to internal processes that cut across many functions and which cannot be directly related to any one functional requirement. This is increasingly true as you get into lower-level elements. The design documentation cross-reference should be restricted to those aspects of the design that have fairly direct functional significance. A person who understands the specification (or a section thereof) should incorporate anything read in the design documentation that makes functional sense and ignore anything that appears to be an internal system matter.

The cards produced by this pass should be merged with the specification cross-reference. The result after filing and editing is a combined cross-reference with at least one entry for every pertinent functional requirement that came from the specification and (presumably) at least one corresponding entry that came from the design documentation. The subject list will expand, and in most cases the design documentation will result in additional categories not explicitly specified. Once the two files are merged it is possible to go through the index, subject by subject, to confirm that:

1. Every specified subject is represented in some aspect of the implementation.
2. That which is to be implemented corresponds to that which is specified.
3. That which is to be implemented but not specified does not contradict the specification.

3.4. The Data-Base Cross-Reference

The data base and associated data dictionary is a rich source of test design ideas for independent functional testing. Like so much in testing and quality assurance, the act of doing it is as important as the results of doing it. The data-base cross-reference is a cross-reference of all data objects in the data base, including type, range, and values, for those objects that have reasonably direct functional significance. The majority of objects in the data base are concerned with internal issues and cannot be directly related to functional requirements. A complete cross-reference that included all data-base objects would be unwieldy and very expensive to produce. If the person(s) who creates the data-base cross-reference has previously done the specification and system design cross-reference, then it should not be difficult for her to determine if a given data-base item has or has not direct functional significance.

Details on the construction of the data-base cross-reference and additional information regarding these indexes in general is to be found in *Software Testing Techniques*, Chapter 8—"Data-Base-Driven Test Design" (BEIZ82). It's done the hard way, by reading the data dictionary one structure, one field, one value at a time. Because a reasonably complete data dictionary is prerequisite to this process, it cannot be initiated until the one-third to halfway point in the project's schedule. Every object in the data dictionary is examined, and if it can be related in a direct way to a functional requirement, an entry for that object with appropriate subject keys is created. The entry, as before, contains references back to the data dictionary section or page, with the object's mnemonic taking the place of the paragraph number.

3.5. Expanding and Editing the File

The merger of the cards produced by reading the specification, the design documentation, and the data base results in a master cross-reference index for the entire system. In addition to its obvious use as a working cross-reference, it has several other, equally important benefits.

1. The creator of the index should file the cards herself and edit as she files. There is a distinct advantage to not using a machine or clerk for this process. The act of filing the cards, if the filer reads them at the same time, makes ambiguities and contradictions obvious. If this part of the process were automated or delegated, then you would have to go back through the entire file, subject by subject, to find the contradictions.
2. The file organizes itself into a cohesive and sensible structure for planning system-wide functional testing and/or formal acceptance test.
3. Ideas for tests come into your head as you file and subtleties are revealed.
4. Ambiguous areas that need clarification are revealed.

The basic program (which produced only one card for every subject key specified) was therefore expanded with controls that would allow several other kinds of cards to be produced (in multiple copies) at the same time.

TEST CARDS—A card created whenever an entry triggers an idea for a test. An additional note is added that outlines the test idea. Fields are provided to allocate the subject to a test area.

CLARIFICATION CARDS—A command is used to create additional copies of the entry with the word "CLARIFICATION" on top. These are used whenever an area (in the specification, the design documentation, or data base) needs further clarification. These cards are filed by the name of the person or section most likely to provide the clarification.

WHAT-IF CARDS—These fall between test ideas and clarifications. I call them "what if" cards because they usually start with the phrase, "What if the system is subjected to. . ." Most of these cards are produced to get the designers thinking about particularly subtle or nasty problems.

CONTRADICTION CARDS—Cards that denote a clear-cut contradiction of the specification to itself, the design to itself, or the design to the specification.

TEST ISSUE CARDS—Some functional requirements can be very difficult to test. In some cases, we might not have the slightest idea of how to design a test for the purpose. The test issue cards are used to note such problem areas.

I also use "DON'T KNOW" cards for anything that I can't find a reasonable place for, and "PROCRASTINATION CARDS" for issues that I'm too lazy to resolve at the moment, or for which there are insufficient details for resolution.

As the cards are produced and filed, the index grows and must be edited. A typical system can be broken down into ten to twenty functional areas with five to ten subareas in each area. You start with the specification subjects because maintaining some correspondence with the specification's organization is helpful in convincing the buyer that the specification is being implemented. However, as editing proceeds, some areas become lopsided—either too large or too small. The subjects are rearranged so that each area and subarea are approximately the same size. The number of cards in an area are roughly proportional to the programming and test design effort required for that area. The act of editing the cards also brings clarification cards into conjunction with specification, design, and data-base subject cards. Approximately half of the clarification cards disappear, because the conjunction of information from the several different sources provides the clarification; there's no point in bothering designers with questions you can answer yourself.

3.6. Interviews and Confrontations

3.6.1. Objectives

An independent quality assurance team, under the guise of obtaining information on which to base an independent system functional test or a formal acceptance test, can, if properly prepared, exert a beneficial effect on the system's quality. The act of getting the information needed and following up on that information eliminates far more bugs than the tests produced based on that information. There are overt and covert objectives involved:

OVERT OBJECTIVES

1. Obtain information from the designers on which to base system-level functional tests or a formal acceptance test.
2. Resolve all actual and seeming contradictions of the specification to itself, the design to itself, and the design to the specification.
3. Organize the test plan, design the tests, and cooperate in defining test facilities and test data bases.
4. Point out missing functions, ambiguous functions, or improperly implemented functions.

COVERT OBJECTIVES

1. Perform an informal, private, independent, and continuous review of the design.
2. Get the designers to see and correct ambiguous and contradictory functional areas before they are coded so that testing for such problems is never required.
3. Get the designers to correct internal interface problems and contradictions themselves.

4. Assure that all designers, at all levels, understand the functional requirements and specification that apply to their area and level.
5. Represent the buyer's interest—act as the devil's advocate.
6. Create an informal and private communication channel between all concerned parties that gets issues resolved informally if at all possible.
7. Nudge the design towards a better structure, fortify weak areas, and correct deficiencies through informal and private means rather than formal, public means.

The covert objectives are more important than the overt objectives. Problems are resolved before things get coded, before formal action is required, and long before testing begins. Private and informal methods are more cost-effective than formal and public methods. The question of whether or not the covert objectives should remain QA's secret weapon is interesting. It doesn't matter. I've found that although the programmers, designers, section heads, and such are told in advance what the covert objectives are—as I think they should be—it doesn't really impact the method's effectiveness.

3.6.2. Prerequisites and Climate

The climate and the people that do this interviewing work are crucial. I don't think it can work if QA is handled by a totally external group. It can work for a QA subfunction within the project organization or a closely coupled QA organization within a software development entity. Close cooperation is required, as is an open attitude and a free flow of information. If that climate cannot be achieved, or if QA is viewed as a threat, then this method will be a waste of time.

The key to the method is the interviews conducted, as discussed in the next section. The interviewers must not only be competent with respect to test design and QA, but must also have significant personal design experience in that application. Typically, then, these are intermediate-level design people who are assigned to QA for the duration of the project. They must be competent because they must be respected by the programmers—who are notorious for only respecting their own kind. The people must be level-headed, mature, sensitive, and self-confident, because they will have to examine the work of many other programmers without being judgmental. This is a key point. The interviewers must never overtly express *any* value judgment concerning a design, no matter how bad that design might be. If they do, the informal channel will be broken and that person's effectiveness as an interviewer destroyed. If a bad design is found, then the designer is turned towards a better method by indirect means—by discussing tests that will highlight the design deficiency, for example; by asking the right kind of "dumb" question, and by other indirect means.

3.6.3. The Interviews

Two, possibly three, different interviews are involved. The purpose of the first interview is to obtain a clarification of any questions you might have. The purpose of the second interview is to ask what-if questions, and the purpose of the third interview is to get the material you need to set up a confrontation for contradictions.

The clarification interview is the easiest. I walk into the designer's office and ask him or her my questions, one at a time. I have the cards in my pocket, and a batch of blank cards in another pocket to write new questions on. You'll never know what questions may be raised as a result of this conversation. I conduct the first interview in the designer's office—it's a territorial issue. You are the novice coming to the guru for knowledge. We all like to talk about our work. You can't be harmful if you come in asking, "Please help me understand . . ." This is *not* the time to bring up contradictions and what-if cards. A cooperative designer will give you an answer, an explanation, and will identify further references in the specification or design documentation that will help you understand. However, be careful. Some designers feel that if you don't understand all the gory technical details of their work, then to hell with you. Or they'll point you to some awesome document that would take you months to read. You are trying to relate things back to the functional requirements. If you get bogged down in a morass of technical details, the item's significance is probably internal and technical and the item doesn't relate in a useful way (from a test design point of view) to the functional requirements. You must control the interview so that it doesn't deteriorate into a learned discourse on the implementation. Keep steering back and back again to the functions. As soon as you see that something is not a direct functional issue, put the card in your pocket (you'll tear it up later out of the designer's sight) and go to the next card. Each of these sessions should take about an hour at most. If one person is the key to many areas, it's better to hold several sessions a few days apart than to hit that person for hours at a time.

The second interview is different. This is the what-if interview. I think it's only fair to warn the designers about this one. I drop the stack of "what-if" cards (not more than ten at a time) on the designers' desks when they're not looking or are out of the office. We've established an understanding and some ground rules. Each card concerns a nasty or tricky test case. The designer reads the cards and jots the answers on the back. Most questions, about 90% in a good system, can be answered this way. I check back a few hours later to see if they've been answered. You must be a little bit of a pest in this phase. It's understood that the cards *must* be answered and returned. Here are the kinds of answers you can get and what to do with them.

1. *A satisfactory answer.* Put the card in the test-card file if the issue seems important enough to test. Otherwise, leave the card in the functional file.
2. *No answer.* The issue remains to be answered and will be in the future. It's understood that there should be an approximate date when the issue is to be resolved. Get the date from the designer during the interview. Put it in an open-issue file which you check periodically for resolution.
3. *No answer. No future resolution.* Save the card for the interview.
4. *Unsatisfactory answer.* It seems to contradict the specification. Save the card for the interview.
5. *Contradictory answer.* It contradicts an answer or a statement you've got from another designer. Create contradiction cards and keep this one for the interview.
6. *You don't understand the answer.* Save the card for the interview.

You should have only a half-dozen cards for second interviews, and a few that concern questions that are too complicated to detail on a card. Take the contradiction cards along for this interview also. The first thing to do is to ask for a confirmation of the information on the contradiction cards. If a designer has made a statement for which you know there is a contradiction, don't confront the person with the contradiction just yet. Ask for clarification and confirmation. You'll probably hear something like, "I told you that already."

To which you can reply, "Yes, but I wasn't sure. Please say it again—dumb little me didn't understand it last time around."

You will get the confirmation, so mark the card as confirmed and hold it for the confrontation (discussed in Section 3.6.4). After all the contradictions have been confirmed, you're ready for the business part of the second interview.

You're no longer the meek acolyte seeking knowledge from the guru, but the devil incarnate, come to challenge, hassle, trouble, and destroy. Ask your what-if questions and *demand* satisfactory answers. "Show me how it works!" Force the programmer to cover the missing path in his mind. Push until both of you understand the problem, the issue, and the resolution. But because the designer is more expert than you, expect to "lose" 75% of the time. Expect to be wrong; expect to have raised a tempest in a teapot; expect to have misunderstood often, and don't be bothered by it. If you're usually right, it's an abominable design and probably doesn't need testing to prove it won't work.

The results of the second interview are interesting. Some programmers will thank you (assuming it's one of those 25% of cases when you're right) for having discovered the bug or deficiency. Some will invent a resolution on the spot, and it will hold water, but they'll not give you the satisfaction of letting you know you've caught a bug. Some will clam up and stop talking. And a few, a thankfully small few, will throw you out of their office. Don't be intimidated, give them a few days to cool off, and raise the question again (and again, and again, and again, if necessary). Eventually they'll be convinced that you're not going to give up and they'll come around. In extreme cases, you may have to write an official memorandum concerning a design deficiency. Sometimes the programmer will admit that you're right, but the issue must be resolved at a higher administrative level. Then you may also need an official memo to point out a design deficiency.

Another variation on this game, if you have the right kind of people, is to play the old policeman's game of good guy/bad guy. Good guy asks for information and education as well as confirmation of positions regarding contradictions, from which bad guy constructs the nasty questions. Afterwards good guy can go back and commiserate with the designer. If good guy/bad guy works for you, try switching roles around to keep the design team off guard as to who'll be who the next time. You can match the roles to the personalities involved. A woman may be the best bad guy for a certain man, while for another she would be better in the good guy role. Similarly, a man may work in some ways for a woman, or sex may have nothing to do with it. I use every psychological advantage I can, because all bugs are inherently rooted in the human psyche and you need every trick you can use to exorcise them. Incidentally, don't bother keeping this method a secret from the designers. They eventually catch on to the game, but that doesn't seem to diminish its effectiveness at all.

3.6.4. The Confrontation

You have determined that there is a contradiction in the design or in the minds of two or more programmers. It's time to arrange a confrontation. Time to switch roles again. This time you play the part of a referee—an impartial, incorruptible officiator who does not care how the conflict is resolved as long as it is resolved quickly and correctly. Do it now! Let's say there's a conflict and you've got one designer's version of it and have got it confirmed. Go back to the other designer and get an *immediate* reconfirmation (you've got the cards in your pocket). Get the two of them together as soon as possible. I like to use hallways for this. It's neutral territory. My office is too intimidating, and either designer's office gives one of them an advantage; do it in the halls. The conversation goes, "Bill says . . ., but you, Jane say not. . . . It doesn't seem to matter, from the point of view of functional requirements, which way it goes, and here's the specification reference, which is ambiguous or just doesn't say. I don't care how it's done, but get it done." Stick around long enough to get an answer or to be convinced that they are on their way to a resolution of the conflict. Put the cards with the date of the confrontation and a short statement of the resolution (if any, at that time) into a follow-up file. Follow it up and look for a change in the documentation. Resort to official memos and design deficiency notices only if it seems that the problem has been swept under the rug.

3.6.5. The Resolution

The result of the interviews or confrontations must be:

1. You understand the issue.
2. Both programmers in a conflict understand the issue.
3. A design change that will resolve the issue has been implemented or scheduled for implementation.

Design tests whose difficulty is proportional to the apparent conflict and the effort required to resolve the issue. If it is a simple issue, only simple tests are required, and no special tests are needed if the functional issue is covered elsewhere. If the resolution of the problem was protracted, if it required a lot of agonizing, redesign, memos, or even meetings, test the issue into the ground. Design functional tests that will confirm the proper resolution of the issue. Go over those tests with the designer as a final confirmation of everybody's understanding—especially if it involved a contradiction. Then both designers should confirm that the test will effectively demonstrate the effect.

3.6.6. Scope and Effort

Our model project will last two years and consume 40 man-years of labor. The total effort in independent functional test design and execution will take approximately five man-years. Unit testing, integration testing, and system testing are not included in independent testing but are part of the 40 man-years of effort. Creating the master file and all the cards, editing the file, and setting up for the interviews will take on the order of two to three months for one person. The interviews, resolution of conflicts, and the rest will take an additional three to six man-months but can be divided among various members of the QA test team. The entire game gradually loses effectiveness as project emphasis shifts from design to coding, to unit testing, and to integration testing. After one year on a two-year project, the game's practically useless. Once past the initial round of this kind of testing, you reach a point of diminishing returns, because integration testing will be more efficient at discovering the kind of bug that this kind of testing can discover.

4. SYSTEM FUNCTIONAL TESTING AND ACCEPTANCE TESTING

4.1. Perspective

4.1.1. Similarity and Difference

There's not a whole lot of difference between a final system-wide functional test and a formal acceptance test, and in fact both can be accomplished by the same effort. The differences are more quantitative than qualitative. Furthermore, the formal acceptance test can be a subset of the system functional test. Here are some points of similarity and difference:

1. Both tests must provide a convincing demonstration of the system's functionality in detail, covering the entire specification as well as all functions that were not explicitly specified but are understood in the context of that application.
2. Both should be as independent of the design as possible to guarantee an unbiased point of view.
3. The system functional test is bigger because it must also contend with functions and facilities that were not explicitly specified, and with tests whose necessity is a direct consequence of the design approach rather than a consequence of the specification.
4. Both must be formal in that tests are defined in advance and formal paperwork is required when a test has failed. The acceptance test will be more formal than the system functional test, though.
5. Both tests will have been through a dry run prior to the official run.
6. The formal run of the acceptance test can be held to a predefined schedule and duration. The run of the system-wide functional test cannot be so constrained.
7. They can share common data bases and setups.
8. The test team personnel differ. The system-wide functional test is staffed by design personnel and possibly QA personnel. There is no buyer representation. The formal acceptance test is staffed by QA personnel, design personnel is available for consultation, and there is buyer representation either as direct staff or as witnesses.

Both kinds of tests tend to be large and labor-intensive. If a formal acceptance test is augmented by system tests of interest to the system designers, and if there is reasonable independence, the two tests can be merged, with the formal acceptance test being merely a subset of the final version of the system-level test. There is usually a lot of independence, even if the test is wholly

.designed and run from within the design group, because in the typical project the individuals who programmed the element are unlikely to design or conduct system-level tests aimed at that element. System-level tests are usually run by a test team.

4.1.2. Use of Prototypes

One effective way to get a system into operation and to minimize risk is to develop the system through a set of **prototype systems**. A prototype is a functionally complete subset of a system. That is, it includes all error recovery and exception paths for a system. This is to be contrasted with a backbone, which is enough of a system's functions to permit testing and integration. In prototype design, a subset of the system's functions is scheduled for initial implementation and complete testing. System-level testing of the functions provided by the prototype begins when the prototype has been fully integrated. The prototype is then expanded in stages, functional area by functional area, until the entire system is in operation. A prototype development plan has several advantages:

1. There is early visibility. Buyer confidence is created because the system can be observed to do meaningful work relatively early in the game.
2. If the schedule should slip, it may still be possible to field the prototype as developed to that point, and thereby minimize the impact of the slip.
3. Scheduling and staffing can be managed more effectively. There's less uncertainty and less disruption. Cost is reduced.
4. It's easier to add a new functional area to a working prototype than to get several functional areas in operation simultaneously. Test and design issues are clearer.

There are several disadvantages:

1. The system may never be subjected to a complete, system-wide retest, and therefore some bugs will remain that would have otherwise been caught.
2. Each addition to the prototype results in a changing environment and test data base. Retesting is more uncertain as a result.
3. QA and buyer lose influence and control. This can be prevented if each prototype stage is required to go through a formal test.
4. Early fielding of a partially complete prototype makes subsequent system testing very difficult, and for some kinds of tests (e.g., stress test) impossible. Unless there is a development system available on which to continue testing (as contrasted with off-line or background time on the real system), testing

depth and thoroughness will be compromised for the functions added to the prototype in the field.

5. The buyer, having accepted the prototype, now controls it. All testing therefore becomes public.

4.1.3. Who Designs the Tests?

Three possible parties can design a system-wide functional test or a formal acceptance test: 1) the designers, 2) independent QA, 3) the buyer or a surrogate (e.g., a consulting organization). The real issue is not so much the organizational entity that designs the test, but the degree of real independence the test designers have, and the price paid for that independence. Consider independence on a scale from 1 to 10, with 1 being totally dependent and subservient to the design hierarchy, and 10 completely independent, such as an external consultant that doesn't even have the buyer's biases and axes to grind. An internal QA function that reports directly on project lines but operates in accordance with well-defined and protected independence could be more effective and independent than an external consultant who has been "bought" by a corrupt design organization. Here are some of the consequences of dependence and independence:

1. The dependent test is dominated by structural concerns at the expense of functionality. It may result in a robust, reliable, bug-free system that the buyer hates because it doesn't really address the buyer's problems. The independent test cannot get into design details and therefore is dominated by functional testing, particularly those functions that were explicitly specified. It may well be what the buyer asked for, but not what the buyer needed. What is implemented may not work in areas not explicitly specified, such as robustness, recovery, expandability, maintainability, and so on.
2. The dependent test will be efficient in that coverage will be assured. Independent tests will include tests of many things to no real purpose. Less will be covered, and that which is covered will not be as thorough. Dependent tests can suffer from sins of commission, independent tests from sins of omission.
3. Dependent testers are much more vulnerable to compromise, pressure, coercion, and dishonesty in the interest of short-term goals and superficial contract fulfillment. Independent testers are much easier to fool with "Mickey Mouse" fixes and patches that seem to solve problems but really don't.
4. Application subtleties are better understood by dependent testers. Operational realities are better understood by independent testers and buyers.

These observations are to be taken as tendencies rather than as absolutes. There are some noteworthy exceptions that can reverse these tendencies:

1. If the system is one in a long line of similar systems that have been in operation for a long time, or a replacement for an existing system, the buyer can create a very good functional test based on the experience gained with the system being replaced. Similarly, the buyer can, over the course of several similar systems, develop a good independent test plan which can evolve, system by system, as the systems themselves evolve.
2. The buyer can hire another implementer (e.g., an independent software consultant) to design and execute an independent test. Presumably the consultant knows all the dirty tricks that can be played.* The same can be done in a large organization with several software development groups—one group can be used to test another's system.
3. The independent tester can, by agreement with the builder, have some test personnel participate in the design at various stages. These designers/testers, whose ultimate loyalty is to the buyer, then become the seed of the independent testing cadre. This is a way to infuse the independent test team with the required technical knowledge. The same can be done within a development entity by shifting design personnel over to quality assurance at a later stage in the project.

4.2. The Test Plan

4.2.1. General

There's so much in common between a formal system functional test plan and a formal acceptance test plan that they can be discussed simultaneously. The acceptance test plan is the more formal document, and will therefore be used as a basis for discussion. A formal test plan document must be produced. Although most of QA's benefits resulted from the act of creating the test plan

---

*This is a good ploy to use if outright dishonesty is suspected. The buyer in such cases is often disdained by the builder (perhaps correctly) as ignorant or naive. If the buyer is wise, he will not correct that perception and will keep the expert consultant totally in the background, not letting the unscrupulous designers know that there are "big guns" at work. If things are that bad, the consultant can do the job based only on tangible, documented evidence and need not personally participate in face-to-face confrontations with the designers. The pretense of ingenuousness works well for supposedly naive buyers, who don't remain really naive for long. As for dirty tricks, I've found that when things are that bad, the designer may actually expend more effort, ingenuity, and creativity in attempting to cover things up than would have been required to do the job correctly. It's not unusual for the consultant to learn a whole bunch of new and dirtier tricks. In such instances, the real purpose of the effort is, unfortunately, data gathering in support of impending litigation.

rather than from the act of executing it, without formal documentation and structure there cannot be any formal testing. The document itself is massive—for our model project, about four to five thousand sheets. Lest this be considered excessive, it should be compared to the system documentation, including design documents, code listings, cross references, and data dictionary, which should be of the order of ten times larger than that. The following organization is suggested as a starting point:

SECTION A—General and Introductory
    A1—Generalized verbiage and introduction to the test plan documents.
    A2—Glossary of terms used.
    A3—Reference list to specifications, subsidiary specifications, design memoranda, correspondence, and so on.
    A4—Test design standards and conventions.
    A5—Test running order, procedures, summary sheets, and control sheets.

SECTION B—Test Data Base and Code
    B1—General.
    B2—Test data base documentation and cross-reference. One subsection for each variant data base.
    B3—Support programs or code documentation for test data generators, drivers, and load generators.
    B4—Test configuration specification. Specification of hardware and software configurations needed for different tests.
    B5—Test tools hardware and software.
    B6—Verification hardware and software.
    B7—Miscellaneous support hardware and software used to generate and execute the test.

SECTION C—The actual test specifications.

4.2.2. Section A—General

The A section is generalized and can usually be adapted from previous test plans by outright copying and/or modification. Once you've created the first one, the next test plan is that much easier to develop.

    A2—*Glossary.* Most systems have their own vocabulary. Different organizations working on the same problem may use different terms to mean the same thing. The test plan documentation must be understood by designers, QA, and the buyer. A printed glossary helps avoid a lot of useless debate and misconceptions.

A3—*References.* The specification is not a complete document in itself. It may refer to other specifications and standards. Furthermore, there are pertinent correspondence and agreements, minutes of meetings, approved changes of scope, and so on that modify or contradict the original specification. The test plan documentation should include sufficient references to all such sources so that conflicting opinions over functions can be quickly resolved.

A4—*Test Design Standards and Conventions.* The test plan is a formal document no less structured than code. If there are coding standards, there should be comparable test plan standards and conventions. These cover the structure and content of every test input or scenario. In communications system testing, as an example, we include rules for the construction of message addresses, sources, date and time, and every character of text. One of the standards makes every message unique, and where possible the message text itself identifies the test area, the purpose, and intended outcome. Similar rules and conventions cover the construction of the data base, allocation and naming of terminals, allocation of resources, test scope, input method, verification methods, and so on.

A5—*Test Control.* While the test plan may be a linear document that starts with test group C1 and ends with group C20, because different data bases and configurations are needed, it is not possible to guarantee that the entire plan can be executed in the documented order. Furthermore, discovered flaws, the need for retesting, or schedule or personnel problems may force changes in the running order. Test control documents are needed to specify the running order of the test, and to monitor progress and status of what could be a few thousand subtests.

4.2.3. Section B—Data Base and Code

A complete test plan can rarely be executed using a single data base and a single setup. Each such data base and setup must be documented as formally as the real system's data base. In addition to the data base, there may be many hardware and software tools, or software modifications that are used to support testing. Each of these must also be documented, either directly or by reference.

B2—*Data Base(s) Documentation.* The number of test data bases should be minimized because each variant data base must be tested and debugged. Variant data bases are used when 1) there is no other way to create the condition needed by the test, 2) when test execution time would be excessive under the normal data base, 3) when test design can be simplified or made more effective by using a special data base, 4) when inadequate hardware resources (e.g., memory) does not permit testing all features at their extreme points under a single data base.

B3—*Support Software Documentation.* Special programs may be written for generating transactions or load. Alternatively, a pre-existing load generator with parameters set for the test may be employed. All such code or specifications must be documented either directly or by reference as part of the test plan documentation.

B4—*Test Configuration.* The test bed may be a superset of actual installations for multi-site systems or may be a subset of an ultimate configuration which is not fully implemented in the test bed. Either of these situations means that there is more than one hardware configuration to deal with. Similarly, there may be several different operating systems under which an application system is to run. Each such hardware/software test configuration must be defined and documented in detail.

B5—*Test Tools Hardware and Software.* Documentation of all specialized test tool software and hardware not covered elsewhere. Directly if unique to this test plan, indirectly by reference with an appropriate specification of controlling parameters if pre-existing hardware and/or software is used.

B6—*Verification Hardware and Software.* Some aspects of testing, such as performance testing, may require specialized hardware and/or software for verification. Specially installed instrumentation software or hardware used to confirm transaction flow paths, or off-line historical or log analyzers may be used. All such hardware and software must be documented directly or by reference.

B7—*Miscellaneous Support Hardware and Software.* A catch-all for anything not covered in the above categories. For example, program patches or modifications that are used to abet testing if they are used in more than one test area.

4.3. Section C—The Tests

4.3.1. Structure and Scope

Over the course of several different test plans, we've evolved to a four-tier organization of the tests into the following scheme: **group, subgroup, test,** and **subtest.** A three-level heirarchy proved too limiting and resulted in too many tests in any one area. A five-level hierarchy was clumsy and had too much redundant paperwork and controls. The following characteristics apply to each level.

GROUP—The broadest functional subdivision of the system. A typical system will have ten to twenty test groups, some of which are discussed in Section 4.3.2. below. A typical test group might be the hardware configuration group, which tests all the variant hardware configurations.

SUBGROUP—A functional subdivision of the group which can be designed and executed independently of any other subgroup. For example, a configuration test that shows that any disc drive can serve in any functional capacity would be covered under the rotation test subgroup.

TEST—A test is a subdivision of a subgroup that contains one or more subtests. Every subtest in a test, in addition to covering closely related functional areas, shares the same setup, terminals, verification method, and data base with every other subtest in that test. In principle, once a test has been set up, its component subtests can be run through mechanically.

SUBTEST—The smallest division of the test plan. A relatively microscopic subdivision that includes a detailed specification of inputs and outcomes. In principle, each subtest has exactly one input and one outcome. A subtest is indivisible. When a subtest consists of several steps, the entire subtest must be repeated from the beginning for it to make sense. If the system fails any part of a subtest, the entire subtest must be repeated.

As an example, operator commands form a group. Configuration commands are a subgroup. Each configuration command is subjected to three tests: 1) command syntax errors, 2) command field value errors, and 3) command functions. Each command syntax error test has one subtest for each syntax error possible for that command.

4.3.2. Sample Groups

The following groups can be applied to most real-time, on-line systems that have automatic switchover to standby hardware in the event of failures.

STARTUP AND INITIALIZATION—Tests of the system's ability to be bootstrapped into a workable hardware/software configuration. All steps leading to a hardware/software complex capable of accepting commands and inputs. If there are several different configurations of hardware and software, each may require its own startup and initialization tests. All hardware is confirmed as being in the right state, and all tables in the data base are confirmed as loaded with the correct data. Remote loading of remote hardware subsystems is also tested in this group. This is a natural first group to execute.

OPERATOR COMMANDS—Tests of all operator commands from the point of view of syntax error tolerance, data input error tolerance, robustness, terminal initiating the command, and the functions to be performed by the command. There's a lot of flexibility in this area because it may prove more effective to test some operator commands in the context of the functional areas to which they apply. This is a natural second group of tests.

CONFIGURATION CONTROL—All operator commands and automatic features used to change the physical/logical relation between hardware components. Placing hardware subsystems on-line, off-line, automatic reaction to hardware failures, excepting the CPU, assignment of functions (e.g., files) to devices, and so on.

INTERFACES AND PROTOCOLS—It's an on-line system that communicates with specialized and generalized terminals via telecommunications links. All such interfaces operate under a protocol (e.g., free running, polled, duplex, half-duplex). Every such interface and protocol must be tested in detail.

RESTART—Tests of the system's ability to automatically restart when confronted with software-detected illogical conditions that permit restart and do not require a switchover. Tests of transaction and data base integrity despite the restart.

SWITCHOVER AND RECOVERY—Tests of the system's proper response and switchover to standby hardware for simulated failures that force a switchover. Test of operator commands that force a switchover to the standby. Confirmation that transactions are neither lost nor created as a result of the switchover (as required by the specification).

PERFORMANCE TESTING—Validation that the system meets all specified performance requirements with respect to throughput, delay, number of simultaneous transactions in progress, and whatever else may be part of a quantitative performance specification.

STRESS TESTING—Demonstration that the system can operate reliably at the limits of each of its resources.

TERMINAL MANAGEMENT—Tests that confirm the system's ability to put terminals into and out of service, to change terminal characteristics, restrictions, and capabilities.

OFF-LINE DATA-BASE GENERATOR—Where a special-purpose off-line data-base generator has been constructed, this group tests the generator's ability to create a valid data base from the source data provided to it. Tests of all source syntax errors, data value errors, and data correlation errors.

ON-LINE TABLE CHANGES—Where part of the data base must be modifiable on-line without interrupting the system's operation (except for the affected terminals, say) this group tests all operator commands, command restrictions, preconditions, errors and illogical commands, and whatever else is needed to confirm that such changes can be safely made on-line without compromising the system's integrity or data.

SECURITY TESTING—Whatever testing not covered elsewhere that may be needed to demonstrate the system's invulnerability to deliberate coercion or control by external sources. Tests of passwords, password change mechanisms, security kernel tests, and so on.

These groups must be expanded or contracted in accordance with the system's functional requirements. Many of these groups disappear for software systems that operate under a pre-existing operating system: the operating system should have been through all of these tests at some point in its life. In communications, for example, user terminal interfaces and protocols are expanded into several groups, with each group corresponding to a class of related protocols. Input tolerance disappears and is replaced by message format testing groups. Most of configuration testing is reduced to trivia in an unduplexed system and greatly expanded for a multi-computer complex. Restart may be totally subsumed under switchover and recovery, or vice-versa if there is no standby processor to switch to.

4.3.3. How Many Subtests?

Our model system will be subjected to a final acceptance test that consists of 1500 to 2500 subtests. It's better to aim for more subtests than can be reasonably run in the initial part of test plan design than to aim for fewer. Under this rule, the initial aim is to specify 3000 to 4000 subtests. These are developed top-down, starting with group, subgroup, test, and subtest. At first, the subtests are merely numbered, listed, and defined in one or two sentences. It's easy to list a lot of subtests this way. Later, these must be culled down to a more reasonable number because each subtest must be documented, inputs must be created, data-base objects specified, the subtest must be tested, and so on. Just listing proposed subtests and publishing them makes the design team aware of what is to be tested. Reading the list of subtests for a functional area will motivate the designers to examine their programs with those subtests in mind. The greatest part of the benefit has been obtained at that point.

The subtests must be culled for practical reasons of budget and schedule, but also because many of them are redundant. It's easier to specify too many subtests and to cull the redundant ones before there is any heavy labor investment in them than it is to continually coordinate the test designers.

4.3.4. Test Sheets

Each subtest is documented on a self-contained test sheet and its extensions. The test sheet is the control document for the subtest. It should contain the following information:

1. GROUP, SUBGROUP, TEST, SUBTEST identifier number and text.
2. Date released, date tested, date formally executed.
3. Status—pass/fail/scheduled for retest.
4. A brief statement of the subtest's objectives.
5. Initial conditions and setup.
6. Data base and configuration reference.
7. Specification references and/or design documentation references which this test is intended to confirm.
8. Special operating instructions (e.g., necessary patches).
9. Detailed (character by character, keystroke by keystroke) specification of the inputs.
10. Detailed specification of all outcomes.
11. Method of verifying the outcome (e.g., observe the output at terminal X, audit the data base, examine the history file).

I found that the subtest itself should be labeled as an error condition or a normal condition subtest. This prevents confusion. In the heat of testing, it's possible to get confused as to whether or not a specific subtest is supposed to result in an input rejection or acceptance. Much of the testing consists of hurling junk at the system. The system properly rejects the input, but we forget that it was supposed to. Valuable time is then wasted chasing nonproblems. Marking each subtest as normal/abnormal action circumvents this problem.

4.3.5. Productivity and Planning

Assuming that the test designers know the application and have experience in test design, the average productivity is approximately two to five complete subtests per day. This includes necessary research, interviews with programmers, subtests that were culled and not completed, subtest documentation, test data base design, test debugging, and dry run of the entire test plan. Treat each test with its component subtests as equivalent to a subroutine. Each subgroup is like a program, and each group is like a subsystem. The productivity varies enormously over different types of tests. For example, input format validation, syntax and field value errors, or operator command syntax and field value errors go very quickly. Ten complete subtests per day is not unusual. Furthermore, for a given input format or operator command, the number of tests can

GROUP _____OF_____
TEST   _____OF_____
SUBTEST _____OF_____
PAGE   _____OF_____
REVISION_____

SPECIFICATION REF._____

VALID ACTION TEST _____
INVALID ACTION TEST_____

TEST DESCRIPTION _____

SUBTEST DESCRIPTION_____

SUBTEST OBJECTIVES_____

SETUP_____

INPUT SPECIFICATION, MESSAGE, OR REFERENCE(S)_____

EXPECTED OUTPUT(S), SPECIFICATION, MESSAGE, OR REFERENCE(S)_____

RELEASE / /   FIRST RUN / /   FORMAL RUN / /   STATUS   PASS/ FAIL
RETEST / /   _____

Figure 6-2. A Sample Test Sheet.

be doubled and the total labor will increase only 20% to 30%. Conversely, almost any test that involves file management and related error conditions tends to go very slowly. Files must be structured, debugged, initialized, loaded with prepared contents, and so on. One or two tests per week for this area is reasonable. With experience, you learn to estimate the number of subtests required for each area, and to predict expected productivity, just as you've learned to estimate the number of lines of code and their difficulty. The detailed estimates of the number of subtests aren't much better than similar estimates of lines of code, but because the test plan is subdivided into relatively small segments, the average tends to be reasonably accurate.

The entire test plan must be designed. The design should be top-down, starting with group definition and subgroups within groups. This is best done after the cross-references are done. With groups and subgroups defined, groups can be assigned to test designers. Their first task will be to outline the individual tests in each subgroup. Tests and subtests are numbered by 10's to allow subsequent insertion of additional tests. At the first stage, each test is described by a single sentence or a one-line title, and an estimate of the number of subtests in each test. This outline is reviewed and discussed. Then the total number of proposed subtests is counted. This is usually two to three times what will be needed. It is usually possible to spot redundant tests at this stage. Redundant tests come about because it is easier to specify them than it is to coordinate the test designers at that level of detail. A test designer working on file management, say, may well specify tests for related operator commands and device assignments which are also covered in the operator command group and in the configuration group. I like to put the entire test plan outline (groups, subgroups, tests) on a rotary card file, with one card per test. The cards can be easily rearranged, duplications and holes spotted, groups and subgroups redefined, and so on. The resulting outline with an explanation for each test group and subgroup is then documented and distributed to all concerned parties (test designers, project management, and buyer). This is the official outline, but it will still contain more tests than should be implemented. The groups are returned to the test designers, who then expand the test definitions and provide a one-line description of each subtest. This is done subgroup by subgroup, or group by group. A major part of the chief test designer's work is to coordinate the individual test designers, to cull redundant tests, and to prevent any one group or subgroup from getting out of balance.* The next round of culling will

---

*There always seems to be trouble with culling. You can say it over and over again, but the buyer always seems suspicious when you cull redundant tests, especially if the redundancy isn't obvious. It's important to make this principle clear—that the test plan will be developed through a series of planned cuts that will bring the total down to the projected 1500 to 2000, or whatever is appropriate. It's interesting, though, that the same persons who argued against the cuts are all for them when the test is actually run.

occur after the subtests have been documented in detail, but before the effort required to prepare inputs, to debug them, and so on has been expended.

Planning and control is as for any other multi-person technical job, such as programming. You monitor progress at the group and subgroup level, number of tests designed, documented, inputs prepared, data-base definitions made, tested and debugged, and dry run, using the usual charts and graphs for the purpose.

4.4. Execution

4.4.1. The Dry Run

An acceptance test plan is a formal procedure which often has legal and contractual implications—for example, the builder doesn't get paid until the acceptance test has been run. There are two phases to running the test plan: the dry run and the real run. Bits and pieces of the dry run have been executed as individual subtests were tried and debugged. When a subtest demonstrated a bug's existence, the software was modified and the subtest rerun to confirm the validity of the fix. Similarly when a test bug is discovered. In either instance, there is rarely time to do regression testing of all other areas that might be affected. A smart buyer expects that the entire test plan will have been rehearsed and dry run prior to formal run, and a smart builder should accommodate those expectations because:

1. The test plan is complicated: rehearsal is essential to prevent cockpit problems.
2. The dry run is yet another form of regression testing and will usually show up some bugs in the system or in the tests.
3. A formal acceptance test is an expensive procedure and is usually staffed more heavily than the dry run. Wherever it's done, a lot of people are tied up for two to three weeks, with attendant hotel bills and per diem.
4. There will be witnesses present during parts of the test who have little or no experience with the system and who may get the wrong impression over harmless slipups and test errors.
5. There will be more than enough slip-ups despite the rehearsals to make the actual run realistic enough for the most suspicious critic.

4.4.2. Staffing

The key persons on the staff are the test director and the customer's counterpart—the chief witness. Here is the rest of the test staff:

TEST DIRECTOR—A high-level test designer with a congenial personality who doesn't panic easily. Emphasis on calmness under pressure, and a thorough knowledge of all requirements. This should typically be the number-two person on the test plan development team: the one who did all the hard work.

ASSISTANT TEST DIRECTOR—An essential person who must be developed along with the test director. The test director's job can be a strain and he needs relief. Furthermore, you can't let a big complicated test come to a halt because someone is sick.

CONFIGURATION MANAGER—Keeps track of all the data bases to be used, does the hardware and data-base setup for each group or subgroup of tests, monitors terminal and equipment status, acts as liaison with hardware service personnel, coordinates remotely located terminals and test sites.

RECORDER—Keeps track of all paperwork, test and subtest status, schedules retests, finds the right paragraph in the specification, and most important of all, carries the cross-reference rotary file on the airplane to the test site.

TECHNICAL SUPPORT—At least two, but perhaps more, individuals from the design team who can between them understand and/or explain, and/or correct any deficiencies discovered during the run. Individuals who can take dumps and who can communicate with design personnel to solve problems (possibly by telephone) as they turn up. This support can be effectively provided by the individuals on the design staff who will supervise the system's cutover to live operation after formal testing is done.

CHIEF WITNESS—The test director's counterpart on the buyer's side. The chief witness could have been present at and perhaps participated in the dry run. An unflappable person is also good in this role. This is the buyer's main representative and should have the power to accept or reject a test or subtest.

ASSISTANT CHIEF WITNESS—For the same reasons that an assistant test director is needed. If there's reason to have hostility, it's politic to let the assistant chief witness do it.

CO-RECORDER—The recorder's counterpart on the buyer's side. Every subtest passed and action taken should be countersigned by the co-recorder.

CHIEF OPERATOR—This person takes an operational point of view. The chief operator should have been tracking the system and test development all through, so there should be relatively few surprises. It's effective and politic if as many as possible of the operator actions are executed by the buyer's operator. Everybody has more confidence as a result.

ASSISTANT OPERATORS—Terminals must be manned, remote site staffed, inputs inserted and witnessed at many different places. Assistant operators should be drawn equally from the builder's and buyer's staff. The builder's technical support personnel can double in this capacity, because when they're needed for technical reasons there's no testing going on and when testing is in progress there's no need for their expertise.

The most important thing about all these people is that they be knowledgeable in their area of concern. The next most important thing is that they not be excitable, hostile, or defensive.

4.4.3. Staging

Let's face it, if the test plan has been dry run and rehearsed, then its execution is a ritual and should be accorded all the respect due any somber ritual. Therefore, in addition to the purely technical aspects of designing and running a test, attention must be given to the dramatic and subjective aspects of that run—the **staging**. The ritual doesn't prove anything objective, but recall that the purpose of the test is to be a suitably convincing demonstration that the system works as intended and not a proof. Therefore, the conduct of the ritual must leave all parties with the belief (assuming that the belief is warranted) that the system works. Let's take the same design, a good design, and run it under two different environments:

The test doesn't run smoothly. There are a lot of cockpit errors, and time and again testing is halted to explain away some apparent, but unreal problem. Schedules are not adhered to. There are no breaks, and everybody works long hours alternated with standing around with nothing to do. The witnesses are hostile and the builder's staff is defensive. The system is perceived as a lousy system, and the buyer will be forever convinced that it is so.

The test team is well rehearsed. They know exactly which terminal to use for what. There is a prepared agenda and schedule for every day of the test. All supporting documentation is available as needed. Team members are not only competent, but they look and act confident and competent. If bugs are claimed, the claim is recorded and verification testing is scheduled. Time has been left in the schedule for breaks and for such follow-up and retest activities. The whole thing comes off very smoothly. The buyer accepts the few bugs or problems that were discovered and is convinced that the design staff will correct the deficiencies. There's a positive feeling for this system that will remain throughout its operational life.

Staging is paying attention to a lot of little things, such as:

1. Every piece of code, every data-base structure, table, and file is backed up in triplicate* and is preferably available on two different media (e.g., magnetic tape and removable disc pack).
2. An adequate supply of printer and terminal paper has been ordered and delivered—at least twice as much as anybody expects to use. Printers are checked twice daily for adequate paper and refilled during lunch times and other breaks.
3. There's an adequate supply of printer and terminal ribbons, cartridges, type heads, daisy wheels, and any other consumable supplies.
4. Wherever possible, all inputs are prepared in advance on paper tape, magnetic cartridges, floppy discs, and so on. All are available in triplicate. Each is clearly labeled as to group, subgroup, test, and subtest, and color coded if possible.
5. Test scenarios that must be executed by persons at terminals or control consoles are preprinted using a large legible font. A master copy of all such test directions sheets (the **score**) is available, and several copies as well.
6. Library suppliers have magnetic labels used for identifying book stacks. These are about 2cm by 10cm and will attach to any steel surface. There are never enough terminals available to have one terminal for each functional role. The functional assignment of most terminals must be altered as testing progresses. Furthermore, terminal failures are common and the physical terminal used for a given set of tests may have to be changed. By using a preprinted magnetically attached label** for all functional changes of terminal assignments, such changes can be taken in stride. If the lettering is neat and legible (use a label maker), the witness can glance around the test site and immediately identify the functional role of each terminal. The same technique can be used for shifting functional assignments for tape transports, disc drives, computers, printers, and so on.
7. All system documentation, especially test plan documentation, is available on-site, at least in duplicate.
8. A portfolio that defines everything needed at every test position for each day is prepared in advance. Think of it as having a conductor's master score, with additional scores for every instrument in the orchestra.

---

*How many times have you destroyed both the primary and its backup while creating a new backup? More times than I care to admit.
**So when we got there, we found that the site's test terminals were later models that had plastic cases to which the magnetic labels wouldn't stick. We bought steel self-adhesive tape at a local auto supply store to solve that "sticky" problem.

9. There are adequate communications facilities for reaching the design staff. You can't conduct a test if there isn't a telephone with direct outside lines available and you have to go through an operator for each call.
10. There are adequate bookshelves, file cabinets, and storage cabinets to hold all the stuff. Furthermore, they all have locks.*

4.4.4. Orchestration

The formal run should be planned like a concert or a symphony. The test director sits on a high stool with the master score and calls out the moves. Every position is staffed, and everyone has his or her own score. The order in which the test groups are run must be based on a reasonable pace, must provide interesting interludes alternating with dull ones. Here are some concepts to use in **orchestrating** the tests.

1. An off-line data-base generator program (if part of the test plan) can create a lot of printer activity, especially if the group is dominated (as it should be) by source syntax errors and data-base definition goofs. There's nothing as dramatic as starting the testing with something that will get printers going, tapes rocking, and discs shrilling. Everybody likes that kind of movement.
2. Most parts of the test are very, very dull and may have no obvious visible outcome. We are all primitive savages at heart and can more readily believe a tangible outcome such as printed output, terminal chatter, and so on than an intangible hypothetical setting of some bits in a hypothetical memory location. Alternate dull tests with physically active tests.
3. Schedule the routine stuff that everybody knows must be plowed through, and that nobody expects to fail, immediately after lunch. Schedule the important stuff for about ten in the morning so that even the late risers won't miss it.
4. Schedule those things which you perceive to be the buyer's primary concern as early as reasonable—get the fears and anxiety over with earlier rather than later—but save something for the end.
5. Invite the buyer to submit their own tests and make room in the schedule for them. It's better if their tests are run intermixed with yours than if they're run later. That way, the orchestration remains under your control.

---

*A communication system installed in a North African country had the main site about two kilometers away from the line termination frame. The two sites were connected underground by a large, expensive, multi-conductor cable. The dry run ran fine, but the night before the formal test was due to start, the Arabs dug up and stole the cable.

6. Leave blocks of time available for breaks, for new setups, for ad-lib tests, and for rerunning tests that have to be rerun for whatever reason.

7. Don't schedule more than six hours of testing on any one day—that's an exhausting pace after the third or fourth day. Don't schedule second-shift or weekend testing—everybody hates it and the system as a consequence. Try to break early on Friday afternoons—everybody appreciates it.

8. Make all corrections, data-base modifications, patches, fixes, or anything else needed to correct bona fide system or test bugs that somehow slipped through all previous testing, during the second shift and at night. Just because the buyer's going to get a good night's sleep doesn't mean you will. Try to have all real and supposed problems resolved by the following morning.

9. Get partial sign-off on each subtest and continue testing even if a subtest has been failed. Similarly for tests within a subgroup and subgroups within a group. Don't allow the process to grind to a halt over a few inconsequential subtests—keep the momentum up—but be sure to resolve all issues as soon as practical.

4.4.5. Conclusion and Celebration

There cannot be a satisfactory conclusion unless there is concurrence as to what the conclusion of the formal acceptance test means. Sometimes the disparity in the buyer's and builder's understanding doesn't surface until after the test is finished: then the system won't be accepted and ill feelings towards it will abound. It must be understood that completion of the acceptance test, with a predefined (small) percentage of unpassed subtests, is a satisfactory basis for acceptance. The principle that *if every subtest of a test has been passed, then the test has been passed* must be understood and accepted by all. Similarly for the relation between tests and subgroups, subgroups and groups, and groups and the system. The buyer should have agreed that the proposed test is an adequate test, and all objections to it should have been resolved before the formal testing started. One condition which has been at times forced on the builder is totally unacceptable: the buyer insists that if an error is found, then the entire test must be rerun from the beginning. This is an appropriate position for hardware reliability and environmental testing, but is unrealistic for most software testing. If there is a sensible operational reason for that kind of a test, then that test should be done separately, and only after the main part of the formal acceptance test has been run and satisfactorily concluded. The number of outstanding, unpassed subtests allowed should be small—certainly less than one percent of the total (e.g., 10 to 20 subtests). Acceptance should be acknowledged even if all 20 subtests are in 20 different groups. If all of these conditions have been documented and agreed to in advance, then the satisfactory conclusion of the formal test is obvious and a celebration is justified (the outstanding problems, must of course be corrected).

The celebration (say dinner for all at a good local restaurant) is part of the ritual and should not be omitted. True, the builder and the buyer have been through a lot of work and need and deserve to unwind. But more important, it's a way to seal the (hopefully) positive feelings towards the system that the successful acceptance test has engendered—feelings that will result in a better, smoothly operating system in the future, as builder and buyer cooperate to remove the bugs that inevitably slipped through all previous testing.

5. TASKS FOR A QUALITY ASSURANCE DEPARTMENT

1. Design and/or acquire the tools that will be used to create and maintain the specification, design, and data-base cross-reference indexes. Establish the creation of the indexes as part of the QA function for each project.
2. Establish a standard for terminology glossaries. Create a glossary for each project and get concurrence on it from designers, QA, and the buyer.
3. Examine the master cross-reference to: assure the designer's intent to comply with the specification; determine ambiguities and contradictions in the specification, the design, and the data base with one another and within each.
4. Establish an informal review/interview procedure based on the master cross-reference. Get concurrence with management regarding the overt and covert objectives of this activity.
5. Select and train individuals with design experience who are inherently good at interviews and can avoid being judgmental.
6. Nudge the designers towards a better system by the studied use of threatened tests. Bolster weak areas by proposing many tests which will lead the designer to a self-realization of the weakness. Allocate interview time not only in proportion to the perceived complexity of an area, but in proportion to the perceived weakness of the design. Use indirect and informal methods rather than direct criticism and formal deficiency reports whenever possible.
7. Make sure that management understands, approves, appreciates, and rewards the accomplishments of the indirect methods used.
8. Define beforehand, for each project, who is to design and execute the system-wide functional test and the formal acceptance test. Obtain prior agreement on the extent to which the two test design efforts can be merged or must be separated.
9. Design and adopt a standard for the formal system test or acceptance test

plan document. Define all permanent sections and their contents, define test design standards and conventions, test data-base standards and conventions, all necessary forms for summary sheets, test sheets, input preparation and definition, status reports, and so on.

10. Identify all test tools (hardware and software) that will be used, that must be modified, or that must be acquired for the project. Include sufficient time in the schedule and sufficient cost in the budget to obtain the working tools.

11. Propose to centralize the acquisition, modification, and development of test tools under QA in order to reduce the incidence of redesign of tools for one project after another and in order to build a library of increasingly more sophisticated and effective tools over the course of several projects.

12. Establish a hierarchy of tests, such as: group, subgroup, test, and subtest. Define a sufficiently broad set of groups and subgroups to cut across all projects. Develop first- and second-level outlines (subgroup, test) for all groups to form a skeleton on which subsequent acceptance tests or system tests can be based. Refine this outline, project by project, to eventually construct a library of test plans from which the bulk of any test plan can be started. Just as the designers try to save code from one project to the next, try to save tests.

13. For each project, do labor and cost projections for the system test and/or the acceptance test, based on the final number of subtests to be implemented. Get management concurrence up front that there is sufficient time and money to design and conduct the test, and concurrence from the buyer that a test of the proposed scope is adequate. Establish the principle of selective, successive culling as test development proceeds.

14. Define formal test staffing as early as possible, identifying the necessary participation from the design staff, from QA, and from the buyer. Acquire all necessary consumable supplies and other resources and facilities and get them to the test site. Ask for twice as many terminals as you think you need, which is four times what you'll be offered.

15. Get the principle of incremental sign-off at the subtest level, and conditional system acceptance after a specified percentage of all subtests have been successfully run, accepted as the basis for the successful conclusion of the test.

16. Rehearse the entire formal test at least once, preferably twice, before the formal run.

17. Prepare all test documentation, scripts, scores, and associated paperwork in advance and in triplicate. Be sure there is adequate backup for all files and programs.

18. Pay attention to orchestration, staging, and celebration.

7

CONFIGURATION, RECOVERY, AND SECURITY TESTING

1. SYNOPSIS

The testing discussed in this chapter does not usually apply to software written as application packages designed to run under a commercial operating system, but does apply to the testing of that operating system. This testing applies to most embedded and dedicated systems, particularly those that have automatic switchover to redundant hardware in the event of failures. It also applies to on-line systems that communicate with remote user terminals.

2. CONFIGURATION TESTING

2.1. What Is It?

Figure 7-1 is a functional block diagram of the FAA's Weather Message Switching Center in Kansas City, produced by North American Phillips. This center handles a large variety of aviation and weather messages gathered from many sources and distributes those messages to several thousand terminals throughout the United States and its possessions. The system was designed to operate 24 hours a day, 365 days a year and has more than achieved its target failure rate of less than one outage in ten years. While five different functional computers are shown, any one of the five physical computers can serve in any of the five functional roles. Furthermore, only two of the five computers must be working for the system to fulfill its primary mission. The assignment of functions to different physical computers is dynamic and changes from time to time as computers fail and are repaired. A similar scheme is used for tapes, moving head discs, fixed head discs, and other devices. The hardware elements interconnect by means of a configuration switching network.

A more typical example is shown in Figure 7-2. All critical devices are at least duplicated. There are two sets of front-end terminations, any one set of

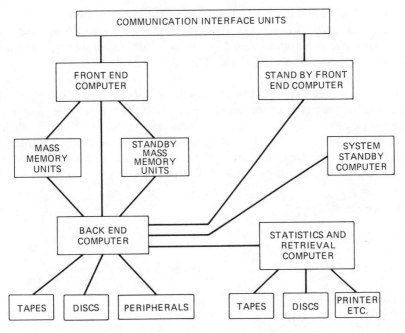

Figure 7-1. FAA WMSC Multi-Computer Complex.

which can handle all the terminals. There are two CPU's and two device controllers for each kind of device. Discs, for example, are doubly connected to two buses and can communicate with either CPU via either controller. Similarly for tapes. A viable, fully working configuration might consist of one front-end complex, a CPU, three discs, and five tapes. The lines shown connecting

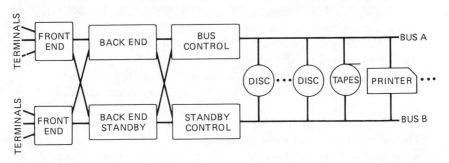

Figure 7-2. Typical Duplexed System.

the devices indicate the potential connections that can be achieved through the configuration switching networks. If N devices of a given type are required, the system is typically equipped with $N+1$ or $N+2$ devices of that type to allow continued operation despite failures. The system has at least two operational states—working and failed—but may have more. For example, the system's design might allow all functions to be accomplished with only one available disc unit, but the performance might depend on the number of units that were operating on-line. There are too many variations possible to discuss in depth from the point of view of design. More design information can be obtained in BEIZ71. Our immediate concern is the testing of configuration capabilities, which to a great extent is design detail independent.

2.2. System States

2.2.1. Device States

At any instant of time, a device can be in any of the following states:

1. Working and on-line.
2. Working and off-line.
3. Working and in standby.
4. Failed off-line.
5. Failed on-line.
6. Failed and in standby.

A state graph for one device is shown in Figure 7-3. The dashed lines indicate transitions that will occur automatically, while the solid lines indicate transitions that can be initiated by operator commands. This is a typical state graph because many variations are possible:

1. There may be several different functional modes—i.e., different ways of working on-line. For example, a disc unit could be used for historical recording, or for storing system files and programs.
2. There may be several different kinds of standby, either for each functional role, or a common standby for all functional roles.
3. There may be working, off-line operational states of different kinds.
4. Other transitions, either automatic or manual, may be incorporated.

For the purpose of analysis and testing, a device is considered as failed or DOWN if it is not available for use either by the on-line system or for some other defined role such as standby or off-line processing. For example, if the

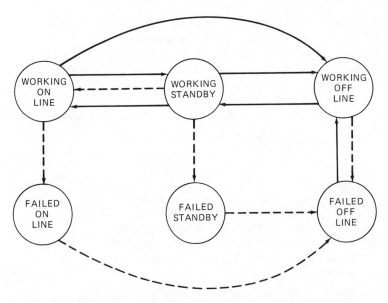

Figure 7-3. State Graph of UP/DOWN States of a Device.

device is undergoing testing by maintenance, even though it has not actually failed, it is DOWN as far as the system is concerned.

2.2.2. Device Type States and System States

At any instant of time, the system has a number of devices of each kind UP and the rest of those devices are DOWN. To a first order approximation, the states of the system with respect to any one device can be depicted by Figure 7-4. Actually it's more complicated, because one should really take into account the device's functional role, how many are in which role, the number of different standby options, and the number of different off-line options. In

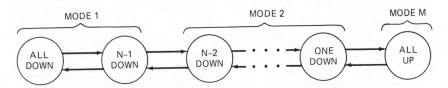

Figure 7-4. Multiple Device UP/DOWN States and Modes.

practice, the usual concern is with the number of devices UP versus DOWN. The probability of N devices UP can be calculated by:

$$P_i = \frac{MTBF_i}{MTBF_i + MTTR_i} \qquad Q_i = \frac{MTTR_i}{MTBF_i + MTTR_i}$$

$$P_i(k;n) = \frac{n!}{(n-k)!\,k!}\,P_i^k Q_i^{n-k}$$

$$P_i(k,m;n) = \sum_{s=k}^{m} P_i^k(s;m)$$

where:

P_i = Probability that a device of type i is up.
Q_i = Probability that a device of type i is down.
$MTBF_i$ = Mean time between failure for device type i.
$MTTR_i$ = Mean time to repair for device type i.
$P_i(k;n)$ = The probability that k out of n devices of type i are up.
$P_i(k,m;n)$ = The probability that k to m devices of type i are up.

The system has different operational modes depending on how many of a given device are UP. The above expressions are used to calculate the probability that the system is in one of the specified operational modes. The **system state** is defined by the number of each type of device which is UP or DOWN, and the probability that a system is in a particular state is given by the product of the probabilities of the device states, or:

$$P_x = \prod_{i=1}^{m} P_i(k_i, m_i; n_i)$$

where k_i, m_i, and n_i define the range of UP devices and the total number of devices of type i for state X.

For more details on how to calculate system states, the mean time in each state, and the expected performance including the failures and restorals of devices, see BEIZ71.

When we take into account the device states and their possible functional assignments, the combination of assignments possible for each device type, and furthermore the combination of device types, the total number of possible system states is astronomical. A system such as the WMSC has of the order of 10^{50} states. A relatively simple duplexed system could have of the order of 10^{10} states. State coverage would require us not only to test the system in each state, but to test all transitions between states—a clearly impossible prescription. States can be grouped in accordance with the system's performance in that state. For example, it doesn't really matter (or shouldn't, if there are no bugs) which tapes are UP and which are DOWN, and in some sense all states with say five tapes UP are equivalent if configuration switching provides complete, unbiased, interchangeability. If we can, by testing, confirm that only the count of UP/DOWN matters rather than the specific device that are UP or DOWN, then the total number of states that must be considered have been reduced by several orders of magnitude—still too large to handle, but better. If by further testing we can show that it is possible to treat each device's failure modes separately from the failure modes of other devices, then the number is reduced by several more orders of magnitude. By making a sufficient number of assumptions of this kind, and by executing tests that confirm the validity of those assumptions, or *by redesigning the system so that the assumptions are valid,* the total number of states and tests can be reduced to a practical level.

2.2.3. Strategy

The following strategy is used:

1. Confirm the operability of all configuration changing commands.
2. Show that all interchangeable devices are really interchangeable so that subsequent testing is based only on the number of devices which are UP or DOWN and not which specific devices are UP or DOWN.
3. Repeat the above tests for all device types.
4. Select representative states that correspond to each identifiable performance level and confirm the system's operability in each representative state.
5. Do additional testing, if possible, such that the sum of the probability of the states tested exceeds the required system availability.

2.3. Configuration Command Tests

The solid lines of Figure 7-3 showed the configuration changes that could be made by operator commands. Each such transition must be tested. Actually it's a bit more complicated, because the command may be allowed or forbidden depending on the number of devices of that type that are UP in that system state. It may also depend on the state of other devices. For example, although there is a command to take a disc, say from the working on-line state to the standby state, this command may be permitted only if there are four or more discs on-line. Most properly designed systems will not execute a command that would cause the system to crash. Or if allowed, then special confirmation procedures will be invoked that are not required in other states. Another way to look at this is to say that there is not a single state graph for Figure 7-3, but many, and each of them must be tested for all transition causing commands.

Testing that the proper transition occurred (or was forbidden) is only the start. What must be shown is not just that the transition occurred, but that it occurred without disturbing the system's operation: that the transition was made without compromising ongoing transactions. This does not mean that there will be no pause in processing the transactions, or even that the transaction will not be lost. The concept of "disturbing" or "compromising" is application dependent. For example, in telephone systems it is permitted to "lose" a call for which dialing has been started up to the point where the called party picks up the receiver; but it is not permissible to lose a call once it has been successfully connected. In some process control systems it may be permissible to lose or duplicate some input and/or output control signals, but not others. In telecommunications systems, loss of incoming packets or duplication of outgoing packets is allowed, but the loss or duplication of complete messages for which the system has accepted responsibility is not permitted. To verify that transaction compromise does not occur, all configuration tests should be run with active background transactions, set at near stress level loads. Test design consists of:

1. Design all syntax and field value error tests as for any other operator command, taking into account that permissible field values may depend on the system's state.
2. For each hardware device type, draw all the appropriate state transition graphs (one for each pertinent system state), or if possible one graph for all pertinent states, showing which commands can force which transitions for that device type.
3. Find a reliable method (e.g., operator commands) for getting the system into each interesting state. If the necessary commands are lacking, then augment the operator command set to allow you to get into any system states. Such commands can be disabled later.*
4. Full coverage, both positive and negative, must be shown for all device states and transitions. That is, show not only that allowed commands in a given state work, but that disallowed commands are rejected without harm.

For each command and transition tested, confirm that:

1. The correct transition occurred, by confirming the state of the devices that participated in the transition.

---

*We always install special commands to simulate equipment failures and to force switchovers. Such commands must, of course, be removed before the system is commissioned.

2. No incorrect transition occurred.
3. The device that came on-line was properly initialized.
4. The device that came on-line is working.
5. No active transactions were compromised.

This last item may be difficult to confirm and may require extensive off-line processing of historical records and logs. Typically, the confirmation is done by processing historical records for a batch of tests. If a compromise is detected, and if the execution of the tests was tightly controlled, then it is possible to bracket the tests that were executed when the compromise occurred. The tests must then be rerun (typically one test at a time, with all subtests in that test) and confirmed one at a time, to find which command actually caused the compromise.

2.4. Rotation and Permutation Tests

Every physical device in the system has three identities: a physical identity (the number painted on the cabinet), a logical identity (the number by which the device is accessed), and a functional identity. Logical and physical identity may be identical in simple systems, but in most systems the relation between physical and logical device identity can be modified. Whether the logical/physical relation is modifiable or not, the functional/logical relation is always changeable in a system that permits configuration changes. The objective of **rotation** and **permutation tests** is to show that every physical/logical and every logical/physical permutation works for every device. Let's clarify this by an example (see Figure 7-5). Say that there are three tape stations whose physical

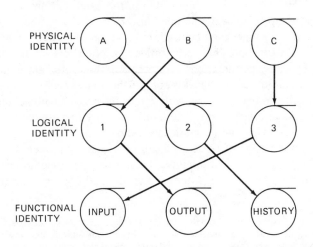

Figure 7-5. Physical, Logical, and Functional Device Identity Permutations.

names are "A," "B," and "C." Furthermore, the logical identity of the three can be changed by instruction to any of "1," "2," and "3."Logical tape units can furthermore be used for input, output, and history, say. There are rules that specify the number of different logical and functional units. For example, the system rules might be that the physical/logical permutations of A, B, C into 1, 2, and 3 must be **one-one**. That is, there must always be one and only one logical unit 1, 2, and 3. A different set of rules governs the relation between logical and functional position. The proper operation of all of these must be confirmed separately for the physical/logical transitions (if any) and for the logical/functional transitions. If the system is simple, and there are only physical/functional permutations to contend with, and while the job is considerably simplified, it's complicated nevertheless.

The most common bug in this area arises as follows. The programmer inadvertently assumes that the on-line computer, say, is always number 1 or that the three functional tape units (input, output, history) are always assigned to physical devices A, B, and C respectively.* It's never as blatant as all that, especially if there's an intermediary physical/logical assumption to contend with. This fallacious assumption tends to bury subtleties, initialization problems, implicit assignments, bootstrapping problems, and so on. If allowed to remain, and if not tested, the system seems to go through a complete acceptance test with honor, and somehow goes through one mysterious crash after another when the operators start using it. These are really bad bugs and, if present, are an operational nightmare.

In principle, it is necessary to test every permutation of a physical/functional assignment, taking into account that there could be permutation restrictions that depend on the system's state. For example, if there is only one tape station available, it must be used for input; if two, for input and output; and only if three or more tapes are available must history be implemented. Furthermore, up to three history tapes may be used, but no more than two input tapes, and so on. The number of possible permutations for N devices is much larger than N factorial because permutations with one, two, three, etc., units out of service must also be considered. Just as it is not possible to test every path in a routine, it is not possible to test every permutation of physical/functional or physical/logical/functional assignments. The equivalent of complete cover is obtained by a series of **rotation** and **permutation tests**.

Insight to the design of these tests can be helped by proper notation. Let's consider the physical/logical assignment tests under the assumption that every assignment must be one-one. Number the physical devices from 0 to N and

---

*It happens out of convenience and habit. The programmer sets up test cases that correspond to a specific assignment and may indeed test other permutations during unit testing. However, another programmer who calls the routine makes the mistake of assuming a fixed physical/logical or logical/functional assignment.

number the logical assignments from 0 to N also. Say that there are 8 devices of a given type. A sequence of integers, such as 01234567, means that logical device 0 is physical device 0, logical device 1 is physical device 1, and so on. Similarly, permutation 13576240 means that logical device 0 is physical device 1, logical device 2 is physical device 3, and so on. Enough tests must be designed and executed to assure that the integers 0 through 7 appear in each position. For four devices, one such set of permutations is clearly 0123, 1230, 2301, and 3012, or a simple set of rotations or cyclic permutations. This is the minimum number required to achieve coverage. Unfortunately, cyclic permutation tests tend to have holes, because the first correction of configuration bugs often takes care of all cyclic permutations, but no others.* The test needed are:

1. A sufficient number of permutations to show that every physical device can operate in every logical identity.
2. Another set of tests to show that every logical device can operate in every functional role.
3. A different set of permutations is potentially required for each system state with respect to that device type. For example, the rules governing tape transport assignment are different for 0, 1-3, 4-7, and 7-15 tapes on-line. A different set of tests must be designed and executed, or the same tests repeated (if appropriate) for each of the four cases.
4. Greater confidence can be obtained by using permutations that are related by pairwise interchanges, such as 0123, 1032, 2301, 3210. This avoids cyclic assignment bugs.
5. Even more confidence can be obtained by including the complement of the permutations in addition to the normal permutations. The complement is obtained by complementing each integer with respect to N, yielding 3210 for 0123. Note that the set of permutations in 4 are self-complementary so no additional permutations are needed.
6. For each configuration permutation tested, confirm by means of a set of standard transactions, with background transactions in operation, that all functional requirements of all functional devices are met.

2.5. Degradation and Restoration Tests

The system has N devices of a given type. At any instant, some of these, say M, are in operation and N-M have failed, are being serviced, or are otherwise

---

*The tests needed for N devices can be determined using the theory of finite groups, which is beyond the scope of this book. In general, complete cover requires of the order of $(2N+1)\log_2 N$ tests, which is excessive for most applications if N is large. For small N, typical of most systems, common sense will provide a solution. For the mathematically inclined, the test set required is the basis of the group. For large N, say 20 or greater, some theoretical treatment is warranted to provide a reasonably irredundant test set that provides coverage.

unavailable. In principle, every configuration state must be examined, and what is worse, every automatic and manually initiated transition from state to state must be considered. Just as all paths cannot be covered, all configuration states and all transitions between them cannot be covered. The total number of states and the transitions between them can be considerably reduced without practical compromise by the following assumptions:

1. Only one device will fail at a time, and the system will stabilize in the new state before the next failure.
2. Restorals occur only one at a time, under control, and from a stable state. A failure will not occur while restoral or initialization of a restored unit is in progress.
3. Operator commands and logical/physical rotation tests have been completely tested, and it is unlikely that configuration action will be sensitive to which device is going up or down.
4. The system state and operation with respect to one kind of device is not materially affected by what happens to another kind of device. For example, tape failures can be treated and tested independently of disc failures.

If the system design or behavior is such that it is not possible to make these assumptions with a clear conscience, *then the best approach to configuration state testing is to redesign the system so that such assumptions are valid.** That course, as drastic as it may seem, is really easier than designing, executing, and confirming all the tests that would be needed, in the absence of these assumptions, to prove that the system is capable of working despite hardware failures. The tests specified are augmented to include a *limited* number of cases which are not bound by the above assumptions. The test design strategy is:

1. Identify, for each device type, the different operational regimes corresponding to the number of available devices of each type.
2. Find different methods for inducing or simulating malfunctions in each device (e.g., pull the plug, special commands, etc.) Design tests that show that the system properly removes the malfunctioning device for each such method. Pick the simplest method for use in these tests.

---

*The probability of simultaneous failures or failures while state transitions are underway is (or should be) very small. The simplest approach to handling such cases is to turn configuration control over to the human operator when such conditions are detected or suspected. Alternatively, in any such situation do an orderly system shut-down. Surprisingly, this approach yields a more reliable system, with a higher availability. The software required for simultaneous and coincident failures is very complicated, large, and bug prone. The bugs avoided by not using the "sophisticated" multi-failure approach have a higher cumulative probability than the sum of the probabilities of failures occurring while a failure is being reacted to.

3. Start with all devices up. Fail one device and show the proper assumption of that device's functions by a standby unit. Restore the failed device and show its proper assumption of a standby role.

4. Repeat the above with fewer and fewer standby units up, so that all configuration states with respect to that device type have been tested.

5. Repeat 3 and 4 above for all device types.

6. Select multiple device type failure states (e.g., some discs and tapes failed) based on availability calculations and the probability of being in the specific configuration states. Pick enough states to cover 99.999% of the system's operational domain.

7. Pick triple-and-higher level failures only if required based on system availability calculations to achieve 99.999% coverage.*

8. Design additional tests to cover failures while restoration is going on, or failures during recovery from failures only if the recovery period for the first failure exceeds a few seconds. For example, if a recovery requires a protracted disc copy, then failures while the disc copy is in progress should also be tested.

9. Design triple simultaneous error states if and only if there is a pressing need, an adequate budget, and sufficient time.

All of these tests require confirmation of transaction integrity. They should all be done under high background load, approaching stress levels.

3. RECOVERY TESTING

3.1. What Is It?

Recovery testing is testing performed to confirm that a system with switchover capability properly resumes processing without transaction compromise following hardware restoral. Systems with automatic recovery must have the following components as hardware or software or as a combination of them:

1. Methods of detecting CPU failures and malfunctions.
2. Removal of the failed CPU.
3. Switchover and initialization of the standby CPU.
4. Records of ongoing transactions and system states that must be preserved despite the failure.

---

*Not .99999 availability, but that the sum of the probability of the configuration states tested exceed .99999. Some of these states could be failure states. However, if the availability requirements should exceed 0.99999, then you must design and execute enough tests to cover the states by which such availability is achieved. It gets very expensive.

CPU failures are detected in two primary ways: 1) self-detection by software, typically as detected illogical conditions, and 2) hardware detection by a switchover/alarm unit, or by another computer. Self-detection of failure occurs when the program responds to a detected illogical condition which is deemed serious enough to warrant recovery. The details are application dependent. Some examples are: loss of resources; illogical linking of chained resources such as queues, data buffers, or disc space; excessive interrupts; excessive time spent in any one program, where timing limits are specified for each program; failure of diagnostic check calculations. Hardware detection can be done by a special monitor and switchover unit, or the same functions can be implemented as software in the standby computer. The on-line computer is required to send periodic check messages to the monitor unit. These can range from simple messages to multiple messages at several different frequencies, with complicated diagnostic information embedded. If the monitor unit detects an error in the content or the timing of the check messages, it will usurp the current on-line CPU, disconnect it from the configuration by logical or physical switches, and then initialize the standby CPU which will take over and do the recovery processing.

Recovery is based on resuming processing from a known, logical state, not only for the system, but for every transaction in the system that must be protected through the failure. The system and transaction states are recorded periodically in a recovery file or **ledger**. This can be done either by stopping the processing periodically and recording all pertinent information in duplicate on fixed-head discs, say, or by recording changes to the system and transaction states as those changes occur. Usually a combination of methods is used, with part of the information recorded cyclicly, whether changed or not, and with part recorded as the changes occur. The recording of changes will typically be done in batches. All processing is arranged so that, with the given information regarding a transaction, it is possible to reprocess that transaction from the last recorded state without error. This is the crux of recovery testing.

Arranging the processing as a set of discrete recoverable steps has deep implications throughout the design. For example, no copy of data can ever be destroyed until that data has been safely stored in duplicate. If work is done on a transaction, say, it must be done on a copy of the transaction. Almost all processing routines must be reentrant. Whatever paths a transaction might take through the processing routines, all paths must periodically merge at the point where ledger information is recorded, prior to going on to the next step in the processing. In other words, the design of a recoverable system is not merely the addition of failure detection, data recording, and recovery modules to a nonrecoverable system, rather, recoverability must pervade the entire system design, from the lowest-level subroutines to the highest executive levels. Consequently, while a system may function perfectly in the absence of failures, this is no guarantee that the system will work in a recovery mode.

3.2. Restart and Recovery

The simplest aspect of recovery is **restart**. **Restart** is the act of discarding the present system and transaction states, fetching the most recent ledger, and initializing the system and transactions to the states recorded in the ledger. Restart retains the current CPU and hardware configuration. A restart may be self-initiated when an illogical condition is detected, or it may be used when there is no standby to switchover to, or it will be the first thing done by the upcoming standby that takes over processing after the primary computer's failure. Restart consists of the following steps, each with its own test requirements.

1. Identify all points in the program and all methods that can force a restart. Design methods to initiate such points, usually by patches that are driven by operator commands inserted to force the restart. For example, a special operator command is implemented that bypasses normal processing, and on the basis of a supplied parameter value can jump to any of the defined restart initiation points. This command should be removed prior to commissioning the system to live operation. All restarts should eventually come to a single, unique restart point in the recovery program.
2. Restart begins by aborting all ongoing peripheral activities and re-initializing all devices. Each device has at least two possible states—busy and not busy. Most will have several different busy states. Each device type must be tested in each state. Patches are inserted to assure that the switchover will occur with the device in the desired state. The device's ongoing operation is aborted (if busy) and it is initialized to a quiescent state which must be confirmed.
3. The system state (e.g., peripheral device assignments, mode of operation, control terminal assignment, and so on) must be fetched from the ledger. There are at least two copies of the ledger. Each copy contains self-checking information, serial numbers, and such that allow it to be validated. If faulty, then recovery will be based on an earlier ledger. Every possible ledger fault for the system state must be simulated and tested. Recovery with both the primary and the secondary ledgers must be simulated and tested. Once the system has acquired a valid ledger, the system configuration state must be confirmed.
4. Using the ledger data, the system now attempts to reconfigure and initialize all peripheral devices back to the appropriate configuration state. This must be confirmed as successful for all devices. However, the time elapsed from the failure that caused the restart to the actual restart is arbitrary, and could in case of a complete outage occur hours after the failure; therefore, there is no assurance that the peripheral device states match the states in the ledger. Every state conflict of this sort for every device must be simulated and tested, and the system must be shown to acquire a proper replace-

ment or take other appropriate action as a result. The conclusion of these tests shows that the system is capable of correctly reconfiguring itself into a viable configuration.

5. The system now must load and initiate recovery programs. The next step is to fetch the transaction recovery data from the ledger. If transaction state data was recorded as change information, the system must first reconstruct the state of each transaction from the change information. This process must be simulated and tested. Eventually, the system recovers all transactions and is capable of processing new transactions. The state of each transaction recovered must be confirmed. The structure of all dynamically allocated resources and queues must be confirmed.

6. The system now loads and/or initiates normal processing.

7. At some point in the above process, depending on the application but typically after the configuration has been established but before all old transactions have been recovered, the system is ready to accept new incoming transactions. If new processing is allowed during transaction recovery, that must also be simulated and tested.

8. Recovery is rarely perfect. Some transactions may have to be re-initiated as a result of the malfunction, warning messages distributed, ongoing transactions curtailed in an orderly manner, and so on. The specifics are application dependent. Whatever those specifics might be, each must be simulated and validated.

In addition to the automatic restart and recovery actions, most systems can initiate restart and/or recovery by special operator commands. All such commands must, of course, be tested as part of restart/recovery testing.

3.3. Switchover

Switchover is the act of changing the controlling central processor—that is, the CPU in which the system executive software is run. This is not neccessarily the largest CPU in a multi-computer complex. Switchover can be initiated in a variety of ways. Furthermore, the system can be in a number of different states when switchover is initiated. Each combination must be tested. Switchover can be initiated by:

1. Operator commands.
2. Self-detection by the on-line processor (i.e., abdication).
3. Detection by the monitor unit or processor that serves as a monitor.

There may be variations on each of these methods that must also be simulated and tested. The possible system states during a switchover are:

1. No available standby—in which case switchover is reduced to a restart.
2. A standby is available but it is engaged in off-line processing under an off-line executive program. The tests must show that the off-line processing was successfully terminated in an orderly manner, with all off-line peripherals brought to specified states.
3. An available standby operating in a switchover-ready backup mode.

In some systems, such as the WMSC's front-end computer, the standby processor accepts inputs and is continually updated by the on-line processor. This is done to prevent input loss. Such systems are called "no-break" systems. At no point in the process of switchover and restart are input transactions curtailed or lost. Consequently, the entire process of restart must operate with active new transactions, while old transactions are being recovered. When more than two computers are involved, as in the WMSC, the number of possible system states when a switchover is initiated is vastly increased. In other multi-computer complexes, instead of a simple primary-standby configuration, the system may have several different levels of capabilities depending on the number of computers that are available. Each such state must be tested. The method of initiating the switchover and the system state can usually be separated so that the combination need not be tested. However, in the above example, the switchover-forcing operator command may not be allowed if there is no standby computer available, causing thereby an interaction between the switchover initiation method and the system state that will force the combination of the two to be tested.

Switchover testing must also confirm that there is no built-in bias as to which physical processor is to be the on-line processor and which is to be the standby. Most systems are designed so that either processor can function in either role. If not designed that way, then the principal advantages of a standby as a means to improve the system's availability is lost. While this symmetry between on-line and standby should have been tested as part of configuration rotation testing, it should be retested in the context of switchovers. One simple way to do this is to do all the switchover tests in sequence, so that first one and then the other processor is the on-line processor.

Restoral of the failed computer to the standby or off-line state must also be tested. The designers tend to focus on the act of going down and recovering from the failure at the expense of comparably thorough testing associated with the repair and restoral of the computer. In the case of a multi-computer complex, where the system state is represented by a complicated state graph, as with all state-driven operations, full coverage is required and all states, and all automatically and manually initiated transitions between those states, must be tested. Full coverage here is in the sense of covering the processor state graph and not the entire system state graph.

3.4. Transaction Fidelity and Accountability Loss

3.4.1. General

Several things can happen to a transaction as a result of failure:

1. The transaction itself is lost, but the fact of that loss is known.
2. The transaction is lost and the fact that it's lost is not known.
3. The transaction is not lost and that fact is known.
4. The transaction is not lost, but that fact is not known.

In other words, we must distinguish between the transaction loss and loss of the knowledge concerning the transaction's state. The fourth case above can lead to transaction duplication, which in some cases can be more damaging than transaction loss: for example, a purchase order, a money transfer, or a control signal. Every system has rules that govern the circumstances regarding transaction loss, duplication, or transaction **accountability**; that is, loss of information concerning the transaction's state or the fact that there was a transaction. Transaction loss and accountability loss are two different issues. In many communication systems, transaction loss is tolerated for some messages, but transaction accountability loss is never tolerated. In general, the rules governing transaction loss and accountability loss depend on the transaction type, and may depend on the system's state. The first step in accountability and transaction fidelity testing is to clearly define those rules.

3.4.2. Transaction Fidelity Testing

This is an inherently difficult kind of test to design and execute. The object of transaction fidelity testing is to confirm that:

1. No transaction is lost.
2. No transaction is unknowingly duplicated.
3. No transaction is merged or interlaced with another transaction.

The above are interpreted in the context of the rules for each transaction type. We assume that all of the above have been thoroughly tested in a static mode, or dynamically, with active background transactions. The mass of previous testing that has taken place to confirm the system's proper operation should have, as a matter of course, examined the system to show that fidelity was maintained in the absence of failures and switchover. That's a prerequisite to showing that fidelity is maintained despite failures. This is a difficult kind of testing because the bugs we are after are all timing and circumstance dependent. Furthermore, it is impossible to postulate and explicitly test all the timing circumstances, all the sequences of interrupts, and all the points at which failures can occur that could result in transaction fidelity compromise. The approach must be statistical. That is, we force the system to process vast quantities of transactions while simultaneously forcing one switchover after another. If no fidelity compromise is detected, then we can be confident (but not sure) that transaction fidelity goals have been met. Here is an instance in which long test runs are legitimate. For example, run the system at full load for 200 hours with a switchover every half-hour.

A prerequisite to transaction fidelity testing is a means of confirming that fidelity objectives have been met. This is done by examining historical logs recorded for every transaction. It is not necessary that the system record all transactions in a history file, even though this is desirable. A log that identifies the transaction, time of arrival, sequence numbers, and other data that allow it to be correlated to outgoing transactions, source, type, and so on is sufficient. If the system does not record this kind of information, then it is impossible to verify transaction fidelity. The exception is if the transactions are produced by an external load generator, and if there is a clear rule that allows the load generator/monitor to correlate responses and output transactions unambiguously with input transactions. Let's assume that either the system itself or the load generator produces a log file from which it is possible to verify transaction fidelity. If not, then the system or the test bed must be augmented to provide such a log file.

An off-line balance program must be created and executed to confirm transaction fidelity. In principle, it means matching every input transaction or transaction component with every corresponding output. This is complicated because the sequence of input-output differs with each transaction type. Some inputs may engender several outputs or no outputs. Some outputs may be generated automatically, with no stimulating input. Whatever the rules are, the off-line balance program processes the logs and historical data and matches inputs and outputs, and flags all inputs and all outputs that appear not to follow the rules.

Testing consists of forcing the system through one switchover and/or restart after another while it is processing a stressful load. It is easier to stress the system while forcing recovery in the hope that the situation which causes transaction fidelity loss recurs than to design statistically meaningful explicit tests. This is one area in which random test data is useful, because it forces the system down many more paths than would be exercised with simpler, fixed data, and therefore increases the probability that fidelity losses will occur. This kind of testing, particularly when done in conjunction with stress testing, not only always exposes fidelity loss when first run, but also causes system crashes in profusion.

A test in this context, then, consists of forcing the load, doing the switch-overs, and then doing the confirming off-line verification runs. As such, it can be done while other parts of system testing is going on. It's a good idea. Most of the rest of system testing explores strange situations and error conditions. That's done simultaneously from several different terminals. Perhaps, at another terminal, there's penetration testing going on (see Section 4 below). Furthermore, through all this, there's heavy, stressful, background traffic, and switchovers are done at random. Close the log files every hour, say, and process them to confirm transaction fidelity. If transaction compromise is suspected, then it must have been caused by one of the activities that took place during that hour.

In some systems, such as secure, military communication systems, the issue of transaction fidelity and accountability is so important that an explicit test is used for the purpose. The system is required to run under heavy stressful load for a period of, say, 100 hours while being subjected to continual switchovers. A limit on the maximum number of unexplained fidelity losses is established. Outright crashes must be examined and explained, and the bug corrected. The test is restarted following each such crash, for a new 100-hour period. Unexplained fidelity losses that do not cause crashes, when compared to the number of transactions run without fidelity loss, provide a basis for a statistical prediction of the system's probability of fidelity loss.

3.4.3. Accountability Testing

Accountability testing is not different than fidelity testing, but is merely more of the same with a few additional factors thrown in. The same kind of load generation must be used, and the same off-line processing done. The difference is that the input load must be completely and carefully metered. Not only must input and output balance, but recorded input must exactly match the supplied input. This is practically impossible to test and confirm without an external load generator. The comparison is threefold. The generator's input and output are balanced and confirmed, the system's data records and data log records are balanced and confirmed, and then the two sets of records are balanced against one another.

4. SECURITY TESTING

4.1. The Problem

4.1.1. The Concern

There is an increasingly justifiable concern over the security of systems, particularly on-line systems that can be accessed by remote terminals. As systems get larger and handle larger and larger cash flows or the equivalent, they have become more attractive targets for criminals and also more vulnerable to criminal attack (see LEIB74). Once, the act of penetrating a system's defenses and possibly corrupting data was considered a harmless prank. Today such acts are increasingly being treated as felonies. As a consequence, some form of security testing is becoming part of all on-line systems.

4.1.2. Objectives

The problem of proving that a system is secure is similar to the problem of proving that a system is bug-free.* The most elementary form of security compromise is **sabotage****—the denial of service by the saboteur to legitimate users. Any system that can be crashed by a bug can be sabotaged, and therefore a prerequisite to proving that a system is secure is to first prove that it is bug-free; a proof which is known to be both theoretically and practically impossible. Just as proof methodologies have been developed and explored for bugs, research has been conducted concerning proofs of security, and again the never-ending regression of assumptions crop up: to prove security, you must also prove that the security prover is secure (and bug-free), and so on, and so on. Therefore, the objective of security testing is not a formal proof, but the establishment of a sufficient degree of confidence that the system is secure. That degree of confidence is, of course, application dependent, and therefore so is the cost of security testing. Security testing for highly sensitive systems can equal or exceed the cost of all other testing combined.

Security, like recovery, is not achieved by merely emplacing security measures over an otherwise unsecure design. Like recovery, security pervades the entire design, from low-level common subroutines to the executive. Consequently, security testing consists not of new kinds of tests, but primarily of confirming under ordinary testing that security has not been compromised.

4.1.3. The Criminal Programmer

If you were building a safe you would have some hypotheses concerning what a safecracker was likely to do and what the safecracker's skills and tools were.

---

*In one instance, the buyer specified that the security of a system be formally proven, even though the theoretical possibility of such a proof had yet to be proven. The contractor agreed to this specification clause and only examined its implications after contract award. The hassle surrounding the *proof* of security was one of the contributory causes to the contact's eventual cancellation.

**From the French word "*sabot*" meaning wooden shoe. A wooden shoe tossed into the works is sure to do much damage.

Similar hypotheses are needed as a prerequisite to security testing. What are the criminal's goals and resources? Possible goals include:

1. Sabotage—denial of service to legitimate users by causing crashes or overloading the system with trash.
2. Intelligence—illicit and undetected reading of transactions or files.
3. Transaction fidelity compromise; always accompanied by transaction accountability compromise. Duplicating, hiding, destroying, modifying, or passing transactions or data through internal security barriers.
4. Modification of the system's operation by program or data-base changes. The ability to affect entire classes of transactions, rather than individual transactions.
5. Identity compromise—the ability to mimic another user—to steal time, resources, or cash from another user or under another user's identity—electronic forgery.
6. Usurpation of control. Compromise of the system's security to the point where the penetrator can run the system, and all that that implies.

This is not a complete list. Every known crime in recorded history (short of rape but including murder) can be theoretically executed by a criminal programmer. As more and more of our society becomes pervaded by computers, more and more opportunities for computer-related crime will exist.

The criminal's resources include:

1. The criminal is a criminal and has the amorality and disdain for society that all criminals implicitly or explicitly have. The criminal programmer is not the nice kid down the street who does clever things to the bank or telephone computer using his home computer as a terminal. She's a hard-nosed, vicious, antisocial felon who'd just as soon kill you as install a controlling patch in your program. That's a more personal, productive, and realistic way to look at it.
2. The criminal programmer is skilled—in fact, brilliant but warped. He has all your documentation, all the listings, and knows everything that's worth knowing about the system except the details of the current operational state and the current passwords.
3. The criminals are not alone. They are organized and disciplined and can bring as much manpower as needed in proportion to the expected payoff. For example, subverting the stock market might warrant an effort of several hundred man-years; subverting the defenses of the United States would warrant several thousand.
4. The criminal is a legitimate user with some level of access to the system, and some legitimate passwords. Who ever heard of a safecracker who didn't

first "case the joint"? Who ever heard of a spy who didn't have secret or top-secret clearance?

5. The criminal has all the communications lines, support hardware and software, smart terminals, microcomputers, and whatever else is needed to breach the system's security, if it can be done.

Like all security methods, computer security must make the cost of breaching security higher than the expected payoff multiplied by the probability of not being detected. The main methods used by the criminal to achieve penetration and control are:

1. Breaching input tolerance and robustness.
2. Overloading.
3. Browsing through garbage.
4. Exploiting nonexistent resources and denied services.
5. Random attack.
6. Use of illicit channels.

4.1.4. Inside Jobs

The criminal may violate the system's physical security by changing codes, changing wiring, or by any and all means that can be done by having an accomplice or spy in the physical computer room or in the organizational entity that runs the system. Suitably placed insiders can circumvent any built-in security measures and any executed tests for those measures. Protection against insiders is not a testing issue. It is a matter of establishing and administering a security policy (e.g., security checks, badges, identities, bonding, guards, and so on). One form of inside job is a quality assurance and testing concern: the use of **Trojan horse programs** or **trap doors.**

Trojan horse programs are programs or program segments, often stored as data, that when activated turn control over to the criminal. A **trap door** is the specific key that provides access to the Trojan horse. For example, a rarely used path has a "bug" which will cause the execution of data—data which gives the penetrator control over a password list, say. The Trojan horse is activated by the penetrator just long enough to get control, and is thereafter wiped out. The Trojan horse is possibly coded-in during system development or test, or at some other time when access to the system is relatively easy for practical reasons. Audits of all paths, not once but several times, and several times independently at all system levels, is the best protection against the embedment of Trojan horses. Create an environment that questions "clever" code or unexplained constructs. Note that an automatic audit program that seeks Trojan horses is useless. The Trojan horse's planter is smart enough to gimmick the analyzer so that his Trojan horse will not be detected. Once installed, there is probably no reliable method for discovering Trojan horses, except in the simplest systems, or the crudest form of Trojan horse.*

4.2. Frontal Attack Methods

4.2.1. Frontal and Flank Attacks

The fundamental rule of strategy and tactics is the concentration of available resources against the enemy's weak spots in order to achieve a local superiority even though the enemy may outnumber you overall. The inherent advantage to the defender is typically three to one. That is, the attacker must typically have three times the resources that the defender has in order to succeed. If that cannot be achieved globally, then it must be achieved locally, such as by attacking an exposed flank or an unprotected rear. The would-be computer system penetrator has the same problem and the same solution. The system's security must, of course, be tested for invulnerability to frontal attack—but must also be tested for invulnerability to flank or rear attack. That means that security measures must guard not only against one source or problem, but against simultaneous attacks and problems. Just as there are systems that can handle a single transaction at a time without difficulty and yet fail when several transactions are to be processed simultaneously, a system's security measures may be adequate against a single penetrator, but vulnerable to simultaneous attack. The frontal attack is a diversionary tactic intended to activate the security processing module, say, which is unfortunately not reentrant or adequately protected. The simultaneous sneak attack then actually uses the security handling routine's weakness as the method of achieving penetration.

Security concerns must pervade the entire design, as I've said, but it's almost impossible in the context of a single routine to foresee or even understand the implications of a simultaneous attack. Consequently, security-related testing should be conducted under stressful loads while other kinds of error condition testing is going on with several different kinds of attacks tested simultaneously.

4.2.2. Input Tolerance and Robustness

Most attacks begin with an input. Exploiting the lack of input robustness is the simplest form of frontal attack. Therefore, a secure system must be especially

---

*Don't be naive. All that has to appear as code is a single jump instruction—and even that needn't be the case if the "bug" involves instruction modification. Explicit code is stupid and crude, and code stored as permanent data is only slightly subtler. Anything that can be caught by static analysis or cursory audits is amateurish. Trojan horses can be embedded only because the criminal knows that his devious abilities, ingenuity, and labor will be grossly underestimated.

robust and tolerant of input errors and garbage. Normal input syntax testing and field value validation testing must be increased beyond that which would be used for an unsecure system. Whereas the unsecure system need be tested only for a few simultaneous format or value errors, the secure system must be tested with many more double- and triple-error conditions. Particular attention must be paid to input field value errors, especially to limit values. A common ploy is to hurl an incredible number of bad transactions or transaction segments in an attempt to force wrap conditions. A smart terminal or microcomputer can be programmed to generate such transactions as fast as the protocol can accept them. The defense against this kind of attack is to keep track of the number of erroneous inputs and to either initiate a security alert or to turn the offending line off, or both when an error-count threshold value is exceeded. If such protection is provided and tested, the would-be penetrator is then effectively forced to be a legitimate system user. It doesn't solve the problem, but it does make penetration riskier and more expensive. What's more, now that the criminal must have legitimate access to the system, there's at least a suspect list that the police can start with. It's a whole lot better than trying to trace a telephone booth in Arkansas.

4.2.3. Overwhelming

Denial of service to others can be achieved by overwhelming the system's resources.* The objective is sabotage rather than control. Protection is provided by establishing resource usage limits for each user and denying the use of excessive resources. The system's response is either to hold the offending user to prespecified limits (each of which must be tested) or to deny service to the offending user. Resource usage monitors that provide alarms under excessive resource demands or under bizarre patterns of usage allow security personnel to examine a user's operation for possible illicit intentions. However, this is a delicate issue because strange usage patterns could be just that, and there may be privacy and civil liberty concerns involved.

Overwhelming resources can be used as the frontal part of a two-pronged attack. The criminal knows that when certain resource usages reach predefined levels, the system's operational mode changes. For example, when fixed-head disc is overwhelmed, files are continued onto moving head disc extensions. While the system's security is adequate in the primary mode, it is inadequate

---

*The operators were furious over layoffs that occurred when a new system was installed. Erroneous inputs were normally routed to service positions for examination and correction. If the correction was in error, the errored correction was sent to a service position, but the original error was also retained in a service position queue. The operators created paper-tape loops that caused the same error to be repeated recursively every few seconds, depleted all available resources in a few minutes, and brought the system down.

or ineffectual in the exception mode. For example, fixed-head disc files may be protected against browsing (see below), but not their moving-head disc or tape extensions. Whenever the system has different modes of operation or provides different kinds of service in response to resource utilization thresholds, the system's security must be retested in each such mode of operation.

4.2.4. Recovery Penetration

A system has no-break front-end and is designed to accept new, incoming transactions while switchover is taking place. This is provided as a user convenience so that, except for momentarily garbled outputs, the user does not know that a switchover has taken place and that recovery processing is underway. The criminal's attack consists of finding an unambiguous and reliable method of crashing the system, forcing it into switchover and recovery, and then doing the real penetration attempt while recovery is underway. As an almost trivial example, we found that a time-shared system could be easily crashed. As a convenience to the user, it restored all users that had been logged in prior to the crash. However, the automatic telephone input handler permitted new users to dial up and get connected without logging in only while recovery was underway. The result was that we could create a "tap" on a legitimate user's line. Getting that user to spill the beans was trivial. We prepared tapes that mimicked the entire log-in sequence and simply asked the unsuspecting user for his password, which he dutifully gave us. After a few days we caught a system programmer and obtained the passwords needed to control the system.*

Philosophically, this is just an extension of the idea that the system may be vulnerable when resources are stressed. The basic principle is that any program that's active when users are on-line, or any program mode that can be activated by on-line users, must be subjected to security testing, including especially restart and recovery modes.

4.2.5. Systematic and Random Attacks

You can, given enough time, open any safe by trying enough combinations. The safe is secure because it's unlikely that the right combination can be found before the safecracker is discovered. The automated safecracker uses a com-

---

*All anecdotes in this chapter concerning security breaches and penetration attempts refer to legal and legitimate attempts done in the course of security testing. I am not, nor have I ever been, nor have I ever knowingly consorted with, criminal programmers.

puter and tries thousands of combinations per second. Either systematic attacks or random attacks can be used. The design fallacy here is that the programmer discounts trying the thousands or millions of cases that must be tried. While the most obvious place that security can be compromised is by trying random file names or random passwords, there are many other places where random attacks can be used to penetrate the system. Two principles are employed to squelch random and systematic attacks.

1. Returning the minimum amount of information on a failure.
2. Keeping records and track of all unsuccessful attempts.

As an example, the MULTICS operating system does both. Assume that I have a valid password and the name of a file for whose security I am not cleared. An attempt to access that file, or even an attempt to access a directory on which that file appears, will result in a message that the file does not exist— not that it exists but I have no right to it. If I access a directory, only those file names to which I have legitimate security and privacy access are listed without apparent gaps. For me those other files do not exist. The second half of the protection is that the legitimate user or security personnel are informed of every unsuccessful access attempt. While not preventing random and systematic attacks, this turns the problem over to humans who can deal with it in an appropriate manner.

Testing for vulnerability to random and systematic attack consists of showing that gratuitous information is not supplied to the attacker and that the proper alarms are sounded (or recorded) when the attack is made. The principles are clear, but it is in general not possible to design an explicit test for every possible place where the system is potentially vulnerable to random or systematic attack. Direct tests of the protection mechanism should and can be made. The rest can be verified by a spot check and by extending the normal testing. Anything that the random or systematic attacker will attempt has been tested, at least one error at a time, in the context of normal testing. We extend erroneous input tests (e.g., syntax errors, field value errors) by repeating the erroneous inputs a sufficient number of times to trigger the security measure.

Several weaknesses should be looked for. Say that the basic error monitoring scheme allows no more than N errors of a given type in a specified time period. You must check that a successful input does not wipe out or reset the error counter, or that a new kind of error does not wipe out the counter. If that happens, the penetrator can merely do N−1 bad inputs, reset the alarm with a good input, and then go on with more bad inputs. Reentrance of the error monitor should be tested by having several attackers reach the error limit simultaneously.

4.3. Indirect Attacks and Data Attacks

4.3.1. Browsing and Garbage Cans

This is the simplest form of attack. It is an attack on data, especially data required to obtain seemingly legitimate access to secure areas. Every espionage agency knows how valuable garbage is. Spies can glean a lot of national secrets by picking through a diplomat's garbage cans. That's why we burn classified documents and use paper shredders. Garbage is gold to the criminal. There is no such thing as meaningless data or useless garbage. If the system's garbage is examined long enough and carefully enough, eventually that garbage will yield important information, such as passwords, security codes, decryption keys, and so on. A computer system's garbage is stored in resources such as main and mass memory buffer blocks, purged records and files, temporary duplicate records, temporary backup records and files, and so on. **Browsing** is the organized examination of the contents of discarded resources to which the browser has legitimate or illegitimate access. There are three steps to an attack by browsing:

1. Access to garbage.
2. Reading and interpreting the garbage.
3. Using the results of browsing (e.g., a discovered password).

The third step has no direct testing implications. The first step is the more complicated, so we'll deal with reading and interpreting the garbage first.

The penetrator has gotten hold of a buffer block or file record, say, which contains some garbage from a previous user. Reading and interpreting the data is a question of programming. The browser knows what he's looking for (crypto keys or passwords, say) and because, as postulated, he has the system's documentation, he knows precisely what format he's looking for. The garbage can be interpreted as binary, as decimal, as alphanumeric, or as object code instruction format. The attacker's analyzer program first examines the garbage under the hypothesis of each different format type and, based on stored statistics, determines the most likely data format for that piece of garbage. A parser appropriate to the garbage type is then activated for the next phase of the analysis. For example, if the garbage is instruction mode, the parser might look for privileged instructions, security mode instructions, or immediate operands. If alphanumeric, the parser might look for keys or passwords. If something interesting turns up, the data is stored for later human examination, and the browser attempts to get another piece of garbage to look at. The penetrator may have to run the program for days or weeks until something interesting turns up, but if there's any breach in the way secure resources are handled, eventually, by chance, the penetrator's automated browser/analyzer will find it.

A first, and naive, line of defense is to put all classified and unclassified resources in totally separated pools. This does not work, because the penetrator has legitimate access to secure resources—usually at the highest level. Consider this. The penetrator is, or mimics, a legitimate user. Passwords are treated at the highest security level. Legitimate users are allowed to create their own passwords and keys, and to modify those passwords or keys so that even operational personnel cannot tell which passwords are in use. Therefore, legitimate users, operating in their own security domains, may indirectly access secure resources and therefore may indirectly have access to someone else's secure garbage.

A more potent defense is to assure that all resources, of whatever classification, are wiped clean after use. This provides assurance that there is no garbage to browse through. However, most programs are not written that way. Programmers learn to do things efficiently. Most operations involving resources are done by manipulating things that refer to the resource rather than the actual resource. For example, we don't transfer the content of a data block, but only a pointer to that block. We don't wipe a resource clean, but only mark it as clean. This is done in the interest of processing efficiency. If this kind of indirect incineration was not done, then most file operations would be doubled or worse, and cleanup processing could easily be more time-consuming than normal processing. There are two generic situations with respect to garbage cleanup—systems in which all garbage is destroyed, and systems in which garbage is only selectively destroyed in the interest of processing efficiency or performance.

In either case, what must be verified is that garbage was cleaned on all paths in which garbage must be cleaned. The testing issue is analogous to the resource loss problem. All systems, particularly in the early phases of testing, lose memory resources. This happens because while a programmer must get a resource to process a transaction, and always knows that a resource must be obtained, the routine's operation is not affected if the resource is not returned to the pool. Strange paths, particularly those caused by error-related interrupts (e.g., such as might be caused by a forced crash), can result in resource loss because the resource return is bypassed on the exception path. The same thing happens with garbage cleanup. Garbage may be cleaned on all normal paths, but be bypassed on abnormal or failure-related paths.

If universal cleanup is used, then testing consists of installing a resource monitor which is to be active during the course of all normal testing. The resource monitor is activated whenever a resource is assigned to a user from the pool and again when a resource is returned to the pool. The monitor checks the resource character by character to confirm that it has been cleaned, or, equivalently, it does not check but wipes, because cleanup may be less expensive than checking: for example, the computer has a multi-word clear instruction. The processing penalty is, of course, horrendous. The system is frozen and halted whenever an unclean resource is discovered.

A similar scheme can be used with systems that use selective cleanup. But then, it is no longer possible to install the necessary software in a unique program, such as a resource manager. Garbage monitors or assertion statements must be installed at every point in the program where it is assumed, for security reasons, that the resource is clean, and this fact must be confirmed in the course of normal testing.

4.3.2. Nonexistent Resources and Objects

Garbage is not the only thing to browse through. The penetrator can also browse through things that do not logically exist, but which physically exist. For example, say we have a record whose maximum length is 1024 characters. At any point in time, the valid data in the record is less than that, say N characters. Thus while the logical record's length is N characters, there is still a physical record of 1024 characters, and therefore there can be 1024–N characters of garbage in that record. Accessing that garbage is the act of accessing something which doesn't have a logical existence, but does have a physical existence. As another example, in one system we penetrated we found that the user was allowed up to three logical tape units, which were actually implemented as moving-head disc files. If we dynamically declared logical tapes 4, 5, 6, 7, and 8, say, the operating system came back with an error response and denied the tapes. However, once requested and denied, those files could be read. They were, of course, someone else's files.

Opportunities for this kind of penetration, and subsequent browsing, abound because the processing cost of assuring that all logical file and record properties at all times match physical file and record properties is usually more than the buyer is willing to pay for security. Thus the penetrator can read beyond the end of record, beyond the end of file, beyond the end of tape, read the printer, read the card punch, open an opened file, close a closed file, read a closed file, read before the beginning of a record, read and write records in the wrong format, and so on. You object—you say that the system doesn't allow such operations—that all such operations result in an error—and of course you're right—but you're underestimating the criminal. First of all, she's working in as much assembly language as she needs to get physical access to things. Secondly, did you ever check what was in the input buffer after you attempted (and were prevented from) reading beyond the end of file? You wouldn't—it would be a silly thing to do in the context of normal code and normal programming. And there's the crux of the testing implications. In normal test design we might not go down certain paths because such paths, although possible, could never harm the system or do anything but give the user garbage responses and operations. It's assumed that the user will abort such attempts, because, after all, "Garbage in equals garbage out"—isn't that just dandy?

The testing implications therefore are:

1. To confirm that there is no accessible garbage following a rejected and illegal file or record operation.
2. Expanding the tests to include scenarios that make no operational sense and transaction flows that result in no known useful results.

Furthermore, garbage searching through illegitimate operations should also be attempted following an induced crash, because recovery is always a vulnerable time.

4.3.3. Illicit Channels

An **illicit channel** exists when a user transfers material or data from a classified area to an unclassified area.* That's a simple example. The channel may exist between two areas or users who are not allowed to transfer certain kinds of transactions to each other but do. Both users are assumed to be legitimate users with all necessary accesses. For example, the bank manager can legitimately access his account and my account. He transfers $1000 from my account to his by an illicit channel. Every transfer of information from one user to another is done by a logical channel. The channel has security- and privacy-related rules that dictate what kinds of information can be transferred in what directions over that channel, and may furthermore have such transfers conditional on security keys, passwords, authorizations, and so on. Putting it in the context of data transfers seems harmless. Talking about transferring classifed data from a secure file to an unclassified file seems a little more threatening. But if we transfer and thereby transform an information request to a paid-up purchase order and deliver five thousand computer terminals as a result to an empty barn in Arkansas, then that's another matter. If there's one thing the seasoned computer criminal knows how to do, it is to transform raw information into cold, hard, laundered cash.

---

*The word "channel" in this context is not limited to physical I/O channels. A channel exists when routine A passes data to routine B, when routine B reads A's data, or when B can access A's garbage. The most bizarre example of a channel is one in which A modifies resource utilization with a junk program and B monitors the system's response time. A's modification pattern is a Morse-code message. Low utilization for a "dot" and high utilization for a "dash." Channels can be strange when security is considered. This last example was of a **covert channel**. There is no known means of providing security against covert channels between cooperating legitimate users. Our discussion is limited to **overt channels**.

One way to assure that illicit channels do not exist is to centralize all information transfers through a security monitor. Then testing consists of normal testing of that function. Note also that illicit channels can exist by shared usage of nonexistent resources. A creates the garbage, which B then picks up. If channel checks are more diffused, then normal testing should be augmented to include security/privacy violations tests in addition to exercising the usual normal and abnormal functions. You should also confirm that the denied transfer did not actually take place. For example, if the security check is done by the receiving routine (which is a security bug), it could reject the logical transfer because of a security/privacy violation, but only after the physical transfer had taken place. The receiving routine's scratch area contains the data nevertheless, which can be accessed by an assembly language browser: so even though the transfer seems to have been blocked because of a security violation, it has nevertheless taken place!

4.4. Tiger Teams

A **tiger team** is a team of penetration experts hired to attempt to breach the system's security. Their primary virtue is that they represent another independent attack on the system's integrity. They do not suffer from the same misconceptions and complacency that the system designers suffer from (they have other misconceptions and complacencies), and they can also be effective when insider work is suspected. However, a tiger team, no matter how expert, will not prove that a system is secure, nor is it a substitute for methodical security testing. If security is a real concern, then after all other testing is done, after the system has been through the formal acceptance test, and after it has been declared bug-free and secure, hire not one but two or more tiger teams, so that the system is assaulted simultaneously from several different directions and points of view. If the system has not been thoroughly tested beforehand, the tiger team is a waste of money—because breaking buggy systems is like taking candy from a baby.

5. RETROSPECTIVE ON TESTING COSTS

One of the tragedies of testing is underestimating testing costs when such things as recovery, accountability, switchover, and security must be implemented. Let's say that system testing and related independent quality assurance is 25% of the software development effort in the absence of the above. We know that recovery, acountability, security, and the rest must materially increase the cost of design, if properly done. What are the testing cost implications?

1. Transaction recovery adds 20% to 25% to the testing cost. Independent testing and QA is now 31% of design cost.
2. Simple configuration testing for a duplexed system adds another 15%. Test costs are raised to 35% of development costs.
3. Accountability testing adds another 15%. We are now up to 39% of development costs, which have also been increasing by a similar amount.
4. Transaction fidelity testing over a protracted time period with induced crashes adds another 5%. The count is now 40%.
5. Escalation of normal testing to provide adequate input tolerance testing, accountability testing, transaction fidelity testing, and so on, as suitable to security concerns, multiplies testing labor across the board by 50%. We're up to 60% of development costs.
6. Design and executing test scenarios for frontal and flank attacks, for penetration attempts, and all the rest, adds another 10%.
7. Garbage collection and cleanup testing adds another 20%.
8. Audits and security measures to prevent Trojan horses, to create the software in a secure environment, and all the rest multiplies the total test labor by another 25%, for a count of 84%.
9. Checks of illicit (overt) channels adds another 20%.
10. External, independent testing and tiger teams adds another 10%, for 92% of the development cost.

But the software's development costs have been increasing in a like manner. The net result is that a secure, recoverable system's cost is not just twice, but of the order of four to five times as expensive as a nonrecoverable, nonsecure, equivalent system. Furthermore, the test and debug labor shifts from 50% to 80% or 90% of the total cost. Half of that test and debug time is spent by independent QA and related security auditors. If security is really important, it would not be out of line to have software development costs be six or seven times as great as the insecure equivalent. Furthermore, system design, unit design, coding, system integration, system testing, documentation, and all the rest would only be 20% of the system's cost, with the rest of the labor expended in independent QA and verification efforts.

These realities should be sobering. The buyer must understand that recovery and security are expensive commodities. The builder must also understand this and must adjust proposed costs, budgets, and schedules accordingly. The development groups must understand that the balance of power and personnel has been drastically shifted from its traditional position. Design's new objective must be to design code and systems that can be easily tested and verified. Because testing costs are so high, the hardware must be increased in speed and the memory must be expanded to compensate for the relative inefficiencies of highly testable code. Doubling program memory and CPU speed would not be out of line for testability alone. Security (as for garbage cleanup) can increase it further. Finally, the hardware side of the builder's shop must be reconciled to the possibility that software costs can now be larger, possibly by an order of magnitude (decimal, not binary), than the cost of the hardware in which that software is to run. Failure to appreciate these realities is probably the single largest source of project failures in secure, recoverable, system development efforts.

6. TASKS FOR A QUALITY ASSURANCE DEPARTMENT

1. Determine the hardware configuration(s) of the system and include a sufficient level of configuration testing to assure that the system works under all permutations of physical/logical/functional assignments. Base schedules and planning under the assumption that effort will be proportional to NlogN, where N is the number of hardware devices that can participate in the assignments.

2. For multi-computer systems, or other systems that exhibit multiple levels of performance based on hardware availability: create an accurate model of the system's availability states (devices up/down) and let configuration testing be guided by a probabilistic coverage of all states and transitions sufficient to assure .99999 coverage or the availability goal, whichever is higher. As a rule of thumb, each additional "9" in the availability requirement compounds testing costs by 20%. That is, 0.9999 costs 20% more to test than 0.999, but 0.999999 costs 75% more to test.

3. For simpler systems, identify all configuration states and all permissible manually and automatically initiated transitions between such states. Design enough tests to assure that all states and all transitions have been covered.

4. For every device type, where there are N devices of that type, design a sufficient number of tests to test all device up/down transitions from every state of that device, under the assumption of only one failure or restoral at a time.

5. Identify every failure detection method to which the system must respond and initiate a restart and recovery and/or switchover. Design reliable means for exercising or simulating all such methods.

6. Define the required degree of accountability and fidelity required for the system and implement appropriate tests. Create or modify the transaction generation, log recording, and analyzer tools needed to confirm transaction fidelity and accountability.

7. Define security objectives in as concrete and quantitative manner as pos-

sible. Obtain buyer and management guidance concerning the level of security and security testing that they are willing to pay for. Be sure to point out that security testing is more open-ended than normal testing and much, much more expensive.

8. Participate with a security department or cognizant agency in all aspects of physical and personnel security that might impact system security. There's no point in spending millions on software security testing if inadequate physical and personnel security can totally circumvent your efforts by an inside job.

9. Implement auditing procedures aimed at exposing the more obvious forms of Trojan horses, more as a deterrent than anything else.

10. Crank up input tolerance testing if the system is to be secure.

11. Make stress testing a mandatory prerequisite to security testing.

12. Design and implement resource monitors and test tools to confirm proper garbage disposal.

13. Go back through the entire acceptance test plan and augment it for security testing concerns, in addition to the few extra tests that will be added for explicit testing of security-related areas.

8

BACKGROUND, STRESS, AND PERFORMANCE TESTING

1. SYNOPSIS

Background loads are used to make testing realistic. **Stress testing** is testing the system under high loads to probe its viability under resource overload. **Performance testing** is aimed at quantitative predictions of load-handling capacity. All three require a controlled source of transactions with which to load the system.

2. TRANSACTION GENERATORS

2.1. General

Realistic testing should include not only forcing the system to handle test transactions, but also forcing it to deal with input loads that simulate the real environment. Five methods are available for supplying the system with transactions.

1. Manual load generation.
2. Real loads.
3. An external (to the system) load generator system.
4. Cogeneration of load by a copy (possibly modified) of the system.
5. Self-generation of load by the system itself.

I've listed manual load generation as a method because it's often attempted, usually with little success. It's not an unreasonable method for very slow systems, for small systems, or for batch systems. But it's totally hopeless for any real-time, large-scale system that handles loads measured in transactions per second rather than transactions per day. The main problem is human unreliability. Even if the transactions are prepared in advance there is no repeatability of timing, and there are cockpit errors and other sources of uncertainty that make such loads almost useless in a testing context. If a manual input crashes the system, it's unlikely that that particular crash (if load rather than function dependent) can ever be reproduced. There is no reliable measurement of transaction arrival rates. Errors are erratic rather than controlled. Humans tend to get into ruts that inadvertently bias the load's statistics, sometimes far away from what was intended. Besides all that, it's expensive, time-consuming, and mind-dulling work.

2.2. Real Loads

This is both the best and the worst kind of load to use. It's good because there's no compromise with reality. Real loads provide a proper measure of error conditions, anomalous cases, bursts, and so on. It's bad because more data logging and instrumentation hardware and software are needed than for simulated loads. Another limitation of real loads is the difficulty of achieving saturation. The operators of a credit-checking system, say, will not tolerate artificially induced overloads in the interest of seeing if the system will crash because of resource saturation, or in support of determining the system's capacity. Yet, when a system is first commissioned, the actual load is far short of the system's capacity (or should be). The final difficulty with real loads in performance analysis and testing is that the characterizing parameters of real loads are far more scattered than they would be for a similar load provided by a test-bed load generator. This implies that sophisticated statistical analysis methods must be used to determine the system's capacity—methods which are unnecessary on the controlled test bed.

Whether we like real loads or not, every system when put into operation will be tested under real loads by definition, but that does not mean that one can forgo testing under simulated loads. That's like saying that because an aircraft will be tested in operation, there's no need to test it in a wind tunnel first.

There is one often overlooked subtlety with real loads. While the real load is ultimately more realistic than a simulated load, that may not happen until the system has been in operation for several months. The input and cockpit errors in the first few months of operation are higher than they will be after the system and its users settle down. Furthermore, the initial system parameters are probably ill-set, and consequently not only is the system subjected to an unrealistically high error rate, but it is ill-tuned to boot. This provides additional stress, which is good for testing but bad for performance assessment.

2.3. Load Generators and Simulators

2.3.1. General

Load generators and simulators can range from a simple, predetermined set of transactions presented to the system under a job-control language to the entire real-time simulation of a complex environment. The simplest example I can think of is a paper-tape loop loaded on a teleprinter to provide a repetitious load. Among the most complicated are the Apollo mission simulator used by NASA and the FAA test facility at Pomona, New Jersey. The FAA facility can provide realistic loads for an air traffic control system, including pilots, aircraft, and controllers. A combination of automatic and manual simulation (for pilots and controllers) is used. The facility can test new programs, new hardware, new traffic patterns, and hypothetical or previous emergencies under a wide variety of assumptions and conditions.

Whether simple or elaborate, a load generator is a source of statistically specified transactions. That load may be generated on-line or off-line. Because a load generator often incorporates test and measurement hardware and software, it can be as, or more complicated than the system it's intended to test. Furthermore, because the load generator is itself a real-time system, its reliability and load-handling capacity cannot be ignored. Elaborate load generators are effective when they are used to test many different systems, or to simulate many different environments, or when no other approach is feasible or safe.

The block diagram of a typical load generation system is shown in Figure 8-1. It consists of three parts: an off-line data generator, an on-line load generator, and an off-line analyzer. In practice, the three may be merged or reallocated in different ways to on-line and off-line processing.

2.3.2. Data Generator

The input to the data generator is a specification for a run, typically in terms of statistical parameter values for transactions, including such things as: mean arrival rates, distribution characteristics, special-application-related probabilities, and so on. As an example, a simulator for an international telephone system could generate traffic scenarios with the following parameters: mean call arrival rate minute by minute over a period of several days, the distribution of call durations, the probability and characteristics of user misdials and wrong numbers, the busy probabilities of the receiver, the user's behavior for busy or blocked calls, detailed statistical characteristics of all caller errors, and the destination country and its network's behavior.

The data generator is in principle simple but in practice complicated. It consists of long chains of controlled random number generators, each of which

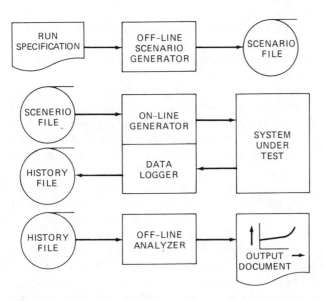

Figure 8-1. Load Generator Block Diagram.

adds another component to the specified transaction. For the telephone example, the process starts by generating the time to the next call from the previous
call, based on the mean call generation rate probability distribution specified
for a class of callers. The dice are then loaded and rolled to determine what
kind of call this is to be—whether or not it's to be dialed correctly, and if
incorrectly, just how incorrect and at which digits. The dice are also rolled to
determine the user's hesitation between digits, whether or not the called party
will be busy, whether or not the international trunks will be available, how long
the call will last, who will hang up first, how long the second party will wait
before hanging up, and so on. A script for the call is constructed one factor at
a time and stored in a transaction record. Proceeding in this way with various
transaction types, with subtypes within types, for fields and options, an entire
scenario, lasting from seconds to hours, can be constructed. The data generator's output is a detailed scenario file that will be used by the on-line load
generator.

There are several reasons for using an off-line generator that creates a scenario file rather than incorporating these functions into the on-line load
generator:

1. It's possible to generate the transactions using a higher-order language or
   simulation language and thereby reduce programming costs as compared to

developing the data generator in a language that can be hosted by the on-line generator.

2. It's no longer necessary to use the same computer for data generation and load generation.

3. On-line crap shooting (e.g., random number generation) is very slow and not particularly efficient in the typical real-time system hardware that is used for on-line generation. There are so many places that the dice must be thrown that the processing time to create a simulated transaction can easily exceed the time to process a real transaction by a factor of a hundred or more.

4. On-line generation means that the scenario cannot be repeated. If the system crashes, or a bug is found, it's not possible to exactly duplicate the situation. A stored scenario generated off-line and executed on-line can be exactly repeated.

5. Statistical data generators, like simulators, may need time for the statistics to stabilize. A ten-hour scenario might have to be generated as the last ten hours of a twelve-hour simulated run. If transaction generation is done on-line, the initial stabilization period may subject the system to unrealistic loads.

2.3.3. On-line Load Generator/Data Logger

The on-line load generator takes transactions from the scenario file and attempts to issue them to the tested system at the time marked for that transaction. I say "attempts" because if the tested system is saturated and is delaying inputs, the attempt may fail. Then the load generator must act in accordance with the instructions in that transaction's specification. For example: discard the transaction, try again N times, try again only once, and so on. The on-line generator is further complicated because it must have all protocols (human and machine) implemented. Where a transaction involves interactive behavior, the on-line load generator must simulate that behavior. It is, therefore, a system in its own right. It is in most respects simpler than the tested system because:

1. Recovery from malfunctions is not necessary, nor is switchover, rigid accountability, and so on. It's easier to fix the bug and rerun the test.

2. There are far fewer error paths and exception conditions than in the tested system. The load generator does not usually interpret the transactions or received outputs, but merely passes them to the tested system at the right time and logs the responses.

3. It's not usually necessary to test every detailed protocol glitch, transaction

error type, format variation, and so on to get a meaningful simulation of load. Simulated user errors are a subset of real user errors, as are formats, and variations.

In some respects the load generator is more complicated and must be more efficient than the tested system because:

1. If the load generator saturates before or at the same load that the tested system does, it will not be possible to determine which saturated. Typically, the load generator should have two to three times the transaction-handling capacity of the tested system.
2. The load generator may require resources not available to the tested system, and consequently, more handlers for discs, tapes, and so on.
3. The load generator, in the interest of minimizing processing time, may use much more memory than an equivalent function done in the real system.
4. The load generator usually incorporates data logging and system performance monitoring hardware and/or software.

Load generation, performance monitoring, and data logging are almost always done in the same system because:

1. The scenario specified by the scenario file and the executed scenario will differ with respect to timing, transaction execution orders, and rates because of saturation, throttling, and delays in the tested system. Consequently, it's the executed scenario and not the attempted scenario that counts.
2. Transactions involve interactions. Some performance factors, such as delays, can only be measured by the response delay between input and output. Only if all outputs are monitored and logged by the same computer can such interaction delays be simulated and measured.
3. To correlate the driving transactions with the responses of the tested system to those transactions, would require that the hypothetically separate logger store enough information to make such correlation possible at a later time. Storing that information can require more processing than doing the correlation on-line.
4. There is so much in common to a generator and logger that separating them would entail needless hardware and software duplication.

The output of the data generator/logger is a history file that combines the original scenario and the history of the tested system's responses to that scenario. Because of the problems of generator saturation, as much as possible of subsequent correlation and analysis processing is left to an off-line analyzer.

2.3.4. Off-line Analyzer

The off-line analyzer is an off-line program that takes the history/log files produced by the generator/logger and does all necessary statistical and accountability calculations. Its first step is to correlate inputs with corresponding outputs, or to otherwise gather up all the pieces that belong to a particular transaction (if those pieces occur scattered throughout the log file). Input/output balance calculations are done to detect any loss of transaction fidelity or accountability. Accountability must be based on a comparison with the tested system's version of what it handled during that scenario. Finally, all timing and related parameters and counts must be processed to recalculate the probabilities that were used to generate the scenario. That way, the scenario's statistics as run can be confirmed against the scenario's statistics as specified. If the source statistics and the run statistics calculated from the log files do not match, the discrepancy must be explained. It can be caused by bugs, transaction loss, transaction fidelity or accountability loss, or saturation.

2.4. Cogeneration

Cogeneration is using a copy of the system to supply load for another copy. Cogeneration is applicable when the load generator's requirements and the tested system's requirements are almost identical. In communications systems, as an example, both the load generator and the system must have all protocols and message analysis facilities implemented. Both must be able to store messages and output them on specified lines when those lines are free. In process control systems, the symmetry between the behavior of a controlled system and the system that controls it can be exploited to convert the control system into a load generator. Cogeneration is cost-effective when the modifications needed to convert the tested system into a load generator are *small*. The main advantage to cogeneration is the low cost of producing a load generator. There are several limitations to cogeneration, though:

1. You could be using a buggy system to test a buggy copy of itself.
2. The generator and the tested system will saturate at approximately the same throughput. As a load generator for performance testing, it's limited and must be used cautiously.
3. It's almost impossible to simulate transaction errors.
4. It's difficult to generate realistic transaction arrival rate statistics, and other statistically defined transaction parameters. For example, a mean rate can be easily generated, but the variance or higher moments or the arrival rate distribution itself cannot be.

5. It's difficult to disentangle cause and effect, especially as it relates to transaction processing delays and performance.

One way to improve the situation is to strip out all but the essential parts of the system to create a generator. In many cases, this is possible because most of the error conditions represent paths that will not be executed in the load generator. For example, while the tested system must properly handle input errors, which could be generated by the load generator, it will not output errored responses (or shouldn't) to the load generator. Therefore, the processing paths for such errored responses can be stripped out of the generator. The actual creation of the driving transactions can be done on-line. Usually this would mean inserting patches or modifications to the system's program, because systems are not usually designed to autonomously initiate transactions. Alternatively, if the system has the facilities needed to retrieve and output previously stored transactions, then the transaction can be created and analyzed off-line as discussed in Section 2.3.

2.5. Self-Generation

Self-generation is cogeneration taken to the logical extreme. The tested system is used to produce its own driving load. The prerequisite to this approach is that output transactions with suitable modification, or with program patches, can be interpreted by the system as valid input transactions. If this can be done, then it is possible to physically connect output lines to input lines so that every output becomes a new input. With further modification, as discussed in Section 3 below, the load can be made to either increase with time, decrease with time, remain steady, or be otherwise controlled. The preconditions that apply to cogeneration obviously apply to self-generation, because now the opportunity to make patches or other modifications that convert the tested system into a load generator are almost nonexistent. The primary advantage to self-generation (when it can be done) is that it's even less expensive than cogeneration and doesn't tie up a set of duplicate hardware. The disadvantages are similar to that of cogeneration, only worse:

1. "Both" systems saturate at the same throughput.
2. It's not possible to overload the system, because if input is saturated, the driving output will slow down—the self-generated system perforce throttles itself.
3. There is almost no control over transaction statistics, other than the transaction arrival rate.
4. Cause and effect are intertwined. They are inherently inseparable.

5. Input and output transactions are correlated and tend to be lock-stepped to one another. Randomized timing is lost.

As a load source for performance analysis and measurement, self-generation can only be used in simple situations, or where all the artifacts of self-generation are understood. As a method of providing a constant background load, or for stress testing, it has no equal.

3. LOOPS AND SNAKES

3.1. What Are They?

A large part of generating an artificial load is the off-line portion of the load generator. When a statistically correct scenario is required, this may be the only way to do it. However, if our purpose is merely to provide background load to keep the system busy while testing, or if it is to provide a crushing load that will stress all resources, then statistical niceties can be dispensed with in the interest of getting a simple generator; use self-generation. The principle is straightforward. Take a transaction output, transform it so that it looks like an input transaction, and output it. Then, by patching or modification, or directly if possible, take the input transaction and use it (after all processing) as an output transaction, either directly or after suitable modification. The generic situation is shown in Figure 8-2.

A transaction is started on the loop by some initialization process. It is injected into the system and goes through a transaction's normal output processing. The resulting response is transmitted on the outbound line to an external transformer (e.g., a cogenerator, a microcomputer, a piece of wire) which generates a new input transaction that now enters the system in the normal

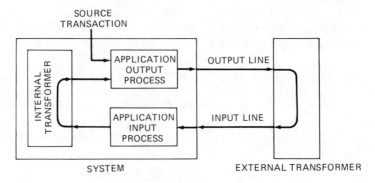

Figure 8-2. Basic Loop Structure.

way. In communications systems, the external transformer is especially simple: it is a piece of wire that connects an output line to an input line. Once a transaction is started, it will continue to circulate in this loop until terminated by placing either the input or output line out of service, or by some other command that will kill it. There are several prerequisites to generating loads in this way:

1. Input and output transactions must occur one-for-one. Every output can be transformed into a suitable input and vice-versa.
2. The external transformation is simple, or can be done with existing hardware and/or software.
3. The internal transformations can be done without inducing major artifact that will distort the entire process.
4. The protocol used is relatively simple and symmetrical, at least along non-errored paths.

The external transformer can be moved internally by interposing its functions within the input processing part of the program. For example, if the output is a response to a request in an information storage system, the requested data can be constructed to look like a valid request. The transformation then consists of stripping and inserting characters as needed to create a valid request, between the point where the transaction has been recognized as having arrived, but before it has gone through input format validation. Similarly, the internal transformer can consist of activating a stored response, or of "misrouting" the correct response to the desired output line rather than the output leg (assuming a full-duplex line) of the line along which the request came. Alternatively, if input and output line processing is handled by a dedicated microcomputer, or if it is to and from a smart terminal, they can be programmed to do the required transformations. The variations are endless and application specific. It will be assumed that the required transformation can be programmed and inserted at the most convenient point. The rest of this section will describe things in terms of communications systems because: 1) the transformations required are the simplest possible; 2) any system for which this kind of load generation can be used must have at least the rudimentary communication facilities that make such generation possible.

3.2. Simple Snakes and Loop

Figure 8-3 shows the scheme expanded to include several simplex lines (unidirectional lines). If lines are full-duplex, each half can be considered a simplex line. In communications systems, the external transformation is a piece of wire and the internal transformation consists of modifying the message's address.

The incoming transaction is entered at an input terminal or otherwise

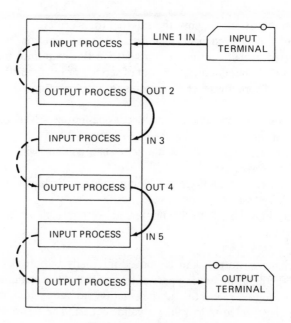

Figure 8-3. Basic Snake.

injected by a suitable command after it is fetched from storage. It goes through normal processing, and by internal routing, it is transmitted on output line 2, which is physically patched to input line 3, and so on. Details of input and output processing are left out to simplify the picture. Physical (external) connections are shown by solid lines, while internal (logical or routing) connections

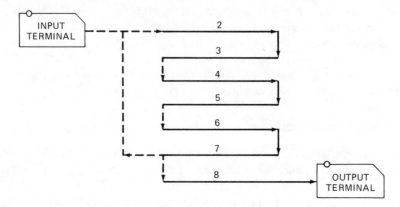

Figure 8-4. Multi-Line Loop.

are shown by dashed lines. Every message injected results in 3 input and 3 output messages. If there are N input legs and N output legs, input and output rates are multiplied by N. If the source terminal can generate one message per second, and there are 10 pairs of lines, the total throughput has been multiplied by 10. If there are a hundred lines, the throughput is multiplied by 100.

Suppose now, that instead of dumping the output transaction at the output terminal, we arrange to feed it back internally as well as externally, at the end of the loop, as shown in Figure 8-4. The original transaction is injected at the input terminal and is internally routed to output on line 2. It then follows the loop until input line 7, where it is routed in duplicate to output line 8 and to the output terminal, and also back to line 2 for output. The loop's operation is now distinctly different. Once a transaction has been inserted it will circulate in the system until one of the lines is shut off. Throughput can now be increased to the point where the lines (or the system) is saturated by injecting more transactions at the input terminal. Each new transaction entered forces one more transaction onto the loop, and one more transaction circulates the system. The number of transactions that the loop can handle is the round-trip time for the loop divided by the duration (after all protocol overhead and processing delay) of the transaction. Additional transactions entered beyond loop saturation do not increase throughput but do deplete resources, which can be useful in stress tests. The throughput is the number of transactions passing any given point per second multiplied by the number of input (or output) lines in the loop. The output terminal, to which the end of the loop was doubly terminated, acts as a monitor for the loop. Its output is exactly $1/N$ of the loop's throughput. If there is a bug, the loop will invariably terminate and so will the monitor terminal's output. If full-duplex lines and terminals are used, then the input terminal and the monitor terminal can be the same.

3.3. Linear and Exponential Loops

If instead of just routing one copy of the transaction to the loop-starting point and another to the monitor terminal, yet another copy is internally looped back to enter the loop, then each time a transaction reaches the end of the loop, another transaction is added to the loop. With N passes through the loop, there are N more transactions on it. This process doubles the number of transactions on the loop each time through. A counter can be fitted to prevent this from happening each time, so that any rate increase from a simple linear growth to doubling can be accommodated. I call these **linear loops** in contrast with **expo-nentional loops** whose growth rate is much higher.

Faster growth rates can be achieved by doing the equivalent of a duplicated output at every output point. This creates N^M messages for N circuits and M passes and hence the name "exponential loop." The system reaches saturation very, very, very quickly. The throughput rate is limited by the lines and the system's processing power and soon reaches the saturation point. What happens thereafter is the justification for the use of exponential loops. In a matter of seconds or minutes, mass storage, queues, buffer blocks, and all other memory resources, even if measured in billions of bytes, are depleted. By controlling transaction types, lengths, and other characteristics, linear and exponential loops can be used to saturate resources in almost any desired sequence. This permits full testing of resource limits without having to resort to small test values, or to the creation of millions of transactions—the system does it to itself.

3.4. Duplexed Loops

The principle of loop and snake design with full-duplexed circuits is the same, but a bit more complicated. Several loop and snake structures are shown in Figure 8-5. Keep in mind that now, each input line has a corresponding output line. As before, physical connections are shown by solid lines and logical connections by dashed lines. The system is assumed to exist on either side of the physical connections—wherever dashed-line logical connections are shown.

Figure 8-5a shows a pair of **duplexed Siamese snakes** constructed from 8 full-duplex lines. The points marked "input" are input terminals, and those marked "output" are output terminals. There are two snakes here, one that enters at line 1 and traverses the following sequence of physical connections (bold-face) and logical connections (normal type): **1-2**, 2-4, **4-3**, 3-5, **5-6**, 6-8, **8-7**. Its siamese twin travels in the opposite direction. If now, 7 is logically connected to 1 and 1 is logically connected to 7, we obtain two counter-rotating loops instead of snakes. Figure 8-5b converts the Siamese snakes into a single, long snake that traverses all circuits first in one direction then in the other.

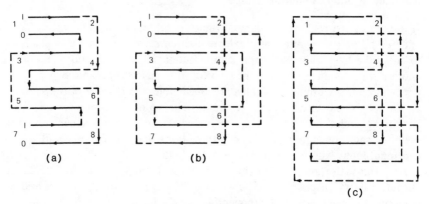

Figure 8-5. Duplex Snakes and Loops.

Connections are skipped in a pattern to force the snake to go through all circuits, with both input and output done at line 1. A similar scheme can be used to build a counter-rotating duplexed loop shown in Figure 8-5c. There are several rules that must be followed in designing loops and snakes:

1. Physical connections must always match in pairs—i.e., if output of 1 goes to input of 2, then the output of 2 must go to the input of 1.
2. Logical connections need not follow that rule.
3. Logical self-connections and physical self-connections (output of 1 to input of 1) are usually not allowed under the applicable protocol.
4. An odd number of nonsymmetrical logical connections are needed to make long loops, an even number for long snakes.

The advantage of long loops and snakes for full-duplex lines is that they cut the number of physical terminals needed for input and output in half. In most cases, with full-duplex lines and terminals the same terminal can be used to inject transactions into the loop and also as a monitor terminal.

3.5. Loop Control

Loops are stopped by breaking either a physical line or a logical connection or, equivalently, by putting any line out of service. With suitable controls you can extract exactly one transaction from a loop. This is done by having a fictitious logical terminal that simply discards one transaction when ordered to do so; alternatively, it can be done by diverting a transaction from its normal routing in the loop to the monitor terminal. The latter is preferable because it keeps all logs and records straight. Use existing operator commands, existing control mechanisms, and normal terminals to inject transactions, control the loops, and do the logical connections whenever possible. Anything out of the ordinary added to the system such as patches, while they may be more convenient than using an existing facility, cast doubt on the veracity of the transactions generated by the loops and snakes, and therefore on the tests that will be run using them.

4. BACKGROUND AND STRESS TESTING

4.1. Background Testing

4.1.1. General

Background testing is any kind of testing carried on with a simultaneously active source of transactions. These can be provided by an external load generator, cogeneration, or self-generation. The statistical characteristics of the background load are not important, because background is not used for quantitative performance evaluation. The most important thing about background load is that it exists and that it be used as early as possible in testing, from unit level up through and including system testing. Background load levels should be set sufficiently high to assure that there are more than two transactions actively undergoing processing simultaneously. If at all possible, background loads should be set higher than the expected load—at the highest level consistent with reasonable testing procedures.

4.1.2. Why and How It Works

Background testing can discover a lot of bugs, especially interactive, time dependent, or race condition bugs. Reentrance problems and data-base corruption are also caught by background testing. There's no mystery to this. If background load is used while other testing is underway, then you have forced the conjunction of a strange path (the test path) with a normal path (the background path). The more testing is conducted under high background load, the more likely it is that the conjunction of the test cases and the normal cases provided by the background will reveal bugs. The bug revealed by background does not necessarily appear in the context of the test being run. Typically, the bug shows as a program halt caused by a detected illogical condition, often in the background load. It may also be discovered only after a history log audit is run that shows that either transaction fidelity or accountability were lost.

4.1.3. Correction Procedures

A test failure with background loads active cannot be interpreted in the same way as a test failure without active background. In a normal (nonbackground) test, the usual procedure is to rerun the test to confirm the bug's existence. Confirmation usually occurs. Then, by rerunning smaller and smaller segments of the test and monitoring intermediate results, we can usually determine at exactly which step the failure occurred. If background is used, the test verification procedure must be modified.

1. Rerun the test without background. If the symptoms are confirmed, then you're back to ordinary testing.
2. The test results are not confirmed when background is turned off: repeat the test with active background. The results are either confirmed or not.
3. The test results are confirmed only with background active: repeat the test several times to assure that the effect does indeed recur.
4. The test results are not confirmed when the test is rerun with the back-

ground active. Rerun the tests with ever higher load levels, up to the maximum the system can handle.

It is possible that reruns will fail to reproduce the test failure. If the test was passed without background but failed with background, then the problem is clearly a result of either the interaction of the test transaction with the background transactions or the fact that both were being processed simultaneously. Because timings are not absolutely controlled in a test situation, it is possible that the specific race conditions and interactions will never recur under test. If the symptoms are a system crash, then things are relatively easy because we can take dumps and such and can often find the cause of the crash. If the symptoms are relatively localized processing errors, then things are more difficult indeed. The first step in debugging such problems is to determine if the symptoms are associated with test transactions, with the background transactions, or with both. This should have been done when the test failed, because it may not be possible to reproduce the failure.

We seem to be faced with the same test and debugging problems that we will have to face when such unexplained and unreproducible events occur in the field. That is the case. And there lies background testing's virtue and weakness. We have introduced more uncertainty as the price of more realistic testing. This increases the possibility of unreproducible results and of knowing that there are bugs which have not been fixed. In most cases in which a bug shows up under background but not without background, it will be quickly isolated and corrected, so that the system is better as a result of background testing. The unexplained bugs and failures would have been there whether or not we used background testing. However, they would have been noticed only in the field, where experimentation is expensive, or often impossible—the very experimentation we need to do (e.g., reruns with ever-increasing background) to explain such interactive bugs. Therefore, background testing not only helps us find and remove such bugs, but it gives us more knowledge concerning those that we noticed, could not reproduce, and could not as a result remove.

All such unreproducible and unexplained failures should be logged and documented. The associated documentation should include detailed descriptions of the tests run to attempt to reproduce the failure. The explanation may come only later in testing. The documentation should be reviewed periodically to see if any of the symptoms can be explained in terms of bugs that were discovered subsequently.

4.1.4. Extensions

The background idea can be extended to discovering bugs in data handling. The data base is configured to the maximum possible size, especially main memory. Input and output lines should also be defined to the maximum possible number. Lines for which there are no physical terminals should be placed out of service. That part of the data base or files which should not be modified by any of the tests is filled with repetitious information, or systematic information that can be easily verified by a program. The system is then run with active background. When testing is interrupted to close logs and history files, a data-base audit program is activated. This program examines all parts of the data which should not have changes and flags any that have. Because database bugs are usually wild cards, if there are more items in the data base that should not be used than items that should be used, it is more likely that a bug will modify one of the unused areas whose modification is easy to detect by the audit program.

The effectiveness of background can be further increased by allowing several independent tests to occur simultaneously. For example, there's no reason not to simultaneously enter three or four different input errors at three or four different terminals. Again, this increases the probability that the conjunction of little-used paths will reveal an interactive race condition or reentrance bug. Simultaneous testing should be reserved for the later phases of testing, say for an acceptance test dry run, so that there is confidence that the units worked correctly by themselves, and that the problem is in the fact that things were happening simultaneously.

4.2. Stress Testing

4.2.1. What Is It?

Stress testing is testing with high background load, to the point where one or more, or all resources are simultaneously saturated. It is to system testing what destructive testing is to testing of physical objects. The intention of a stress test is to "break" the system; to force a crash; to send it down in flames.* I've yet to run a stress test that didn't have that effect. Self-generation is especially effective as a stress test load because it typically stresses processing and resources more than normal loads do (albeit the stress is abnormal).

4.2.2. Why It Works

One might naively argue that a system doesn't know or care how many transactions it's processing, and that, unlike physical systems, it does not get "tired"

---

*Stress testing wasn't in the customer's mind when they asked us to build a load generator for their system which was intended to handle ten transactions a second. The on-line portion of our generator was capable of twenty transactions per second, which was more than enough to demonstrate the system's capacity, which was what the generator had been designed to do. It stressed the system at 0.1 transactions per second by crashing it. And kept on crashing the system, 0.1 transactions per second at a time, up to 4 transactions per second. Our demonstration became the ultimate stress test, and the system's designers took to calling it "the trash masher."

or stressed by heavy load. With the exception of electromechanical hardware, that's mostly true—the transistors don't get tired.* However, stress testing, despite the above does reveal many bugs. Here are a few examples of bugs caught by a stress test.

1. The programmer used a cyclic interrupt buffer to store successive interrupts while earlier ones were being processed. Stress testing showed that buffer wraparound controls had not been properly designed. Under stress, the interrupts overwrote each other and the resulting illogicals brought the system down.

2. Portions of the operating system worked at two different priority levels. The system was cyclic, so that the lower-level processing typically followed in a fixed order: three routines, A, B, and C, normally executed in that order. However, routine B was a lower-priority routine. Under stress, the actual routine's execution order was A B' A B' C, where B' indicates different segments of the interrupted B. Interlocks to assure the execution order were missing because the programmers had thought that no other sequence could occur.

3. A high-priority input interrupt driven routine fetches resources and normally holds them for a short time. It bypasses normal resource checks because the holding time is so short. A higher-priority routine under stress protracts the execution time of the guilty routine and also depletes the resource. This set of events results in a resource lockup where the resources required to clear the resources in use are not available, and as a consequence, the system crashes.

4. A fixed-head disc transfer optimizer has a bug which forces superfluous rotations when more than 64 transactions are scheduled in one revolution. Under stress, the bug is revealed by the system's catastrophic performance loss.

5. A resource management routine examines thresholds of resource utilization to trigger resource recovery actions, load throttling, and alternate processing paths (e.g., such as extending files to other media). The threshold settings are dynamic and load dependent, but the logic is faulty. Wavering load in the neighborhood of the thresholds makes the system initiate the recovery action at lower and lower loads, to the point where threshold values permit no input whatsoever and the system is in a permanent recovery.

6. A hardware problem in the logic design of a disc controller does not surface

---

*But actually they can and do. Repeated execution of some instruction sequences in a very tight loop over a long period of time can cause the doping impurities in some semiconductors to migrate to the point where the semiconductor fails. This happened to a satellite. It was brilliantly repaired with a 500-mile-long screwdriver. They found a set of commands that when executed in a tight loop reversed the impurity migration and healed the failed semiconductor.

unless the transfer rate exceeds a specified value. Similarly for logic design bugs in a system's main bus. With several hundred of these computers in the field, these hardware problems emerge only under stress testing.

Stress testing works because it does the following:

1. Forces race conditions.
2. Totally distorts the normal order of processing, especially processing that occurs at different priority levels.
3. Forces the exercise of all system limits, thresholds, or other controls designed to deal with overload situations.
4. Greatly increases the number of simultaneous actions.
5. Depletes resource pools in extraordinary and unthought of sequences.

I said earlier that one of the effects of interrupts was equivalent to the interposition of a jump to, and return from, an interrupting routine after every instruction in the interrupted routine. This increased the true number of possible processing paths in a program to unthinkable numbers. Furthermore, it is almost impossible, even if were practical, to create such situations statically. What stress testing does is to sample a small portion of these strange paths.

4.2.3. When to Stress Test

Our earlier practice had been to do stress testing last—after all other testing had been done. Recently, with good results, we've taken to doing stress testing early and repeatedly. This has several beneficial effects:

1. The bugs caught by stress testing tend to be subtle—if left to last, the project staff has been depleted and the people best able to recognize and fix these bugs are no longer available.
2. The bugs in question are rarely wild cards or simple goofs. They are often design flaws that may have implications in many areas. Getting these out early decreases the probability that the bug's symptoms will be fixed in several units where they appeared as symptoms, rather than in the unit that is actually at fault.
3. Repeated stress testing is a cheap form of regression testing. A stress test after every new version, new system assembly, or new compilation always reveals a few bugs.

The procedure, then, is to big-bang a backbone system capable of surviving element-level testing. As soon as possible, background load is tried. When background load has been debugged, the system is stressed to the breakpoint.

Stress testing continues until no further bugs are revealed by it. Then element-level testing continues. Stress testing is activated whenever possible: whenever it doesn't interfere with other testing—overnight, over weekends, at lunch. This kind of stress testing is based on normal, error-free load that of itself does not exercise strange paths. It is set to the highest level that the system can sustain with the available resources.

The above is a lot easier to do than it seems. Once background load is debugged, stress load can usually be applied to the system in a matter of minutes. Therefore, there's no difficulty in setting load to stress levels over lunch, or whenever the system's not being used for normal testing. Done in this way, over the project's life, it's not impossible to claim that the system has operated under full load for several thousand hours by the time it's delivered. Everybody has more confidence in it then.

4.2.4. Stress Test Parameter Control

Besides the stress test done as part of normal testing, as described above, specialized stress tests should be designed and implemented to test every system resource and tuning threshold. Let's consider a simple example in which a system uses queue blocks to control transactions and buffer blocks to store the transaction's data. Normally both of these resources are in main memory but can under overload conditions be extended to fixed-head discs. Similarly, the fixed-head disc pools can be extended to moving-head discs. Each of the two resources has at least two, but typically three, thresholds.

1. The threshold at which the extension is initiated.
2. The threshold at which the extension mode is stopped.
3. The threshold at which the extended data blocks and queue blocks are returned to the main memory pools.

If there were only one threshold that initiated the extension in one direction and also stopped it and recovered from the extension when traversed in the other direction, the system could be dynamically unstable. A snowball situation could occur that would deplete the pools. Think of a thermostat. The temperature at which the heating system is turned on is not the same as the one at which the system is turned off—if they were, the controls, the motors and relays would soon wear out as the system was cycled on and off several times a minute.

Every extendable resource pool has such thresholds. Other thresholds and tuning values include:

1. Maximum bounds on the number of transactions of a given type that are to be processed by a given program.

2. Bounds on the maximum duration (or number of items) to be fetched from or stored on a given media in either a given time period or a batch.
3. Maximum execution time for specified routines.
4. Maximum elapsed time between specified processing events.

It's not unusual for a real-time system to have several dozen such parameters. Individual stress subtests should be designed, if at all possible, to traverse each such threshold in both directions (up and down), thereby forcing the system to contend with all high load situations, at least one at a time. This is accomplished by:

1. Controlling the transaction arrival rate.
2. Specific transaction characteristics (e.g., length).
3. If necessary, by patching the parameter's value.

In communications systems where we use self-generation for load, we can stress all important parameters by controlling the message input rate, the length of the messages, the number of routing indicators in each message, and the duration of the test run. Analogous methods can be implemented for all systems.

4.2.5. Staging

A high-stress test should be part of every system's acceptance test. Staging the stress test is probably the most important piece of staging you can do to build the buyer's confidence. Think about a typical contemporary system's operation. What is there to see? Almost nothing. If the system runs smoothly and is well tuned, then even disc activities appear infrequent because the disc isn't seeking all over the place. At best, some tapes may show signs of activity, but that's likely not to be proportional to load. Even if there are console lights to look at, their pattern doesn't differ by much when the system is active or inactive. And many modern systems don't even have console lights to look at. Furthermore, if the system's not busy doing productive work, it's at work full tilt running exercisers. In other words, there's nothing to see—nothing to show that's in any way tangible, that indicates whether the system is busy or loafing.

We are all savages at heart and can relate better to tangible, physical evidence of work than we can to a printout that claims that the system processed 10,000 monetary transfers in the previous hour. The buyer may intellectually accept the claim that the system has achieved a certain throughput, or that it has been stressed, but that has nothing to do with the subjective belief that he's being hoodwinked—a belief that will persist until the system proves itself by doing the job for which it was designed. Staging the stress test does not mean playing games to deceive the buyer, but conducting the stress test in such a way as to provide the maximum tangible evidence that the system is being stressed. Here are several ways of providing that evidence:

1. Use an audio monitor if the computer has one, or a transistor radio. The audio monitor on early computers sampled several bits of the main memory bus. The result was a sound. If you don't have an audio monitor, try a few cheap transistor radios and an antenna wire inside the CPU's cabinet near a memory bus. FM usually works better than AM. Try it with your calculator if you don't believe me. Exercisers and bug loops produce high-pitched whistles. Interrupt-driven systems sound like a flock of chirping birds. Cyclic systems sound like donkey braying or a jazz drummer or a combination of both. The sound generally gets louder and more complicated with increased load. After a while, you can tell what the system's doing from the sounds it makes. It can be a legitimate and dramatic indicator of system activity. It depends on the system. Use it if it works.
2. Use a lot of small loops with a monitor terminal on each loop. Use teleprinters for this rather than CRT terminals. Increase the load one loop at a time, with one transaction at a time per loop. Add transactions and loops to build the load. Eventually, all the printers are going full blast. Although each monitor's activity only represents a fraction of the load, with twenty or thirty printers going the clatter is deafening enough to satisfy the most cynical critic.
3. It's a stress test, therefore anything that creates stress is legitimate even if it wouldn't be done as part of normal operations. If the system produces an end-of-day report, say at 2359, set the system clock to that time and get the high-speed printers and discs into the act as well. Set up some file searches if that'll get the discs chirping and tapes spinning.
4. If you've got an external hardware monitor that can give you periodic reports on CPU activity, disc activities, and so on, put that on a printer and get the report out.

There's no need to fake anything. Most systems can produce tangible outputs which are proportional to the system's load and which can be used in a convincing demonstration that the system is being stressed. I've always loved the excitement of a formal stress test (after all the rest has been thoroughly tested). The test director calls out, "Turn on loop seven," and a few minutes later that loop's monitor teleprinter joins in. Then he calls for loop 8, and 9, and so on. The person injecting the transactions responds each time by repeating the command (he doesn't say, "Aye, aye, sir," but it's a temptation). It's a scene out of *Star Trek* or a World War II submarine movie. The audio monitors blare, the tapes rock, the discs chirp, and soon everybody's sure that the floor is shaking under the strain. After fifteen minutes of this racket, the chief witness shouts, "Okay, okay. I'm convinced," and its time to make the reservations for the acceptance celebration. Try it. It's good.

5. PERFORMANCE TESTING

5.1. Objectives and Prerequisites

5.1.1. Objectives

Performance testing can be undertaken to: 1) show that the system meets specified performance objectives, 2) tune the system, 3) determine the factors in hardware or software that limit the system's performance, and 4) project the system's future load-handling capacity in order to schedule its replacements. All of these objectives can also be done with varying degrees of success by analytical modeling and by simulation. However, only live measurements on the real system, with a real load, can provide an accurate assessment of its performance.

Tuning is defined as optimizing the allocation of system resources—for example, by trading processing time for space, by reallocating memory pools, by putting more labor into time-critical routines, by buying new hardware, and so on. Tuning cannot be done without understanding the performance-limiting factors (objective 3 above), nor can projections of a system's ability to handle a future load. All performance-testing objectives reduce to measuring the system's performance under a real or simulated load. The first time this is done is when it's done to show that a system meets specified performance objectives—i.e., in a system performance test. This is also usually the simplest case and the only case that will be discussed in this book. Further information on analytical modeling, tuning, and performance measurement and analysis can be found in BEIZ78.

5.1.2. A Bug-Free System

Performance testing presumes a robust, working, debugged, and stable system. The debugging in question is not limited to bugs that affect a system's function, but must also include removing bugs that do not affect a system's function but which only affect its performance. Consider first bugs that affect only a system's functions. The worst such bug is one that crashes the system. In the presence of such bugs the system's performance is nil and no rational performance testing can be done. Many system bugs that affect function also affect performance. A less severe example than a system crash is a bug that forces a periodic restart. Resource loss is often recovered by a restart and lack of resources shows up as a performance degradation. Bugs can cause any protocol, such as might be used for communication links or for device handlers, to traverse retry paths more often than they would if the bug wasn't present. Erratic and illogical performance (such as decreased processing delay or decreased resource utilization with increased load over a small range) is often a sensitive symptom of a deeper, function-related bug.

Assume that all bugs that have an impact on the system's function have been removed. What remains are bugs that cannot be discovered except by performance testing. There's a spectrum for such bugs, ranging from poor strategy to poor implementation. For example, a bug that forced a disc to seek to the home position prior to the correct seek would affect performance and probably little else. A bug that allocated a chain of resources rather than a single resource will deplete the pool prematurely and therefore impact performance. Poor strategies can range from minor to outright idiocy and can also affect performance. At some point we might say that a design is so poor that even though it meets all functional requirements, it must be redone because of its performance impact.*

Thus while the objective of performance testing may be to show that a system meets specified performance objectives, most of the time spent in performance testing will be spent rooting out bugs that affect function but which are only discovered in performance testing, bugs that affect only performance, bad design strategy and tactics, and mistuning.

5.1.3. Prerequisites

Given a smoothly running, reliable, robust, bug-free system, performance testing has the following components:

1. A clear statement of performance objectives.
2. A source of transactions to drive the experiment.
3. A controlled experimental process or testbed.
4. Instrumentation to gather performance-related data.
5. Analytical tools to process and interpret the data.

The source of transactions was discussed under load generation in Section 2 above. The remaining factors will be discussed in subsequent sections.

---

*The hardware had no multiply instructions. Two numbers had to be multiplied. The first ranged from 1 to 30, the second from 1,000,000 to 5,000,000. Multiplication of these numbers was done in a loop by over-and-over addition. Which number did the programmer add how many times?

5.2. Performance Objectives

5.2.1. Background and Reality

It may seem self-evident that before one can measure performance in order to compare it to performance objectives, there should be a clear statement of what those objectives are. Self-evident it may be, but such statements are also infrequent, and therein lies one of the big problems of performance testing. Murkiness with respect to performance objectives takes the following forms.

1. There is no statement of performance objectives, or a statement so vague that it cannot be reduced to a quantitative measure.
2. The only statement of objectives is that which was made in a proposal. It may be quantitative, but its relation to reality is arbitrary. It's no more than salesman's hype because the proposer never expected the bluff to be called.
3. There is a detailed and clear statement of objectives. It's quantitative but unmeasurable in the practical world. It requires resources or effort in excess of the contract value, or an experiment duration that exceeds the system's expected lifetime.
4. There is a detailed and clear statement of objectives, but the objectives are unachievable at reasonable costs. No objections to it were raised by *any* bidder, because none wanted to risk disqualification and all expected that it would go away or be modified.

All the above lead to problems concerning system performance—problems that are sometimes resolved only after costly arbitration or litigation; solutions that may leave the buyer with wholly inadequate performance, or that may force the vendor to supply double or triple the original hardware capacity, or double the software development cost, or all three. While performance verification may not be a contractual requirement, if one of the above scenarios or a variation applies, performance testing in some form may be initiated by a vendor as a defensive move or by the buyer in support of litigation. A clear understanding by all parties of performance objectives and validation criteria is, therefore, the single most important prerequisite to performance testing.

5.2.2. Performance Measures

Performance measures and requirements are quantitative—that is, numbers: numbers that can be measured and confirmed by rational experiments. A performance specification consists of a set of specified numbers. The system's actual performance is measured and compared to the specification. The measured numbers either are less or more than the specified values. If less, the system fails, if more, it passes the performance requirements. Everything else is a variation of these simple ideas. If it can't be reduced to measured numbers (perhaps in the form of probability distributions), then it isn't a performance specification and has nothing to do with performance testing.

What is the difference between a microcomputer and a supercomputer? Assume that both can access as much memory as might be needed. Both the smallest and the largest computers can be programmed to do exactly the same job. A programmable calculator with access to a disc or tape, such as a HP41CV (for an inconceivable number of program overlays and data-base fetches), can be programmed to do the same job done by an airline passenger reservation system, say. The difference between the two is the rate at which transactions can be submitted and the delay that the completion of those transactions will entail. If transactions are submitted at a rate faster than the system can handle, the system is said to be **saturated** and the delay is infinite. The rate at which transactions are submitted to the system is called the **load**. The rate at which the system processes transactions is called the **throughput**. These are not necessarily the same. Figure 8-6 shows the typical relation between throughput and processing delay. Load is measured in arriving transactions per second. Processing delay is measured in seconds. Every system experiences a finite, non-zero delay at zero throughput. That delay is at least the delay required to process one transaction, but may include other internal delays due to overhead processing and a variety of other factors. Every system has a maximum steady-state throughput, called the **saturation throughput**, at which some resource (CPU execution time, channel transfer rates, disc access rates,

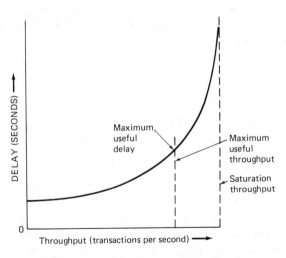

Figure 8-6. Typical Throughput-Delay Function.

memory) is fully occupied. At that throughput, if allowed, the delay would be infinite. In practice this doesn't happen. A poorly designed system will crash, but a properly designed system will take steps (such as delaying input polls) to forestall the new transactions. Such delayed transactions, while not delayed within the system because they are prevented from entering, experience an external waiting delay. If the tasks are presented to system at a steady saturation rate, even though not delayed within the system, considering the global system that consists of the processing equipment and the user population, the transactions suffer an infinite delay nevertheless. As interesting as the saturation throughput might be intellectually, pragmatically every proper performance specification states requirements in terms of a maximum useful delay and an associated minimum throughput. What constitutes a maximum useful delay is context dependent. A processing delay of a few milliseconds is intolerable in an antiaircraft missile control computer. A few tens of milliseconds might be tolerable for a nuclear reactor controller. Telephone users get angry when dial tone delays exceed a few seconds. Stockbrokers become exasperated when the system takes half a minute to answer their query. Employees get frantic and go on strike when payroll checks are a day late. Congressmen start investigations when the census bureau's statistics aren't available in time to reapportion districts prior to the next election. Each user of a multi-programmed system, such as a time-shared system, while resident in the system can be looked upon as a source of transactions. Collectively, all the users represent a source which, while usually described as "degree of multi-programming" or "number of simultaneously active users," can also be reduced to an equivalent transaction arrival rate or throughput.

So you see, it doesn't matter if the system is large or small, real-time or batch, uni- or multi-programmed, commercial or technical—in all cases, a performance specification can, and must, be reducible to a relation between throughput and delay.

5.2.3. Complications and Variations

The above is a simple case and assumes only one throughput and one delay. As such, it applies only to the simplest systems. Real systems have much more complicated measures:

1. There is more than one kind of throughput. Throughput may be expressed by a mix of different transaction types, or by a set of probability distributions for different transaction types. There could be a different measure for each type. Throughput could be expressed as a function of the different types in specified proportions.
2. Each transaction type could have a different maximum useful delay speci-

fied. Alternatively, several different mixes of types could be presented, with each mix having a different maximum delay specified.

3. Assume one transaction type and one delay specification. The delay is not defined by a single number but by the parameters of a distribution. For example, "The probability that the delay at a throughput of 4 messages per second shall exceed 2 seconds shall be less than .05, and the probability that the delay at a throughput of 8 messages per second shall exceed 8 seconds shall be less than .02, and the probability over the entire range of throughputs that the delay will exceed 120 seconds shall be less than 0.00001." Variations with multiple transaction types and multiple specifications of delays for mixes, with distributions, also occur.

4. Performance may be intertwined with a quantitative reliability/maintainability/availability specification. Different throughput-delay relations are allowed under different hardware failure conditions. Not only must performance be measured for the all-up state, but for degraded states as well.

The most insidious complication, however, is that which comes about through specification changes. As the project progresses, but before it's finished, changes are made—new functions are added and previous functions enhanced. All of these must adversely impact performance. There is no free lunch. If the processing time per transaction is increased, then the saturation throughput must decrease, the throughput at which the maximum useful delay occurs must decrease, and the delay at any throughput must increase. That's physics, not programming. Yet, because of the practical difficulties associated with analyzing the performance impact, the performance specification is not changed and the builder doesn't usually remind the buyer that there is a performance impact. If it gets bad enough, it may lead to litigation. I don't really know why performance impacts are so often swept under the rug only to emerge at performance testing time—but they are. Because they're swept under the rug is perhaps the reason that there's more chicanery, obfuscation, outright dishonesty, and trauma associated with performance testing than with any other form of testing I know.

5.2.4. Difficult and Impossible Measures

Just because there is a clear performance specification doesn't mean it's measurable. One of the more difficult types of measures to employ is one which involves transient response times and time-varying loads. Almost all performance analyses and measurement of computer systems are done under the assumption of steady-state load. The analysis and measurement of computer systems under time-varying loads that cannot be reduced to steady-state loads or quasi-steady-state loads is in its infancy, and what there is of it is beyond the scope of this and many future books. In process-control systems, where there is a long history of analytical techniques, the transient behavior of systems and the measurement thereof is not so bleak, but also beyond the scope of this book.

Transient problems aside, what makes a measurement difficult is the lack of proper measurement tools. Processing delay can be difficult and expensive to measure. It may take a lot of external monitor hardware to clearly identify the input and the output to that occurred as a result of that input. Systems, especially those that use communication links, can suffer queueing delays caused by devices and other systems that are external to it. What is measured then is the combined global system and total delays which must be accurately subdivided into external and internal components. Finally, there is the problem of **artifact**. **Artifact** is a distortion of the measured value caused by the act of measurement. For example, instructions inserted in an on-line program to measure a processing delay contribute to that delay and therefore distort the measured values. Artifact must be disentangled, typically by analytical means, from true delay. If the artifact is severe, the entire measurement may be invalid.

The final prerequisites, then, are that in addition to a quantifiable relation between throughput and delay, there must be means to measure that delay and throughput. Builder and buyer must agree to the acquisition of the necessary tools to measure the performance parameters and to correct the measurement if necessary to get rid of measurement-induced artifact.

5.3. Instrumentation Issues

Performance testing requires instrumentation to measure performance parameters. Instrumentation takes two principal forms: hardware and software. Hardware instrumentation is almost always augmented by some form of software instrumentation, and this combination is often more effective than either method alone. Whatever is used, it is used to measure or record things of interest—call them **events**. Examples include I/O operations, transaction delays, interrupt counts, number of calls to subroutines—anything that makes sense in the context of performance testing and tuning. We can subdivide what is recorded regarding an event into four categories:

1. *Logging.* All the information of interest concerning an event: start and stop time, system state, register contents, and so on. An event log can be made as simple or as complicated as you wish, but if software is used for logging, then the more complex the log, the more the artifact. Event logging, because it is a software means, is especially artifact prone.
2. *Event Counts.* In many cases all that's necessary is a count of events over a

specified period. For example, a count of input and output transactions. Event counts are accumulated in counters and periodically logged. Event counts are simpler and induce less artifact than event logs, but lose the identity of the individual events.

3. *Event Durations.* The duration of events or processes can be measured directly by hardware or software means. Just as we can discard information to reduce artifact by using event counts instead of event logs, we can accumulate event durations for specified events. Dividing by corresponding event counts gives us mean event durations. Event durations can be accumulated or recorded only if there is a clear way of recognizing the start and stop of an event.

4. *Sampling Methods.* Further artifact reduction and precision improvement can be achieved at a loss of information concerning individual events by using statistical sampling methods. For example, instead of accessing the clock to get the start and stop of a specific disc access, and then subtracting to get the duration of that access, you can sample the activity of the disc. By keeping count of how often a 100-millisecond sample, say, of the disc activity was active, you obtain the mean disc utilization. For example, out of 1000 samples it was active 435 times. The utilization is therefore 0.435.

5.4. Software Instrumentation

5.4.1. Control

The basic processes of logging, counting, timing, and sampling can be done by software: by inserting code. Logging is the most artifact prone because the most data is recorded with an event log. Software instrumentation, while giving precise and copious information, cannot be inserted into a program wholesale lest the system spend all its time processing artifact and instrumentation rather than doing honest work. Means are required to turn software instrumentation on and off. Some methods are:

1. *Conditional Logic.* All instrumentation software is fitted with bypass-control logic (e.g., flags) which jump the program around the instrumentation code. Only the software probes needed at the moment are active. This introduces relatively little artifact, except for program space. Processing time can be affected in systems with cache and paged memories. Page boundary crossing frequency may be affected, as may working set statistics. The biggest price is object code space. It is effective when such logic can be centralized and is inherently small. We've put sampling software into systems permanently with very little artifact.

2. *Conditional Compilation or Assembly.* An obvious method to use if availa-

ble. Only those software probes that are to be active are assembled, and only those result in object code. There is no space penalty. However, because space does change in accordance with which probes are activated, page boundary statistics may be affected. Another source of artifact is subtler. An optimizing compiler may produce different codes and different run times depending on which probes are activated. The biggest headache with conditional compilation for inserting software probes is that, in the context of a full system, recompilation could be a very time-consuming process. The next biggest problem is the proliferation of variant object programs.

3. *Patching.* Object-level patching provides the greatest control for the greatest effort. Almost all artifact, except that which is directly involved in the measurement, can be eliminated. The patch is done the usual way—by an unconditional branch to the instrumentation area followed by a return to the patched instruction. It has several serious problems that must not be ignored. Patches are inherently buggy, dangerous and misunderstood. Patches come loose after recovery or reload. They are rarely properly recorded.

5.4.2. Software Probes

1. *Event Logs.* Software is used to recognize events of, interest, and, when recognized, the associated data is recorded in a log buffer. Logs are accumulated until the buffer fills in order to take advantage of batch operation efficiency—e.g., large block transfers to a disc. Elaborate logs should be avoided because of artifact. Wherever possible, use existing system records even if this may require a lot of off-line processing. Start by listing the events of interest and then examine by-product and historical files to see how such information can be gleaned from the history records. Sometimes, all that's needed may be one or two missing numbers to allow the entire set of data to be derived from the normal system logs or accounting data. If specialized logs are required, keep the on-line processing to a minimum. Record things as integers, and do all normalization and scaling operations off-line.

2. *Event Counting.* This is a software probe's strongest point. It is much easier to recognize a significant event from within the software than by hardware means. The probe's logic detects the event and increments the appropriate counter. Clearly, counters must be periodically recorded, and then reset. Alternatively, counters can be recorded when they overflow. Periodic resetting is the cleaner method. Use very large counters—say 32 bits—so that the probability of wrapping is nil. Keep them in a block, and store and reset them periodically. The artifact is minimized and no time is wasted checking for overflow.

3. *Event Duration Measurements.* This is a software probe's weakest point. Event duration measurement requires access to a real-time clock or incrementing specified counters under an interrupt while the event is in progress. If time is recorded, then two logs are required, or an on-line subtraction. If interrupts are counted, there's conditional logic at every interrupt. Besides the inherently high artifact induced by on-line event duration measurements, there's additional uncertainty. Application programs may not have real clock access—but access only after high-priority programs have returned control to the application level. While not a significant error for events that last minutes, this error is very significant if you are trying to measure disc seek times, say, which last a few hundred milliseconds.

5.4.3. Sampling Methods

Sampling methods, whether used for event counting, logging, or timing, can be the most accurate and can minimize artifact. Software instrumentation samples all events, counters, etc. (although not all at the same rate). The probe point (i.e., the software instrumentation point) is used to set and reset event flags, and to increment and reset event counters. The sample is triggered by a periodic clock interrupt, and, in accordance with coded instructions, all memory locations of interest are recorded. Efficiency is obtained by keeping such memory locations in a contiguous memory block.

Computers and operating systems with subroutines and/or priority stacks are especially amenable to sampling methods. If the clock interrupt operates at a high priority level (the highest, say, except for hardware fault interrupts), the top of the stack can be sampled and the identity of the interrupted routine can be recorded. Typically, this is a program counter value. Subsequent off-line analysis, based on knowing the subroutine's object-level locations, can then be used to determine which subroutine was executing when the interrupt occurred. Sufficient samples of this kind can be used to determine the effective elapsed time for all routines in the system. Depending on how much you wish to incorporate of the program's map, you can focus on individual routines, segments of programs, etc. We've instrumented systems by making the subroutine's identity part of the call. The instrumentation is then relocatable, and the subsequent mapping operation is not needed. Accuracy can be increased by increasing the number of accumulated counts. If means are provided to measure the execution time of the entire program, then the elapsed execution time for individual routines can be accurately determined. Note that the artifact is constant and depends only on the processing done at the clock interrupt level. Because the program counter can only be in one location at the time the sample is made, the artifact is always the same, no matter what the system is doing— a constant amount for each clock interrupt. Analytical correction to remove the artifact is then trival.

5.5. Hardware Instrumentation

5.5.1. Hardware Monitors

A hardware monitor is typically a mini- or a microcomputer that has probes which are used to sample hardware elements within the instrumented computer. Connectors or probes are attached to the bus, I/O channels, memory data ports, memory address ports, interrupt lines, etc. The connector or probe is a high-impedance device so that the hardware operation of the monitored system is not affected.

5.5.2. Hardware Event Detection

Event detection in a software monitor is implicit. The programmer inserts instructions in the running program whose execution is dependent on the occurrence of the event. The logic associated with detection of the event can be, in the software monitor, as elaborate or as simple as circumstances require. Consequently, events detected by software monitors are meaningful from the point of view of application, but the price for this is artifact. This is the fundamental trade-off between hardware and software monitors. Hardware monitors are free of artifact, but simplistic and limited.

Hardware monitors detect events by wired (plugboard) or programmed logic. Programmed logic in this context does not mean a normal computer's program, but the operation of a programmed logic device or microcode that can evaluate truth functions of a bit pattern. The idea behind a hardware monitor is to recognize events that occur at bus or memory speed. Logic hardware looks at the bit patterns traversing the probe lines and evaluates those patterns for a hit. The logic can range from simple masking to ranges of values, to combination or sequences of values. Examples are:

1. Any memory address above 17777777.
2. A bus data line value between 234 and 336.
3. A memory data value of 12345671.
4. A bus sequence of "Z C Z C."
5. A boolean expression in line values.

The event, once detected, is logged and recorded. What happens subsequently depends on what the monitor has been programmed to do with that event.

Hardware logic is limited. Consequently, events with elaborate criteria must be recognized partially by the hardware and partially by software executed within the monitor. While the execution of programs within the hardware monitor to extend the limited hardware logic is possible, such programs consume monitor resources. And even though the hardware monitor's operation does not create artifact in the measured system, the monitor is itself susceptible to saturation and artifact. For example, if it takes 20 microseconds of monitor CPU time to record an event, the monitor cannot record more than 50,000 events per second. If the hardware monitor is operated close to saturation, it, too, will run out of buffers, fall behind in time-tagging events, or otherwise fail to keep up with what it is recording. This is an indirect form of artifact which must be considered. As with software monitors, the answer may lie in splitting the measurements over several runs, with different probes activated in each run.

5.5.3. Event Logging

Event logging consists of detecting the event, time-tagging it, and recording the data. In the first two parts of this operation, the hardware monitor is superior. The event might be signaled by addressing a specific memory location, assuming that the monitor was monitoring the memory address bus. The artifact associated with time-tagging the event which occurs in a software monitor does not exist. Typically, one attempts to get the memory address as a by-product of normal processing: i.e., the event causes a jump to a specified location. The monitor detects the jump on the memory address lines. At worst, you have to insert an instruction to write junk to a memory location whose address is used as a code for the event.

5.5.4. Event Counting

This is where the hardware monitor's superiority is clear. Instead of time-tagging the event, the monitor (under monitor software/hardware control) increments (decrements) specified counter(s) in the monitor's memory, when the event is detected. Software in the monitor records and resets the counters in accordance with programmed schedules and criteria (e.g., periodic reset, reset on overflow, etc.).

5.5.5. Event Duration Measurement

Two events are required. One event must be detected that initiates a timer, and another that terminates the timer. The timer is updated at specified rates by the monitor software. For example, the first event is the detection of the I/O instruction that initiates the disc seek operation on the disc channel. The second event is the detection of the seek-complete interrupt (say) associated with the same channel. The first event is programmed to start the counter and the latter to stop the counter. While most counters are programmed and implemented in monitor memory, some monitors use hardware counters and are consequently fast but limited. The completion of the time measurement causes the event, the duration, and the completion time-tag to be recorded.

5.5.6. Internal Events

The typical monitor is a minicomputer. It can, therefore, detect and record internal events. For example, you can specify that event duration measurements be recorded in a set of counters that are used to record a distribution of, say, seek times. Monitor software, on-line, checks the range of the time interval and increments the associated counters. As with software monitors, there is no limit to sophistication other than monitor resources and saturation.

5.5.7. Sampling Methods

Sophisticated monitors can be programmed to turn probes on and off and can therefore be used to sample events, thereby reducing the probability of monitor saturation. Just what can be sampled depends on the monitor's logic ability and the architecture of the system it is monitoring. For example, microcomputers offer few opportunities to insert probes into the system. Conversely, large main-frame machines may be fitted with probes on ALU's, cache memory, etc., including hardware elements that are not directly monitorable by pure software techniques.

5.5.8. Monitor Data Processing

On-line processing and data reduction by a hardware monitor is avoided for the same reason that it's avoided with software monitors. The hardware monitor is a computer and is also subject to artifact and saturation. Typically, the monitor's data is recorded for subsequent analysis, or is recorded on a compatible medium so that it can be processed by another, more powerful computer.

5.6. The Experimental Process

5.6.1. Real Versus Test Beds

There is a profound difference in measurements taken in support of performance testing on a test bed and the same measurements done in the field. While satisfactory performance can be demonstrated using a few data points on the test bed, the same prediction when based on live data from the field may require thousands of data points and sophisticated statistical methods to produce a valid prediction. That kind of analysis is worthy of a book in its own right. For more information see BEIL77, BEIZ78, DANI71, DRAP81, and FREI71. The present discussion will be based on test bed measurements.

The use of random load—that is, input transactions with parameters created by a randomizing process—is appropriate to performance testing if that random load's statistics match the statistics specified by the buyer. However, note that as the simulated load is made to more closely approximate the real load, its variability increases and so does the analysis required to confirm the system's performance. A perfect load simulation is identical to a live systems and must be analyzed by the same statistical methods.

The above, however, is not the real issue regarding the use of random loads or "realistic" loads in system performance testing. The real issue is that the buyer hasn't got the foggiest notion of what the statistics should be. I hear the buyers screaming "foul" in the background—but that's the truth, and they're not to be blamed. Here are some reasons why it's almost impossible to get meaningful statistics concerning transactions beyond projected input rates and a few simple, key parameters.

1. There's never been a system like this before. It's a new service in a new market. The buyer has hopes and guesses, but no hard evidence. The system provides a variety of services and functions. After a few years of operation, some "neat" functions will have never been used, and some "unimportant" functions which had been added as an afterthought, or for developmental and test convenience, will be more popular than any other feature.
2. It's a replacement system. Every department in the user's organization has been asked to make projections of load and characterizing statistics. They individually produce a combination of what they're actually doing, what they think they should be doing, what they'd like to do if given the resources, and drop what they think they shouldn't be doing. There's puffing and exaggeration all along the line, as well as rampant conservatism. Then middle management doubles the estimates, cost accounting chops them in half, and upper management fudges the budget. What do such statistics mean?
3. It's a replacement system and there are good statistics and good projections. But no one can properly gauge how the replacement system will affect user habits and the operational environment. That changes the statistics.
4. Wars, depressions, inflation, strikes, embargoes, mergers, acquisitions, deaths, suicides, births, love and hate—all these conspire to make any projection uncertain. Load projections and statistics ultimately are a measure of how people will behave (process control and similar applications are a notable exception).

Just how bad are such statistics? I'm delighted with any load projection and statistics that prove to be within 25% of reality. I hope that designers will consider the possibility that any system parameter (other than raw load) could vary by $\pm 50\%$, and that they provide sufficient tuning flexibility to accommodate such variability. The test bed experiment is based on projected load characteristics. There's no point in providing the full variability of real loads, because that variability is too uncertain. The mean values should be realistic and should correspond to specified values (e.g., mean transaction arrival rate, mean length, mean duration, mean error rates, etc.), but the variation (e.g., standard deviation) can be kept deliberately small. This will considerably reduce the subsequent processing and interpretation labor, as well as simplify the experimental process. The final point to consider when comparing test bed results with real results is that it takes a long time—six months to a year—for systems to stabilize. During that working-in and familiarization period, the load is so loused up with cockpit errors that any statistical inference is hardly worth the paper it's printed on.

5.6.2. The Actual Experiment

It is an experiment and should be treated as such. There are three rules to follow:

1. Everything should be controlled.
2. Change one thing at a time.
3. Redo the run if rules 1 and 2 are violated.

No other testing should be going on while performance tests are run. Hardware should be run under exerciser and diagnostic programs to confirm their operability. In duplexed systems, a preliminary set of performance testing runs should be done to confirm that the performance is the same for all configurations and permutations.*

It's easier to describe the experiment as if an external load generator is used, although the same principles apply to cogeneration and self-generation.

1. Verify that all initial conditions are satisfied. Clear the system, boot it, load the data base (fresh for each run), and start the system.

---

*Don't assume that identical computers made by the same manufacturer run at the same speed. Don't assume it—prove it or disprove it by measurement. I've measured speed differences of 30% between two computers—differences that didn't show up until we started performance testing. Configuration speed differences can be bizarre. Computers A and B working with discs C and D respectively operate at the same speed, but A working with D and B working with C are much slower. It's tough to prove. And you may have to resort to some special benchmark runs to demonstrate it. Even then, you'll have to rub the manufacturer's nose in it before they'll admit to the problem and correct it. I wouldn't get upset about a speed difference of under 5%, because that could be due to an unavoidable difference in the length of cables and the only way you could equalize the speed would be to slow the faster computer.

2. Do the same for the load generator.
3. Run a few standard tests to confirm that the load generator works, that the system works, and that they can talk to each other.
4. Use fresh media for each run—e.g., don't mix several different runs on the same disc pack, tape, or floppy.
5. Mark the time and all pertinent data in a test log book.
6. Run the generator for that data point.
7. Close all log files and remove them from the on-line system.
8. Duplicate the log files and protect the primary from inadvertent destruction and overwriting—if the run is long and expensive, triplicate the data.
9. Confirm that the system was working after the run.
10. Run the data gathered through an analytical program that calculates the same statistical parameters that were used by the off-line generator to generate the scenario file. Confirm that the statistics match, and explain if they don't.

5.6.3. Analysis

Analysis of the results can be a complicated thing, particularly if performance is multidimensional and specified statistically. Let's say for the moment that the system's performance measure consists of determining the relation between throughput and delay. However, there are several different kinds of transactions that go into the throughput. Instead of working with delays, it's easier to work with the delay's reciprocal, which I call the system's **subjective rate**. I call it the subjective rate because it is the rate which one user sees as the system's effective processing rate at that throughput. The system might be servicing ten users simultaneously, each of which is introducing a transaction every 10 seconds. The throughput, or **objective rate**, is one transaction per second. Suppose that each user, because the system is servicing other users, sees a delay of 5 seconds per transaction. To that user, the system seems to be capable of processing 1/5 of a transaction per second. The advantage of the subjective rate curve over the throughput-delay curve is that the subjective rate is nearly linear for many systems. In fact, for the simplest, ideal, queueing system it would be a line sloping downward at a 45-degree angle. Figure 8-7 shows the subjective rate curve corresponding to the typical throughput-delay curve. Instead of a maximum useful delay, we have a minimum useful subjective rate. Saturation occurs when the subjective rate becomes zero. Figure 8-8 shows a real subjective rate data set taken from a large communication system. Notice the relative high degree of scatter caused by the variability of the real data (among other things). The higher control over the test bed situation almost completely eliminates the scatter.

If there are several components to the throughput (e.g., several different

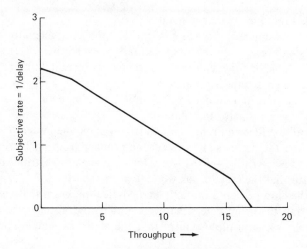

Figure 8-7. Typical Subjective Rate Function.

transaction types), then it is necessary to do runs not only with different load levels, but with different mixes of loads. The total throughput is expressed as the sum of the component throughputs, and algebra or regression analyses can be used to break the data down to determine the impact of different load mixes. From data gathered over several different mixes of load it's then possible to predict what the system will do under a load mix that was not tested. This is one of the ways in which unrealistic test bed measurements (say, because of load generation method limitations) can be extended to predict the system's behavior under more realistic loads. A word of warning, however. When using

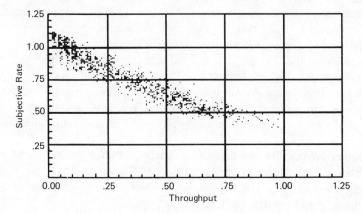

Figure 8-8. Subjective Rate Data for a Real System.

mixes of loads, it's important that there be no linear relation between the different components of the load. Choose odd numbers and primes. If you do not randomize the data points this way, you may inadvertently establish a functional relation between the various mixes that makes the data for the different mixes mathematically equivalent—a lot of processing and effort will go into it, and you'll have to do it over again.*

5.6.4. Detailed Analysis

Once you have confirmed that the system's overall behavior is reasonable, you're ready to start examining details in that behavior. Either with additional runs or from the data already gathered, determine the following:

1. For the range of throughput, the processing time for all major software elements, particularly those that are believed to be limiting the performance.
2. Divide the percentage of time spent doing a process by the throughput to obtain the expected processing time per transaction as a function of throughput for each process.
3. Are the per-transaction processing times for different components reasonable and according to expectations? Confirm or explain if not reasonable.
4. Rank the per-process times in decreasing order and do additional runs that break the largest ones down into their components. Try for 10 to 20 processing components the largest of which consumes no more than 10% of the total processing time.
5. Examine the per-process processing time–throughput curve for any sharp breaks, wiggles, notches, and other discontinuities. They are usually indicative of bugs. Repeat the run at such points with additional data gathering and probes activated.
6. A per-process curve that slopes gradually downward with increasing throughput is typical of batch operations—overhead remains constant with increased load and is amortized over more transactions.
7. A continual rise indicates a function that gets less efficient with increasing load. Typical of scan operations, sorts, mergers, searches, and so on.

---

*For the analyst, here is what I'm talking about. The throughput mix is expressed as a linear function of the form $a_0 + a_1x_1 + a_2x_2 + a_3x_3 ...$, where x_i is throughput component i. In any one run, you vary the load from zero to the maximum, while holding the relative value of the coefficients the same. A different mix is a different set of relative coefficients. If the different mix vectors are linearly related, when you attempt to determine the system's response as a function of different mixes, you'll find that the matrix you have to solve is singular. You had 10 variables in the mix and therefore had to test at least 10 mixes, but they were inadvertently linearly related—there's nothing to do but repeat a tedious and expensive experiment.

8. A fall followed by a rise is a combination of 6 and 7 above and may mean nothing.
9. A rise followed by a fall is almost always indicative of a bug or a poor design.
10. Rank system resources in decreasing order of utilization at the throughput of interest. Note any resource that is saturated and that was wasted even though it was the performance-limiting resource.
11. Examine the system both at zero and saturation load. Saturation load data gives you the system's saturation mechanism and is a guide to tuning it at lower throughputs.

For more information on analyzing the results of performance tests, tuning, and performance measurements see BEIL77, BEIZ78, BUNY74, DANI71, DRAP81, DRUM73, FERR78, FREI71, and BORO79.

5.6.5. Reconciling the Results

Do not expect the results of performance testing to be easily comparable to the specified requirements. If the system was oversold, or sold in anticipation of higher future loads, then the measured results may exceed the specification by a large margin and everybody's happy. More typically, the measured results (which we'll assume are correct) fall short of requirements or are close to the specified values. Then comes the time for reconciling the measurements to the specification. Several steps should be taken before the subject is broached:

1. Confirm and validate all analyses used to get the results. Don't mark it confirmed until you've gotten the same results three times in a row.
2. Confirm the source data and redo runs or portions of runs if necessary.
3. Review all design changes and enhancements that could have affected performance. Did the runs include such changes, and were performance expectations changed to match?

If you have good data and a controlled test bed, it may be necessary to temporarily disable the new features to demonstrate that the system would have met the requirements had the changes not been made. This may not help, because an enhancement or new function might affect things across the board. It might not be possible to remove, or removing it might not affect performance. If you can reconcile the measured performance to the specified performance by setting up an experiment that demonstrates the impact of changes and enhancements, then that's the best way to do it. Barring that, it may be necessary to use the measured data as the basis for an analytical model and then to modify that analytical model to demonstrate the impact of the enhancement. The very best way, though, would have been to have had an earlier performance analysis that was updated as specification changes were made, to have analytically determined the impact of each and every change, and to have obtained relief from the buyer in the form of a revised performance specification for every change incorporated that had a performance impact. That way, there's nothing to reconcile.

6. TASKS FOR A QUALITY ASSURANCE DEPARTMENT

1. Include load generation for background, stress, and performance testing as a major budget item—probably to be shared equally between software development and quality assurance.
2. Select load generation methods (external, cogeneration, self-generation) appropriate to schedule, expected residual value, need, and validity. Start load generation development at the same time as software development.
3. Plan software instrumentation in support of performance testing as part of the system design rather than as an afterthought. Develop, publish, and discuss embedded software instrumentation as early as possible.
4. Tie down load statistics and parameters as early as possible in the project and in contractually binding written form.
5. Establish a method (e.g., continual revision of models) for tracking performance impacts of buyer changes just as you track cost and schedule impacts—it's no less important.
6. Include background testing as part of element-level testing, as soon as it is feasible. Test reports should include whether or not the tests were run under background.
7. Start stress testing as early as possible in the program. Subject the system to stress whenever possible—after every revision, after every new version, after every major data-base change, and so on.
8. Include a well-staged stress test as the highlight of the formal system acceptance test; be sure to rehearse it.
9. Accept no performance criteria that cannot be measured and validated with the allocated personnel, schedule, and monetary resources. Conversely, be sure that all persons involved are aware of the cost and time that might be associated with validating specific performance parameters.
10. Plan performance testing as a specific, recognizable activity to be done on a test bed, and if necessary in the field. Be sure to allow enough time for the system and users to stabilize before attempting field performance testing.
11. Run performance tests intermixed with other system tests to detect bugs whose primary symptoms are performance-related. Validate the system's performance by a test run after every major revision, version change, data base change, and so on.

9

QUANTITATIVE METHODS

1. SYNOPSIS

Methods for measuring complexity, predicting bugs and programming difficulties, McCabe's metric, Halstead's metric, the state of software reliability theory, the Hitachi method.

2. QUANTITATIVE MEASURES AND METRICS

2.1. Philosophy

One of the characteristics of a maturing discipline is the replacement of art by science. Science is epitomized by quantitative methods. Early physics, in classical Greece say, was dominated by discussions of the "essence" of physical objects, with almost no attempts to quantify such essences. They were struggling with what questions should be asked. Quantification was impossible until the right questions were asked. By the sixteenth century, physics began to be quantified—first by Galileo and then by others—a trend that has continued to today. In the eighteenth century we called physical scientists "natural philosophers," recognizing that all the right questions hadn't been asked, and that all was not yet, even in principle, amenable to quantitative analysis. Today, physics is as hard and quantifiable a science as one can get and far removed from its speculative roots in philosophy.*

Computer science (I think that the term is still presumptuous—we're still more of a craft than a science) is following the same trend towards quantification. Ultimately we hope to be able to convert a specification by mechanical

---

*But very modern particle physics borders on mysticism and seems to be ready to make a full circle back to speculative nonquantitative philosophy.

means into precise estimates of labor, resources, and reliability. Ultimately. If there's a note of skepticism it's because so much of what we want to quantify is tied in with humanity and its erratic behavior. Should we expect greater success over a shorter period of time than economists and sociologists have had? Our objective, then, is not necessarily the ultimate truth, the "real" model of how programs and systems behave, but a partial, practical truth that is adequate for the practitioner. Does it matter whether our models of program complexity or software reliability are right or wrong in some abstract sense so long as they correlate well with reality? We have programs to write and systems to debug. We can leave the search for truth to the theorists and be content with pragmatism. What works is what counts. For metrics in general, see GILB77 and PERL81.

2.2. A Historical Prespective

I've no record of programming labor estimates on ENIAC, but I'm sure they fell far short of reality. The first programmer, Lady Lovelace, who coded for Charles Babbage's wonderful but unfinished computer in the nineteenth century, I'm sure often said, "Just one more week, Mr. Babbage, and it'll be done." Lucky for her the hardware was never finished, so she never did have to go beyond desk checking. By the mid 1950s individual programmers (highly individualistic programmers, I may add) had coalesced into programming groups, which meant there was now a new profession: programmer manager. The managers, who were ultimately responsible for productivity and quality, soon began to measure software effort in terms of "number of lines of code." That was used as a basis for predicting programming costs, testing costs, running time, number of bugs, salaries, the gross national product, the inflation rate of the peso, and who knows what else. It is today still the primary quantitative measure in use: "Count the number of lines of code, and you know all there is to know." A landmark study by Weinwurm, Zagorski, and Nelson (WEIN65, NELS67) debunked any such simplistic measure. They showed that cost was heavily influenced by such things as the number of meetings attended, the number of items in the data base, the relative state of hardware development (if new hardware), documentation requirements, and other factors that didn't relate directly to simple measures such as lines of code. The study also debunked popular programmers' myths, such as "Real-time software is much more difficult than batch processing." The study is important because it's among the first serious large-scale efforts to quantify the issues in programming. Furthermore, the base for this study was not a bunch of small homework exercises, but a large group of system programs, spanning the entire range from subroutines to systems. As a basis for cost estimating, these studies have yet to be surpassed by anything that's been published.

2.3. Objectives

Our objective in this book is not to quantify all of computer science, but only to explore those measures (or **metrics**) of software complexity and reliability that have proven their worth in practice. To see what kinds of metrics we need, let's ask a few questions:

1. How much will it cost to develop this software?
2. How long will it take?
3. How good will it be when it's done?

I won't try to answer all of questions 1 and 2, because that would be a book on programming management and would require us to get into design, development, coding, documentation, training, and the rest that's outside of testing and quality assurance. Our limited objective is to answer questions 1 and 2 to the extent that the incidence of bugs is a measure of test and debug labor and therefore a component of development cost and duration. Question 3 is a straight reliability question; at least that's the only way we can attempt to answer it. If a program has been through all required functional testing, and is believed to be bug-free, and its operation has been approved by the buyer (perhaps after negotiations and arbitration), then functionality plays no role in the determination of "how good" the program is. All that remains to ask is what is the probability of failure, or the expected time between failures or malfunction, or how many bugs remain—that is, what is the software's reliability?

3. COMPLEXITY MEASURES

3.1. General

What do we mean by "complexity" as applied to a piece of software, and why? The "why" is the easier question. Without defining "complexity," using only our intuitive notion of software complexity, we expect that more complex software will cost more to build and test, and will have more latent bugs. Therefore, an appropriate measure of software complexity should be a component in the answer of all three questions in 2.3. above. Any useful measure of complexity should satisfy several basic, minimal requirements:

1. It can be calculated for all programs to which we apply it.
2. It need not be calculated for programs that increase in size or for programs that in principle cannot be debugged.
3. Adding something to a program (e.g., instructions, storage, processing time) can never decrease the measured complexity.

The first requirement states that it's a usable measure. The second says that we won't try to apply it to unreasonable programs, and the third is formalized common sense. It's another way of saying that the program is at least as complicated as the sum of its parts. Under theoretical equivalents to these assumptions, it can be proven (BORO72) that, contrary to our intuition but in agreement with our experience, there are gaps in complexity. For example, have you noticed that there are many programs that take less than fifty man-years, and many that take more than a hundred, but few between fifty and a hundred? Borodin's gap theorem doesn't tell us anything practical about where the gaps are or even if they're within the range of program size being written today—just that they exist, wherever they are, for every reasonable complexity measure. So although we don't know where the gaps are, we shouldn't reject a complexity measure because applying it seems to lead to discrete jumps in complexity.

3.2. The Simplest Metric: Lines-of-Code

3.2.1. What Is It?

Count the number of lines of code in a program and use that number as a measure of complexity. If, then, bugs appear to occur at 1% per line, a 1000-statement program should have 10 bugs and a 10,000-statement program should have 100. I can think of a simpler measure: Weigh the listing—or if you don't have a scale, measure its thickness with a ruler. Why not? Is it really less scientific than counting? Think about it. There's a high correlation beween the weight of the listing or its thickness and the number of statements in it. On a large project, it probably correlates to better than 90%. Within a project with all paper supplied by the same vendor, and all listings done under the same operating system utility, the formats are probably very regular. I think that if you were to gather statistics over one large project or many small projects (that used the same paper), the weight of the listings would correlate as well to the bug rate and test efforts as do lines-of-code. Yet "lines-of-code" sounds reasonable and scientific, and "listing weight" seems to be an outrageous put-on. Who's been putting whom on?

3.2.2. How Good (Bad) Is It?

Thayer, Lipow, and Nelson in their monumental software reliability study (THAY76) showed error rates ranging from 0.04% to 7% when measured against lines of code, with the most reliable routine being one of the largest. Furthermore, there was no simple nonlinear law that related number of bugs per line to number of lines, except in the grossest sense. The same lack of useful correlation is shown in Rubey (RUBE75). Curtis, Sheppard, and Milliman (CURT79A) show that length is as good a measure as others for small programs, but is optimistic for large programs. Feuer and Fowlkes (FEUE79B) indicate that length is useful in determining maintenance effort. Moderate performance is also reported for length metrics by Schneidewind (SCHN79A). The definitive report on the relation between program size and bug rate is Lipow's (LIPO82). In his study of 115,000 JOVIAL statements, he found a nonlinear relation between bug rate per lines of code and program size; but also included other factors that related to language type and modularization. Small programs had an error rate of 1.3% to 1.8%, with large programs increasing from 2.7% to 3.2%. Lipow's study, however, and most of the others, only included executable lines of code and not data declarations. The bottom line of it all is that lines-of-code is reasonably linear for small programs (under 100 statements) and increases nonlinearly with program size. It seems to correlate reasonably well with maintenance costs. It is certainly a better metric than sheer guesses or nothing at all.

3.2.3. Inherent Limitations and Weakness—The Hidden Assumption

Every metric has hidden assumptions concerning the source and nature of bugs. A metric that excludes data definition and data initialization statements (e.g., declarations) assumes that data-base errors are not significant. A metric that ignores comments assumes that the frequency of interaction and interface bugs between modules is not affected by the quality of documentation. The major hidden assumption in the line-of-code metric is that it assumes that typographical errors and wild cards dominate bugs. If the bug counts included syntax errors (as most of these studies did) that were caught by the compiler or assembler, the validity of this bias is enhanced. However, since testing can't even begin until such bugs are removed, because they should be considered strictly private (except insofar as they impact the individual programmer's productivity), they really shouldn't be counted at all. Typographical bugs do not dominate bugs, and that invalidates the basic assumption.

3.3. McCabe's and Related Metrics

3.3.1. What Is It?

McCabe's complexity metric is a count of the number of decision statements in a program. Actually it's a count of the decisions plus one. The addition of one is related to keeping things correct when considering the complexity of an assembly of several modules. Complexity is additive. If unit A has a complexity of 7 (six decisions) and unit B has a complexity of 9 (eight decisions), their sum has a complexity of 16. Refining things a little more, multi-way branches such as ON...GOTO or case statements are reckoned at one less than the number of possible branches. Thus, a ten-way case statement is counted as equivalent to nine decisions. This is correct because it would take nine binary decision statements to code a ten-way case statement. Myers (MYER77) has suggested a further refinement of McCabe's metric. A decision can be complicated. For example, the decision could be based on the satisfaction of a statement of the form "(A = B) & (C − D = 0) & (X$ = "abcd")...." Each component clause of the overall decision is in its own right a decisionlike statement. The refinement consists of counting each such clause as if it is another decision. Other ways of calculating McCabe's metric are discussed in BEIZ82 in detail. McCabe's metric, despite its simplicity, is based on deep properties of program structure and is also related to the minimum number of paths required to achieve coverage. Its principal virtue is simplicity. The number of equivalent decisions can be trivially counted, either by hand or automatically, with almost the same ease that one can determine lines-of-code.

3.3.2. How Good Is It?

McCabe's metric achieves significantly better correlation of complexity to bugs and debugging difficulty than lines-of-code does. Zolnowski and Simmons (ZOLN77) show good correlation to the programmer's intuitive notion of complexity. Additional reports that relate McCabe's metric, or other metrics that are almost equivalent, to bugs and debugging effort are reported in BELF79, CHEN78A, CURT79A, ENDR75, FEUE79A, FEUE79B, LIPO77, SCHN79A, SCHN79B, SCHN79D, SHEP79C, THAY77, and WALS79. Although the statistics are sparse, the consensus is that McCabe's complexity metric is a useful rule of thumb that's much better than raw lines-of-code. McCabe advises partitioning routines whose metric exceeds 10. Walsh (WALS79) confirms this advice by citing a military software project to which the metric was applied. They found that 23% of the routines with an M value greater than 10 accounted for 53% of the bugs. They also showed in this study of 276 routines that programs whose metric was greater than 10 had 21% more bugs per line of code than those with lower values. There appears to be a discontinuous jump in the per-instruction bug rate in the neighborhood of M = 10. Manzo (MANZ80) uses the metric as a component of programming management. He gives greater scrutiny to programs whose metric exceeds 10 (but does not legislate an artificial partitioning to get the metric below 10) and adjusts estimates of programmer productivity, schedule, and testing time to the value of M by taking into account the apparent jump in the neighborhood of M = 10. Other references related to McCabe's metric are BAKE79A, BAKE80, PAIG75A, PAIG78, and WOOD78.

3.3.3. The Hidden Assumption and Weaknesses

The hidden assumption in McCabe's metric is that bugs are proportional to control-flow complexity—that processing complexity, data-base structure, and typographical and wild-card bugs are immaterial. Another weakness* is its failure to distinguish between different kinds of control-flow complexity. For example, a simple "IF-THEN-ELSE" statement is judged at the same complexity as a loop—this is contrary to intuition and experience, because the loop is probably three times as likely to have worse bugs. Case statements are judged overly harshly, despite the fact that they can materially improve understanding. A string of nested IF-THEN-ELSEs interposed with processing would be given the same complexity as a straightforward case statement with a direct branch to the appropriate processing. Complexity for subroutines is additive. McCabe doesn't ignore the additional complexity caused by modularization, but the interface complexity is no worse than a simple branch. The final weakness is that a thousand straight-line instructions are judged to be as complex as a single instruction. It's easy to create a program that circumvents this metric. Conversely, pathological programs aside, within a fixed environment, application, and programming style (e.g., within a programming group or project), McCabe's metric is an easy to use and useful rule of thumb for comparing alternate approaches and for estimating debug labor.

3.4. Halstead's Metrics

3.4.1. What Are They?

Halstead's metrics are based on a combination of arguments derived from common sense, information theory, and psychology. The clearest exposition and justification is still to be found in Halstead's *Elements of Software Science* (HALS77). It's an easy-to-read little book that should be read before applying these metrics. The following exposition is intended only as an introductory overview aimed at getting us a bug predictor. The set of metrics are based on two, easily measured, parameters of program:

n_1 = the number of distinct operators in the program (e.g., keywords)

n_2 = the number of distinct operands in the program (e.g., data base objects).

---

*To be fair about it, I'm judging the weakness of a metric relative to its validity: the better the metric, the more harshly I pick at it.

From these Halstead defines **program length**, which is not to be confused with the number of statements in a program, by the following relation:

$$H = n_1\log_2 n_1 + n_2\log_2 n_2 \qquad (1^*$$

In calculating the Halstead length, paired operators such as "BEGIN...END," "DO...UNTIL," "FOR...NEXT," "(...)" are treated as a single operator, which is what they actually are. For any given program it's possible to count the actual operator and operand appearances.

$$N_1 = \text{program operator count}$$
$$N_2 = \text{program operand count}$$

The actual Halstead length is evidently:

$$N = N_1 + N_2 \qquad (2$$

He also defines a program's **vocabulary** as the sum of the number of distinct operators and operands. That is:

$$n = \text{vocabulary} = n_1 + n_2 \qquad (3$$

The central claim of Halstead's theorem (equation 1) is that the program's actual Halstead length (N) can be calculated from the program's vocabulary, even though the program hasn't been written. It does not tell us how long the program will be in terms of instruction counts (not directly), but it is an amazing claim nevertheless. Its immediate importance is that it's often possible to get an operand count and to estimate operator counts before a program is written. This is particularly true when the program is written after a data dictionary already exists. If a program is written using 20 keywords out of a total of 200 in the language, and it references 30 objects in the data base, its Halstead length should be $20\log_2 20 + 30\log_2 30 = 233.6$. The key question is how well does H (the predicted Halstead length) compare with N (the actual Halstead

---

*The late Maurice Halstead used "N" for this metric, as has the rest of the literature. I have several reasons for departing from that practice. The use of "H" for "Halstead length" is a fitting tribute to Halstead's contribution to computer science. The term usually used for this metric is "program length," which is easily confused with program instruction count. "Halstead's metric" or "Halstead length" cannot be so confused. Finally, the form of the definition is reminiscent of information theoretic information content, to which it is related. In information theory, the information content is denoted by "h" and is calculated by a similar equation.

length measured on the program). The answer is, very close. The validity of the relation has been experimentally confirmed, many times, independently over a wide range of programs and languages. Furthermore, the relation appears to hold when a program is subdivided into modules.

The bug prediction formula is based on the four values, n_1, n_2, N_1 and N_2:

$$B = (N_1 + N_2) \log_2 (n_1 + n_2)/3000 \tag{4}$$

All of which are easily measured parameters of a program. A program, then, which accesses 75 data-base items a total of 1300 times, and which uses 150 operators a total of 1200 times, should be expected to have $(1300 + 1200)\log_2(75 + 150)/3000 = 6.5$ bugs.

In addition to the above equations, Halstead also derives relations that predict programming effort and time which also seem to correlate with experience. The time prediction is expectedly nonlinear, showing 2.4 hours for a 120-instruction program, 230 hours for a 1000-instruction program, and 1023 hours for a 2000-instruction program. While the correlation is not perfect, it at least got into the right order of magnitude. Over a set of 24,000 instructions, the predicted 31,600 man-hours agreed with the actual 36,000 to 12%. While not perfect, it certainly seems to be way ahead of whatever's in second place.

3.4.2. How Good?

Confirmation of these metrics has been extensively published by Halstead and others. The most solid confirmation of the bug prediction equation is by Lipow (LIPO82), who compares actual to predicted bug counts to within 8% over a range of program sizes from 300 to 12,000 executable statements. The analysis was of post-compilation bugs, so that syntax errors caught by the compiler are properly excluded. However, of the 115,000 statements in the experiment, only the 75,000 executable statements were examined. It would be interesting to see if better accuracy would have been obtained had all declarations been included in the analysis. Ottenstein, in an earlier report (OTTE79), showed similar superb correlation. Curtis (CURT79A) shows that Halstead's metrics are at least twice as good as lines-of-code and are not improved by augmenting them with lines-of-code or with McCabe's metric.

The experimental confirmation appears to be coming in from all sides, and it's evident that if ever a true software science emerges, it will be based in no small part on Halstead's work. Other confirming studies include FEUE79A and FEUE79B. Critiques are to be found in CURT79A, DEYO79, DUNN82, LASS79, SHEA79C, and ZWEB79.

3.4.3. The Hidden Assumptions and Weaknesses

Since Halstead's metric is the best we have, it's fitting that it be subjected to the harshest criticism. There are far fewer hidden assumptions in Halstead's work than in any other comparable effort, but some assumptions and weaknesses still remain.

1. *Modularity.* Modularity is not ignored, because each call, together with the parameters of the call sequence, will contribute to the values of n_1, n_2, N_1 and N_2 and therefore to the predicted bug count. Note that Halstead treats each distinct subroutine call as a unique operator and not just as the one keyword "CALL." In this respect, the impact of hypermodularity on bug rate is not ignored. The criticism is that Halstead does not distinguish between a programmer's "own" subfunctions and a subfunction provided by another programmer. Each are given equal weight. The metric might be improved by fudging the weight given to external calls by multiplying it with a constant k_f, larger than one, which is a measure of the thickness of the semantic fog that exists whenever two programmers attempt to communicate. For own subroutines and modules, the index is equal to one and Halstead's criterion relating to optimum module size (see HALS77) holds. For external calls, the fog index might be as high as five (depending on the documentation clarity) and would result in larger units and subunits produced by a single programmer. Common subroutines and macros in a library are treated as language extensions and have a unity fog index as for built-in language features. If this isn't valid, then documentation must be improved to the point where such calls are no more difficult than built-in keywords.
2. *Data-Base Impact and Declarations.* Halstead isn't to be faulted on this one. It's just that most evaluators and confirmers have continued the erroneous practice of ignoring nonexecutable statements such as declarations and data statements. Which is to say that most initialization and data structure bugs are ignored. The evaluators can't be faulted for this entirely, because in many cases errors in data declarations and initializing data statements are not even counted as bugs. If a true bug count is used, one that includes declaration errors and data statement bugs, then declarations and data statements, equates, constant declarations, and any other statements that affect not just what code is produced, but what data is loaded, should also be counted in determining Halstead's metrics. If such bugs are ignored, then the corresponding declarations of course cannot be counted.
3. *Code-Data Ambiguity.* There is a hidden assumption that code is code and data is data, and never the twain should meet. If Halstead's metrics are

rigidly applied to an assembly language program that does extensive modification of its own code (ugh!), it will predict the same bug count as a routine that performs the same operations on a fixed data area. Trying to expand the bug prediction or program length equations to such dynamically varying junk would make it impossible to do a static calculation of the metrics. Only a dynamic count would do. In principle, the method still works. Each modified instruction, after each modification, would increase the operator count. Say that a programmer implemented a flag by changing a NOOP instruction to an unconditional branch (a common practice at one time); that instruction, in addition to its appearance as a unique operand, would also contribute two unique operators. The bug prediction would be clearly raised. Whether it would be increased to the point where it would correctly predict the catastrophic impact of instruction modification remains to be seen. The issue in code-data ambiguity is not with instruction modification, but with code masquerading as data. That is, with data whose actual function is control—as in jump tables, finite state machines, undeclared internal languages and their interpreters, and similar effective and useful programming tactics. There is nothing inherently weak in Halstead's approach if we count such things correctly. Control and instructions in the guise of data are operators and not operands. State tables are tables of operators and operands. In the same vein, in languages that permit subroutine names in a call, each value of a subroutine name parameter should be treated as if it were a different operator. Similarly for calls that permit a variable number of operands—each value constitutes a different operator.

4. *Data Type Distinctions.* In strongly typed languages that force the explicit declaration of all types and prohibit mixed type operations unless a type conversion statement has been inserted, the weakness does not exist if we count all type conversation statements, whether or not they result in object code. If we count all declarations, including user-defined type declarations, there is no weakness in Halstead's metrics. The problem arises in the more common languages which permit mixed operations (e.g., integer–floating point addition) and which have no user-defined types. In principle, each use of an operator must be linked with the type of data over which it operates. For example, if a language has integers and short and long operands, and if mixed mode operations are allowed in any combination, then each of the basic arithmetic operators (add, subtract, multiply, divide) actually represents six operators, one for each combination of operand types. If a language has four types of arithmetic operands, then each of the basic operators corresponds to ten operators, and so on for all combinations of data types and all arithmetic operators.

5. *Call Depth.* No notice is made of call depth. A routine that calls ten differ-

ent subroutines as a sequence of successive calls would actually be considered more complex than a routine that had ten nested calls. If the totality of the routines and all that it calls were considered, the bug prediction would be the same for both because the total operator and operand counts would be the same. A non-unity fog index associated with each call, which would be multiplicative with depth, would raise the predicted bug rate for deeply nested calls. This would be more realistic.

6. *Operator Types.* An IF-THEN-ELSE statement is given the same weight as a FOR-UNTIL, even though it's known that loops are far more troublesome This is an example of a broader criticism—that operators and operands are treated equally, with no correlation to the bug incidence associated with specific operators or with operand types.

7. *General Structure Issues.* Of these, the fact that nesting is ignored (nested loops, nested IF-THEN-ELSE, and so on) is probably the most serious critique. A BASIC statement such as:

$$100 \ A \ = \ B \ + \ C \ @ \ D \ = \ SIN(A) \qquad\qquad N = 9$$

is less bug prone than:

$$100 \ D \ = \ SIN(B \ + \ C) \qquad\qquad N = 6$$

but is claimed to have a higher bug potential. This claim is true if it is assumed that bugs are dominated by typographical errors, but untrue in reality. The first structure is more prone to typographical errors, but is clearer. The second structure is less prone to typographical errors, but is more prone to nesting errors. If we counted $SIN(B + C)$ as a different operator than $SIN(A)$, this problem is taken care of, but this may be an overly harsh use of operator counts. In general, then, a nested sequence of operators, be they loops or logic, is more complicated than an unnested sequence with the same operator and operand count. The possible solution might be a nesting fog index that increases by multiplication with increasing depth.

The gist of the above criticism is not so much with Halstead's metrics, but with the way we should apply them. They have proven their worth, but that doesn't mean we should accept and apply them blindly and in a doctrinaire, orthodox, immutable, and rigid manner. It's too early for that. The above critique implies methods of improvement—some of those suggestions may in practice prove effective and most will probably prove to make little difference or to be outright wrong. It is only by trying, by making variations, by meticulous and honest recording of data, that we will find what components and what interpretations are really useful and the context to which those interpretations apply.

3.5. Other Metrics

The appearance of McCabe's and Halstead's metrics has spurred the proposal, development, refinement, and validation of a host of similar and related metrics, or totally different alternatives based on different assumptions. Some of those cited below preceded McCabe's and Halstead's work and some followed. It's too early to tell which will be experimentally confirmed independently over a large range of projects and applications, no matter how rational and sensible their basis might be. Some of the more interesting and promising alternatives are presented in BAKE79, BAKE80, BELF79, CHAP79, CHEN78A, DEYO79, FEUE79B, GILB77, LIPO77, MCCL78B, PAIG80, SCHN79B, WHIT80, and ZOLN77. Most of these metrics and their variations recognize one or more weaknesses in the popular metrics and seek to measure reliability and/or predict bug counts through refinement or alternative formulation of the problem. It is inevitable that increased predictability and fidelity can only be achieved at a cost of increased sophistication, complexity of evaluation, and difficulty of use. The proposed refinements of Halstead's metrics discussed in 3.4.3. above are clearly a case in point.

3.6. A Plan for Action

We've discredited lines-of-code as a useful measure of complexity or as a bug predictor and are left with two, relatively easy-to-apply metrics—McCabe's rule of thumb and Halstead's bug formula. How should they be used?

1. Educate programmers, section leaders, and managers on the use of McCabe's metric as a handy rule of thumb that's useful for qualitative comparisons of control structure complexity.
2. Get programmers to use McCabe's metric, particularly in the design phase. This should be a continual practice and should lead to simpler, cleaner control structures and therefore to less bugs.
3. Modify source language processors, or do the count by hand, if necessary, to automatically calculate McCabe's metric for compiled or assembled code. Keep records that will allow subsequent correlation of bug rate, development time, debug effort, test design effort, and test execution effort with M. Establish simple, local fudge factors based on the gathered statistics that will provide a sharper prediction. For example, count each subroutine call in the program in addition to the decision counts.

4. Modify the source language's processor (the parser particularly) or build or buy a language postprocessor that will evaluate the components needed to calculate Halstead's length and bug formula. Keep it flexible so that it can be modifed and made sharper as data comes in.
5. Have predicted bug count (better to call it a "buggyness index") printed with each compilation, so as to influence the selection of design approaches that are inherently less bug prone.
6. Gather statistics that will allow you to compare actual bug counts to predicted counts (this needs cooperation with the programmers because most of their bugs should be eliminated in private testing). Find the weaknesses in your version of the bug prediction equation and update the calculation to reflect a more precise determination.
7. Track the appearances of discontinuities in the actual bug counts (note that Halstead's bug equation is already nonlinear). Examine all such discontinuities to determine what qualitative change caused the discontinuity. This may lead to new management techniques or new, sharper prediction methods.
8. Track the literature to see what others are doing in this highly volatile area—benefit from others' experiences in addition to your own.
9. Keep the programmers informed about what components of the bug predictor formula dominate and how it works. Hope that they will try to "cheat" by designs that will lead to lower predicted bug counts—which is precisely what you want them to do.
10. To the extent that your ultimate bug predictor formula correctly reflects the kinds of bugs you have, the above approach is self-invalidating. The better and sharper your predictions, the more influence they will have and the more new code will be influenced to invalidate your predictions. If the overall bug rate doesn't go down, your effort has been in vain. If it goes down but doesn't change (vis-a-vis the type of bug predicted), then you're not getting as much out of the effort as you might.
11. If you implement the above, be willing to pay the price. Agree to letting bug rate (honestly counted) be a major component of the evaluation of quality assurance effectiveness. It should span more than one project, though, and be judged over a period measured in years, not months.

4. SOFTWARE RELIABILITY

4.1. General

The primary objective of software reliability prediction is the same as for hardware: given a system, what is the probability that it will fail in a given time period, or, equivalently, what is the expected duration between failures? In hardware, if the expected time between failures (MTBF) is too small, then more-reliable components are substituted for less-reliable components, or redundancy is used to achieve the required improvements. In software, the approach to improved reliability is more testing—which, if you think about it, is the prerequisite to replacing unreliable components (buggy code) with reliable components (debugged code). Unfortunately, that's where the similarity stops.

Hardware reliability predictions are done as follows:

1. Components (including solder joints and connectors) are subjected to extensive life testing under realistic conditions. For example, 50,000 integrated circuits of a given type might be tested at their temperature limits for several thousand hours. These tests provide the basis for assigning a failure rate to each component.
2. When components fail, the nature of the failure is examined, and, if possible, the manufacturing or assembly process is modified to prevent or reduce that failure mode. Eventually the failure rate stabilizes as all economically feasible and recognized improvements are made. More-reliable components are typically available at a higher price, though.
3. Components are sampled and tested regularly. Field failure data is also noted. Both of these provide continual feedback to assure that the failure rate of the components remains stable or improves.
4. Calculations of subassembly reliability are done using standard reliability formulas—to a first order approximation, the failure rate of a subassembly is calculated from:

$$F_S = \sum_i f_i N_i$$

where F_S is the subassembly failure rate, N_i is the number of components of type i (including solder joints and connector pins), and f_i is the failure rate of component type i.
5. Where warranted and affordable, subassemblies are also tested as components, to verify the predicted subassembly reliability. The same kind of feedback that was used for components is used for subassembly. Life testing of subassemblies is not as extensive as for components, because subassemblies are significantly more expensive.
6. The same process and philosophy is carried upwards, through assemblies, subsystems, and systems. The further up we go, the less reliance there is on actual bench testing and the more there is on predicted failure rates based on reliability calculations. This is primarily because the closer we get to a system, the more expensive such tests become. When systems employ

redundant hardware to automatically recover from hardware failures, live testing can only demonstrate that the system does not meet its reliability objectives and can never prove that it does. The reason is that such systems could have system MTBF's measured in centuries and there could never be enough accumulated test hours to warrant a valid reliability prediction based on a reasonable test duration. Furthermore, failures of large-scale, computer-based systems are dominated by software failures, something which hardware reliability prediction methods cannot possibly predict.

Using hardware reliability methodology as a philosophical base, let's examine its methodology to see where any method of measuring or predicting software reliability must differ.

1. The basic component of software is an instruction. It cannot fail, no matter how often it is written on a coding sheet or how often it is executed. The problem is rarely with the instruction or keyword, anyhow, but in how it's used. You can put an add instruction on a test bed (e.g., in a loop), or on a thousand test beds for a thousand years, and the only things you'll measure are initial hardware design flaws (which once recognized should be assumed fixed forever), hardware failures, and alpha particle hits (about which there's nothing you can do).
2. Subassembly reliability (e.g., subroutine failure modes) do not follow from instruction reliability. Just as with instructions, it doesn't matter how many copies of the subroutine you exercise, it will tell you nothing about its reliability. Although its behavior under a set of tests will give you some insight, repeating those tests can tell you nothing new. Furthermore, while subassembly failures caused by subassembly interactions can generally be ignored in hardware reliability, that's one of the principal causes of software failures, particularly after system testing is done.
3. With proper quality assurance and feedback, the same error will never recur with software once it has been discovered. Every single, discovered and corrected failure improves the unit reliability. The unit after repair is not the same unit it was before the failure was detected.
4. Continued testing and correction leads to a more reliable system. As a correlary to this, because continued field operation is a form of testing, the more you run a software system, statistically, the better it gets*—exactly the opposite of what happens for hardware.
5. Hardware failures are dominated by the gross aggregation of components rather than by how those components interact. The more reliable a piece of

---

*Assuming it's not modified or enhanced—a rarely valid assumption.

software becomes, the more likely it is that the remaining bug results from the interaction of components than from flaws in the components (e.g., units) themselves. The assumption that component failures are independent, which dominates hardware reliability thinking, is invalid for software and becomes increasingly more invalid as the system continues to be refined.

We can summarize the difference by noting that hardware reliability prediction assumes (for the most part) independence of failure and also that the reliability measuring process does not effect the failure rate (or shouldn't). Software reliability must assume interdependence of unit failures and implicitly takes into account the role of testing in improving the reliability. On the whole, software reliability theory is inherently more difficult than hardware reliability theory.

4.2. The State of the Art

A clear exposition of the state of the art of software reliability theory is to be found in Dunn and Ullman (DUNN82). They discuss more than a dozen different models and their variations, with extensive references to the literature. The proliferation of models is not dominated by deep philosophical differences between the modelers, but rather by an attempt to more closely approximate reality. Some of the fundamental assumptions and how they vary from model to model are discussed below.

1. Most models assume a fixed but unknown number of bugs when testing starts.
2. Bugs are universally assumed to be independent.
3. Most models assume perfect debugging. That is, the debugging process introduces no new bugs. However, some of the later models take into account that not all detected bugs will be fixed, and that the debugging process itself may introduce new bugs.
4. Most models assume that test time and calendar time are the same. The Musa execution time model (MUSA75, 79A, 79B) separates the bug discovery rate from the correction rate and allows a different environment for testing than for operations.
5. The models assume that failure is proportional to bugs remaining. This implicitly means that bugs are assumed to cause single failures and each failure can be related to one bug.
6. The models assume path homogeneity—that is, data are entered randomly and such data uniformly exercise all code. This is in direct contradiction to the reality that the statistically significant paths cover a small percentage (say under 10%) of the code.

The principal differences among the models are in the extent to which the above assumptions apply or do not apply, the kind of probability distributions assumed for the occurrence or detection of failures, and the methods by which the measured data is to be fitted to the models. Most of these models have been tested on data gathered from real systems, and most have been confirmed experimentally to one degree or another. No one model of software reliability appears to have a distinct superiority to any other, and none seems ready for practical application. For more information on the state of the art, a historical perspective is to be found in Schick and Wolverton (SCHI78) and applicable philosophy is discussed in Littlewood (LITT78). Pertinent information on various models are to be found in DUNN82, BASI73, CHEU78, GOEL79A, GOEL79B, GOOD80, HAMI78, JELI73, LAPA73, LAPA75, LEHM80, LIPO77, LIPO79, LITT78, LITT80, MIYA78, MORA72, MORA78, MUSA75, MUSA79A, MUSA79B, MUSA80, PERL81, RAMA80, RUBE75, SCHI78, SCHN75, SHOO72, SHOO73, SHOO78B, REMU79, SUKE78, SUKE79, and THAY77, to name just a few of the thousands of papers that have been written on the subject. The reader is advised to read DUNN82 for an overview before digging into the literature.

4.3. What's Missing?

The fundamental problem with all existing theories is that they are far from reality. The second problem is that they are far from providing simple, pragmatic tools that can be used to manage software development. If a theory were realistic, we could tolerate mathematical and statistical sophistication because the payoff would be worth it. Here are some more general criticisms of the state of the art—most of which are known and understood by most modelers, but which have to date proven too difficult to incorporate in a reasonable theory of software reliability.

1. There is no notion of bug severity. An error in the tenth digit of calculation is judged as harshly as a crash-causing bug.
2. Despite some models (MUSA75) that distinguish between test and operation time, all other aspects of the difference between test behavior and live behavior are ignored. It is implicitly assumed that testing is random and matches operational statistics—in other words, there's an implicit assumption that testing is done at its worst instead of at its best. Good testing is not random nor in any sense uniform across the set of program paths. Good testing focuses on improbable paths. No model offered takes into account the tester's ingenuity, cunning, and dedication to making the system crash.
3. High-load crashes are more frequent than low-load crashes. Some bugs will only appear under stress testing. Therefore, bug discovery is not only a func-

tion of the number of transactions executed under test, but also of the rate at which those transactions were presented to the system.

4. The efficiency of debugging is assumed to be independent of the system's reliability. Not only is debugging imperfect, but that imperfection increases with time. The longer the system's been in operation, the subtler the remaining bugs are and the dumber the debugger. Both of these lead to a constant number of bugs in the system after some time. The system stabilizes with remaining, detected problems that will never be explained or corrected.

5. The program is assumed immutable except for the correction of bugs. The impact of maintenance is ignored. Combine the continual modification of the program to accommodate new requirements with the increased subtlety of the remaining bugs and the decreased efficiency of the available debuggers, and the number of bugs doesn't remain constant, but increases, eventually to the point where the program must be scrapped. With maintenance included in a theory of software reliability, the theory should predict that software *does* wear out in the sense that it is no longer economically modifiable.

6. Bug discovery rate is assumed proportional to test intensity, or constant with time, or decreasing with time. It really goes up and down. It's high in initial testing; low during the middle period when thousands of boring variations are tried, high again under stress testing, peaks yet again just after cutover, and so on. Bug discovery rate is heavily influenced by testing strategy.

4.4. Where Does That Leave Us?

It's much easier to criticize a theory than to correct it. Furthermore, a software reliability theory that satisfied all the above objections would probably be so complicated that it would be impractical. The purpose in providing this perspective on the state of the art of software reliability theory is to warn the reader about the premature application of very young theories and the danger of management based on such theories. No person in their right mind today should agree to contractually binding software reliability requirements or predictions. That is, making a proven minimum mean-time-between-failures, say, a contractually binding component of system acceptance. As Littlewood points out (LITT78), such measures may not even exist for software. This does not mean that we have no requirement to demonstrate that our software is reliable—such as in subjecting the system to a thorough test, a stress test, and a detailed formal acceptance test. Such testing demonstrates reliability, but tells us very little about the expected number of remaining bugs, or about how often such bugs may cause the system to fail. No proposed future theory should be accepted or applied until it satisfies the following requirements.

1. A clear statement of the basic assumptions underlying the nature of bugs and the way in which their removal affects reliability.
2. Recognition that all bugs are not equally severe.
3. Recognition that neither the testing process nor the operating environment are random and that they are very different environments.
4. The theory has been verified over a large number of large projects, independently by different workers, and the circumstances of these projects match the circumstances to which the theory is to be applied.

5. WHEN WILL IT BE DONE?

5.1. Retrospective

We asked three questions at the beginning of this chapter and found that we had means of predicting the approximate number of bugs to expect in a routine and no really effective method to determine how many bugs remain after testing. The question of when the system will be ready for cutover seems at first glance to be intimately related to the number of bugs remaining—but it doesn't have to be. Suppose we've designed a set of tests which we believe will constitute an adequate check-out of the system. The builder and the buyer have agreed that when that set of tests (e.g., the formal acceptance test) has been passed, the system is ready for operation, no matter how many bugs remain, be it one or a thousand. You can be a purist and object—but think about it. From the beginning we said that it was neither possible nor practical to prove that a system is bug-free. If we've agreed to back off from absolute objectives in an absolute sense, shouldn't we also agree to back off from absolute objectives in a statistical sense? The completion of testing is a seduction—a seduction in which both builder and buyer agree that the system is ready for live operation. The pragmatic issue, then, is not how many bugs remain but when is the system considered to be useful—or at least sufficiently useful to permit the risk of failure. Granted that a good software reliability theory would allow us to hedge our bets a little closer and to minimize the risk that both buyer and builder were engaged in mutual self-delusion, but I never saw a system not go into operation because we couldn't predict how many bugs it had.

5.2. Hitachi's Method

5.2.1. Project "Bankruptcy"

Hitachi Software Inc., in a paper by Abe, Sakamura, and Aiso (ABEJ79), defined a project as **bankrupt** if it suffered a 20% schedule overrun. The authors further expressed concern if the project overran for *one day*. How many projects do you know of where anybody gave a damn about a month or half-a-year, never mind a single day? Before you shrug off concern over a one-day slip as Japanese obsession with quality and schedule, let me point out that their concern is based on the rational evaluation of the pertinent economic issues. If the software in question controls a large industrial factory or process whose cost is $500,000,000, at an interest rate of 10% per year that works out to $137,000 per day in interest costs, or in terms of prevailing programmer costs, a burn rate of 15 man-months per day. It doesn't take very many days before the nonproductive cost of the idle plant has exceeded the cost of the software several times over. If you, as a software supplier, were liable for the waste and interest associated with project delays, would you be looking at days or minutes? And if you were personally liable as an individual, would your concern shift to seconds and milliseconds? With that background and point of view, it's no wonder they looked for and developed methods which seem to be capable of predicting completion to within a few days of target.

5.2.2. Prerequisites and Setting

The prediction of possible overruns starts with the onset of integration testing. In the typical 24-month project, the earliest integration of modules is not likely to start before the sixth month. Therefore, there remain approximately 75 weeks of additional work to the end of the scheduled completion time. It is understood that, at any instant of time, some modules are in unit testing, some are undergoing integration testing, and if a backbone exists, some system-wide functional testing is underway. It is further assumed that all units will undergo proper unit testing prior to an integration attempt and that all bugs caught at the unit level have been corrected. The following are assumed to be known or available:

1. A scheduled completion date.
2. The number of items or test cases that are to be checked over the remaining time.
3. A method of recording the number of bugs discovered once integration starts.

The first requirement needs no elaboration—it's that date that we all tend to ignore. The second item presupposes formal design of test cases. It also implies fairly microscopic tests, such as those I've advocated. Granted that not all subtests are equivalent. Some may take hours and some minutes. However, if all requirements and testing have been subdivided into the smallest cases that make sense, then the typical system will be scheduled for 1500 to 3000 subtests.

In that context, the variability of individual subtest difficulty is swallowed by the large number of subtests.

The bug count and the rate at which they're discovered and corrected can be obtained from,a patch log, or any other reasonable form of record keeping. Note that all tests here are public tests, so there should be no problem in getting these counts if things are under control. Note also that incorrect fixes cause multiple bug counts, which is proper.

5.2.3. The Basis

The Japanese project bankruptcy study was based on an examination of 23 projects which collectively included over a million lines of code. The projects included operating system software, language processors, and large-scale, online systems. The projects included wholly new code, major modifications to old code, and combinations thereof. The studies showed a remarkable similarity across all projects in the rate at which test items were completed. The use of test item completions is inherently sounder than bug detection rates. As we've seen, even if we know how well we're detecting bugs, we've no reliable way of knowing what percentage of existing bugs we've eliminated. We can at any time know exactly what percentage of tests have been successfully passed. Furthermore, the study showed that the rate of bug detection was a poor predictor of project completion. A very high detection rate could mean either that the software was miserable or that the debugging crew was very good.

Figure 9-1 shows a summary of the Japanese experience in plotting test case completion rates across the 23 projects. The cases are normalized to percentage of cases completed and percentage of allowed time elapsed. It's only when things are normalized this way that the crucial and consistent pattern emerges.

They showed that test completions follow three different phases. In the first phase, completion progress is slow, because there are many bugs and not much of the system is running. Phase 1 is the period in which we're trying to get a sufficient backbone working so that we can get into serious testing. The second phase is the boring phase, in which test completion progress is high. This is where most of the testing is done. If unit testing has been good, relatively few bugs will be found per test, but because the test completion rate is high, so is the overall bug detection rate. The third phase shows another slowdown. This slowdown occurs because the bugs found in this phase are subtle, interactive, and inherently more difficult than bugs discovered in the earlier phases. They found the following:

1. The average duration of the first phase, across the 23 projects, was 22% of the available time.
2. If the onset of the second phase was delayed beyond the 55% point, bankruptcy was inevitable.

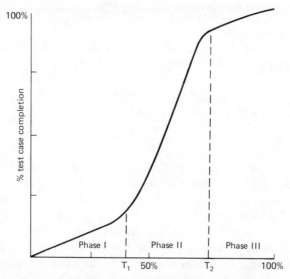

% test case completion

Phase I   Phase II   Phase III

T_1 50% T_2 100%

% of time (normalized) from start of integration to completion

Figure 9-1. Test Case Completions History.

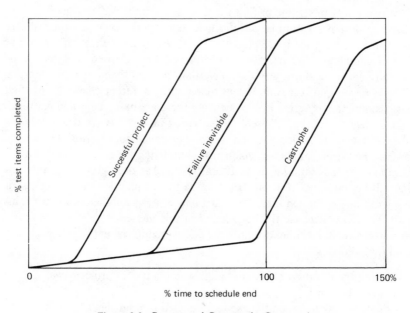

% test items completed

Successful project

Failure inevitable

Castrophe

0   100   150%

% time to schedule end

Figure 9-2. Success and Catastrophe Compared.

3. For the successful projects, the average duration of the first phase was 15% of the available time, and for the bankrupt projects it was 97% of the available time.
4. The duration of the second phase for successful projects was 57% of the time, and for bankrupt projects 29% of the time.

Figure 9-2 summarizes these findings. The data suggest that the test completion rate during the first phase was relatively constant across all projects (successful or failures) and that it was the *duration* of the first phase that determined success. In other words, the primary difference between the good and the bad project is the point at which transition from the first to second phase occurs. The third phase seems to be relatively insensitive to the project's prior history. It seems to take the same amount of time to clean up the subtleties, with relatively small variations. Note also that the slope of all three cases is the same in the second phase. If anything, test completion rate (slope) is slightly better for the catastrophes than for the successes (understandable). The fact that the slopes in the three phases are relatively constant across good and bad projects means that project failure occurs because the late onset of the efficient second phase moves all schedules out. Note also that the longer the duration of the first phase, the fewer the tests that will be run in the efficient second phase. As an extreme, if the entire project were dragged out to several times the initial schedule, the efficient second phase would disappear and only the inefficient first and third phases would remain. The key to this method, then, is *to plot and detect the time at which the transition from phase 1 to phase 2 testing occurs.*

5.2.4. A Refinement

A second measure is based on the bug detection rate and the rate at which bug detection is accelerating or decelerating. A cumulative plot of the total bugs detected and corrected is maintained. From this, the bug detection rate (bugs/week) is determined, as is the derivative of the bug detection rate. This is divided by the peak bug detection rate occurring prior to the crucial schedule midpoint. They found that if the value of the figure determined in this way exceeded -0.3, then project failure was inevitable. The range for failed projects was from $-.3$ to $+2$ and for successful projects from -0.3 to -10.* The rationale behind this metric is subtler. If the bug detection rate does not start to decrease after a certain point, it means that the bug density is remaining high despite the fact that test cases are being completed. We should expect the bug

---

*If you read the original paper, which I recommend, don't be confused by the fact that my definitions are reversals of theirs.

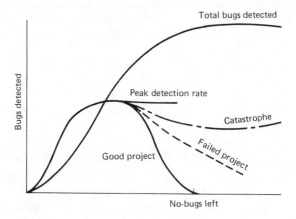

Figure 9-3. Bug Detection Rates.

detection rate to peak and then decrease. This would lead to a negative derivative for the bug detection rate. If the ratio of peak detection rate to the derivative at the 50% point in time is not strongly negative, then it will take a long
time for the remaining bugs to be cleared. See Figure 9-3.

5.2.5. Procedure

1. Plan all testing in advance and require estimates of the number of test cases
   expected for each element's element-level testing, integration, functional
   testing, and system acceptance testing. Uniform standards are needed for
   subtest scope to assure reasonable homogeneity across subtests.
2. Once integration testing starts, plot subtest completion rates and cumulative
   bug detection rates.
3. For long, large projects the data should be relatively smooth. If not, use the
   regression techniques discussed in Section 5.2.6 below.
4. Monitor these curves weekly to find if you are in the first or second phase.
   The second phase is marked by a dramatic increase in the test completion
   rate. If this is delayed beyond the 25% schedule point, corrective action is
   warranted. If delayed beyond the 50% point, a catastrophe is inevitable.
5. Monitor the bug detection rate for a peak. This should occur approximately
   midway during the test period. After the rate starts to drop, calculate the
   critical value (i.e., derivative of the bug detection rate divided by the peak
   bug detection rate). If this is positive, it's time to panic.
6. The cumulative data should be examined at least weekly, and revised predictions of the phases produced weekly.

5.2.6. Regression Analysis

For long-term projects with large staffs and thousands of test cases, the data should be relatively smooth, and simple manual graphing of the points will suffice. For smaller projects (18 months with a staff of 25, and 2000 subtests, say) the data tends to be rocky, and simple plotting will not suffice. The Japanese study solved this problem by fitting a regression curve through the subtest completion data. Unfortunately, the method they used was analytically dubious and inherently insensitive. They used a six-term polynomial to fit the data. Such a fit, while possible, has potentially bad behavior at the end points. A better fit can be obtained with less effort by using a function which is inherently "S" shaped, such as:

$$C = 1 - \exp(a_1 t + a_2 t^2 + a_3 t^3) \tag{1}$$

Where: C is the percentage of tests completed,
t is the elapsed time
a_1, a_2, a_3 are constants to be derived by the regression.

Since C has been normalized, we can define a new parameter, N, the percentage of tests not yet completed, which is evidently 1–C. Equation 1 then becomes:

$$N = \exp(a_1 t + a_2 t^2 + a_3 t^3) \tag{2}$$

Taking the logs of both sides,

$$\log_e N = a_1 t + a_2 t^2 + a_3 t^3 \tag{3}$$

Substituting $X_1 = t$, $X_2 = t^2$, and $X_3 = t^3$ linearizes the problem and converts it to an ordinary linear regression which can be done by any high-quality calculator or personal professional computer such as the HP41–CV or the HP–85. It's better to avoid higher-order terms if a reasonable fit to the data can be obtained with only a quadratic. Given the regression coefficients, you can either plot the regression curve over the data to see where the transition is occurring from phase 1 to phase 2 testing and from phase 2 to phase 3. Alternatively, you can find those points analytically by calculating the radius of curvature of C as a function of time. The onset of phase 2 is marked by a peak positive curvature. The middle of phase 2 is marked by zero curvature, and the onset of phase 3 is marked by a peak negative curvature. The zero curvature point (middle of phase 2) is a better basis for extrapolating the bug detection rate than the peak rate used in the study. The radius of curvature is given by:

$$R = C'' (1 + C'^2)^{-3/2}$$ (4

where C' and C'' are the first and second derivatives of C with respect to time, respectively. Let:

D = bug detection rate (bugs per week)
D$_o$ = bug detection rate at the midpoint of phase 2, as determined from zero curvature (R = 0)
D' = The derivative of the bug detection rate with respect to time.

then D'/D$_o$ is monitored to see if the bug detection rate relative to the peak is decreasing as it should.

5.2.7. Interpretation

A successful project appears to be based in part on accomplishing the following:

1. Keeping phase 1 as short as possible.
2. Getting the highest possible slope in phase 2 testing.
3. Keeping phase 2 testing going as long as possible.

Both phase 1 and phase 3 have small slopes, and therefore progress is slow. Phase 1 can be minimized by accelerating the point in time at which effective parallel testing can start. That means getting a backbone into operation as soon as possible. Nothing should be allowed to interfere with getting that working backbone up and running, because testing is inherently inefficient without it. Say that the elements of which the backbone is composed consist of half of the program's software. If you did complete integration and unit testing on the backbone elements, then you would perforce delay the onset of phase 2 to the mid-life of testing, and possibly bankrupt the project. Alternatively, if only those parts of the backbone element that are essential to backbone operation are tested and integrated first, then efficient phase 2 testing can begin. You can project this strategy backwards to the onset of the design phase by defining the testing backbone first, coding its elements first, giving those elements priority in unit testing—all aimed at getting phase 2 testing started as early as possible. The same emphasis should be given to nonbackbone test tools and utilities, and the design of the test data base. Instead of leaving such things until last—until after coding and unit testing—get them done first to maximize phase 2 testing efficiency and duration.

Phase 2 testing slope is limited by the availability of testing resources and personnel. The time to go into heavy overtime and around-the-clock testing is not towards the end of phase 3 (in a panic, as usual) but at the *onset* of phase 2. Overtime and around-the-clock testing increase human and mechanical resources and therefore increase the phase 2 slope. A good backbone permits simultaneous testing by several individuals and therefore also increases the phase 2 slope.

Phase 3 testing is slow and it's interesting to see why:

1. The bugs are subtler and therefore hard to find.
2. The project staff is winding down quantitatively—there are fewer people available for testing.
3. The project staff is winding down qualitatively—senior personnel and key designers are needed on other projects. Intermediate levels dominate.

The impact of the above is multiplicative and is inherently self-defeating. Not only are the problems tougher, but there's a smaller, less experienced staff to deal with them. We can delay the onset of phase 3 testing by several strategies:

1. Keep staffing high.
2. Keep key people on.
3. Get the phase 3 bugs out early.

The first strategy is bound to be ineffectual. It may be your only choice if the project's in trouble, but it can only be done at a high increase in cost and management problems that goes beyond your project. Other projects will suffer from late starts due to unavailable personnel, and/or part of your crew will be on the beach waiting for new projects. It prevents a smooth transition from project to project and results in a net cost increase and overruns (but not on your project). The same can be said for the second strategy, but not as strongly. The key people are not necessarily the best designers, but the best debuggers and testers. They're not necessarily the same. Key designers should be available for consulting on the problems, but they do not necessarily have to remain on the project. Some of the best testers and debuggers may be at the intermediate level. Recognize that design and test talent are not equivalent and plan your phase 3 staffing in recognition of that fact. Also recognize that by the time you get into phase 3 testing, the problems are (or should be) system-level and interactive issues, and independent testing is no less efficient, and can be better. There's no need to keep a designer on past the integration of his or her units, unless that designer also happens to be one of your better testers.

Phase 3 bugs can be brought out early, in phase 2, if we recognize what kind of bugs tend to dominate phase 3. These are rarely bugs directly related to microscopic functional issues; almost all of them are interactive, system-level issues that involve data-base corruption, interrupt handling problems, reentrance issues, resource management, load dependent bugs, and performance problems. By getting as much as possible of phase 2 testing done under a background load, by doing repeated, early stress testing, and by doing initial performance testing as early as possible in phase 2, you maximize the likelihood that phase 3 bugs will be shifted to phase 2 where there is time and resources to correct them. Our decision to use background during integration and to do repeated stress tests early in the game was based on Hitachi's experience. It seems to have worked for us. However, that experience is merely anecdotal and doesn't substitute for a formal, controlled experiment. At present, all I can say is try it if it seems reasonable to you.

5.3. Other Methods of Tracking

5.3.1. What to Track

Sophisticated theories aside, almost anything you do to keep honest track of bugs and testing progress is better than nothing at all and will give insight into what's going on. Using normalized time and percentage of completion is a good idea, because it allows the comparison of progress across projects that differ in size and scope. Each of the suggestions below can be applied three times: during unit- and element-level testing, during integration testing, and during system testing. If system testing and formal functional testing (acceptance test dry run) are separate, then there are four places to track things. The lower-level inputs (e.g., unit-level data) are merged to produce the higher-level charts.

1. Coverage percentage achieved (unit, element, subsystem, system) as a function of normalized time.
2. Private to public transitions—for example, calculate the Halstead length for all elements and the Halstead length of the system and plot percentage of Halstead length that has successfully passed formal element-level testing.
3. Integration completions—either based on element counts or, better yet, on Halstead length.
4. Cumulative number of bugs detected, cumulative number of bugs corrected, and number of outstanding uncorrected bugs.

5. Bug detection rate, bug correction rate, bug accumulation or depletion rate.
6. Number of unexplained crashes, malfunctions, mysterious occurrences, and so on—both a cumulative count and a rate.
7. Cumulative number of test bugs, cumulative number of test bugs corrected, outstanding number of uncorrected test bugs, and all associated rates.
8. Cumulative number of data-base errors, cumulative number of data-base corrections, outstanding uncorrected data-base problems, and associated rates.
9. Cumulative number of patches, number of outstanding patches.
10. Time between versions and releases, number of paths required to get a release to pass regression testing.

You don't want to keep track of all these. I assume you've got a QA function or project to run and that testing manpower and progress is more important than research. Most of the above are interrelated and most can be gleaned from your current paperwork with very little effort. If properly defined, it can be done by a clerk. Alternatively, and better, put it on a personal computer so you can plot the data, do the regressions, and present sexy looking reports for management that explain why you're doing so well, or why you aren't.

5.3.2. The Pit of Extrapolation

Tracking data is merely recording history. If you've been meticulous you can't get into trouble. However, when you extend a curve beyond the last measured point, you are engaging in an act of blind faith. Everything we've learned shows that bugs and progress do not follow neat linear patterns or even simple curves. There are gaps and discontinuities. Extrapolating a smooth curve or a straight line is dangerous enough; extrapolating trends in the light of possible discontinuities and nonlinearities borders on suicidal. In principle, you have no right to extrapolate a trend unless you have some notion (e.g., a law, preferably a nonempirical law) that tells you what to expect. That's what the software reliability theorists are trying to do, albeit without great success. So remember, whenever you extend a line beyond the measured points, keep it dotted and fuzzy, and let it get broader and more uncertain as it goes out.

The second point regards noise in the data. There was a hardware problem—so of course progress is reduced. Similarly for holidays, major discovered problems, vacations, new personnel, and so on. You don't get nice smooth data unless the project is very large and very protracted. Real data is a bunch of scattered points. If you do your extrapolation by connecting the dots, you'll oscillate between the exhilaration of grossly optimistic projections and pessi-

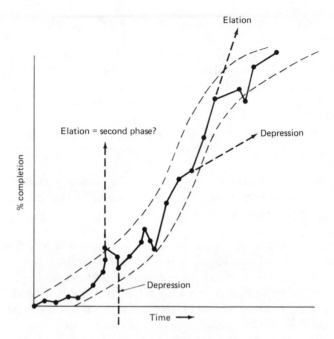

Figure 9-4. How to Make a Wreck of Yourself.

mistic devastation—see Figure 9-4. You need to run reasonably smooth curves through the points and not get optimistic or depressed over short-term trends obtained by connecting the dots. At any instant, the real projection lies in a broad band, indicated by the outer lines in Figure 9-4, that follow the center curve. One of the advantages of using regression analysis is that it doesn't hug the dots and is unbiased. If you use a polynomial regression package to extrapolate trends, don't get sucked in to using higher-order polynomials. There's very little of interest in engineering that can't be fitted with a cubic. The higher the order of the polynomial, the better it fits the points—and the closer it approaches to connecting dots—which is emotionally wearing.

6. TASKS FOR A QUALITY ASSURANCE DEPARTMENT

1. Implement the general use of McCabe's metric as a design rule-of-thumb measure of complexity, as an aid to productivity evaluation, and as an indicator of test complexity.
2. Implement the neccessary tools for calculating Halstead's metrics automatically from source code. Produce bug predictions as a starting point for determining expected test effort.

3. Modify the metrics you use by continuing feedback over several projects with the intent of making them better. Keep an eye on the literature for promising new metrics, especially those whose validity has been independently confirmed.
4. Be sure that management understands the differences between hardware and software reliability and the state-of-the-art of software reliability theory. Protect the contract signers from premature agreement to the use of a software reliability prediction model of dubious validity.
5. Track the literature in hope that useful methods of predicting software reliability emerge—hopefully before the end of this century.
6. Try the Hitachi method for predicting test completion rate. Try it at several levels—for programs, their test cases, and schedules; for subsystems, their test cases, and schedules, and for the whole system.
7. Track other progress measures that are easy to implement from existing paperwork and testing by-products. Use normalized times so that you can compare large projects with small. You might find a new, useful relation.

10

ACHIEVING QUALITY SOFTWARE

1. SYNOPSIS

How quality software can be achieved. The practical problems of quality assurance and quality assurance management.

2. TESTABLE DESIGNS

2.1. Changing the Perspective

The prevailing attitude in programming is to glorify design and denigrate testing. The primary question in the programmer's mind is "How can I implement this feature?" and the corresponding question in the programming manager's mind is "How can it be done within budget and schedule?" Testing concerns don't even come up as primary questions. Testing and debugging are necessary evils that will fritter away half of the labor and two-thirds of the schedule. With this point of view, the programmer is tacitly encouraged to try shortcuts. Go ahead, jump out of the middle of a loop and merge into the tail end of a subroutine to utilize common code. Use whatever trick you can to get the code done and running in record time. Don't waste time on planning and high-level designs. Don't worry about the niceties of system conventions and standards. Don't bother with modularity because it gets in the way of production. We know that these attitudes don't work in the long run because the resulting code is unmaintainable. We also know that they don't work for large systems because the complexities of large systems force us into cleaner and simpler designs. But each project leader is not dealing with a large system, nor is the programmer. Each deals with a component of a system, and within that component, they feel that formality and structure are unnecessary—even though they might agree to the necessity of structure at the system level.

If testing and debugging take half the effort, then shouldn't the programmer give them explicit recognition by asking "How can I test my implementation?"

Similarly, the project leader should ask "How can I get the program properly tested within the budget and schedule?" If equal emphasis was given up front to testing, then I believe that good code would follow, because the things that we recognize as good in coding are the same things that contribute to easy testing. If testing is easy, then it will be thorough. If testing is thorough, the software will have quality. In other words, the single most important thing that can be done to achieve quality software is to design the quality in. That's more important than how the quality assurance department is structured, who it reports to, what testing is independent, what kind of reviews are held—more important than the entire contents of this book, of *Software Testing Techniques,* and of the next ten books published on software quality assurance. If you achieve nothing more than getting project leaders and programmers to ask "How can this be tested thoroughly?" *before* they design it, then you will have achieved more for quality software than anything else you might do.

2.2. Techniques for Testable Design

Each testing technique reveals another way in which a design can be made more testable. Here is a summary of the techniques and their implications for design:

Path Testing. A routine with fewer paths is more testable than one with more paths. Jumping around within code, unnecessary GOTO's, "sharing code" instead of using a subroutine or macro, all increase the complexity of the code and the number of paths. Program flags that are used to control paths, block paths, and so on create additional states for the routine and make more of the paths process dependent. The ideal routine has no memory. The execution of the program at a point is independent of how it got to that point.

Loops. Simple, explicit loops have explicit loop control variables and can be tested in a few cases. Concatenated loops can be tested independently. Cleanly nested loops can be tested in a finite number of combinations. Convoluted, ad hoc loops cannot be simply tested.

Logic-Based Testing. Simple IF-THEN-ELSE constructs and case statements, or decision-table-based logic are explicit and easy to evaluate for all 2^n cases of interest. The variables that direct the paths are explicit and identifiable. Convoluted, ad hoc logic can be a nightmare to disentangle.

Syntax Testing. Explicit separation of input validation into syntax, field-value, and correlation analysis, in that order, makes it possible to do syntax testing independent of field values and subsequent processing. Field values and types can be tested independently of syntax. And the correlation between field values can also be tested independently of syntax. This separation modularizes testing and eliminates most of the complicated interactions that would otherwise have to be tested.

Transaction Flow Testing. If the system controls the operation done on transactions by means of a set of transaction control tables, rather than ad hoc code, most of testing consists of showing that the transaction control mechanism works. Testing the various transaction paths is then a question of testing the contents of the control tables. Just as simple paths are beneficial in path testing, they are beneficial in transaction-flow testing.

Interface Testing. Formal interelement interfaces with standardized calling sequences make interface testing a comparative snap. There's no need to learn how each pair of programmers agreed to communicate with one another—they must all communicate within the limits of the interface standards. There is only one standard against which to judge and not N^2 for N programmers. Because all interfaces are explicit, there's no need to design tests for the implicit interfaces.

State Testing. The modules that benefit from an implementation in terms of a finite state machine—such as device handlers, protocol controllers, resource threshold managers, and so on—are all designed as finite state machines with explicit state transition tables, documented states, documented transitions, and documented outcomes for each transition. There's no need to waste countless hours trying to figure out what the states are and what factors contribute to the states.

Data Base Testing. Testing the construction of the data base, its initial values, how fields and structures are used, is much simpler when there is a centrally designed and managed data base and associated data dictionary. The almost complete elimination of private space eliminates most reentrance bugs. Problems of leftover garbage, data-base corruption, hidden data modification, and the like are reduced significantly, and testing for such conditions is considerably simplified.

Integration. It's easier to add and test a small module than a big one. It's easier to integrate a single-function module than a multi-function module. Modules with single entries and exits, with explicit entry-exit parameters, are much easier to integrate than multi-entry multi-exit modules. Well-modularized code with explicitly specified functions for each module means that the backbone is more likely to consist of selected modules that are completely tested rather than selected paths though partially tested elements. The former creates a more reliable and robust, and therefore more effective, backbone than the latter.

Specifications. An explicit, documented specification for every element at every level is an explicit guide not only to what must be implemented, but also to what must be tested. If modules are created on the basis of verbal understandings, then not only is the module's intention hazy, but so are testing requirements. Independent testing without specifications is far more expensive, because valuable time must be wasted to create the missing specification.

Higher-Order Languages. Good higher-order languages get more coding done in less time, with fewer bugs than assembly languages. It's not so much the language as its processor. A bad compiler can make the best language worthless, and a superb compiler for an old language can go a long way to preventing bugs. Every language feature that abets the detection of dubious and potentially dangerous constructs (e.g., mixed-mode arithmetic) is welcome. Every kind of cross-reference produced (and used) reduces bugs. To the extent that the language forces the explicit declaration of objects and their attributes, it reduces bugs.

2.3. Tools

I don't know any programming tool that isn't more valuable as a test tool. We can't impose rigorous testing and expect programmers to do it with stone axes. The most important tool, of course, is access to the computer. That means enough terminals, enough machine time, quick turnarounds (preferably on-line testing and debugging).We can't ask programmers for copious documentation and deny them simple documentation tools. That means word processors and text editors. We can't expect people to keep on top of changes if those changes aren't made and distributed in a timely way. That means adequate clerical help, easy access to duplicating machines, or on-line documentation access. Before you worry about the fancy computer-oriented tools, are you sure that the mundane office tools are there and accessible to the programmers?

Following are the kinds of tools that are and should be available in support of quality software. All of these can help reduce the testing labor and also aid documentation of test progress.

Cross-References. There are just never enough different kinds of cross-reference available. The ideal cross-reference generator would allow the programmer to specify what is to be referenced against what, and in which order the cross-reference should be produced.

Style and Standards Checking. Permits the declaration of stylistic rules, standards, and coding and naming conventions. Checks code for conformance. This catches most wild cards.

Charters and Graph Generators. Generators that on the basis of static analysis produce a flowchart of the code. Better yet, an abstraction of the code that shows its graph (e.g., node-to-node) paths. Call tree generators are useful. A top-down call tree generator lists all the subroutines that can be called from a given point. A bottom-up generator or cross-reference produces all the possible callers for a given module.

Coverage Certifiers. Often coupled with a data generator, but not necessarily. These analyzers keep track of what path segments (links) were covered under a series of tests and identify any uncovered code.

Test Drivers. Test drivers are indispensable in unit testing and at any time when a working backbone isn't available. The drivers organize test cases, initialize the routine or system to known conditions, fetch and insert inputs, compare actual outcomes to predicted outcomes, and so on.

Instrumentation Tools. These help the insertion of instrumentation code without incurring the bugs that would occur for manual instrumentation, do the appropriate data gathering and storage, and some subsequent analysis.

Complex Tools. There are appearing some complex test tools such as SADAT (VOGE80) that automate much of test execution labor. SADAT performs an analysis of the code, creates the static flow chart, finds the decision-to-decisions path segments, automates selection of paths, automates the insertion of instrumentation code for those paths, and automates path sensitizing.

A complete survey of test tools is beyond the scope of this book. The reader is advised to examine and compare test tools, to question manufacturers on what's available for their hardware, and to pressure for adequate tools. The consensus on tools is that they're well worth the price, if someone else pays for them. Good, detailed surveys of test tools are to be found in DUNN82, JENS79, MYERS76, RAMA75A, and REIF77. Articles on specific tools and experience with tools are to be found in FOSD76, HOLT79, HUAN75, HUAN79, PANZ78, RAMA75B, RAMA76, RYDE79, and VOGE80.

2.4. Performance Impact

The most often heard reason for not using higher order languages or for not using well-designed code is that the proper design will have a deleterious impact on the system's performance. It is argued that structured code and higher-order languages are incompatible with tight, efficient software of the kind that's needed in time-critical software. Before I debunk that myth, let me state that I never expect a machine to be able to produce faster or more efficient code than a dedicated programmer who's really working at it. By the time machines and programs can beat us at that game, they'll be doing all the programming, reading all the books, and probably writing them also. Okay, so the machines can't beat the dedicated programmer who spends three months writing the ultimate 10-instruction bootstrap. But what about the average? And does it matter?

Most of the code in a real-time system doesn't operate in real time. Half of the code is probably off-line software used to generate tables, analyze on-line operations statistics, do billing, and so on, where timeliness in the millisecond and second range is just not that important—certainly not as important as maintainability. Of the on-line code, only about 10 to 15% operates on normal paths. The rest concerns low-probability exception conditions where ineffi-ciency can be tolerated. Of the critical on-line software, less than a third has any real performance impact. In other words, the real performance impact of fast or slow code is probably tied up in less than 5% of the system's software. We could afford tight code in those areas if we had more testable code in the other 95%. With regard to higher-order languages, while an optimizing com-piler can't beat a dedicated human, most humans aren't dedicated. The com-piler can do a better job optimizing the usage of registers, fetches and stores, and the like, than most humans can on an average. The human can only see a dozen instructions ahead or behind, and isn't willing to do it all over again when an initial strategy proves ineffectual. The optimizing compiler will try as long as you let it. It produces more efficient average code.

The last point concerns space. The use of explicit structures, clean, testable programs, modularity, and all the rest do have some space impact. They may take more main memory. So what? If you're designing software that's to go into a watch, calculator, home computer, automobile, or other consumer prod-uct that's going to be sold in the millions, then it probably does pay to squeeze or worry about a few bytes. But most systems are single-shot systems. I used to say that the cost of the extra memory was far less than the design, test, and debug labor required to get around the memory shortage. That's no longer true. The cost of the extra memory is typically less than the cost of arguing about it. There's probably nothing cheaper with a better payoff than giving a pro-grammer sufficient memory in which to create that nice, testable, structured code. There's nothing worse you can do than to take it away.

3. WHO WANTS QA?

3.1. Motives, Ulterior and Otherwise

Why does a programming organization that has not had a formal, explicit, quality assurance function agree to one? The right reason is that they believe that it will work, and that it's a more cost-effective way to achieve the required software quality. This is the reason that's always stated, yet it's often not the real reason. To the extent that the real motives and stated motives differ, the job of quality assurance will be made possible or impossible. Here are some real motives.

Over My Dead Body! The programming staff has a history of catastrophes. Productivity appeared to be high, but as time went on, more and more serious field problems were related to software. Management, recognizing the fact that there's a software quality problem, creates and imposes software quality assurance from above. It won't work. Management didn't go far enough. They should have scrapped the entire software department and started fresh with a combination of good designers and cooperative quality assurance. They've built-in the conflict between QA and design and it's inevitable that in the ensuing struggle to the death, QA will lose.

Lip Service. Whether the software is good or bad is unimportant. QA has been called into being to satisfy a contractual requirement or to create a good image. Management doesn't believe in software QA. So hire the most simple-minded dolts you can find, who can talk a good game and know all the buzz words, give them a fancy rubber stamp, and call that QA. The software will get gradually worse. Some people may take QA seriously and stop worrying about testing because that's QA's job. They all go down the tubes together, eventually.

It's the Latest Thing. Everybody just knows that QA is the latest and bestest thing. QA will cut bugs to a tenth, QA will do this, that, and the other thing. Build a big organization, staff it to the hilt, produce copious memos and standards, hold meetings, and be busy, busy, busy. Going to extremes for the wrong reasons is also not effective and may not produce better programs.

Software quality assurance cannot be imposed from above on an unreceptive programming staff. It must be a grass roots movement. It must evolve from the gradual realization by the programmers and programming managers that an explicit QA function is not only the way to get better programs, but the way to reduce cost, improve schedules, and remove some of the uncertainties associated with large programming efforts. Ideally, there already exists an informal, distributed, operational quality assurance function that's ready for formalization. The trigger to that formalization could be a few catastrophic experiences on one or another projects—it's not a bad trigger if most of the programming staff agrees that a formal QA function is the way to avoid future disasters. It could be triggered in response to an external requirement, or because they realize that its time has come. Any of these could be a proximate cause. Whatever the trigger, though, if there isn't grass roots understanding and belief, it won't work.

3.2. Up-Front Understandings

Assuming that QA is being started as a formal activity, for the right reasons, it's important that the ground rules be established in advance, and be written down. Of these, the question of independence, discussed below, is the most important. Other understandings that must be clarified include:

1. *Budget.* QA can't live off the dregs. At present, proper software QA takes approximately 20% of the project cost; it will go up in the future. The money's got to come from someplace. In some applications, that figure could go much higher (e.g., in nuclear reactor controls) and must be figured as part of the cost. There can be no independent quality assurance without an independent budget.
2. *Staff and Facilities.* QA is staffed much like a programming project except that it requires a higher share of clerical help because there's much more documentation to handle. Facilities are similar to programming facilities but may require more bookcases, files, and conference rooms. Staffing tends to be more senior than programming, and office facilities should be adjusted accordingly.
3. *Computer Time and Test Facilities.* Just as budget must be allocated, so must computer time and other test facilities. QA needs a fair share, including good shifts and bad shifts. Typical computer facility usage ranges from 10 to 25% of that used by the programming staff.
4. *Capital Budget.* Capital expenditures run higher for QA than for a programming group of comparable size. You can't expect an individual project to pay for generalized test tools—hardware or software. If such tools must be bought or developed for a specific project, then it's likely that the tool will be useful only on that project or not acquired at all. QA needs a capital budget to acquire existing test tools, to modify test tools, to create new test tools, or to adapt test tools developed by a project for more general use. Capital equipment or computer time is also needed for computers to host cross-reference generators, to maintain test data bases, and so on.
5. *Interaction.* QA's effectiveness and costs are at the mercy of the project to which it's being applied. If the software's rotten, then QA's costs and schedules will escalate. Conversely, don't be surprised if management hears the same story from the project side (i.e., budget and schedule were destroyed by QA's meddling).

3.3. Independence

Independence of QA from the project hierarchy is probably the most important doctrine that can be established. If there is true independence, then budgets, staff, and facilities follow. It's very easy to see if a QA function is independent or not. Go up the management tree from the project side and up the management tree from the QA side, and find the point at which they merge. If the person in that slot has project management responsibility, then QA is not independent. Actually it's not an absolute thing, because everybody up to the chairman of the board has some degree of project responsibility. The point is, how much muscle does QA have? If it reports to a divisional vice president, say, who has P&L responsibility, and also controls sales, development, and production, then if QA reports at that level, it's likely to have the requisite degree of muscle and independence. Muscle means the ability to overrule the project hierarchy when this is essential to meet quality objectives. Muscle means the ability to cause schedule slips and large expenditures of additional labor and money in order to meet mandatory quality objectives. Muscle means that management may decide to scrap the project rather than make the investment needed for the required quality. Muscle means the ability to set the quality standards and the test standards to which software development will have to conform.

Muscle, however, is not a license to kill. Remember that every time the beneficial conflict between project and QA erupts into a confrontation, both are damaged. If QA attempts to impose unrealistic goals, to make the software development effort noncompetitive, to impose a burdensome overload of nonproductive paperwork more concerned with form than function, then again software quality will suffer and, eventually, independent QA will disappear.

Independence is also a spectrum. Clear guidelines must be developed that delineate QA's rights and responsibility at every stage from unit testing to system testing. Independent testing means independent test design and not the minor act of running tests independently that were designed by the software designers. QA cannot function effectively in structural testing, and therefore independent testing by QA is perforce functional testing. Define independence in the following terms:

1. Make a clear identification of what constitutes a unit, program, subsystem, system, and any other meaningful levels inbetween.
2. At each element level, define who (QA or project) designs the structural tests, who designs the functional tests, who witnessess what tests, what paperwork must be produced for that level, and who sees to it that all quality assurance measures appropriate to that level have been accomplished.
3. Define QA's role as an arbitrator between the buyer and builder. Define just how far QA can go in taking the buyer's side. To what extent can QA "blow the whistle" to the buyer without fear of losing job and livelihood?
4. Define the channels to be used to overrule or to force changes in software for every level element from unit to system. Define the channels of appeal.

This is to be complemented by equivalent channels on the project side. The project leader needs a mechanism to overrule QA, to appeal, and so forth. It must be a two-way street with equal power on both sides.

4. STAFFING AND MANAGEMENT

4.1. The Halt, the Lame, and the Blind

"Give me your tired, your poor . . . the wretched refuse of your teeming shore, send these, the homeless, tempest tossed to me." Did Emma Lazarus write this for the Statue of Liberty or was it a staffing plan for quality assurance? I won't apologize for the cynicism. I can't speak for others in this business, but I've had my share and fill of the "wretched, the poor," the incompetent, the neurotics, the psychotics, the alcoholics, and the halt, the lame, and the blind. Would that I had more of the halt, lame, and blind, because there at least there is intelligence and competence that can more than compensate for physical disability. If a person's an idiot as a programmer, what will make him a mavin in quality assurance? A lazy goofball is of no use to either programming or to QA. And if a person is so screwed-up emotionally that they can't program from one day to the next, how will she fare in the more stressful environment of quality assurance? Don't delude yourself into thinking you've got independence if you can't hire and fire. Don't think you're going to do a job using programming's castoffs. That also means, indirectly, that QA salaries will be at par with programmers—not less, because only by offering decent salaries can you attract good people.

I have noticed one thing, however, that shouldn't be ignored in evaluating a programming staff "castoff." Sometimes a person can be a so-so programmer but turn out to be a real asset to quality assurance. It may be a question of creativity, or the kind of creativity that a person has. There are some excellent literary critics who are busts as writers. Knowledge of a subject doesn't mean you can teach it. There are a lot of similar parallels, and it's been gratifying to take a person who seemed to be a mediocre programmer (but never stupid or lazy) and find that in a QA environment he turned into a real tiger. But don't go thinking that every mediocre programmer has QA potential.

4.2. The QA Worker

Now that I've said what the QA worker isn't, what do we want? The following is an amalgam of the qualities that I've observed to be beneficial in a good QA worker.

1. *Experience as a programmer.* Three to five years of hands-on programming experience in the system and application to which the person will be assigned. At least one year in the organization on a project before being assigned to QA.
2. *A thick skin and a good sense of humor.* QA personnel take a lot of heat and abuse—it isn't a place for hypersensitive individuals who take things personally. Humor is important because it's a good way to defuse tensions. It's better to get quality by cajoling than by command.
3. *Tolerance for chaos.* People react to chaos and lack of structure in two ways—one caves in, the other attempts to create structure out of chaos. Test design and quality assurance must start when many things are undefined. If you wait for definition, it's too late. The QA worker must be able to pick things up and drop them when blocked. It's an inherently more chaotic world than the programmer's world.
4. *Tenacity.* The picture of an English bulldog fastened on the burglar's ass comes to mind. A QA worker has to go after an objective and hold on either until she's satisfied or until the objective has been redefined. The programmer must know, from the QA worker's personality, that the problem will not be allowed to go away. QA workers are inherently organized. They use files, indexes, records, and all the other tangible accouterments of an organized mind as second nature. There's too many things for QA to look after to trust to memory. If QA is committed to seeing to it that the little things are noticed, then there's no room for scatterbrained individuals.
5. *Skeptical.* That doesn't mean hostile. There's no room for an accepting personality. I mean skepticism in the sense that all is fit to be questioned, and that nothing is taken for granted—only the tangible evidence in documents will suffice, not comfortable, reassuring words.
6. *Cunning (or "low cunning" as Gruenberger put it).* Insidious, devious, diabolical. "Street-wise" is another good term, as are fiendish, contriving, wily, canny, and underhanded.
7. *Bold.* You can't intimidate them, even by pulling rank. They've got to be fearless lest they succumb to compromise. That also means that they must function within an organization that provides them with backing, as high as necessary, to get the quality that's needed.
8. *Self-sufficient.* If they need love, they don't get it on the job, that's for sure. They can't be looking to the interaction between them and programming as a source of ego gratification or nurturing.
9. *Honest.* Fundamentally honest and incorruptible. Agony over perceived compromise. A dedication to "right."

To these I can add the ability to communicate in writing and verbally, an innate ability to handle people, and a lot of other qualities. The ideal QA worker would be such a paragon that he or she would be after (and getting) the company president's job before long.

4.3. Dealing with Hostility

4.3.1. The Hidden Problem

No one wants to talk about hostility. Why does everyone hate software QA? How does one handle the undisguised or thinly guised hostility? The hostility exists and is tangible in every organization I've seen.

4.3.2. The Source

QA is a destructive process. Dedication to proving that something fails is by nature destructive and hostile. The relation between QA and programming is fundamentally an adversary relation. Nobody likes the person who causes pain, who creates labor, who forces rework, who criticizes. The programmer can tolerate all that in their supervisor because the supervisor dispenses rewards and pleasure in addition to pain. QA dispenses pain and no reward, except a very abstract one, long after the project is done. But software QA is not alone in this respect. Production personnel in a factory don't like QA inspectors either. Bookkeepers don't like auditors. Nobody ever liked the Inspector General.

4.3.3. What Can Be Done?

Ultimately, as software QA proves its worth, as it becomes part of every job and every organization, it will be (perhaps grudgingly) accepted, and with that acceptance much of the hostility will go away. In some organizations that state has been achieved, but not for every programmer and every project. In others, only laws seem to prevent bloodshed and physical violence. Let's assume that management is behind QA and that there's acceptance at most programming management levels—say that the problem of hostility is one that exists mainly between individual programmers and QA personnel. What can be done to alleviate that hostility, and to protect the QA worker against it?

1. Make sure the new QA worker is aware of the potential for hostility. Often it's not recognized, the QA worker is demoralized, and doesn't know why. Expecting hostility won't reduce it, but will make it easier to deal with.
2. Don't be judgmental. If you see a lousy piece of code, don't say so. Design tests that will reveal its weaknesses—or discuss testing methods with the perpetrator. It's the end objective that counts.
3. Be aware of "face." Don't humiliate the programmers, no matter how much their code may deserve it.

4. Pass the buck. Don't critique the violation of coding standards and style. Point out the deficiencies and pass the buck to an amorphous, high-level, standards setter. "I'm just doing my job—it isn't my standards," etc.
5. Keep it private. Always try to get things accomplished within the private domain rather than the public domain. Try to get things improved without resorting to formal memos and deficiency reports.
6. Keep it light. You're dead serious but can't act that way. You can be a complete bastard and still smile.
7. Invoke a common enemy. Make the buyer's QA the common enemy if that suits. Invoke a government spec—divert the heat.
8. Give out rewards—acquire and develop test tools that will make the programmer's job easier. Provide feedback on the kinds of bugs and how to prevent them. Put out upbeat QA memos and reports when there's been a really successful project—praise the programmers for the quality and don't take public credit. Publish and distribute letters from satisfied buyers. Throw an acceptance test party.
9. Help the project managers by giving them test progress feedback, bug projections, test completion reports, and anything else that will make their job easier and more predictable.

4.4. A Tour of Duty

QA work is not something that can be done by most persons indefinitely. Hostility is part of it. The fact that it is perceived to be less creative than programming is another part. Finally, for most programmers it's a career dead end—the reputation for software QA has been so poor that many programmers regard a stint in QA as a stain rather than a kudo. I personally think it's an honor and that it can be every bit as creative as programming. But that belief doesn't change the programmer's perspective. One way out of this and also a way of breaking down the artifical barriers between programming and QA is to use a tour of duty that alternates between programming and QA. Every person who does a tour of duty in QA becomes a better programmer for it. Their code is cleaner, better structured, better documented, better tested, and far more defensive than it had been before. Furthermore, such individuals are typically more open and less hostile when it's their turn to be on the wrong end of the QA stick. In an organization with relatively low turnover, people can be shifted into QA roles and back into programming on a regular basis. Say that the typical project lasts 18 months. The entry-level programmer works on two projects to gain the necessary experience. Instead of a third project, she does QA on a project. Then two more projects and then QA again. Finally, the programmer can do a stint as assistant QA director for a project, followed by assistant project manager, project manager,and then QA manager for a project. Along the way you'll find individuals who have a talent and gusto for QA work. These become part of a permanent QA cadre. What we ultimately want is not just acceptance of QA's role as a necessary evil, but an appreciation of it as a necessary, benevolent part of the programming process. On that glorious day, there will be no more defensiveness or hostility. Rotating the staff is one way to help that day come about.

5. QUALITY ASSURANCE SQUARED

5.1. The Problem

QA work can be divided into three main activities: 1) the creation and enforcement of standards, 2) reviews, audits, and record keeping, and 3) independent test design. The first of these activities consumes a small part of the labor and has no unique quality assurance problem—only the long-haul results will show if the standards were effective or not. The second set of activities, while highly technical, are essentially clerical. Quality assurance over the activity is exercised by supervisors as for any other clerical activity—by reviews, audits, and so on. It is the third activity, the design, documentation, dry running, and execution of tests, that has a unique quality assurance problem—that is, quality assurance squared.

Quality assurance over test designs and testing is essential to a successful QA effort. Consider it from the programmers' point of view. QA puts their work under close scrutiny, designs tests intended to make their programs fail and point out (directly or indirectly) design deficiencies. A test error will not be overlooked or forgiven by the programmers. With a mature attitude on both sides, a low incidence of test errors can be tolerated—just as a low incidence of bugs is tolerated. The test errors, just like the bugs, must be corrected. However, if QA has a high incidence of public test bugs, then confidence in QA's work is eroded. Those who object to QA's intrusions have ample grist for their mills. The result is that QA will be either bypassed and ignored, or held in derision. It is therefore essential that QA provide a level of test quality assurance that is at least as good as that which the programmers do for themselves—and if at all possible, significantly better.

5.2. Programming and QA Test Design Compared

There are many similarities between programming and independent test design done by a QA department. There are also differences. The similarities and differences lead to methods of QA quality management.

1. Tests are less complicated than the programs they test. While a set of tests may require more lines of code or the equivalent than the unit under test,

the tests don't interact with one another. Each represents a path through the routine. A set of finite paths is much simpler than the routine.

2. Tests are to a great extent independent of one another. Or they should be. The concern of any one subtest or test tends to be microscopic and generally does not have a global impact. For example, while a bug in an input processing module might cause a system recovery failure, it's unlikely that a bug in an input processing module *test* can cause the failure of a system recovery *test*.

3. Programmers have elegant tools for catching syntax and other source code errors (e.g., compilers, assemblers). Test designers have no such tools, and because much of what they test involve deliberate errors, such tools may be impossible. Programmers can ignore source code errors that show up as syntax errors, but testers have to rely on manual methods.

4. Programmers have utility software and programming tools that create cross-references, indexes, lists, maps, graphs, and the rest. Testers deal with documents such as specifications and correspondence, whose cross-references cannot be automated.

5. Program designs are for the most part formal and are documented in a formal language (e.g., the source language). The program is either as intended or not, but its interpretation by the computer is immutable. Test designs include informal (e.g., natural language) components whose interpretation is done by humans and may change from moment to moment and from person to person.

6. Programs, when subjected to specific tests, will usually respond in exactly the same way each time they're run. Tests, particularly those that involve simulated operator and user actions, can be executed erroneously. It isn't always clear what was wrong: the program, the test, or its execution.

7. The individual programmer's scope tends to be narrow. Because QA personnel are at about one-fifth the size of programming personnel, the scope of the tester is at least five times greater than that of the programmer. Because only half of QA's work is in test design, the QA test designer has to deal with a conceptual scope that's at least ten times greater than that which the individual programmer deals with. Of necessity that means that the tester's knowledge of any one area is inherently shallower than the programmer's. The individual test designer, then, deals with a scope that corresponds to the technical group leader. The QA leader's technical scope corresponds to that of the system architect. Yet, since individual routines are being tested, the tests must be as meticulous and precise as the routine being tested.

8. Whatever schedule the programmers are working with, the testers must cover the same territory over a shorter period of time. Independent test design can't really be started until most of the design has jelled. That means

a late start for test design. Typically, the tester has half the time that the programmer has.

9. The programmer has to hit a moving target because of specification changes, modifications to functional requirements, and, to a lesser extent, design changes. The tester's target moves more erratically. Not only does every specification and requirement change impact test design, but so does every implementation change, and many bugs. Furthermore, successful tests may invalidate other tests that had been previously run or that have not yet been run. A successful test reveals a fundamental design flaw. The programmers fix the problem and in so doing invalidate a score of previous and scheduled tests. While, in principle, purely functional tests would not suffer from this problem, functional coverage can only be achieved by taking some advantage of structure to reduce the number of tests required. If the structure changes, it's inevitable that some tests will be made ineffectual and that some new tests will be required.

5.3. Test-Testing and Debugging

The procedure for test-testing and debugging parallels program testing and debugging, but there is a much higher reliance on manual methods. Of these, desk checking is the most important.

1. *Design.* The test design documentation must include references to the appropriate specification. If the test designer takes advantage of structure to simplify testing, then the test design documentation must explicitly list just how the structure was used; what it was about the structure that allowed the elimination of tests, and what assumptions were made—so that if the structure changes, it's possible to go back and redesign the tests if necessary.

2. *Coding.* This consists of documenting the initial conditions, the inputs, the data-base assumptions, and the expected outcomes of each subtest in meticulous detail down to the last character. Also required is a specification of the method used to verify the outcomes. Often this may be simple (e.g., "Observe output XYZ on terminal 101") but in some cases may involve substantial off-line, after-the-fact, verification processing. The test designer must create the equivalent of subroutines for initial conditions, inputs, data base, and verification.

3. *Desk Checking.* This is where most test design bugs are caught. The "code" is a document, such as the subtest specification sheet. It must be examined manually, character by character, for a match to intentions. At least 30% of the effort required to design and debug tests should be involved in manual desk checking and reviews.

4. *Audits and Reviews.* Peer reviews are very helpful here. Test designers should work in pairs so that one designer can cross-check the other's work. QA managers should audit (read in detail) all tests.

5. *Independent Testing.* If a test is properly designed, then it should be capable of being run by any competent person. I strongly advocate the principle of having a different person do the dry runs for a test than the person who designed it. Furthermore, the test-tester should work it cold, with little or no input from the test designer. This practice shows up ambiguities and test design and documentation deficiencies very quickly.

6. *Reruns.* Every failed test (that is, a test whose outcome was not as predicted by the test designer—in that case it was the test that failed and not the system) must be repeated, not just once but several times. If test drivers are used, then this problem goes away for many tests. However, test drivers can only provide simulated operator actions and user behavior. Ultimately, scenarios must be run from real terminals where there's lots of room for cockpit errors.

7. *Cooperation with Program Designers.* Most test bugs are obvious and easily corrected. Some, however, are subtle. It isn't always clear what went wrong. Did the program fail the test? Was it a test design bug? A test execution bug or cockpit error? A specification error? The problem can sometimes only be resolved by discussions with the cognizant program designer. So even though we're talking about independent test design, it's neither possible nor effective to cut all communications between the test designer and the program designer.

8. *Cooperation with the Buyer.* Let's rule out controversies in which the test designer is forced to appeal to the buyer for the resolution of a fundamental conflict between QA and programming—that's not a test bug issue. The resolution of an apparent test bug may sometimes come only after the buyer's intentions are revealed. We have a controversy—say that programming claims a test bug while QA claims a program bug (I've also seen it the other way). It involves questions that have never been asked—how does the buyer want the system to behave under these conditions? If there's an open, informal channel between programming and QA to the buyer's representative, such questions can be resolved. Often only the buyer's operational know-how can resolve the question. Appeals to the buyer of this kind should be minimized, and made only when there's no other way, lest the buyer gets the false impression that the system is no good.

9. *Automation and Tools.* Test designers should strive to automate as much as possible. The ideal is to approach the formality that we normally associate with programs. The more we make test design and debugging like code design and debugging, the more we reduce uncertainty and confusion.

5.4. The QA Manager's Role

The primary force for test quality is the QA manager or QA project leader. However you structure QA for a project, there should be at least one person who has primary technical responsibility. On a large project, this would be done by a lead technical person, typically the assistant QA manager with technical responsibility. On a smaller project, that job is the QA project leader's. I estimate that 25% of my time is spent on QA[2]. That means reviewing tests, reading test documentation, catching errors, and so on. In other words, doing another, independent desk check. Since so much of test design is test documentation in the form of test sheets, I've found it effective to do the reviews on a word processor directly. That way I can read, edit, and correct all in one go. The word processor automatically flags all changes, so that the individual test designers can confirm if the correction is valid or not.

As the project progresses, more and more of the manager's time must be spent on this odious but essential task. It has several benefits. Recall that earlier I said that you start test design with more test ideas than you can reasonably hope to implement, and that as detailed design progresses, more and more tests would be culled. The intention of that culling is to create an independent functional test that is thorough, and even-handed across all functional areas. Now, test designers also have pride, and in the final phases of culling we have to cut tests that have already been detailed. The test designers will all assure you that if you cut their tests the system will be a disaster. I always ask the designers to do their own culling—because they can do a better job of it than I can. However, towards the end, every designer has culled to what they feel is the absolute minimum, and we still need to cut 20 to 30% of the subtests. I say subtests here rather than tests because it's rare that a whole test can be sacrificed. In this final cut, all test groups, subgroups, and tests are fully justified. If the cut is to occur, it can only occur at the lowest, subtest level. How can you make a rational decision concerning what to cut if you haven't been through the entire test plan down to the detailed subtest level?

5.5. Be-bugging

One idea for test QA that's been around is the idea of **be-bugging** (GANN79, SCHI78). Gannon (GANN79) used deliberately inserted bugs (be-bugging) as an experimental method to determine the incidence of various kinds of bugs and the techniques that were most effective in catching them. Schick and Wolverton (SCHI78) discuss the use of be-bugging as an aid to predicting software reliability. Gilb (GILB77) has an extensive discussion of the use of be-bugging as a method of predicting maintainability and reliability, as well as the problems associated with realistic be-bugging. Myers (MYER76) discusses the role of be-bugging in reliability prediction, as do Dunn and Ullman (DUNN82). The use of be-bugging in software reliability prediction is intuitively simple and is based on a method that has been used by fish managers. You have a mixed population of fish in a lake (pike, bass, and perch, say) and you want to know how many of each there are, their average weights, and so on. You catch a fixed number—say 100—tag them, and then let them go. Over a period of time fish are caught. If you keep track of the ratio of tagged fish to untagged fish for every kind of tagging, then you can make some precise estimates of what's in the lake. The question to ask is "Can we equate bugs to fish?"

The problem is not with statistics, but with the bug seeding process. One can, given sufficient resources, always create bugs that a particular, finite set of tests, will never catch. Conversely, one can design a set of obvious bugs that almost any stupid test would catch. Fish are fish, and the act of catching and tagging a fish doesn't change a perch to a pike. Bugs are much more slippery than fish. The validity of be-bugging in reliability prediction depends completely on whether or not the seeded bugs share the same statistics as the remaining bugs. Note that if the seeded bugs share the same statistics as the bugs caught to date, that doesn't give you the right to infer that they share the same statistics as the bugs remaining: the act of debugging perforce changes the characteristics of the remaining bugs. The more bugs you catch, the more the remaining population is converted from perch to pike.

5.6. Tit-for-Tat

Be-bugging may prove useful as a method of quality assurance over independent test design. One would expect that if we seeded a hundred bugs into a program, a set of independent tests that caught all one hundred would be better than a set that caught only fifty. Actually, while one would intuitively expect that to be the case, there's no real basis for statistical interference because again we don't know the bias that might be built-in to those hundred seeded bugs.

Let's bypass the statistical problems by not attempting to make a quantitative evaluation of just how good an independent test might be. Let's just consider the impact of knowing that there are bugs on the independent test designer. It must result in more thorough desk checking and therefore better tests. There's no need to create a set of contrived bugs—the real system has enough real bugs, which are more likely to be representative of remaining bugs than any contrived bugs. If seeding is to be done, it should consist of leaving in bugs that were discovered. That means that the seeding is done by the programmers. This has several beneficial effects:

1. The programmers now see the test designers as in the same boat—the power is no longer completely in the hands of QA, and the conflict between QA and programming has been partially defused.
2. We've avoided an ever-increasing hierarchy of test testers. Let QA^2 be handled (in part) by programming.
3. It really becomes a two-way street—in a poor environment, it will accentuate the conflict; in a good environment, it will alleviate it.

The seeded bugs should be selected by the programmers from among those bugs that were caught earlier and that have relatively local impacts, preferably with subtle rather than obvious problems. They must also be bugs that would have a functional impact and that could reasonably be expected to be caught by a proper functional test. The programmers must be fair. Our own experience with this is inconclusive. Test designers didn't object to being seeded—most welcomed the idea of getting something that would help them gauge their own effectiveness. Programmers seemed to be enthusiastic about the prospect. We've yet to implement it from the start on a full project.

6. WHO DESERVES THE CREDIT, WHO DESERVES THE BLAME?

6.1. A Charm Against Tigers

A man in Arkansas wore a big medallion—an ornate thing that weighed more than a pound. "What is it?" he was asked, to which he replied that it was a charm against wild tigers. To which the questioner said, "You fool—there isn't a wild tiger within 10,000 miles of here." "You see," said the medallion wearer, "it works." Is software quality assurance a charm against wild tigers? If the system goes into the field with better than average reliability, then it was the designers who did a superb job. If it's buggy, QA failed to hold its end up. The question of whether or not QA works is difficult to answer. There's one circumstance in which it could be decided conclusively. In some software projects, the application is so critical that the program is written in parallel by two or three different groups (GEIG79). It's an appropriate solution to the creation of reliable software for a nuclear reactor controller, say, but the cost is at least three to four times the cost of a single program. The three programs are run simultaneously and compared. Majority voting decides which program is in error. In this method, software QA is done reciprocally by each independent group against the other. It provides an extremely strong motivation for quality software. It could also represent a test bed in which the effectiveness of QA can be measured. Let two of the groups have extensive QA and one have little or none. Will it prove anything? Perhaps or perhaps not. The group without QA, still recognizing that they are in competition with the other group, may institute self-policing that's more effective than that provided by the external QA.

It comes down to this: the effectiveness of QA is very difficult to measure, especially over the course of a single project. While controlled experiments are essential, they are almost impossible to carry out. If there's a belief in QA's role, then no one will do without it. If there's no belief, a programming staff might be motivated to higher quality and more rigorous internal testing just to prove the point that QA is not essential. Furthermore, some of the most effective QA techniques work against proving QA's worth. For example, by not being judgmental, by trying to avoid confrontations, by getting software changes made through persuasion rather than through dictates, by creating an environment that assures thorough self-testing by the programmers, by not rubbing the programmer's face in every bug caught—by doing all those things, we also reduce the visibility of QA's contribution. I said at the outset that QA's goal had to be bug prevention before bug detection. How do we credit QA for prevented bugs?

6.2. Keeping Records and Public Relations

Just because you should be self-effacing in order to reduce the conflict between programming and quality assurance doesn't mean that you shouldn't document caught and prevented bugs. Working in a spirit of cooperation with programmers typically means that the programmers will get the credit for bugs caught—even if it was a QA activity that revealed it. Keep records so that if QA's contributions are dismissed as inconsequential, if push comes to shove, you'll have documented evidence to prove your claim. If programming managers are aware that you're keeping records, they're more likely to give credit where credit is due.

No small part of getting fair credit is good public relations. Much of what QA does is tangible. If QA undertakes to design and debug a test data base for use by programming and QA alike, document it like you would a program, report its progress, and the rest, so that it can be evaluated as a program. Similarly for test tools that are used by programming and QA. Try to convert as much of your activity as you can into an activity that looks like programming. Accept budgets and schedules, work to specifications, state intentions early, and show that those intentions and objectives were accomplished. And if no one else will give you the credit, be sure the buyer appreciates your role and says so in a letter of commendation (if warranted).

6.3. Reasonable Expectations and Claims

You won't get anywhere if you project 100% bug elimination, or, alternatively, insist that without QA the project will fall. The environment for QA is still fundamentally hostile, and all of software QA must be sold. You can't sell things if you make outrageous claims or have unrealistic expectations. Avoid committing yourself to quantitative predictions, because the state of the art of quantitative predictions with respect to software reliability and latent bugs is still too primitive for that. Furthermore, if you make quantitative claims, you'll be required to demonstrate that you have met them—and that may be impossible.

6.4. Internal and External Comparisons

The best comparisons are internal—projects on which extensive QA was used against projects on which it wasn't. Don't get sucked into making the comparison on a single project—it's only over a set of projects (pre-QA versus post QA, say) that QA's contribution can be proved. External comparisons on similar projects, say bug rate statistics, may prove that you're doing as well as another group or better. Again, such comparisons are dangerous, and care must be taken to assure that the circumstances are really similar. The problem of comparisons is much easier in a huge programming organization—such as that of a computer manufacturer. There are many programming groups, many projects, the hardware is mostly the same, the environment tends to be uniform, and constraints and management's attitude are similar. It's then possible to make meaningful comparisons of QA's effectiveness. In most programming organizations, however, the basis for comparison is too small to warrant quantitative measures—at best you can get agreement that it worked, and that the program was better with than without QA.

Until we get reliable methods for measuring software quality, for predicting bugs, for predicting and validating software reliability, we should not expect to have an easy time of proving that QA was effective, except qualitatively.

7. WHERE TO FROM HERE?

The ultimate form of software QA will not be the same as it is today. Long-term success and long-term recognition of its benefits cannot come in a climate in which a fundamentally hostile adversary relation exists. I would like to see a time in which there is no external QA manager. In which independent QA is unnecessary. In which QA functions are totally integrated within the project hierarchy and so diffused that it is impossible to tell who is concerned with programming and who with QA. Just as individual programmers must shift their hats from designer to tester, I would give them a third hat to wear—the QA hat, to be used first on their own work, and then, because we recognize our own biases, to be used on other programmers' work. I would like to see the software equivalent of the Japanese Quality Circle at work—where everyone has a say and everyone can have an impact on the creation of more reliable software. The artificial division between programmer and QA disappears, and the hostility is replaced by a cooperative spirit, with the right kind of internal controls, checks, and balances that assure that only quality software will be built. Then the QA's manager role will become a delight—it will be to create and emplace those controls, to gather data on what ideas work, and to coordinate, organize, and implement the myriad contributions to quality that are offered up by all programmers.

REFERENCES

ABEJ79   Abe, Joichi; Sakamura, Ken; and Aiso, Hideo. An analysis of software project failures. Proceedings of the Fourth International Conference on Software Engineering, Munich, September 17–19, 1979. IEEE CH 1479-5/79.0000-0378.

           Survey of 23 projects with one million lines of total code. Minicomputer to large computer software. Provides some simple, effective measures of probability that a project will become bankrupt. Impressive results and claims that the probability of not detecting bankruptcy by their method is less than 0.02.

AKIY71   Akiyama, K. An example of software system debugging. Proceedings of the 1971 IFIP Congress, Amsterdam: North-Holland, 1971.

           Bug statistics on routines ranging in size from 700 to 5500 instructions with correlation to the number of decisions and subroutine calls. Proportion of bugs found in unit testing, integration testing, and system testing.

ALBE76   Alberts, David S. The economics of software quality assurance. Proceedings of the 1976 National Computer Conference, Montvale, N.J.: AFIPS Press, 1976.

ANDE79   Anderson, Robert B. *Proving Programs Correct*. New York: John Wiley and Sons, 1979.

BACK59   Backus, J. The syntax and the semantics of the proposed international algebraic language of the ACM-GAMM Conference. Information Processing, Paris, 1959.

BAKE79A   Baker, A.L., and Zweben, S.H. A comparison of measures of control flow complexity. Proceedings COMSAC '79, New York: IEEE, 1979.

BAKE80   Baker, A.L. A comparison of measures of control flow complexity. *IEEE Transactions on Software Engineering* **SE-6**: 506–511 (1980).

BARN72   Barnes, B.H. A programmer's view of automata. *Computing Surveys*, **4**: 222-239 (1972).

General introduction to the concept of state graphs and related topics from a software-application perspective.

BASI73   Basin, S.L. Estimation of software error rates via capture-recapture sampling: a critical review. Science Applications Inc, Palo Alto, Calif., September 1973.

BAUE79   Bauer, J.A., and Finger, A.B. Test plan generation using formal grammars. IEEE, Proceedings of the Fourth International Conference on Software Engineering, Munich, September 1979. IEEE CH 1479-5/79.0000-0378.

Use of state-graph model for processes and the automated generation of test cases based on such models. Examples of application to telephone call control.

BEIL77   Beilner, H., and Gelenbe, E. (editors). *Modeling and Performance Evaluation of Computer Systems*. Amsterdam: North-Holland, 1977.

Conference proceedings of an international workshop on performance evaluation in 1976. Statistical methods and many case studies.

BEIZ71   Beizer, Boris. *Architecture and Engineering of Digital Computer Complexes*. New York: Plenum Press, 1971.

Two volumes on hardware and software architecture of real-time, multi-computer complexes with automatic reconfiguration. Emphasis is on system design. System structure, performance, executive structures, reliability/availability calculations.

BEIZ78   Beizer, Boris. *Micro-Analysis of Computer System Performance*. New York: Van Nostrand Reinhold, 1978.

Analytical models of software processing time, memory utilization, queueing theory, system models, mass memory latency models, model validation, and system tuning.

BEIZ82   Beizer, Boris. *Software Testing Techniques*. New York: Van Nostrand Reinhold, 1983.

Companion to this book. Focuses on unit testing techniques, theory, and tools: expansion of Chapter 3 in details.

BELF76   Belford, P.C., and Taylor, D.S. Specification verification—a key to improving software reliability. PIB Symposium on Computer Software Engineering, Polytechnic Institute of New York, April 1976.

Examines the verification of specifications, use of specification languages, and related subjects.

BELF79   Belford, P.C., and Berg, R.A. Central flow control software development: a case study of the effectiveness of software engineering techniques. IEEE, Proceedings of the Fourth International Conference on Software Engineering, Munich, September 1979. IEEE CH 1479-5/79.0000-0378.

Use of decision-to-decision paths as a measure of complexity. Statistics on bugs caught during design review, unit testing, and system testing based on 24,000 lines of executable code. Statistics show that limiting the module size is not effective and that module sizes of 100 to 200 lines would be better than 50 lines of executable code. Decision-to-decision paths are a better predictor of the number of test cases and development effort required than are lines of code.

BOEH73   Boehm, B.W. Software and its impact: a quantitative assessment. *Datamation* **19:** 48–59 (May 1973).

BOEH75A   Boehm, B.W., McClean, R.K., and Urfrig, D.B. Some experience with automated aids to the design of large-scale reliable software. *IEEE Transactions on Software Engineering* **SE-1:** 125–133 (March 1975). (Also in IEEE, Proceedings of the International Conference on Reliable Software, Los Angeles, April 1974.)

Statistics on software errors.

BOEH75B   Boehm, B.W. Software design and structuring. In *Practical Strategies for Developing Large Software Systems.* (Ellis Horowitz, editor).Reading, MA: Addison-Wesley, 1975.

BOEH75C   Boehm, B.W. The high cost of software. In *Practical Strategies for Developing Large Software Systems.* (Ellis Horowitz, editor). Reading, MA: Addison-Wesley, 1975.

BOEH79   Boehm, B.W. Software engineering—as it is. IEEE, Proceedings of the Fourth International Conference on Software Engineering, Munich, September 1979. IEEE CH 1479-5/79.0000-0378.

Survey of the state of the art in testing and software engineering. Lots of good aphorisms.

BOIE72   Boies, S.J., and Gould, J.D. A behavioral analysis of programming—on the frequency of syntactical errors. IBM Research Report RC-3907, T.J. Watson Research Center, Yorktown Heights, New York, June 1972.

BORO72   Borodin, A. Computational complexity and the existence of complexity gaps. *Journal of the ACM 19:* 158–183, (Jan. 1972).

BORO79   Borovits, Israel, and Neumann, Seev. *Computer System Performance Evaluation.* Lexington, Mass: Lexington Books, 1979.

Readable introduction to performance measurement, analysis, organization of studies, and cost-benefit analyses.

BROW73   Brown, J.R., and Lipow, M. The quantitative measurement of software safety and reliability. TRW Report SDP-1176, 1973.

BUNY74   Bunyan, C.J. (editor). *Computer Systems Measurement: Infotech State of the Art Report Number 18*. Maidenhead, Berks., SL61LD, UK: Infotech International LTD., 1974.

        A panel of experts get together to discuss system performance, analysis, simulation, and tuning. An excellent overview.

CHAP79   Chapin, Ned. A measure of software complexity. Proceedings of the 1979 National Computer Conference. Montvale N.J.: AFIPS Press, 1979.

CHEN78A   Chen, E.T. Program complexity and programmer productivity. *IEEE Transactions on Software Engineering* **SE-4**: 187–194 (1978). (Also in Proceedings COMSAC 77, New York: IEEE, 1977.)

        Defines a complexity metric based on structure and information theory. Shows a discontinuous change in productivity with increased complexity.

CHEU78   Cheung, R.C. A user-oriented software reliability model. Proceedings of the Second International IEEE Conference on Computer Software and Applications, November 13–16, 1978. Chicago.

CHOW78   Chow, T.S. Testing software design modeled by finite state machines. *IEEE Transactions on Software Engineering* **SE-4**: 78–186 (1978). (Also in Proceedings COMSAC 77, New York: IEEE, 1977).

        Testing of software that can be effectively modeled by state graphs with examples from telephony. Categorizes types of state-graph errors and shows relation between type of cover and the kind of errors that can and cannot be caught.

CHUN78   Chung, Paul, and Gaiman, Barry. Use of state diagrams to engineer communications software. IEEE, Proceedings of the Third International Conference on Software Engineering, Atlanta, May 1978.

CICU75   Cicu, A., Maiocchi, M., Polillo, R., and Sardoni, A. Organizing tests during software evolution. IEEE, Proceedings of the 1975 International Conference on Reliable Software, Los Angeles, April 1975.

CURT79A   Curtis, B., Sheppard, S.B., and Milliman, P. Third time charm: stronger predictions of programmer performance by software complexity metrics. IEEE, Proceedings of the Fourth International Conference on Software Engineering, Munich, 1979. IEEE CH 1479-5/79.0000-0378.

Continuation of related experiments (see SHEP79C). Correlation between McCabe, Halstead, and program-length metrics. Halstead's metric appears to be a better predictor than either length or McCabe's metric. Study dealt with small FORTRAN routines.

CURT80B   Curtis, B. Measurement and experimentation in software engineering. *Proceedings of the IEEE* **68:**1144–1157 (1980)
Survey of various complexity metrics including McCabe's and Halstead's. State of the art and current research on software metrics.

DANI71   Daniel, C., Wood, F.S., and Gorman, J.W. *Fitting Equations to Data.* New York: Wiley-Interscience, 1971.
An excellent introduction to the subject of regression analysis with many examples worked out in detail. This book goes as far as most performance studies are likely to need.

DEMI78   DeMillo, R.A., Lipton, R.J., and Sayward, F.G. Hints on test data selection: help for the practicing programmer. *Computer* **4:** 34–43 (April 1978).

DEYO79   DeYoung, G.E., and Kampen, G.R. Program factors as predictors of program readability. Proceedings of the Third IEEE Conference on Computer Software and Applications, Chicago, November 6–8, 1979. IEEE publication 79CH 15125-6C.

DNIE78   Dniesirowski, A, Guillaume, J.M., and Mortier, R. Software engineering in avionics applications. IEEE, Proceedings of the Third International Conference on Software Engineering, Atlanta, May 1978
Good bug categories. Statistics on bugs caught during specification, design, and coding and the kind of testing used to catch them. Also effort required to catch bugs.

DRAP81   Draper, N., and Smith, H. *Applied Regression Analysis* (second edition). New York: John Wiley and Sons, 1981.
A very big book (more than 700 pages). A survey of the entire field of regression analysis covering theory and practice. A primary reference.

DUNN82   Dunn, R., and Ullman, R. *Quality Assurance for Computer Software.* New York: McGraw-Hill, 1982.
Features an especially good section on software reliability theory and related issues.

ELSH76B   Elshoff, J.L. An analysis of some commercial PL/I programs. *IEEE Transactions on Software Engineering* **SE-2:** 113–120 (1976).

ELSH78B   Elshoff, J.L., and Marcotty, M. On the use of the cyclomatic number to measure program complexity. *ACM SIGPLAN Notices* **13:** 33–40 (1978).

ENDR75   Endres, A. An analysis of errors and their causes in system programs. IEEE, Proceedings of the 1975 International Conference on Reliable Software, Los Angeles, April 1975. (Also in *IEEE Transactions on Software Engineering* **SE-1:** 140–149 (1975).

Detailed error categories and statistics on bugs for each.

FERR78   Ferrari, D. *Computer System Performance Evaluation.* Englewood Cliffs, N.J.: Prentice-Hall, 1978.

Overview of the field including measurement, simulation, analytical models, computer selection, tuning, and design.

FEUE79A   Feuer, A.R., and Fowlkes, E.G. Some results from an empirical study of computer software. IEEE, Proceedings of the Fourth International Conference on Software Engineering, Munich, 1979. IEEE CH 1479-5/79.0000-0378.

Study of 197 PL/I routines averaging 54 statements. Focus is on maintainability. Shows that program size is a good guide to maintainability as measured by error density, time to repair, and subjective judgment. Shows that decision density (related to McCabe's metric) is probably better suited to large programs.

FEUE79B   Feuer, A.R., and Fowlkes, E.B. Relating computer program maintainability to software measures. Proceedings of the 1979 National Computer Conference, Montvale N.J.: AFIPS Press, 1979.

Study of 123 PL/I modules in business data processing applications. Relates complexity measure to maintainability. Applies Halstead's metric to maintainability question.

FISC79   Fischer, K.F., and Walker, M.J. Improved software reliability through requirements verification. *IEEE Transactions on Reliability* **R-28:** 233–240 (1979).

FOSD76A   Fosdick, L.D., and Osterweil, L.J. Data flow analysis in software reliability. *ACM Computing Surveys* **8:** 305–330 (1979).

Use of graphs, survey of symbolic execution methods, path expressions derived from flow graphs, detection of data-flow anomalies.

FREI71   Freiberger, W. (editor). *Statistical Computer Performance Evaluation.* New York: Academic Press, 1972.

Collection of papers from 1971 conference on statistical computer performance evaluation.

GABO76   Gabow, H.N., Maheshwari, S.N., and Osterweil, L.J. On two problems in the generation of program test paths. *IEEE Transactions on Software Engineering* **SE-2:** 227–231 (1976).

Construction of constrained paths.

GANN76   Gannon, J.D. Data types and programming reliability—some preliminary evidence. PIB Symposium on Computer Software Engineering, Polytechnic Institute of New York, April 1976.
          Discussion of data types and data-type operands. Summary of errors related to data types. Type error statistics. Shows 10% type errors, most of which could have been caught by a good compiler.

GANN79   Gannon, C. Error detection using path testing and static analysis. *Computer* **12**: 26–31 (August 1979).

GEIG79   Geiger, W., Gmeiner, L., Tranboth, H., and Voges, U. Program testing techniques for nuclear reactor protection systems. *Computer 12:* 10–17 (August 1979).
          Structure-based unit tests, test tools, static analysis tool (SADAT), instrumentation, and bottom-up testing.

GILB77   Gilb, T. *Software Metrics*. Cambridge, Mass.: Winthrop, 1977.

GOEL78B   Goel, A.L., and Okumoto, K. Analysis of recurrent software errors in a real-time control system. ACM, Proceedings of the 1978 Annual Conference.

GOEL79A   Goel, A.L., and Okumoto, K. Time dependent error detection rate model for software reliability and other performance measures. *IEEE Transactions on Reliability* **R-28**: 206–211 (1979).

GOEL79B   Goel, A.L., and Okumoto, K. A Markovian model for reliability and other performance measures of computer software. Proceedings of the 1979 National Computer Conference: 769–774.
          Report on the application of a software reliability model to 320,000 instruction program; prediction of additional test time needed.

GOOD75   Goodenough, J.B., and Gerhart, S.L. Toward a theory of test data selection. *IEEE Transactions on Software Engineering* **SE-1:** 156–173 (1975).
          Limitations of structure-based testing and formal methods of proof. Formal definitions for reliable tests, valid tests, complete tests, and successful tests. Use of decision tables as aid to test case design.

GOOD79   Goodenough, J.B. A survey of program testing issues. In *Research Directions in Software Technology*. (Peter Wegner, editor). Cambridge, Mass.: MIT Press, 1979.

GOOD80   Goodenough, J.B., and McGowan, C.L. Software quality assurance: testing and validation. *Proceedings of the IEEE 68*:1093–1098 (September 1980).
          Comparison of hardware and software life-cycles, state of the

art of: testing, testing methodology, and research. Proposal of design methodology aimed at improving software quality.

GREE76   Green, T.F., Schneidewind, N.F., Howard, G.T., and Parisequ, R. Program structures, complexity, and error characteristics. PIB Symposium on Computer Software Engineering, Polytechnic Institute of New York, April 1976.

HALS75   Halstead, M.H. Software physics: basic principles. IBM Technical Report RJ-1582, T.J. Watson Research Center, Yorktown Heights, N.Y., 1975.

HALS77   Halstead, M.H. *Elements of Software Science*. New York: Elsevier North-Holland, 1977.

HAMI78   Hamilton, P.A., and Musa, J.D. Measuring the reliability of computer center software. Proceedings of the Third International Conference on Software Engineering, Atlanta, May 10–12, 1978.

HANF70   Hanford, K.V. Automatic generation of test cases. *IBM System Journal* **9**: 242–257 (1979).

Use of BNF and syntax-directed software to generate syntactically valid test cases of PL/I code for testing a PL/I compiler.

HANS78   Hanson, W.J. Measurement of program complexity by the pair cyclomatic number, operator count. *ACM SIGPLAN Notices* **13**: 29–32 (1978).

HAUG64   Haugk, G., Tsiang, S.H., and Zimmerman, L. System testing of the number 1 electronic switching system. *Bell System Technical Journal* **43**: 2575–2592 (1964).

HECH77B   Hecht, M.S. *Flow Analysis of Computer Programs*. New York: Elsevier North-Holland, 1977.

A clearly written, deep exposition of the application of graph theory to the analysis of programs. Primarily aimed at questions related to compiler design and code optimization. Large bibliography. For the mathematically mature.

HEND75   Henderson, P. Finite state modeling in program development. IEEE, Proceedings of the 1975 International Conference on Reliable Software, Los Angeles, April 1975.

HETZ73   Hetzel, W.C. (Editor). *Program Test Methods*. Englewood Cliffs, N.J.: Prentice-Hall, 1972.

Basic book on testing. Comprehensive pre-1972 bibliography on testing and related subjects.

HOFF77   Hoffmann, H.M. An experiment in software error occurrence and detection. MS Thesis, Naval Postgraduate School, Monterey, Calif., June 1977.

HOWD76   Howden, W.E. Reliability of the path analysis testing strategy. *IEEE Transactions on Software Engineering* **SE-2:** 208–215 (1976).
Proof that the automatic generation of a finite test set which is sufficient to test a routine is not a computable problem. Formal definition of computation error, path error, and other kinds of errors.

HOWD78A   Howden, W.E. A survey of static analysis methods. In Miller, E., and Howden, W.E. *Software Testing and Validation Techniques.* IEEE Tutorial, New York: IEEE, 1978. (IEEE Catalog No. EHO-138-8.)

HOWD78B   Howden, W.E. A survey of dynamic analysis methods. In Miller, E., and Howden, W.E. *Software Testing and Validation Techniques.* IEEE Tutorial, New York: IEEE, 1978. (IEEE Catalog No. EHO-138-8.)

HOWD78C   Howden, W.E. Empirical studies of software validation. In Miller, E., and Howden, W.E. *Software Testing and Validation Techniques.* IEEE Tutorial, New York: IEEE, 1978. (IEEE Catalog No. EHO-138-8.)

HOWD78D   Howden, W.E. Theoretical and empirical studies of program testing. *IEEE Transations on Software Engineering* **SE-4:** 293–298 (1978). (Also in IEEE, Third Conference on Software Engineering, Atlanta, 1978.)
Symbolic trace, algebraic value trace, reliability of various methods.

HOWD78E   Howden, W.E. An evaluation of the effectiveness of symbolic testing. *Software Practice and Experience* **8: 381-397** (1978). (Also, University of California at San Diego, Computer Science Technical Report, No. 16, (1977).
Shows that path testing is 64% effective.

HOWD80   Howden, W.E. Functional program testing. *IEEE Transactions on Software Engineering* **SE-6:** 162–169 (1980). (Also in Proceedings COMSAC 78, IEEE, November 1978).
Role and use of functional testing as applied mostly to the testing of mathematical software—proposes combined functional/structural testing.

HUAN75   Huang, J.C. An approach to program testing. *ACM Computing Surveys* **7:** 113–128 (1975).
Structure-based testing, graph models, path coverage, path count, path predicates; discusses use of inserted counters in links to measure test thoroughness.

HUAN79   Huang, J.C. Detection of data flow anomaly through program instrumentation. *IEEE Transactions on Software Engineering* **SE-5:** 226-236 (1979).

ITOH73   Itoh, Daiju, and Izutani, Takao. Fadebug-1, a new tool for program debugging. IEEE, Record of the 1973 Symposium on Computer Software Reliability, April–May 1973.
Summary of findings on the utility of path-tracing test tool. Statistics on bug types.

JELI73   Jelinski, Z., and Moranda, P.B. Application of a probability-based model to a code reading experiment. IEEE, Record of the 1973 Symposium on Computer Software Reliability, April–May 1973.

JENS79   Jensen, R.W., and Tonies, C.C. *Software Engineering.* Englewood Cliffs, N.J.: Prentice-Hall, 1979.

KERN76   Kernighan, B.W., and Plauger, P.J. *Software Tools.* Reading, Mass.: Addison-Wesley, 1976.

LAPA73   LaPadula, L.J. *Engineering of Quality Software Systems, Vol. VIII: Software Reliability Modeling and Measurement Techniques.* The MITRE Corporation, Rome Air Development Center technical report number 74-325, January 1–June 30, 1973.

LAPA75   LaPadula, L.J. Software reliability and timeliness. The MITRE Corporation, DDC Document AD A0007773, January 1975.

LASS79   Lassez, J.L., and Van Den Knijff, D. Evaluation of length and level for simple program schemes. Proceedings of the Third International IEEE Conference on Computer Software and Application, Chicago, November 6–8, 1979. IEEE Publication 79CH1515–6C.

LEHM80   Lehman, M. Programs, life cycles, and laws of software evolution. *Proceedings of the IEEE* 68: 1060–1076 (September 1980).

LEIB74   Leibholz, S.W., and Wilson, L.D. *User's Guide to Computer Crime.* Radnor, Pa.: Chilton, 1974.
One of the better "how to do it" books.

LIPO77A   Lipow, M., and Thayer, T.A. Prediction of software failures. Proceedings of the Annual Symposium on Reliability and Maintainability, January 18–20, 1977; pp 489–494. IEEE catalog number 77CH1161-9RQC.

LIPO79   Lipow, M. On software reliability. *IEEE Transactions on Reliability* R-28: (August 1979). Special issue on software reliability.

LIPO82   Lipow, M. Number of faults per line of code. *IEEE Transactions on Software Engineering* SE-8: 437–439 (June 1982).

LITE76   Litecky, C.R., and Davis, G.B. A study of errors, error proneness, and error diagnosis in COBOL. *Communications of the ACM* **19:** 33–37 (1976).

LITT78   Littlewood, B. How to measure software reliability and how not to. Proceedings of the Third International Conference on Software Engineering, Atlanta, May 10–12, 1978. Also in *IEEE Transactions on Reliability* R-28, (1979).

LITT80   Littlewood, B. A Bayesian differential debugging model for software reliability. Proceedings of the Fourth International Conference on Computer Software and Applications, Chicago, October 27–31, 1980. IEEE document 80-CH1607-1.

MANN78   Manna, Zohar, and Waldinger, Richard. The logic of computer programming. *IEEE Transactions on Software Engineering* **SE-4:** 199–229 (1978).

Survey of methodology and limitation of formal proofs of program correctness. State of the art. Examples drawn from numerical problems.

MANZ80   Manzo, John. Private communication.

MCCA76   McCabe, T.J. A complexity measure. *IEEE Transactions on Software Engineering* **SE-2:** 308–320 (1976).

Definition of cyclomatic complexity, subgraphs that lead to structured code, relation of covering paths to complexity. Basic paper.

MCCA82   McCabe, T.J. (Editor). *Structural Testing.* Silver Springs, Md.: IEEE Computer Society Press, 1982.

A tutorial on structural testing and a collection of important, previously published papers on the subject, including MCCA76, CURT79A, WALS79, MYER77, and SCHN79A.

MCCL78B   McClure, C. A model for program complexity. Proceedings of the Third International Conference on Software Engineering, Atlanta, May 10–12, 1978.

MILL74   Miller, E.F., et al. Structurally based automatic program testing. IEEE, EASCON Proceedings, 1974.

MILL75   Miller, E.F., and Melton, R.A. Automated generation of test case data sets. IEEE, Proceedings of the 1975 International Conference on Reliable Software, Los Angeles, April 1975.

MILL77C   Miller, E.F. Program testing: art meets theory. *Computer* **10:** 42–51 (1977).

Survey of the state of the art of testing, vis-a-vis theory and practice.

MILL78A   Miller, E.F., and Howden, W.E. (Editors). *Tutorial: Software Testing and Validation Techniques.* IEEE Computer Society, 1978. (IEEE Catalog No. EHO-138-8.)

MILL78B Miller, E.F. Program testing—an overview for managers. Proceedings COMSAC 78, Chicago, November 1978. (IEEE Catalog No. 78C-H1338-3C.)

MIYA78 Miyamoto, I. Toward an effective software reliability evaluation. Proceedings of the Third International Conference on Software Engineering, Atlanta, May 10–12, 1978 (46–55).

MORA72 Moranda, P.B., and Jelinski, Z. Final Report on Software Reliability Study. McDonnell Douglas Astronautics Corp., Report Number 63921, December 1972.

MORA78 Moranda, P.B. Limits to program testing with random number inputs. Proceedings COMSAC 78, Chicago, November 13–16, 1978. (521–526). IEEE Cat# 78CG1338-3C. New York: IEEE, 1978.

MUSA75 Musa, J.D. A theory of software reliability and its application. *IEEE Transactions on Software Engineering* SE-1: 312–327 (September 1975).
 Guide to trade-off between test effort and reliability, scheduling of test effort, when to stop, comparison of effectiveness of different design methodologies.

MUSA79A Musa, J.D. Validity of the execution time theory of software reliability. *IEEE Transactions on Reliability* R-28: 181–191 (August 1979).

MUSA79B Musa, J.D. Software reliability measures applied to system engineering. Proceedings of the 1979 National Computer Conference. Montvale, N.J.: AFIPS Press, 1979.

MUSA80 Musa, J.D. The measurement and management of software reliability. *Proceedings of the IEEE 68:* 1131–1143 (September 1980).

MYER76 Myers, G.J. *Software Reliability: Principles and Practices*. New York: John Wiley and Sons, 1976.

MYER77 Myers, G.J. An extension to the cyclomatic measure of program complexity. *ACM SIGPLAN Notices* 12: 62–64 (1977).

MYER79 Myers, G.J. *The Art of Software Testing*. New York: John Wiley and Sons, 1979.

NAFT72 Naftaly, S.M., and Cohen, M.C. Test data generators and debugging systems . . . workable quality control. *Data Processing Digest* 18: (February and March 1972).
 Survey of automatic test data generation tools.

NELS67 Nelson, E.A. *A Management Handbook for the Estimation of Computer Programming Costs*. System Development Corporation, TM-3225/000/01, Santa Monica, Calif., March 1967. Also DDC AD648750.

Expansion of WEIN65 and a practical handbook for software development managers.

NTAF78   Ntafos, S.C. A graph theoretic approach to program testing. Ph.D. Dissertation, Northwestern University, Evanston, Ill.,1978.

Path-covering problems and other subjects applicable to automatic test-data generation.

OTTE79   Ottenstein, L.M. Quantitative estimates of debugging requirements. *IEEE Transactions on Software Engineering* SE-5: 504–514 (1979).

Use of Halstead's metrics to estimate remaining bugs. Data on bugs, and use and validation of Halstead's metrics on several projects.

PANZ78A   Panzl, D.J. Automatic software test drivers. *Computer 11:* 44–50 (1978).

PAIG73   Paige, M.R., and Balkovich, E.E. On testing programs. IEEE, Proceedings of the 1973 Symposium on Computer Software Reliability, New York, April 1973.

Structural testing based on graph model; covering.

PAIG75A   Paige, M.R. Program graphs, an algebra, and their implication for programming. *IEEE Transactions on Software Engineering* **SE-1:** 286–291 (1975).

PAIG77   Paige, M.R., and Holthouse, M.A. On sizing software testing. IEEE, International Symposium on Fault Tolerant Computing, June 1977.

PAIG78   Paige, M.R. An analytical approach to software testing. IEEE, Proceedings COMSAC 78, New York: IEEE, November 1978.

PAIG80   Paige, M.R. A metric for software test planning. Proceedings of the Fourth International Conference on Computer Software and Applications, Chicago, October 27–31, 1980. IEEE document 80-CH1607-1.

PERL81   Perlis, A., Sayward, F., and Shaw, M. *Software Metrics: An Analysis and Evaluation.* Cambridge, Mass.: MIT Press, 1981.

A very good survey of the art, pertinent literature, research problems, productivity models, Halstead's metrics, software reliability. Large bibliography.

PETE76   Peters, L.J., and Tripp, L.L. Software design representation schemes. PIB Symposium on Computer Software Reliability, Polytechnic Institute of New York, April 1976.

Survey of methods and models for representing the behavior of programs, including HIPO charts, activity charts, structure charts, control graphs, decision tables, flowcharts, transaction diagrams, and others. Comments on use and experience with various methods. Critiques and suggestions for new representations. One of the most complete surveys of its kind.

PETE80 Peters, L.J. Software representation and composition techniques. *IEEE Proceedings* **68:** 1085-1093 (1980).

Survey of software description models including Leighton diagrams, design trees, structure charts, SADT diagrams, flowcharts, Hamilton-Zeldin diagrams, decision tables, Nassi-Shneiderman model, data-flow diagrams. Design methodologies that use these models.

RAMA75A Ramamoorthy, C.V., and Ho, S.F. Testing large software with automated evaluation systems. *IEEE Transactions on Software Engineering* **SE-1:** 46–58 (1975).

RAMA75B Ramamoorthy, C.V., and Kim, K.H. Optimal placement of software monitors aiding systematic testing. *IEEE Transactions on Software Engineering* **SE-1:** 403–410 (1975).

Discussion of monitor software inserted in code to measure path traversals and to detect errors. Discussion of algorithm for optimum placement of a minimum number of probes.

RAMA76 Ramamoorthy, C.V., Ho, S.F., and Chen, W.T. On the automated generation of program test data. *IEEE Transactions on Software Engineering* **SE-2:** 293–300 (1976).

Structured-based testing; generation of paths followed by symbolic execution, test constraints on input variables, problems of arrays, difficulty of solving constraint equations, random generation of test cases that satisfy contraints. FORTRAN CASEGEN and automated test case generator.

RAMA80 Ramamoorthy, C.V., and Bastani, F.B., Modeling of the software reliability growth process. Proceedings of COMSAC 80, Chicago, October 27–31, 1980 (161–169).

REIF77 Reif, D.J., and Trattner, S. A glossary of software tools and techniques. *Computer 10:* (July 1977).

Discusses 70 different tools and their application to testing.

REIF79 Reifer, D.J. Software failure modes and effects analysis. *IEEE Transactions on Reliability* **R-28:** 247–249 (1979).

REMU79 Remus, H. and Zilles, S. Prediction and management of program quality. Proceedings of the 4th International Conference on Software Engineering, Munich, September 17–19, 1979 (341–349). IEEE CH 1479-5/79.0000-0378.

RUBE75 Rubey, R.J., Dana, J.A., and Biche, P.W. Quantitative aspects of software validation. *IEEE Transactions on Software Engineering* **SE-1:** 150–155 (1975)

RYDE79   Ryder, B.G. Constructing the call graph of a program. *IEEE Transactions on Software Engineering* SE-5: 216–226 (May 1979).
        Algorithm for automatic construction of the call tree or graph of a program.

SCHE65   Scheff, B. Decision-table structure as input format for programming automatic test equipment systems. *IEEE Transactions on Electronic Computers* **EC-14**: 248–250 (1965).
        Use of decision tables in automatic generation of test cases.

SCHI78   Schick, G.J., and Wolverton, R.W. An analysis of competing-software reliability models. *IEEE Transactions on Software Engineering SE-4*: 104–120 (1978).
        A survey of the history, development, and experience with several software reliability models.

SCHN75   Schneidewind, N.F. Analysis of error processes in computer software. IEEE, Proceedings 1975 Conference on Reliable Software, Los Angeles, April 1975.

SCHN79A   Schneidewind, N.F., and Hoffman, H.M. An experiment in software error data collection and analysis. *IEEE Transactions on Software Engineering* **SE-5:** 276–286 (1979).
        Study of 500 modules averaging 480 statements each with a total sample of 250K statements (including comments). Job was a modification of an operating system. Breakdown by error types and the project phase during which the error was discovered. Relation between McCabe's metric and the fundamental circuit matrix or basis. Shows that McCabe's metric correlates well with the number of bugs and the time needed to correct them, but not with the time required to find them. Shows qualitative change in bug density and labor in the region of $M = 5$. This last result, however, is based on a small sample.

SCHN79B   Schneidewind, N.F. Software metrics for aiding program development debugging. Proceedings of the 1979 National Computer Conference, Montvale, N.J.: AFIPS Press, 1979.
        Comparison of several measures of complexity and their relation to discovered bugs. Reachability matrix and uses thereof.

SCHN79C   Schneidewind, N.F. Application of program graphs and complexity analysis to software development and testing. *IEEE Transactions on Reliability* **R-28**: 192–198 (1979).
        Tutorial overview of graph-related concepts. Fundamental circuit matrix and relation to McCabe's metric. Experiments on ALGOL code; 173 bugs found in 2000 statements. Semiautomatic test tools described.

SCHN79D   Schneidewind, N.F. Case study of software complexity and error detection simulation. IEEE, Proceedings of the Third International Software Application Conference, Chicago, November 1979.

SCHW71   Schwartz, J.T. An overview of bugs. In *Debugging Techniques in Large Systems*. (R. Rustin, editor). Englewood Cliffs, N.J.: Prentice-Hall, 1971
    Nature of bugs and their sources. Debugging and test tools. Difference between debugging and testing.

SHEP79C   Sheppard, S.B., Curtis, W., Milliman, P., Borst, M.A., and Love, T. First-year results from a research program on human factors in software engineering. Proceedings of the 1979 National Computer Conference, Montvale, N.J.: AFIPS Press, 1979.
    Experiment using thirty-six programmers working in FORTRAN on small (fifty-statement) programs. The experiment tested the ease of modification and how well the subjects could recall the control structure. The study shows good correlation between McCabe's and Halstead's metrics, but neither metric particularly effective for small routines.

SHOO72   Shooman, M.L. Probabilistic models for software reliability prediction, in *Statistical Computer Performance Evaluation* (W. Freiberger, editor). New York: Academic Press, 1972 (485–502).

SHOO73   Shooman, M.L. Operational testing and software reliability estimation during program development. *IEEE Transactions on Software Reliability* R-22: 51–57 (1973).

SHOO75   Shooman, M.L., and Bolsky, M.I. Types, distributions, and test and correction times for programming errors. IEEE, Proceedings 1975 Conference on Reliable Software, Los Angeles, April 1975.

SHOO78B   Shooman, M.L. Structural models for software reliability prediction. Proceedings of the Third International Conference on Software Engineering, San Francisco, October 13–15, 1976 (268–280)

SUKE78   Sukert, A.N. A four-project empirical study of software error prediction models., Proceedings COMSAC 78, November 1978, (577–582).

SUKE79   Sukert, A.N. Empirical evaluation of three software error prediction models, *IEEE Transactions on Software Reliability* R-28: 199–205 (1979).

THAY76   Thayer, T.A. Software reliability study. Rome Air Development Center, Report No. RADC-TR77-216. (Also: Thayer, T.A.,

Lipow, A.M., and Nelson, E.C. Software reliability study. TRW Defense and Space Systems Group, Final Technical Report, February 1976. (AD-A030798).

The watershed study on software reliability. More than 300 pages of software-related statistics.

THAY77   See THAY76.

VOGE80   Voges, U., Gmeiner, L., and von Mayrhauser, A.A. SADAT— an automated test tool. *IEEE Transactions on Software Engineering* **SE-6:** 286–290 (1980).

WAGO73   Wagoner, W.L. The final report on a software reliability measurement study. The Aerospace Corporation, El Segundo, Calif., August 1973.

WALS79   Walsh, T.J. A software reliability study using a complexity measure. Proceedings of the 1979 National Computer Conference, Montvale, N.J.: AFIPS Press, 1979.

McCabe's measure applied to 276 routines in the Aegis system. Discusses break at $M = 10$.

WEIN65   Weinwurm, G.F., and Zagorski, H.J. Research into the management of computer programming: a transitional analysis of cost estimation techniques. System Development Corporation, TM-27 1/000/00m Santa Monica, Calif., November 1965. Also DDC AD 631259.

Basic statistics on cost, labor factors, and development time in programming.

WOLV75   Wolverton, R.W. The cost of developing large-scale software. In *Practical Strategies for Developing Large Software Systems*. (E. Horowitz, editor). Reading, Mass.: Addison-Wesley 1975.

WOOD78   Woods, J.L. Path selection for symbolic execution systems. Ph.D. Dissertation, University of Massachusetts, 1978.

WOOD80   Woodward, M.R., Hedley, D., and Hennell, M.A. Experience with path analysis and testing of programs. *IEEE Transactions on Software Engineering* **SE-2:** 278–286 (1976).

Using link count as a metric; path testing; and two measures of cover.

YEHR80   Yeh, R.T., and Zave, P. Specifying software requirements. *IEEE Proceedings* **68:** 1077–1085 (1980).

Examines specifications as a source of program bugs and suggests methodology for specification design.

ZELK78   Zelkowitz, M.V. Perspective on software engineering. *ACM Computing Surveys* **10:** 197–214 (1978).

Survey of the state of the art and the issues in software engineering.

ZOLN77   Zolnowski, J.C., and Simmons, R.B. Measuring program complexity. Proceedings COMPCON Fall 1977, New York: IEEE, 1977.

ZWEB79   Zweben, S.H., and Fung, K.C. Exploring software science relations in COBOL and APL. Proceedings of the Third International IEEE Conference on Computer Software and Application, Chicago, November 6–8, 1979. IEEE Publication 79CH1515-6C.

INDEX